Olga Alekseevna Novikova

Skobeleff and the Slavonic Cause

Olga Alekseevna Novikova

Skobeleff and the Slavonic Cause

ISBN/EAN: 9783337412173

Printed in Europe, USA, Canada, Australia, Japan

Cover: Foto ©ninafisch / pixelio.de

More available books at **www.hansebooks.com**

SKOBELEFF

AND

THE SLAVONIC CAUSE

BY

O. K.

HONORARY MEMBER OF THE BENEVOLENT SLAVONIC SOCIETY
AUTHOR OF 'RUSSIA AND ENGLAND'

LONDON
LONGMANS, GREEN, AND CO.
1883

All rights reserved

PREFACE.

SKOBELEFF's biography has not yet been written, and the materials upon which I found this poor tribute to the memory of our Slavonic hero are very incomplete. I cannot pretend to have produced more than a short sketch, and a most imperfect one, of the brief but glorious career of him who has already become a legendary hero of the Slavs.

The cause for which Skobeleff fought in Bulgaria was a very precious one to me as to thousands of Russians. On my present visit to England I was happy to see that the generous sympathy expressed in this country at the moment of Skobeleff's death still existed, and that many of my English friends were still anxious to learn 'something more' of him. That is precisely what I venture to offer.

Even that humble task I have undertaken with much diffidence. Written under the pressure of many troubles, far away from those whose ample knowledge of Skobeleff and his work could guide my pen and my reminiscences, I am painfully impressed with the shortcomings of this book. But, with all its imperfections, I venture to trust that it will enable Englishmen to realise something of the character of my famous countryman, as well as of the cause to the service of which he dedicated his life, and without which he could never have been entirely our own Skobeleff.

O. K.

London, December 1882.

CONTENTS.

PART I.
SKOBELEFF AS SOLDIER.

CHAPTER	PAGE
I. BIRTH AND EDUCATION	3
II. IN CENTRAL ASIA	10
III. THE CROSSING OF THE DANUBE	33
IV. PLEVNA	43
V. IN CAMP AND IN FIELD	110
VI. THE PASSAGE OF THE BALKANS	148
VII. IN SOUTHERN BULGARIA	176
VIII. GEOK TEPÉ	194

PART II.
SKOBELEFF IN POLITICS.

I. THE SLAVONIC CAUSE	223
II. THE ST. PETERSBURG SPEECH	253
III. SKOBELEFF IN PARIS	263
IV. RUSSIA AND GERMANY	285
V. RUSSIA AND AUSTRIA	299
VI. RUSSIA AND ENGLAND	320
VII. SKOBELEFF AND CONSTITUTIONALISM	338
VIII. DEATH	379

APPENDICES.

APPENDIX A.
          PAGE
SKOBELEFF'S ORDERS OF THE DAY   393

APPENDIX B.
BARON FREDERICKS ON RUSSIAN INSTITUTIONS AND RUSSIAN NIHILISTS   401

APPENDIX C.
LETTER FROM WIDDIN ON THE BURIAL OF THE REMAINS OF NICHOLAS KIRÉEFF   407

PORTRAIT.
SKOBELEFF SOON AFTER GEOK TEPÉ   *Frontispiece*

PART I.

SKOBELEFF AS SOLDIER.

1. BIRTH AND EDUCATION.
2. IN CENTRAL ASIA.
3. CROSSING OF THE DANUBE.
4. PLEVNA.
5. IN CAMP AND IN FIELD.
6. PASSAGE OF THE BALKANS.
7. IN SOUTHERN BULGARIA.
8. GEOK TEPÉ.

CHAPTER I.

BIRTH AND EDUCATION.

Skobeleff born 1843—Pronunciation of Skobeleff—The Skobeleff family—His parents—Russian women—Home-training—His first tutor—Sent to a Paris pension—M. Girardé—At St. Petersburg University—Joins the army—In Poland—Dano-German war—Central Asia.

MICHAEL DMÍTRIEVITCH SKOBELEFF[1] was born at St. Petersburg on September $\frac{17}{29}$, 1843. His grandfather, as he used frequently to remind his troops, had been a private soldier, and won his rank as general by his own sword. His great-grandfather, Nikita, was a sergeant in the army at the close of last century. Beyond his great-grandfather Skobeleff did not trace his pedigree. 'Family never made men great,' was his democratic remark; but the soldierly instinct which he inherited from his ancestors contributed not a little to the success of his career. His grandfather, Ivan, did not win his promotion easily. He was

---

[1] Skobeleff's name is accented on the first syllable. In the majority of Russian three-syllabic names the accent falls on the second: Románoff, Souvóroff, Derjavine, Pojársky, Aksákoff, Lobánoff, &c.; but some have the accent upon the third syllable, as Chomiakóff, Gortchakóff, &c., and others on the first, as Skóbeleff, Kóusheleff, &c.

covered with horrible scars, and he left at least one limb on the field of battle. Ivan Skobeleff was a general of infantry, and at one time governor of the fortress of St. Petersburg. He was more than a general; he was also a dramatic author, and in his day, his plays, specially written for military audiences, were very popular in the army.

Skobeleff's love for poetry, like his genius for war, was hereditary.

Ivan Skobeleff had two daughters and eight sons. Most of his children died in infancy. One of the daughters married the aide-de-camp of the Emperor, Colonel Opotchinine, grandson of the celebrated Prince Koutóusoff-Smolénsky. His seventh son, Dmitry, became a cavalry lieutenant-general, distinguished himself in the campaign against the Turks in Asia Minor, and received the Order of St. George of the fourth class.

Dmitry Skobeleff married the beautiful and graceful Miss Poltavtseff. They had one son and three daughters. The eldest married Prince Bélóssélsky-Bélósérsky; the second, M. Schérémétoff; and the third, the Prince Eugène Romanoffsky, son of the Grand Duchess Mary and the Prince of Leuchtenberg, and first cousin of the Emperor.

Dmitry Skobeleff was a Russian of the Russians. Stern, severe, respectful to old traditions, but kindhearted and passionately attached to his brilliant son. There existed between them to the last hour the most perfect sympathy and affection. But I think the moulding influence of his life was that of his mother.

I hope I may be pardoned for confessing that it often struck me that the Russian women have qualities which are less frequent in women of many other countries. They are more idealistic and self-sacrificing, more real and less conventional. There are exceptions, of course; besides I am, probably, very partial. But the number of superior women who impress me, as I used to be impressed by the intelligence of George Eliot, is, I think, greater in Russia than in many other parts of the world.

I did not know Madame Skobeleff intimately enough to speak of all her qualities from personal observation. She chiefly lived at St. Petersburg, I at Moscow; but the latter events of her life proved of what she was capable. She was very fond of her children, and from her Skobeleff learned to love poetry, of which he was passionately fond. His favourite modern poets were Byron and Schiller. It was under the superintendence of his mother that he learnt to love to read, but his first tutor was a German.

This good man was a severe martinet, who flogged his pupil for the least fault. Skobeleff, who, from his youngest days, was of an independent, passionate, and extremely active temperament, was irritated at this treatment, and a bitter feud grew up between the tutor and the boy. Skobeleff played no end of tricks upon his master, and the latter retaliated in his own way. Matters came to a crisis when the young Michael was twelve years old. He had ridden off one day to pay a visit to a little girl of his own age, to whom in boyish fashion he was paying his court, when the hated tutor appeared and slapped the face of his truant scholar in the very presence of his lady-love. The poor boy, blinded with passion, struck out at him with all his might.

After that fracas the father saw that it was of no use persisting with the German tutor, who, with all his cruelty, could not reduce the child to order.

He dismissed the German, and sent his son to a boarding school in Paris, kept by M. Désiré Girardé. The change for young Skobeleff was indescribable. He found sympathy in place of brutality, kindness for cruelty, and constant incentives to diligence in place of the savage blows of his German pedagogue. M. Girardé soon won the love and confidence of his pupil. The turbulent young Russian became the most devoted and assiduous of scholars, and a lifelong affection grew up between them which was only terminated by the death of the younger. Even to the last Skobeleff, the hero of a hundred combats, and the idol of the Slavonic world, never ceased to speak with the reverence and humility of a pupil of his old teacher. Girardé followed him to St. Petersburg, and has remained attached to the family ever since. He was with him in Bulgaria during the war, and followed him to Paris on the famous visit which created so much excitement in Europe.¹

Girardé used to say that, if Skobeleff had not become a soldier, he would have been a scholar, so devoted was he to learning, and so remarkable his mastery over books and languages. Girardé taught Skobeleff to make a religion of duty. It was a good lesson, and one which he never forgot.

His parents, wishing him to finish his education in Russia, brought him to St. Petersburg. The St. Petersburg University was in 1861 infected with foolish and subversive ideas. The students fancied it would be much better to arrange political demonstrations than to study their lessons. Skobeleff was too well trained and too intelligent not to see the folly of all these disorders, and never lost his own ground. He remained from the first to the last true to his duty, to his Tzar, and his country. But the disorders continuing, the Government was forced to close the University, and Skobeleff's university studies were cut short before their time.

He then entered the army as first ensign in a horse regiment of the Guards. In 1863 he was made an officer, and went off with this regiment to Poland, where an insurrection was breaking out. He was

---

[1] Mr. Rose, writing in the *Fortnightly Review*, Oct. 1882, on the 'Russian Bayard,' speaks thus of Girardé:—'I had frequent opportunities of meeting with this excellent man. Possessing little of the sprightliness of his race, he was reserved, shy, and unobtrusive in the presence of strangers, but *en famille* frank and animated in conversation, which displayed, though not pedantically, his profound learning and varied reading' (p. 406).

stationed with the hussars at Grodno, and had his first experience of actual fighting in the affair of Mekhoff. At Mekhoff, and throughout the whole of the campaign, Skobeleff, although only twenty years old, displayed such remarkable courage and ability as to win high praise from his commander. He received a sword of honour for the gallantry which he displayed at the successful action in the forest of Radkovitz, when the band of Shemiote was dispersed. He remained in Poland till the insurrection was at an end, and then, there being nothing more to do, he returned to St. Petersburg and entered the staff academy, where he distinguished himself by his uncommon abilities.

In 1864 he had his first experience of regular warfare as a spectator, when he followed the course of the Dano-German campaign, and witnessed the first success of the needle-gun. He then returned to St. Petersburg, finished his course, and afterwards went on active service in Central Asia.

Skobeleff was drawn to Central Asia, not only by the opportunity which it afforded for an adventure and of distinction, but because, unlike many military authorities, he thoroughly believed that the art of war could nowhere be so well learnt as in active warfare, even against insignificant foes.

'The first essential,' he used to say, 'to a general, or to any officer, is the habit of being accustomed to danger and the responsibility of command under fire.' These habits, he held, were acquired in irregular war in Central Asia, in Algeria, in Afghanistan. Having once acquired them, a general has secured one great secret of success in regular war, and which more than counterbalances the danger that his previous experience will encourage him to take undue liberties with his foes.

CHAPTER II.

IN CENTRAL ASIA.

Central Asia as a school of arms—Skobeleff in Samarkand in 1869—At Krasnovodsk—The march on Khiva—His first wound—First to enter Khiva—A reconnaissance in the desert—Mission to Khokand—The Khan and his treasure carts—The battle of Makhram—Annexation of Namangan—Revolt of Abdurrahman—Capture of Andijan—A night attack on his pursuers—Khokand in revolt—Second capture of Andijan—Annexation of Khokand—Governor of Ferghana—His career in Central Asia—Slandered and vindicated.

WHAT India is to England and Algeria to France, Central Asia is to us—a school of arms, a training ground for soldiers, where a handful of Westerns hold sway amidst millions of Asiatics. These vast regions conquered for civilisation by European arms of precision, secured from anarchy by European habits of administration, offer an irresistible attraction to ambitious and restless youth.

To Turkestan, therefore, Skobeleff hastened as soon as he had completed those military studies of which he was destined to make such excellent use in later years. He had learned the art of war theoretically in the Academy of St. Petersburg. He went to complete his studies by practical experience in the rough apprenticeship of Central Asian warfare.

It was in the year 1869, when he was twenty-six years of age, that he began his military career in Asia, under General Abramoff, a gallant and active officer who raised himself from the position of a sub-captain to that of Governor of Samarkand, where he greatly distinguished himself by his bravery, energy, and justice. It was a good school for the young Skobeleff to serve under such a commander, and he learned his first lessons of Oriental war in Abramoff's expedition on the borders of Bokhara.

Soon afterwards he was removed from General Abramoff's command and attached to the troops under the command of Colonel Stolétoff, at Krasnovodsk. Colonel Stolétoff is the officer whose visit to Shere Ali in 1878 had such disastrous consequences, both for the Afghans and for the English.

Stolétoff placed him in command of a detachment of cavalry, and entrusted him with several important reconnaissances.

He was not long in developing those extraordinary faculties of observation which served him so well in his after life. Nothing escaped his vigilant eye. He discovered wells, before unknown, in sandy steppes; he mapped out new caravan routes; he sketched valuable plans, and made many geographical discoveries in the then unknown regions between the Caspian and the Aral.

After doing good service at Krasnovodsk, he returned to St. Petersburg, and was attached to the staff of the Guards. His promotion was rapid: in

1872 being named aide-de-camp to the chief of the staff of the 22nd division of infantry with the rank of captain. Some months afterwards he was appointed to the command of a battalion in the Stavropol regiment by order of the commander of the army in the Caucasus.

When Skobeleff returned to Central Asia, he found everything being put in train for the Khivan expedition. Four columns were to converge from different points upon the robber Khanate. General Verevkine commanded the column which started for Orenburg, General Lomakine led a third column for Mangishlak on the Caspian, while the fourth, under Colonel Markosoff, started from Tchikishlar.

The expedition set off in March, 1873. Altogether we put 14,000 men into the field, of whom 3,500 were Cossacks, with fifty-four guns, not including some ten or twelve mitrailleuses, rocket tubes and mortars, and nearly 20,000 camels. Colonel Markosoff's column started on March $\frac{19}{31}$, and recoiled from the waterless steppe on May $\frac{14}{26}$ at Krasnovodsk, without camels or provisions, with every man ill.

The northern column, to which Skobeleff was attached, was more fortunate. Its formation was an afterthought. General Kaufmann at first was opposed to the advance from Orenburg or the Caspian, but he yielded. and on $\frac{Feb. 28}{March 12}$ the order was given to the army of the Caucasus to prepare a detachment for an advance on Khiva from Mangishlak, on the Caspian.

The order was joyfully received, and on April $\frac{14}{26}$ Colonel Lomakine had a small, but compact, body of men ready to start. It consisted of 2,000 men, with six guns. Skobeleff, now a lieutenant-colonel, marched at the head of the vanguard, leading the way across a desert hitherto unknown to our soldiers. The heat was intense. The thermometer stood sometimes at 149 degrees Fahrenheit, and the Kirghiz, believing it impossible for Europeans to traverse a region which at that period of the year even desert-born nomads found insupportable, offered no serious opposition to our troops.

In twenty-nine days Colonel Lomakine's column had marched 400 miles of desert, for the most part unexplored. The last seven days they had made forced marches, but they effected their junction with General Verevkine at Kungrad in good time and excellent spirits.

It was in this march across the steppe that Skobeleff received his first wound. Riding as usual in advance of the column, he galloped with a dozen Cossacks up to an encampment of the Kirghiz Tartars. He was received with a volley of musket balls. Nothing daunted, young Skobeleff, followed by his twelve brave followers, charged the Kirghiz.

There were 100 of them, with 180 camels and a large store of provisions. After a desperate struggle, they fled across the steppe, but not before they had inflicted six slight wounds with spears and sabres upon Skobeleff. Fortunately the wounds, although numerous, were not severe, and the next day he was on horseback heading the advance of his column across the plain.

After reaching Kungrad, Colonel Lomakine's troops were joined to the Orenburg column under General Verevkine. The united forces, numbering 5,000 men, with 10,000 camels, left Kungrad on $^{\text{April 22,}}_{\text{May 4,}}$ and marched on Khiva. They had, on their way, repeated encounters with Khivan troops, in all of which Skobeleff displayed his usual gallantry. On $^{\text{May 26}}_{\text{June 7}}$ they arrived in the neighbourhood of the northern gate of the capital of the Khanate, and there they halted, waiting for General Kaufmann.

After two days General Verevkine determined to attack. The town was bombarded on $^{\text{May 28,}}_{\text{June 9,}}$ and the bombardment was continued the next day. Skobeleff was then ordered to storm the north gate. He had only two companies under his orders, but he fulfilled his mission with such skill and audacity that he succeeded in forcing his way in the city. He was the first within the walls. He cleared the streets with rockets, penetrated to the palace, and carried off three cannon to his camp. General Kaufmann then entered from the south, and was acclaimed as conqueror of Khiva. The honour of this campaign was, however, shared by the northern columns, and in these columns no one distinguished himself so much as Lieutenant-Colonel Skobeleff, who was then only in his thirtieth year.

Before any troops withdrew from the Khanate—for,

however strange it may appear to those who constantly accuse us of breaking our word in annexing Khiva, there is not one Russian soldier in Khiva to this hour—Skobeleff volunteered to go on the first of those madcap expeditions of his which made him so famous.

Colonel Markosoff's expedition had failed to penetrate the desert between Tchikishlar and Khiva. Skobeleff undertook to make a reconnaissance of the region over which Colonel Markosoff's column had found it impossible to advance. General Kaufmann gave him permission, and on August $\frac{1}{16}$, he started from Zmukshir, and attended only by three Turkoman guides he penetrated the steppes as far as Ortakuya. Seven days afterwards he returned to Khiva, having ridden 378 miles across a hostile country, without escort, never knowing where he would find water for himself or his horse. This exploit made a great sensation, and, in recognition of his bravery and daring, he was appointed aide-de-camp to the Emperor, and decorated with a St. George's cross of the 4th class, the first decoration, and perhaps the most prized, of the twenty-nine which were borne behind his bier on that day of sorrow when all Moscow followed Russia's hero to his last resting-place.

In the following years Skobeleff was in Turkestan, and trouble being anticipated in Kashgar, an embassy was sent to Khokand to secure the passage of our troops through the Khanate. The envoy, M. Veinberg, was accompanied by Colonel Skobeleff and twenty Cossacks as escort. The special mission with which Skobeleff was charged was the exploration of the pass of Terek Davan, leading from Khokand to Kashgar.

Our mission arrived at Khokand on July $\frac{13}{25}$, 1875, just as the rebellion of Abdurrahman Aftobatcha was breaking out against Khudayar Khan, the cruel and worthless ruler of Khokand. During the few days that the Veinberg-Skobeleff mission remained at Khokand, Skobeleff found an opportunity of making a very thorough examination of the city and its defences. This task was accomplished under great difficulties. The population was very excited. Every day fresh bands went off to join Abdurrahman. A holy war was on the point of being proclaimed. But, cool, collected, and indifferent as he ever was to danger, Skobeleff completed a detailed plan not only of Khokand and all its fortifications, but of all the country for seven miles round. Hardly had the work been accomplished, when the country rose in rebellion, and the Khan determined to fly.

When Skobeleff was in Khokand, he read in the gardens of the Khan the account of the destruction of the British army when in the defiles leading from Cabul in 1842. At any moment that might be his fate. The Kirghiz of the Khokand were not less hostile than the Cabulees. Russia, perhaps, even more than England—in Mr. Gladstone's fine phrase—ever carries aloft the torch of civilisation amid barrels of gunpowder, and at Khokand in that year the gunpowder was lying loose on every side.

Skobeleff was early initiated in the danger of government in the Khanate. A very few days after his first arrival in Khokand, he had to fly with the Khan, and Skobeleff often amused his friends around the camp-fires in Bulgaria by telling the story of their escape. It was a Central Asian version of the old story of the peasant whose sledge was pursued by the wolves.

The Khan set out from Khokand with a military escort of a small army which revolted piecemeal as it marched along, and announced its desertion by salvos of musket balls. The Russian mission was attended by fifty Cossacks, but for whom neither the Khan nor his ambassadors would ever have reached the frontier. The difficulty of escape was enormously increased by the presence of the harem of the fugitive, and a *cortège* of no fewer than eighty carts of silver and other treasure. The revolted army, after fraternising with the insurgents, set off in pursuit of its sovereign. Skobeleff and his fifty Cossacks with difficulty held the thousands of pursuers at bay. They were being driven in by numbers, when a happy thought occurred to the Khan. He ordered a waggon of silver to be unyoked, and the contents dropped in the road of the insurgents. It had the desired effect. As soon as the Kirghiz saw the money, they stopped to pick it up, and fought with each other for the spoil. In the meantime the Khan was hurrying northwards as fast as he could drag his treasure. Once more his subjects were on his trail. Again was the same expedient resorted to, and with equal success. Before they reached the frontier no fewer than sixty carts had been sacrificed in succession. When at last the Khan had reached Russian territory, he had only twenty cartloads left. With these, however, he was by no means badly off, and he has contrived to live very comfortably at Orenburg on the wreck of his fortune. But for the ready wit of the Khan, it is quite possible that Skobeleff's career would have closed almost before it had begun; as it was, however, he escaped safely, and was able to make good use of his experience in the subsequent campaign.

The situation was then not unlike that which threatened Englishmen during the mutiny of the Sepoys. All Turkestan threatened to rise. Our envoys had narrowly escaped from a violent death. Khokand was in open insurrection. In Tashkend every Russian went armed. The clerks in the government offices wrote with loaded muskets on their desks. A holy war was near at hand, and all the fanaticism of Asia was in danger of being let loose upon us.

The rather cold but no less impartial authority of M. Schuyler maintains that all this terrible crisis was brought upon us almost entirely by England's meddling two years before. The natives would have welcomed the annexation of the provinces as a means of relieving them from their detested Khan. 'General Kolpakovsky,' says M. Schuyler, 'saw this, and telegraphed to St. Petersburg for permission to intervene. But the diplomatic storm with regard to that occupation of Khiva was then in full blast, and permission was refused.'[1] The result was a gradual increase of bitterness against the Khan, and indirectly against Russia because she did not interfere with the Khan. Thus we had a war with all its horrors to wage because English diplomacy would be meddling with what it had no more business to concern itself than Russia had to interfere in the annexation of the Punjab. Yet Russians cherish no ill-will to England, while Englishmen pursue Russia with all manner of absurd and unjust suspicions. It is as true of nations as of individuals that it is only the injured who forgive; they never pardon who have done the wrong.

The insurrection, however, broke out. Khokand was besieged, and Andijan and Hodjent.

General Kaufmann took the field with 4,500 men, of whom 1,500 were cavalry under the command of Colonel Skobeleff. The expedition started on $\frac{\text{August 20}}{\text{September 1}}$ for Makhram, where the Khokandians were massed in force. After two days of marching our little army encamped at Karatchkum, and next day the battle was delivered which decided the destiny of Khokand.

It is very strange, but it is on Skobeleff's own

[1] *Turkestan*, vol. ii. p. 279.

word we have it, that our success at Makhram was largely due to the success which England obtained at the battle of Ferozeshah.

Skobeleff was an omnivorous reader, and he naturally read all the books bearing upon English warfare with the natives of India. He had a very retentive memory, and as he never campaigned without his books, he was constantly able to bring the experience of other wars to bear upon the work in hand. How the battle of Ferozeshah helped to win the battle of Makhram I must let Mr. Marvin tell in General Skobeleff's own words. After describing his interview with Skobeleff in 1882, in St. Petersburg, Mr. Marvin says [1] :—

'Do you know the battle of Makhram?' asked Skobeleff. 'That was a splendid battle and redounds to the glory of Kaufmann, whom I admire very much. Poor fellow! his career is finished. Do you know that our operations at Makhram were suggested by Sir Hugh Gough's battle at Ferozeshah? Shall I bore you, Mr. Marvin, if I describe it on paper? It is a most interesting thing. If you will have patience you will see what a great battle this Makhram was.'

While I was expressing my interest in the matter, Skobeleff was placing a pad of foolscap before him, and selecting a number of pencils from a series of thirty or forty, of various coloured leads, lying neatly on the table, all sharpened and ready for use. Drawing his chair close up to mine, he bent his head over the paper, and began sketching the features of the ground at Makhram with wonderful rapidity. Although a mere sketch, he made a

[1] *The Russian Advance towards India*, by C. Marvin, pp. 107-110.

THE BATTLE OF MAKHRAM.   21

scale at the outset, and used the various coloured leads to indicate clearly the positions of the troops and the features of the ground. There was no slurring of details at all; the names of the localities were inserted, and the numbers of the forces noted at the side. When it was complete, it was more finished than many of the sketches that have been published in the recent military works on our war in Afghanistan. While drawing the sketch, he described the battle-field with great spirit and minuteness; he was never at a loss for a word, he stated his facts one after another without displacing their order, and never needed to explain his explanations.

Briefly, the battle of Makhram was as follows:—The fort occupied a position on the banks of the Syr Daria sufficiently close to a chain of mountains for the Khokandese to attempt to bar the Russian advance up the valley by running out a trench towards them, armed with sixty-eight cannon, all pointed towards the invaders, and by continuing the line of defence to the foot of the hills themselves, by stationing in the intervening ground a huge mass of cavalry. At the back of the fort, the settlement of Makhram, with its numerous gardens, was held by infantry; the fort itself was armed with guns, and the hills flanking the position were crowded with skirmishers. On the opposite side of the river the position was rendered unapproachable by swamps. On coming in sight of this barricade, held by 60,000 Khokandese, General Kaufmann reconnoitred the position with his staff. Although he had only a mere handful of troops, he decided to make an attack the next day, to prevent the enemy overrunning the country. Skobeleff may as well relate, in his own words, what followed:—' Having surveyed the position, he turned to his staff and said: " Who knows anything about the battle of Ferozeshah?" I had read all about it, but waited for the other officers to reply. No one knowing anything about it, I described the battle.' Here he drew a rough sketch of the Punjab and said : 'As you know, Mr. Marvin, Sir Hugh Gough, the father of the General in Afghanistan during the late war, pitched his camp alongside the enemy's at Ferozeshah, without reconnoitring the ground, and when they fired into it, he fought at once and lost several thousand men. The next day he reconnoitred the position, and found a hill on the back that enfiladed it. Marching thither, he inflicted a crushing defeat on the enemy with a loss only of eighteen men.' Turning again to the plan of Makhram, he said: 'There was a hill on the flank to the rear of the Khokandese position which corresponded with that at Ferozeshah. It is now called the Peak of Kaufmann. The next day we marched straight in that direction, keeping all the way upon elevated ground alongside the mountains, until the enemy's position was outflanked. Then we changed front; turned our back to the hills and our faces to Makhram, and, marching straight towards it, swept the enemy right into the river. The river was quite black with heads. Twenty thousand Khokandese perished. We lost only eighteen men. I commanded the cavalry that day. The account of Ferozeshah I read originally in French, but more recently in Malleson's "History of Afghanistan." Makhram was a splendid laurel for Kaufmann.'[1]

[1] This was a favourite story of Skobeleff's. He told it to Mr. Rose amongst others, whose version differs slightly from that of Mr. Marvin's. It is as follows:

'One morning he related an incident which illustrates the extent of his reading, and the advantages of accurate historical information to a soldier. In the war in Turkestan he was on the staff of General Kaufmann, and when the Russian expeditionary force swept down on Makhram it found opposed to it an overwhelming native army, numbering by more than ten to one that of the invaders, and occupying a strong position. This position he proceeded to illustrate by a rough diagram drawn on the table with the charred ends of the matches with which we had been lighting our cigarettes. The right flank of the enemy, he showed, was protected by the walled city of Makhram, its

The battle of Makhram was one of the most decisive which we ever waged in Asia. Our loss was trivial, our gains enormous. We captured 39 pieces of artillery, 1,500 muskets, and more than fifty standards. The Khokandian army was crushed at a blow. Our expedition marched on the capital. Skobeleff's maps were of excellent service. Khokand was occupied without firing a shot. After remaining a week at Khokand, General Kaufmann marched against Abdurrahman, who, with 5,000 men, was offering a show of resistance. When he reached Marghilan the town submitted, and Skobeleff was despatched at night with a flying column of Cossacks, a rocket train, and two companies of infantry, conveyed in carts to follow up the traces of the

front was what seemed a wide grassy plain, while the left rested on a low range of stony hills. Skobeleff, in surveying the position, was struck with its similarity to that described in the record of, I think, one of the Napier's Indian campaigns, though unfortunately I neglected to note down at the time the names of the book, author, and city referred to. Skobeleff at once communicated to General Kaufmann his impression, and the latter General sententiously asked him, "And what did Napier do?" Whereupon Skobeleff gave an outline of the Anglo-Indian action : how at first the British troops delivered their attack in front and found themselves floundering in the grassy plain, which proved to be a treacherous swamp ; how the British general had to retire for the night ; how next morning he executed a flank movement and surprised, demoralised, and hopelessly crushed the huge native army, and captured both it and the city. At the close of Skobeleff's recital, General Kaufmann quietly rejoined, "And that is exactly what we will do, except fall into the mistake of attacking in front, and to-night." With the concurrence of his chief, Skobeleff organised his celebrated plan for the movement with his cavalry, and in combination with General Kaufmann's attack on the left front of the enemy, they repeated Napier's plot, completely routed the immense native army, and occupied Makhram.'—Rose, *Fortnightly Review*, p. 414. 1882.

retreating Abdurrahman. This dashing pursuit of the
enemy completed what Makhram had begun. On
September 3, he came upon the rear of the flying
foe, and a slight engagement ensued, remarkable from
the fact, as M. Schuyler says, that the opposing
forces fought almost unseen, owing to the dense clouds
of dust. But even against the invisible Skobeleff
was invincible, and the enemy fled, leaving forty of
their number *hors de combat*. Skobeleff pushed on
to Ush. The city surrendered, and after a few hours'
rest he pressed after Abdurrahman as far as Karasu.
He then returned to Marghilan, after levying a
heavy contribution in food and horses upon Ush.
His rapid pursuit of the insurgents prevented any
hope of rallying. All the other towns sent in their
submission when they heard of the fate of Ush, and
at the beginning of October General Kaufmann was
able to retire from the Khanate with a treaty promising a war indemnity of three million roubles and
the cession of Namangan, the strip of Khokand
lying north of the Syr Daria.

Our troops had hardly crossed the Syr Daria
when news came that our explorers had been badly
treated at Andijan, and that Abdurrahman was once
more at the head of a hostile force. General Troitsky
was at once despatched to reduce him to submission.
The Khokandians at Andijan were estimated at
60,000 strong. They were attacked, defeated, and
Andijan taken by storm. It was then decided that
the troops should be withdrawn. It was in the retreat

from Andijan that Skobeleff distinguished himself by one of the most famous among his many famous adventures. For three days the Khokandians had dogged their retreat; the whole force under Troitsky and Skobeleff did not exceed 1,200 men. The enemy, elated by the retreat of the captors of Andijan, pressed them hard. From morning to night their firing was incessant. On the third day, when our little column was but half way home, the situation was critical. Our ammunition had run short. The Cossacks had only three rounds left. The infantry only fifteen. It was necessary to do something to beat off the enemy, and a night attack was resolved upon. The Khokandians, some 6,000 strong, were encamped in the middle of a plain. Skobeleff, with his usual audacity, insisted on heading the attack in person. He refused, however, to take with him more than 150 Cossacks. Like Gideon, when he led his 300 against the Midianites, Skobeleff divided his little company into three bands, and stole silently through the darkness, past the enemy's outposts, into the camp. Skobeleff then gave the signal for attack by firing his pistol. In a moment, he and all his men charged, shouting and firing, into the heart of the camp. A scene of wild and maddening confusion followed; the Khokandians awoke, to discover, to their horror, the enemy in their midst. 'The effect,' says Mr. MacGahan, 'was tremendous. For a quarter of an hour the plain resounded with shrieks and yells, shots and the trampling of horses, shouts and groans, and all the uproar of battle. Then all was silence. Skobeleff assembled his Cossacks, and when morning came he found that the whole army of the enemy had disappeared, leaving on the field about 40 dead, 37 standards, 2,000 turbans, 2,000 or 3,000 muskets and sabres, all their camp material and baggage. But what was his astonishment to discover on calling the roll, that he had not lost a man either killed or wounded!'

The annals of war record no more brilliant surprise, but Skobeleff's father in 1854 achieved almost as distinguished a success when, with 800 men, he attacked and completely routed 5,000 Turks.

The blow dealt to the Kirghiz had been severe, but as it was followed by our retirement, they imagined they were victorious. The evil consequences of this mistake were not long in making themselves felt.

Our troops re-entered Namangan on October $\frac{5}{17}$. Skobeleff, who had been the hero of the campaign, was created major-general in the suite of the Emperor, and placed in command of the newly-annexed district. It was his first independent post. The troops were placed in winter quarters, and Skobeleff was ordered to remain strictly on the defensive. The country was very unsettled. Most of the natives of the province ceded to Russia were hostile. Khokand was honeycombed with disaffection. The Khan, who had made the treaty with Kaufmann, fled for his life to our camp. Skobeleff at first contented himself with defensive operations within Namangan. He defeated the former Bey, who had taken the field; but, when he was garrisoning a fortified post eight miles distant, the inhabitants of Namangan, assisted by friends from outside, rose against the Russian troops and besieged them in the citadel—exactly as the Cabulees besieged the English General Roberts in the Sherpur cantonments. Skobeleff, however, was not far distant. He fought his way back to the city, bombarded it with sixteen guns, and relieved the garrison. But the situation remained menacing in the extreme. 20,000 men gathered near the frontier at Balyktchi. Skobeleff fell upon them, dispersed them, and captured Balyktchi. None of these lessons, however, induced the Khokandians to believe that their only safety was to acquiesce in the new settlement.

Skobeleff, who saw that the Khanate could never be quieted by standing on the defensive in its borders, determined to strike a blow at the heart of his enemy. He had only a mere handful of men. The whole force under Skobeleff's command was 2,800 men, 9 companies of infantry, 7½ sotnias[1] of Cossacks, and 12 guns.

Thirty thousand Kirghiz, armed to the teeth and strong in the conviction that they were fighting a holy war against a foe whom they had previously defeated, were holding a strong fortified position at Andijan. But Skobeleff had already taught his

[1] A 'sotnia' means a hundred.

troops to think nothing of the numbers of their foes. Young as he was—it was only his second year in Turkestan, for after the expedition to Khiva he had spent a year in close observation of the Carlist war in Northern Spain—he had succeeded in arousing that enthusiasm and devotion which were to be displayed on a much greater scale in Bulgaria.

A little incident is still recorded of the way in which he insisted upon plunging into an icy river at two o'clock on a December morning, at the head of a dozen of his men, in order to drag out a cannon which was sinking beneath the stream. It was a wild night, the wind was high, the sky was dark, the water was breast high; but he insisted on sharing with the men the bitterest of their hardships.

Such a general they were ready to follow anywhere.

With Skobeleff at their head winters mattered as little as the intensest heats. The stronger the enemy the greater the glory of victory.

At the head of his small but intrepid band Skobeleff crossed the frontier, destroyed the Kiptchak settlement at Paita, and marched on Andijan. The citadel was surrounded by a strong wall fifteen feet high and seven feet thick, occupied by 30,000 men.[1] He left Namangan on $\frac{December\ 25}{January\ 6}$, and reached Andijan on January $\frac{2}{4}$. Instead of attacking at once, with that prudence which in him was as remarkable as his intrepidity, he spent four or five

[1] *Turkestan*, vol. ii. p. 299.

days in making the most careful reconnaissances. Day after day he employed himself and his staff in ascertaining all the information which could be gathered as to the best way of approach, and the comparative strength of the various gates. These perpetual reconnaissances dismayed the besieged, like the people of Jericho before the walls fell down. They could not understand the incessant activity of a foe who nevertheless delivered no attack. On one occasion, Skobeleff, attended by his staff and his escort, rode boldly right into the entrance of the town. The garrison, surprised and awed by his audacity, fled behind the walls of the citadel, while Skobeleff, undisturbed by their fire, made his observations as to the strength of their position. At length, when all his information was complete, he fixed January $\frac{8}{20}$ for the assault. As his troops advanced to the assault, the scene was stirring. Behind the walls the whole space seemed to be covered with the white turbans of the defenders. The roll of their drums mingled with the shriller chorus of their trumpets, and the fierce cries with which the Uzbeks excited themselves for the last struggle with the infidel. Skobeleff had less than 3,000 men. Twice he had summoned the city to surrender, and twice they had refused, and the last time they slew his messenger. The hour had now come when they were to learn to repent of their obstinacy. Skobeleff stormed the village of Iskylik and then bombarded Andijan. After firing 500 rounds, he launched two storming columns against the town. In a few hours they forced their way with a trifling loss into the heart of Andijan, which in the course of the next day they completely subdued.

Leaving a garrison in the city, Skobeleff took a small detachment and started in pursuit of Abdurrahman.

On January 30 he overtook the enemy at Assake, and inflicted upon him a severe defeat. So unrelenting was his pursuit of the enemy that when at last Abdurrahman, after three months' alternate fights and flights, surrendered to his conqueror, his first words are said to have been ' Before we begin to talk, let me sleep, for I have not had a night's rest nor a sound sleep for a whole month.'

Civil war was then raging in the city of Khokand, and to restore order Skobeleff occupied the city.

As there was no native Government capable of holding its own, the Khanate was annexed. It became the province of Ferghana, and Skobeleff, whose skill had contributed so greatly to the conquest, was named its first governor.

From a military point of view, I am told that Skobeleff's campaign in Khokand was chiefly remarkable for his aptitude in adapting his operations to local circumstances and for his great attention to all the details of the campaign. The organisation of the division of tirailleurs which always accompanied the cavalry, the readiness with which he converted his cavalry into infantry, the careful prevision for all the wants of his men, the preparations for the march, the acquisition of all kinds of rapid modes of communication, and, above all, the care and the skill with which he planned the assaults upon Andijan, and the genius with which he enabled every man under his command to form an idea of the plan of the battle in which he was to take part, marked him out in the eyes of all who followed those things as an officer destined to rise high in the service of his country. In this campaign of 1875-6, in his capacity as chief of cavalry or military commander of the province of Ferghana, Skobeleff took part in fourteen combats—some, no doubt, trivial enough, but others sufficiently serious to decide the fate of a province. When he left Central Asia he had received the cross of St. George of the third class, a sword of gold, and a sword of gold enriched with diamonds, and he had established a reputation as one of the ablest and most dashing commanders in our army.

Skobeleff's brilliant victories created enemies. Every great man has his enemies! Envy is the shadow of success. He was a major-general decorated with the cross of St. George, and governor of a province as large as Ireland, and he was not thirty-three. It was unprecedented, and all the more unprecedented because it was notorious that he had gained every step by merit. Worse even than the offence of his youth and his success was the campaign which he began against the fraudulent contractors of the supply department. As is not unfrequently the case, he found it more difficult to contend against those who ought to have been his allies than against a declared foe. The bullets of the Turks were much less fatal to our soldiers in Bulgaria than the shortcomings of the contractors, chiefly Jews—but not only Jews—who pillaged the treasury and starved the soldier at one and the same time.

Reckless as ever in the discharge of duty, Skobeleff set to work against corruption and incompetency with the same vigour that he had shown in attacking Abdurrahman and the Kirghiz. Many were alarmed. To stand on the defensive against such a man as Skobeleff was merely to court destruction. They determined to carry the war into their enemy's camp. They sent lie after lie to St. Petersburg concerning Skobeleff's administration. So persistent were they, that at last the late Emperor sent his aide-de-camp to report on their complaints. But Skobeleff preferred another and more effective line. On hearing a part of the monstrous stories forged against his honour, he telegraphed to General Kaufmann for leave, and started for St. Petersburg, taking all the accounts with him, all the documents and proofs. He had no difficulty in proving to the entire satisfaction of the Government that his enemies had infamously slandered him. After all possible investigations and verifications, he received a certificate from the Treasury that his accounts were clear and correct in every particular. In the meantime, events were stirring in Europe which made Skobeleff's return to Central Asia impossible.

CHAPTER III.

THE CROSSING OF THE DANUBE.

The War of 1877—Skobeleff joins the army of Bulgaria—Father and son at Giurgevo—The passage at Simnitza—Under fire—Dragomiroff's report—Swimming the Danube on horseback—Occupation of Shipka—Mr. Forbes on Skobeleff before Plevna.

To DESCRIBE the part played by Skobeleff in the war in Bulgaria one should either be a soldier or a poet. I am neither. I have no qualification for writing this and the following chapters. To tell the story of the hero in that great epic in the age-long struggle of the Slavs for liberty and independence demands much abler pens than mine; nor can I even attempt to supply, save by translations and extracts from the descriptions of English and American eye-witnesses, any account of the military aspect of his great career.

Inadequate as I am, I venture, nevertheless, to string together their narratives in this and the succeeding chapters, in the hope that they may serve, however imperfectly, to give Englishmen some conception of the genius and character of the young hero who might have become the Souvoroff of the nineteenth century.

It in no way falls within my duty to describe the general operations of the campaign, excepting in so far as Skobeleff was engaged in them.

The history of that war has still to be written by soldiers for soldiers. It is not for me to intrude in matters in which I am of necessity profoundly ignorant. My object is to enable my readers to realise Skobeleff—not to describe the campaign in which he was the foremost figure.

There is even less necessity for me to dwell on the origin of the war. To Skobeleff, as to all of us, the campaign in Bulgaria was at once a crusade and a war of liberation. 'No more generous or holy crusade was ever undertaken on the part of a strong race to befriend a weak one. So all true Russians believe.' Such was the testimony of the American Lieutenant Greene; and his testimony is true. Russia could not help doing what she did. It was at once her instinct and her duty and her religion. For the sake of their oppressed brethren Russians do not mind dying. It is part of our life, of our very soul. We did not go to war with the Turks as the English went to war with Arabi, with Shere Ali, and with Cetewayo. Skobeleff was like Sir Philip Sidney. His soldiers were more like the Ironsides or the Crusaders.

Skobeleff came to Russia from Khokand, when the soul of Russia was deeply moved by the events in the Balkan. The atrocities in Bulgaria, the disasters of the Serbian war, the heroism of our volunteers

under General Tchernayeff, which aroused Russia,
did not fail to touch the heart of the young soldier,
who, even in the remotest districts of Central Asia,
had kept himself *au courant* with all that was going
on in the Western world.

When at last, after all the endless vacillations of
a feeble and hesitating diplomacy had been exhausted
and the Emperor had declared war, Skobeleff hastened to join the army at Kisheneff. Although a
major-general, with the most brilliant record of any
of his brother-officers, he was only allowed to accompany the army *en disponibilité*, as a supernumerary
attached to the Grand Duke Nicholas's staff.

When the war began there were two Skobeleffs,
the father Dmitry and the son Michael. Long before
it ended, to all the world there was only one Skobeleff,
for the fame of the son completely eclipsed the by
no means inconsiderable achievements of the father.
Father and son were devoted to each other, and in
the earlier stages of the campaign they were almost
always together. Skobeleff senior was in command
of the famous Cossacks of the Caucasus, whose rapid
march on Braila enabled us to command the Danube
and secure our communications from the Turkish
attacks. At the beginning of June a small army corps
was formed to hold the banks of the Danube about
Giurgevo, near where the crossing was to be made,
and this army corps was placed under the command
of Skobeleff senior, with whom Skobeleff junior was
associated as chief of staff. They lodged in a small

house in front of the boulevard of Giurgevo. The Turks were kept continually on the *qui vive* by the Skobeleff's and their Cossacks. The father was always reprimanding his son for the recklessness with which he exposed himself to the fire of the gunners at Rustchuk, who fired at his white uniform whenever it showed, as it often did, against the bushes at the Roumanian shore. Michael Skobeleff was in the highest of spirits, full of fun and practical jokes, and delighted with the companionship of the young and joyous officers by whom he was surrounded. At Giurgevo, opposite Rustchuk, he had occupied an old earthwork without artillery, and filled the embrasures with formidable-looking cannon—made of straw. The resemblance was sufficiently good to deceive both the Turks and the English correspondents on the other side of the Danube, by whom the Russians were reported to have heavy siege guns in position three weeks before the real guns came down from Galatz. Skobeleff spent much of his time in making reconnaissances of the opposite shore; but, although constantly shot at by the Turkish sharpshooters, he escaped unhurt.

On one occasion, about the middle of June, Skobeleff crossed the river in a steam launch and landed on the Turkish bank. He did this out of no foolish bravado, but because he was told off to lay a sunken hedge of torpedoes across the Danube at Parapou, a village about ten miles west of Giurgevo. It was necessary to prevent the Turkish monitors at

THE PASSAGE AT SIMNITZA.

Rustchuk getting up the river as far as the intended crossing place at Simnitza. The work was carried out in broad daylight, but it only cost one officer killed and seven men wounded. At last, after long waiting, the waters of the Danube fell, and on June $\frac{15}{27}$, 1877, our army forced the passage of the Danube. Michael Skobeleff determined to take part in it as a volunteer; his position as a simple aide-de-camp to General Dragomiroff, a general only slightly his senior in rank, who had never before been in battle, was indeed a very humble one; but he preferred it, as it enabled him to do some real work. Major-General Yoltchine, with the first detachment of troops, embarked at midnight, and landed about two o'clock in the morning on the Turkish bank of the river. The Turks had about 10,000 men in their camps near Sistova. The Russian force consisted of 15,000 men, divided into six detachments of 2,500 men each. They were rowed across in pontoon boats holding from 15 to 40 men each. Skobeleff embarked with Dragomiroff and his staff. An eye-witness who was present with him in the boat thus describes the scene:—

Hardly had we left the Roumanian shore, than the bullets began to whiz around us, dropping on all sides into the water; but none struck the boat. We crossed the river without mishap, and drew near to the little creek of Tekir Dere, where Major-General Yoltchine had already landed, and was maintaining a fierce combat with the Turks. Dragomiroff, who had watched everything that passed as well as he could through the dense smoke and the morning mist, seemed very uneasy. Everything seemed so frightfully confused. From time to time he muttered some comments on the fight. Skobeleff stood by his side, silently watching the combat. Dragomiroff chafed impatiently under the suspense. Suddenly he heard the voice of Skobeleff.

'I congratulate you,' he said.

'For what?' cried the startled General, looking at the radiant face of his companion.

'For the victory,' replied Skobeleff. 'Your brave fellows have the best of it.'

'Where do you see that?' asked the General, puzzled more and more.

'Where? On the faces of the soldiers. Look at them. Watch them as they charge the enemy. It is pleasure to see them.'

Dragomiroff ceased to trouble himself about the general outlook of the scene. Dominated by the influence of Skobeleff, he grasped the mystery which until then he had not known—how to read victory written in the face of Russian soldiers.

They landed at five—three hours after Yoltchine, and Dragomiroff at once took command. By nine o'clock the passage was secured. The fourth brigade of Riflemen and the 14th Division occupied the heights above Tekir Dere. The firing continued on the right flank.

'Is it not time to stop?' then asked Skobeleff.

'It is indeed,' replied Dragomiroff; 'but I have no one to send.'

'May I go?' asked Skobeleff.

'I shall be only too delighted,' replied Dragomiroff; and Skobeleff set off on his dangerous mission. It was his first reckless act south of the Danube. As he had only landed four hours before, he had not lost much time. On the left our riflemen were firing from some vineyard, on the right the Turks obstinately held the heights.

Skobeleff, 'tall, erect, the image of a young English squire,' as Mr. Forbes described him, dressed in his white overcoat, walked with tranquillity into the heart of the combat. When he reached the riflemen he spoke first to one, then to another, delivering the words of Dragomiroff, and thus continuing, with steady step and perfect coolness, he walked the whole length of the line of fire, until he had delivered the word of command to the whole of the troops engaged.

In his official report Dragomiroff declared that he could not sufficiently praise the courage, the cleverness, the self-sacrifice of Skobeleff. From that moment the clouds which had overshadowed our young hero at St. Petersburg disappeared. He gained the confidence of the Commander-in-Chief, the Grand Duke Nicholas, and afterwards his progress was rapid. The passage of the Danube cost 300 men killed and nearly 500 wounded and missing. Before night 25,000 troops were quartered at Sistova, and the great obstacle to the Russian advance was overcome.

Everyone has heard of Skobeleff's crossing the Danube on horseback when the river was still swollen with the floods, and it is usually mentioned to illustrate his recklessness. But it was not done out of bravado. It was an experiment made by Skobeleff in order to test whether it was practicable to bring the Cossacks across in that fashion. Mr. Rose describes the incident as follows:—

Young Skobeleff suggested that the cavalry should swim across, and he offered to demonstrate the practicability of his scheme. No sooner said than done. He mounted his white charger, wound his way down the scarped clay cliffs at Simnitza, across the small bridge which spanned a creek to the island of Ada, and then, entering the river, the gallant horse, guided by Skobeleff's skilful hands, made for the further shore. The bold experiment was watched with breathless interest from the high ground on the Roumanian bank, and no more moved spectator of the daring enterprise stood there than the grey-haired father. With his binocular he eagerly followed the progress of his son and his gallant charger through the swift current. Then his arms began to shake, and his hands refused to hold the glasses to his eyes. He who had headed eight hundred troopers in a fierce onslaught upon five thousand Turks was unnerved at the sight of so venturesome a deed. Prince Tzérteleff, who was by his side, noting the slow course of his comrade in his unequal struggle with the moving waters, in response to the earnest appeals of the old general, reported every circumstance of the exciting adventure. By-and-by emotion broke the voice of the father as he exclaimed, ever and anon, 'Oh, my brave boy! Is he drowned yet?' And when young Skobeleff touched the little shelving bay below Sistova in safety, a ringing cheer was given by the Russian soldiery who had witnessed the rash feat; and the group which surrounded the grey-haired warrior echoed his 'Thank God!' as much for his sake as for the success of an undertaking almost unparalleled in its temerity.[1]

The experiment, although successful as far as Skobeleff was concerned, was too hazardous to be re-

[1] *Fortnightly Review*, October 1882.

peated on a large scale. The Cossacks all crossed by the bridge.

Skobeleff was then placed in command of a brigade of Cossacks of the Caucasus, the 'finest irregular cavalry in the world,' as he used to declare, and with them he was engaged in reconnaissance duty for the next four weeks.

The chief incident in which he took part was the capture of the fort St. Nicholas on the Shipka Pass. He was sent there after General Gourko and Prince Mirsky had twice attacked the position unsuccessfully. Early on the morning of July $\frac{7}{19}$ he took nine companies of the 36th regiment with four guns, and advanced from the north in the same route as that taken unsuccessfully by Gourko the previous day. He found that the Turks had abandoned all their positions, leaving behind them all their material and the mutilated bodies of their tortured prisoners.

He had done none of the fighting, but by singular good luck the most important position occupied by us in Bulgaria fell into his hands.

Before turning to that great siege which made Skobeleff the hero of the war, let us give here a pen and ink picture, sketched by an English correspondent who bore no love either to Skobeleff or his country.

In the dead of the night [(of July $\frac{16}{28}$), wrote Mr. Forbes to the 'Daily News'], that extraordinary fellow, General Skobeleff the younger, turned up in Prince Shahofskoy's headquarters. He is the stormy petrel of the Russian army. If I were riding along a road in a given direction in expectation of seeing a fight, and if I chanced to meet young Skobeleff riding in the opposite direction, without any inquiry or any hesitation, I should wheel my horse and ride in Skobeleff's tracks in the full assurance that I was doing the best thing for myself and your readers. He is in the thick of everything. In the grey dawn of the morning of the crossing, I shook hands with him on the edge of the bank of the Danube, after the bayonet charge in which he had taken part. His face was black with powder, and he, general as he is, carried a soldier's rifle with the bayonet fixed. He was in the fighting at the Shipka, and led the first column which traversed that pass. There seemed some prospect of quietude for some days on the other side of the Balkans, and the Plevna expedition offered a prospect of fighting. Skobeleff is unattached, and can run from flower to flower, from one fighting ground to another. . . . He is a right good fellow, and a staunch comrade. He came to us from Baron Krüdner's headquarters with instructions that he should take the temporary command of Colonel Toutolmine's brigade of Circassian Cossacks, and execute a reconnaissance in the direction of Loftcha. He rode off in the darkness, and came back last night, after having ridden fifty miles, with the tidings that Loftcha was held by five battalions of Turkish infantry, and its rayon infested by Circassians and Bashi Bazouks.

Such was Skobeleff before Plevna.

CHAPTER IV.

PLEVNA.

The first battle of Plevna—The second battle—Skobeleff's first attack—Reconnaissance before Loftcha—A nocturnal adventure—The battle of Loftcha—Victory—The third battle of Plevna—The attack on the Green Hills—Mr. MacGahan's account—Lieutenant Greene's narrative—A Russian report—Plevna invested—Capture of Turkish redoubt—Skobeleff in the trenches—Belief in his invulnerability—Osman Pasha's last sortie—Surrender of Plevna—Skobeleff and Osman Pasha—A famous siege.

Ah! this is a painful chapter to write. We ourselves were not altogether free of blame for our reverses, which makes it only the worse for our feelings. Here are the facts.

Skobeleff had no part in the first reverse at Plevna. When Lieut.-General Schilder-Schuldner, with 6,500 men and forty-six guns, scattered over a distance of seventeen miles, stumbled blindly upon Osman Pasha with 40,000 of the flower of the Ottoman army at Plevna, Skobeleff was doing duty at Tirnova. In the fight of July $\frac{8}{20}$, when our poor soldiers were aimlessly hurled against an enemy four times their own strength, without even sufficient ammunition to last till night, there was no redeeming feature save the bravery of our troops. 2,800 were killed and wounded—sacrificed without gaining a single advantage. When Skobeleff was in the field the battle was never without at least one bright side, even although it was but the silver lining of the dark clouds of defeat.

Startled by this severe reverse, troops were concentrated around Plevna. Prince Schahofsky was ordered back from Osman Bazar, at the foot of the Balkans, and Skobeleff was summoned from Tirnova to take temporary command of the Cossack brigade in Prince Schahofsky's force.

Arriving at headquarters on the night of July $\frac{16}{28}$, Skobeleff was at once ordered southward to reconnoitre the Turkish position at Loftcha—a place where he was destined afterwards to achieve his first great military success in Bulgaria. He found it occupied in force by the Turks, and here turned to take part next morning in the first great attack upon Plevna, which was ordered for July $\frac{18}{30}$.

Krüdner had to attack from the right, Schahofsky from the left. Skobeleff was stationed on the extreme left of Schahofsky, near Krishin, to prevent the arrival of reinforcements from Loftcha.

We had only 32,000 men, 186 guns, and three brigades of cavalry to attack a strongly entrenched force of at least 40,000 men. Krüdner, with the right wing, was unable to make any impression on the Turkish position at Grivitza. Twice with desperate valour our soldiers charged up to the redoubt, but both times they were swept back by the withering fire of the Turks. Prince Schahofsky, who attacked from Radischevo, captured two redoubts on the opposite ridge. The Turks, strongly reinforced, pressed Schahofsky back, after a desperate struggle. Our ammunition ran short, and all hope of success died. Schahofsky's attack had failed as completely as Krüdner's, and, with shattered ranks and heavy hearts, our brave soldiers retreated in the darkness, closely followed by the enemy, without even being able to bring off their wounded. In these two assaults, so bravely delivered, and so severely repulsed, Skobeleff had no part. He operated independently with the Caucasian brigade on the extreme left of Schahofsky.

The official report of the action speaks of Skobeleff's brigade in high commendation. Here is a summary of what it says: At five o'clock in the morning of that fatal day, he advanced with twelve sotnias of Cossacks, one battalion of infantry, and twelve small guns from Bogot, to Krishin, a village lying about a mile south-east of Plevna. Leaving there eight sotnias of Cossacks and eight guns—I am now quoting from the official report—in a very advantageous position, from which it was possible to observe and repulse the enemy coming from Plevna and Loftcha, he himself advanced with two sotnias of Kuban Cossacks and four pieces of artillery within 700 yards of the faubourgs of Plevna. From that point he observed 20,000 Turkish infantry, massed in reserve between the heights of Grivitza and the town. When Prince Schahofsky opened fire, General Skobeleff did likewise with his four pieces. The enemy immediately replied with six guns, and afterwards increasing rapidly his artillery fire, threw forward all his infantry protected in front by a thick screen of skirmishers, and in the flank by a screen of cavalry.

Met by such a resolute attack, General Skobeleff drew back his advanced guard to the principal position, Krishin, taking at the same time measures to cover his rear and flank, and to ensure his communications with the other troops. Afterwards leaving at Krishin three sotnias and twelve guns, he proceeded with the rest of his feeble detachment to attack the enemy, in order to prevent him from getting possession of the height which commands the country south of Plevna. Master of that height, the enemy could have fallen upon Prince Schahofsky's flank. Notwithstanding a murderous fire and most obstinate resistance on the part of the Turks, the height was occupied. The Turks did not, however, allow the little band to retain an undisputed possession. From 10 A.M. till 4 P.M.—Schahofsky's and Krüdner's attack only began at half past two o'clock in the afternoon—Skobeleff held the height. The struggle was very fierce, and more than once the bayonet was used. At four o'clock, having learnt that Schahofsky had assumed the offensive, and that the enemy did not appear on the side of Loftcha, Skobeleff made a vigorous advance, and almost reached the faubourgs of the town. But there he received a cross fire from fresh troops, and a shower of grapeshot, and was compelled to retire to the battery, which continued to keep up an unequal contest with the enemy's artillery. At ten o'clock in the evening he received from Prince Schahofsky the order to retreat to Bogot and Pelischat. Thus the feeble column of the extreme left fought during twelve hours against an enemy eight times its numbers. In attracting the attention of considerable forces, it powerfully assisted the troops of Prince Schahofsky, and saved them from a dangerous flank attack.

Lieutenant Greene, who gives a more detailed account of Skobeleff's operations, says that his force, 'though smaller in numbers, was handled with such skill as to establish beyond doubt the military genius of this brilliant young commander.' The height which was contested between him and the Turks was the second of the famous Green Hills destined soon afterwards to be for ever associated with his name. He attacked the Turks with two companies, two dismounted sotnias, and four guns. When his men were beginning to yield before the 4,000 Turks who opposed them, he sent in three companies he had kept in reserve, and kept up the fight till dark. Then, when the sun sank behind the horizon, and darkness came down over the bloody field, he drew off the remnant of his shattered force. Every wounded man —and 50 per cent. of his soldiers were killed or wounded—was brought off in safety, and sotnias of

Cossacks kept guard in the rear, as the little force marched back singing in the night, says an observer, the wild melodies which they had brought with them from the distant Caucasus. The loss had been heavy, but he had saved Prince Schahofsky from destruction and achieved the only success of that disastrous day.

Russia lost in that 'second battle of Plevna' more than 7,000 men, out of a total force of 30,000. Neither Schahofsky nor Krüdner had been able to bring off their wounded. That was done by Skobeleff alone, and it was in recognition of this that he was summoned to the headquarters of Gorny Studen after the fight to receive the personal thanks of the Emperor.

Only after the second battle of Plevna was it deemed necessary for Russia to put forth her whole strength. The Guards were ordered to Bulgaria, and, awaiting their arrival, the Russian armies in the Balkans and on the Lom stood on the defensive against the attacks of the Turks. Skobeleff was ordered to Selvi with the Caucasian brigade of Cossacks, and there received in addition one regiment and part of another from the newly-arrived Fourth Corps. In order to restore the spirits of the men, disheartened as they were by the reverses of Plevna, and also in order to ascertain the real strength of the Turks at Loftcha, he determined to make a reconnaissance against the Turkish position. He was accompanied by Mr. MacGahan, who sent a graphic account of the affair to the 'Daily News,' from which I take the liberty of reproducing it as a faithful description of the way in which Skobeleff did his work. Mr. MacGahan, writing from the headquarters near Loftcha on $\frac{\text{July 25}}{\text{August 6}}$, says :—

General Skobeleff pushed a strong reconnaissance to-day against Loftcha. Leaving the Grand Duke's head-quarters three days ago, he took five battalions of infantry, his own brigade of cavalry, and two batteries of horse artillery, and came out on the Selvi road half way between Loftcha. His right wing, composed entirely of cavalry, advanced and occupied several villages encircling Loftcha, from the Plevna road to the Selvi road. He then advanced his artillery on the Selvi road to the heights, a mile distant from Loftcha, overlooking the town, opened fire with sixteen pieces of artillery, and pushed forward his infantry.

It was evident from the moment the heights were reached that the reconnaissance could not be turned into an attack. From fifteen to twenty thousand troops could be seen camped in and about the town, while the low hills immediately surrounding the town were strongly entrenched. There is a strong redoubt on a low hill over-looking the Plevna road, while a high, steep hill on the Selvi side is covered with trenches. There were twelve guns in position and a considerable number in reserve visible.

General Skobeleff nevertheless resolved to feel the enemy, and the hills soon resounded with the roar of artillery and the noise of shells. The Turks replied at once, and for a time there was a lively artillery fire.

General Skobeleff pushed forward his infantry, and my attention was soon directed to his side by a heavy fusillade. From where his guns were placed in the road leads down a narrow hollow, whose sides were covered with woods, down to the foot of the steep hill which was occupied by the Turks in intrenchments. The infantry went down partly under cover of the woods, but not unperceived by the Turks, who poured a heavy fire into the woods. The Russians pushed forward, however, and in much less time than I could have thought, had reached the foot of the hill. They announced their arrival with a shout, and to my surprise, knowing no attack was intended, I saw them begin to dodge up the hill two or three at a time under cover of the bushes and little hollows with which such hills are usually covered. It began to look like a real attack. The Turkish fire grew heavier and heavier, until it was one continuous roll, far more terrible than the heaviest artillery fire, because a hundred times more destructive.

It was evident from this fire that the Turks were three times as numerous as the Russians. An assault under such circumstances would be madness, and I was beginning to wonder if Skobeleff could really be madman enough to attempt it. Suddenly I saw a small party of horsemen dashing down the road within full view of the Turks, and within easy range of their fire, and perceived in a moment Skobeleff. He was mounted on a white horse, and wore a white coat, offering a splendid target for sharpshooters. As I afterwards learned, he, like myself, began to perceive that the attack was growing far too serious, in spite of his orders, and was now going forward to stop it. The soldiers were, it seems, determined on an assault, and the officers maintained, when reproached by Skobeleff, that they could not restrain them. I saw Skobeleff stop apparently to give an order, then saw him dismount, get on another horse, while the white Arabian was led back. He had received a bullet. His escort, which had been composed of six Cossacks, was now reduced to three, the others having been more or less seriously wounded, one mortally.

The fire was still raging along the Turkish intrenchments, and the Russians were still pushing forward. Skobeleff, mounting another horse, a sorrel this time, again galloped forward.

He reached the foot of the hill evidently shouting and gesticulating, while his trumpeter sounded the retreat, apparently with effect, for the skirmishers began to withdraw. Then I saw him go down, horse and man together, and I said to myself, 'He has got it this time.' He had had two horses killed under him at Plevna. If it is the horse only, it makes the fourth within ten days. It is impossible for him to go on in this way long without getting killed. He is fairly under the Turkish intrenchments, and within easy range of the Turkish fire, which is growing stronger and stronger. They are evidently getting reinforcements from the other side, where they are only threatened with cavalry. The roar is continuous, and rolls up and down the hollow like one continuous crash of thunder, only broken by the heavier booming of the artillery. The bullets must be falling about there like hail. It will be a miracle if Skobeleff comes out of it alive.

Here a cloud of dust and smoke gathered for a moment, and was swept away by the wind two or three minutes later. I then saw Skobeleff again on another horse, fresh as ever, coming back up the road at a trot. He had not received a scratch. The reconnaissance was now over. The troops retired as they came through the wood under the Turkish fire, which was not here very effective. The whole loss was five killed and twenty wounded on this side—rather heavy for a mere reconnaissance. Had the troops not been stopped in time, they would simply have been annihilated, as several battalions and regiments were at Plevna.

Skobeleff retired about two miles, camped, and made his report.

While Skobeleff was fighting, his topographers were sketching, and when his last soldier was out of danger, he had secured an excellent map of the Turkish position. He found also that the Turks had 25 guns and 15,000 regular soldiers. Their position was fortified by a redoubt and some batteries on both banks of the river Osma, but it was commanded by a ridge running across the Selvi road, about four miles east of the village. Skobeleff withdrew his forces and fell back on Kakrina, to await reinforcements.

He spent the interval in making frequent reconnaissances and in superintending, with his usual care, every arrangement for the benefit of his men. On one of these reconnaissances he was accompanied by General Grant, not the ex-President, but an American who was acting as Correspondent of the 'Times.' After attempting in vain to draw the Turks into a skirmish, Skobeleff and his friends returned to the cavalry camp on the Osma, and took a carriage to Poradim. On their way there the following incident occurred, which General Grant shall describe:

It was nearly dark when we started for Poradim, about fifteen miles distant. After accomplishing about two-thirds of the distance we became aware that we had lost the way. It was now dark, and we had only two Cossack cavalrymen as an escort, while in some places the lines were less than two miles apart, and, therefore, easily passed in the night. By reference to the north star we found that we were travelling directly towards Plevna, a line at right angles to the proper course, and no road leading to the northwards could be found. We turned round several times until we lost the road we had come on (there are no fences, and newly-made waggon tracks lead in all directions over the open fields). Suddenly we came upon a line of fires, only a short distance ahead; they stretched away in a direction different from our own camps. I had been out the night before, as previously narrated, and had seen all the camp fires of the centre about Poradim. Here was a dilemma: if those fires were Turkish, we must be already inside their picket lines. Skobeleff seemed most annoyed by the idea that 'Punch' would have a cartoon of a Russian General riding into the Turkish army in his carriage, and by the fact that he had no revolver, and as, therefore, he could not fight until the Turks killed him, he might be taken prisoner in this uncomfortable way, like a rat in a trap. We were discussing the idea of passing the night in Plevna (if not massacred), and the Cossacks had their carbines at the 'ready.' Finally, we came to a halt, as we were dangerously near the fires, if they were those of the enemy. Again we turned back, and the sensation was becoming most decidedly disagreeable. We had not proceeded far when we were suddenly stopped. Looking ahead, I could see a clump of horses in the road. We listened, and the seconds seemed slow in passing while we waited for a voice to ascertain whether the accents were Moslem or Muscovite. Never did the Russian language seem so melodious in my ear as it did when the escort exchanged greetings with the drivers of several carts loaded with barley which had barred our passage.

In this way, varied by occasional excursions to the Trojan Pass, sometimes by an attack from the Turks, the month of August passed. On August $\frac{11}{23}$ he concentrated his detachment on the left flank of the army of the west in face of Loftcha. It was a movement of extreme temerity. It was a circuitous advance in the face of the enemy, over the roughest ground, across a river with a formidable Turkish force on the right flank. The artillery was dragged with the utmost difficulty over steep, sloping hills, crossed only by winding footpaths; the heat was excessive, and the difficulty of movement so great, that two days were occupied in the march. The Cossacks of the Caucasus, acting as an advanced guard, covered the movement of the main body, and on the evening of the $\frac{14}{26}$ Skobeleff had the satisfaction of seeing his division encamped near the village of Sebria, on the high road between Loftcha and Selvi.

Loftcha, although twelve miles from the most advanced Turkish position at Plevna, covered the extreme right flank of Osman Pasha. It was held by Adil Pasha with 15,000 men, and was strongly defended by earthworks thrown up along the east of the ridge above the river Osma. Behind the town, on a hill to the west, stood a redoubt and several lines of trenches; the ground was rugged and broken, difficult to storm, but easy to defend. Prince Imérétinsky, to whom the command of the attacking force was entrusted, had 20,000 men and 80 guns, without counting the Cossacks.

Skobeleff, who commanded the left wing, made a night march on $\frac{\text{August } 20}{\text{September } 1}$ from Kakrina to the foot of the ridge east of Loftcha. Arriving at two o'clock in the morning, he drove in the Turkish outposts from the north of the Loftcha road, and spent the few hours of darkness in entrenching his position and constructing epaulements for twenty-four guns.

As soon as day dawned Skobeleff, who had been marching, fighting, or digging since the previous sunset, opened fire on the Turkish position on the ridge to the south of the high road. After an artillery fire had been kept up for several hours, he drove the Turks out of the southern ridge, occupied it, and spent the night of September 2 in entrenching his new position and in constructing epaulements for thirty-two guns. As the result of this consecutive work kept up for a day and two nights without a moment's intermission, Prince Imérétinsky found on his arrival with the main body of the troops that Skobeleff had seized the positions commanding the Turkish batteries and that everything was ready for attack.

Skobeleff usually began the attack at five o'clock in the morning, and at that hour, $\frac{\text{August 22}}{\text{September 3}}$, fifty-six guns began to play upon the Turkish lines at Loftcha. General Dobrovolsky soon afterwards joined in with twelve guns from south of Pressiaka. The Turks attempted to crush General Dobrovolsky early in the morning, but their offensive movement was smartly punished, and they were driven back across the Osma.

It was on the left between where Skobeleff was commanding that the decisive struggle took place. The artillery fire was kept up till two o'clock in the afternoon, when the Turkish guns having been silenced, the order was given for an attack in force.

Our troops were advancing rapidly when they came suddenly to the edge of a perpendicular ravine, which intervened between them and the Turkish earthworks; they stopped in some confusion; several fell wounded into the stream at the bottom of the ravine and were drowned. In a few minutes, however, a path was found down the side of the cleft in the hill. Down this some rolled, others slid, and plunging up to their middle, they crossed the water and clambered up the precipitous hill. It was difficult and dangerous. Men stepped on each other's shoulders or struggled up with the aid of poles under a murderous fire from the Turks above. At last a few hundreds gained the summit. The fire of the enemy slackened; with a rousing hurrah our troops flung themselves upon the intrenchments. The Turks turned and fled. The whole of the first line east of the Osma was carried by three o'clock. Skobeleff brought up his artillery into the deserted Turkish positions and pursued the fugitives, through the town, to their second and last line of defence.

Once more the artillery fire reopened, and after two hours' cannonading the order was again given to advance. Skobeleff again led the way, supported on his right by the first brigade of the Second Division under Dobrovolsky and the Rifle Brigade still further to the right. The fighting was very fierce, and the contest was still in doubt when some groups of mounted men were seen leaving the redoubt. 'They are withdrawing their cannon,' cried he to his soldiers, and an indescribable rapture of victory shone on every face. The artillery retreated along the western road, but there was no abatement in the infantry fire from the redoubt. Confident of victory, our officers and men rallied for the final assault. The Turks within the redoubt kept up an incessant and deadly fire. The parapet was 24 feet high, the ditch was wide, and for some time the defenders beat off our attack; but some hundred men having collected in a sheltered spot unseen by the Turks, an attack was made at the side of the redoubt. While they were repelling this, the storming party, headed by a colonel who carried nothing but a cane in his hand, climbed up the wall and plunged into the redoubt. The Turks, seeing all was lost, tried to fly. As they rushed down the long and narrow traverse, which ran the whole length of the redoubt, the exit got blocked by an ammunition cart. The Turks, caught as in a trap, sold their lives as dearly as they could; but in five minutes all was over, and a horrible pile of dead and dying men choked the gorge of the redoubt. The bodies were heaped six feet high—Russians and Turks were intermixed, and so sudden and so resistless was the slaughter, that no fewer than 103 Turks, either unhurt or only slightly wounded, were extricated from the gory pile. Loftcha was won.

The Cossacks pressed the flying Turks for miles across the country. Three thousand are said to have been killed in the pursuit. Adil Pasha's army ceased to exist. Osman Pasha's strongest support was destroyed, our communications with the Balkans were secured, and the first decisive victory since the capture of Shipka restored confidence to our army. Our losses were 1,500 killed and wounded. Next day Osman sent a strong column from Plevna to reinforce Loftcha. It came too late. Skobeleff went out to meet the Turks, but after some skirmishing they withdrew.

From that day the fate of Plevna was only a matter of time. The victory was brilliant and complete, and it can be imagined how popular became the name of Skobeleff in Russia when, after dreary news of repeated reverses, we read the Grand Duke's telegram announcing the capture of Loftcha, which concluded with the brief but emphatic declaration, 'General Skobeleff, junior, was the hero of the day.'

The great attack on Plevna was now pending, and after one day's rest, Skobeleff and Imérétinsky brought their troops to Bogot. On $\frac{\text{August 25}}{\text{September 6}}$ they took up their positions before Plevna. The next day, when Skobeleff made a reconnaissance, he found that Osman had encircled the town with a ring of 18 redoubts and batteries. The cannonade had already begun. It was continued five days before the general assault.

But Skobeleff was already engaged in an attack upon the Turkish position the very next day. He was posted on the left with the advance guard of Prince Imérétinsky's division, with Brestovetz behind him, and the Turkish position on the Green Hills south of Plevna immediately in front. On the afternoon of the 8th he captured, after severe fighting, the three Green Hills in succession, and by five o'clock had come within 1,500 yards of Plevna. The Turks, being reinforced, drove him back to the second hill, and after he was informed that the general attack intended for the 9th had been postponed, he withdrew to the first hill, where he entrenched himself. He lost in that day's fighting 900 men. The next day the Turks made two attacks upon Skobeleff's position, and were driven back. The struggle for the first hill was witnessed by Mr. MacGahan. Here is his description :—

Skobeleff was on the ridge before me, and I was about starting to join him, when the sudden din and uproar of battle, like a thunder-clap, held me spell-bound with admiration. The crest of this ridge suddenly began to vomit flame and smoke. Above this ridge, far higher up, were balls of flames that flashed and disappeared, each leaving a small round fleece of white smoke. The Turkish shrapnel exploding over the heads of the Russians was deafening; and the heavy booming of the distant siege guns slowly pounding away at short regular intervals, as though keeping time, produced a sublime effect. The Turks were in their turn attacking the Russians from the other side, and the Russians had evidently reserved their fire until the Turks were very near, which accounted for the sudden furious outburst. 'That Skobeleff,' said the officer near me, 'how he is giving it to them!' and three or four Cossacks watching with intense excitement depicted on their faces, expressed their satisfaction, convinced that he was there in the middle of the fight, with that charmed life of his, ordering and directing.

In a few minutes the fire began to slacken, and two or three minutes later a loud shout swept along the ridge before us, followed by prolonged cheering. The Turks were evidently beaten back. Then the fire ceased, but shouting continued, going farther and farther away. Skobeleff was evidently going at the flying Turks with the bayonet. Now the fighting is over for the present, but the big guns are still pounding away on our right.

All that fighting was preliminary to the general assault, which took place on $\frac{\text{August } 30}{\text{September } 11}$.

On the night of the 9th, Skobeleff, who until then had been acting under Imérétinsky, was given independent command of the first division of his troops, whilst Imérétinsky, with the second division, was to support Skobeleff in the attack and to protect his left flank. On the morning of the 10th, Skobeleff occupied the second hill with little difficulty, the troops throwing up earthworks, using their bayonets and soup dishes as spades. There they remained until the fatal morrow, when the last great assault was to take place.

I cannot attempt to tell the story of that tragic day. I have not the heart to try. All that I can do is to reproduce here three accounts, one English, a second American, and the third Russian, written by eye-witnesses of Skobeleff's terrible struggle.

Here are a few introductory data. The Russian plan of attack was chiefly directed against three points: the Grivitza redoubt to be attacked by 25,000

Roumanians and Russians in four columns. No. 10 redoubt, the south-east of Plevna, in front of the Radischevo ridge, to be attacked by Generals Kriloff and Schitnikoff with 27,000 men; and the redoubt on the Loftcha road on the Green Hills to be attacked by Skobeleff with 18,000 men. Altogether, 60,000 troops were sent against the redoubts, of whom 7,633 were killed outright, and 10,948 wounded. The Grivitza redoubt was captured, the attack on No. 10 redoubt failed from the first. Mr. MacGahan's description of what he witnessed on the Green Hills that day is as vivid as trustworthy. 'Most of what I relate,' he says, 'I saw with my own eyes, and part I have learned from Skobeleff himself and the officers who took part in the combat.' Here is his account of the battle :—

Early in the morning Skobeleff had occupied the third knoll without difficulty, but up to the moment of the second repulse of Kriloff, Skobeleff had not yet made his assault. He had well prepared the ground, however. At four o'clock he had brought down twenty pieces of artillery to the spur of the ridge overlooking Plevna. Not more than a thousand yards distant from the redoubt I saw an immense volume of smoke rising, and heard a terrible thunder which was not more than five or six hundred yards away on my left. It was evident that Skobeleff, risking his artillery in this advanced position, was determined to make a desperate effort to capture the redoubt in front of him.

The distance from the Russian positions to the redoubt is probably something over a quarter of a mile, up a smooth even slope, where there is not cover for a rabbit. The glacis is a quarter of a mile, or perhaps a little more, in extent. The loss of an assaulting column rushing up over this glacis under the fire of the Turks would be something terrible. The redoubt Skobeleff was attacking was a doubled redoubt in the bend of the Loftcha road down near Plevna. He had advanced his troops down the slope of the mountain to within easy range.¹ As the Turks immediately opened fire upon him from the redoubt, he returned the fire with steadiness and precision, putting his men under cover as much as possible, his cannon pouring a steady stream of shell and canister into the redoubt as well. In fact he worked his cannon so much that several pieces have been spoiled. He had evidently determined to risk everything to capture this redoubt, and if Plevna were not taken it would not be his fault. For three hours he kept up this fire, and just after Kriloff's second repulse, the Turkish fire having somewhat relaxed, dominated by the Russian, he thought the moment had come for making the assault.

He had four regiments of the line, and four battalions of sharpshooters. Still keeping up his murderous fire, he formed under its cover two regiments in the little hollow at the foot of the low hill on which was built the redoubt, together with two battalions of sharpshooters, not more than twelve hundred yards from the scarp. Then placing himself in the best position for watching the result, he ceased fire and ordered the advance. He ordered the assaulting party not to fire, and they rushed forward with their guns on their shoulders, with music playing and banners flying, and disappeared in the fog and smoke. Skobeleff is the only general who places himself near enough to feel the pulse of a battle. The advancing

¹ Lieutenant Greene says: 'They went down the slope of the third knoll in two lines of company columns, preceded by a strong line of skirmishers, *and with all the bands playing*, cleared the Turks out of their rifle-pits at one foot of the slope, crossed the little stream and began ascending the hill.'

column was indistinctly seen, a dark mass in the fog and smoke. Feeling, as it were, every throb of the battle, he saw this line begin to waver and hesitate. Upon the instant he hurled forward a rival regiment to support, and again watched the result. This new force carried the mass farther on with its momentum, but the Turkish redoubt flamed and smoked, and poured forth such a torrent of bullets that the line was again shaken. Skobeleff stood in this shower of balls unhurt. All his escort were killed or wounded, even to the little Kirghiz,[1] who received a bullet in the shoulder. Again he saw the line hesitate and waver, and he flung his fourth and last regiment, the Libausky, on the glacis. Again this new wave carried the preceding ones forward, until they were almost on the scarp; but that deadly shower of bullets poured upon them; men dropped by hundreds, and the result still remained doubtful. The line once more wavered and hesitated. Not a moment was to be lost, if the redoubt was to be carried.

[1] This little Kirghiz followed Skobeleff from Khokand; in his dress of purple silk, and in constant attendance on Skobeleff, he was one of the most conspicuous figures in the Russian camp. Mr. MacGahan gives another picture of the Kirghiz follower, after the reconnaissance at Loftcha, in which Skobeleff's white Arab was shot under him. 'I found him,' says Mr. MacGahan, on returning from the fight, 'sitting on the ground crying over Skobeleff's horse, which he had also brought from Khokand—a splendid animal that did eighty miles the other day without feeling it apparently, while a fine English mare Skobeleff had was completely knocked up, and had to be killed. The Kirghiz, although himself slightly wounded, had brought the horse back from under fire, and finding there was no hope of saving him, killed him, skinned him, cut off his hoofs, came into camp, sat down, and had a good cry without paying the slightest attention to his wound. He had been utterly indifferent when other horses were killed; but this one, he said, was his countryman and brother—the only thing he had to remind him of his far-away home. I saw tears rolling down the poor fellow's cheeks in a stream. He got two bullets through his clothes, one of which made a flesh wound in his arm. He likewise had two horses shot under him at Plevna.'

Skobeleff had now only two battalions of sharpshooters left, the best in his detachments. Putting himself at the head of these, he dashed forward on horseback. He picked up the stragglers; he reached the wavering, fluctuating mass, and gave it the inspiration of his own courage and instruction. He picked the whole mass up and carried it forward with a rush and a cheer. The whole redoubt was a mass of flame and smoke, from which screams, shouts, and cries of agony and defiance arose, with the deep-mouthed bellowing of the cannon, and above all the steady, awful crash of that deadly rifle-fire. Skobeleff's sword was cut in two in the middle. Then a moment later, when just on the point of leaping the ditch, horse and man rolled together to the ground, the horse dead or wounded, the rider untouched. Skobeleff sprang to his feet with a shout, then with a formidable, savage yell the whole mass of men streamed over the ditch, over the scarp and counter-scarp, over the parapet, and swept into the redoubt like a hurricane. Their bayonets made short work of the Turks still remaining. Then a joyous cheer told that the redoubt was captured, and that at last one of the defences of Plevna was in the hands of the Russians.

Having seen as much as I have seen of the Turkish infantry fire from behind trenches and walls, I thought it was beyond flesh and blood to break it,—a belief which had been strengthened by Kriloff's repulse, which I had just witnessed. Skobeleff proved the contrary; but at what a sacrifice! In that short rush of a few hundred yards, three thousand men had been left on the hill-side, on the glacis, the scarp, and the ditch—one-fourth of his whole force. I believe that Skobeleff looks upon such attacks upon such positions as almost criminal, and disapproved highly the whole plan of attack on Plevna; but he believes that if an attack is to be made, it can only be done in this manner, and that, although the loss of men may be great, it is better that the loss should be incurred and the victory won, than half the loss with a certainty of defeat. Skobeleff seems to be the only one among the Russian generals who has studied the American war with profit. He knows it by heart, and it will be seen by those who have studied the great civil war, that in this assault Skobeleff followed the plan of the American generals on both sides when attempting to carry such positions, to follow up the assaulting column with fresh troops without waiting for the first column to be repulsed. If the position proves too strong for the first column, then reinforcements are at hand before they have time to break and run.

Skobeleff had the redoubt. The question now was how to hold it.[1] It was dominated by the redoubt of Krishin on the left already spoken of. It was exposed at the Plevna side to the fire of the sharpshooters, and to the Turkish forces in the wood bordering on the Sophia road, and open to the fire of the entrenched camp. There was a cross fire coming from three different points.

At daylight next morning the Turks opened fire from all sides. The distance from the redoubt at Krishin had of course been accurately measured, and the guns dropped shells into the redoubt with the utmost precision on the exposed sides. The back of the redoubt was a solid rock on which it was impossible to erect a parapet. All the earth had been used for the construction of the parapets

[1] The middle redoubt, which the Russians had taken, as well as the eastern one, which was still in the hands of the Turks, were properly speaking not redoubts at all, since they were only built up on three sides; the front side of each was simply an increased height to the strong line of trench connecting the two, and extending to the west (left) of the middle one; the other two sides were properly mere traverses to this line; and the fourth side—the rear—was wholly open and exposed to the fire from the trench of the camp, only 600 yards off. The ground was hard and rocky, and there were no spades at hand for digging.' Greene's *Campaign in Bulgaria*, p. 250.

F

on the other side. It was evident that the position was untenable unless the entrenched camp on the other side of the Plevna and the Krishin redoubt could be taken. Skobeleff renewed his demand for reinforcements made the evening before. Although his losses had been great, the spirit of his troops was so good that with another regiment he was willing to undertake to capture the redoubt and the entrenched camp, or he would undertake to hold the positions until something could be attempted in some other quarter. Could one or two more positions be carried during Wednesday, say the Krishin redoubt, and one entrenched camp on the same ridge as the Grivitza redoubt, the fall of Plevna might be considered certain. At sunrise the Turks began an attack upon the captured redoubt, and the storm of battle again raged with fury here, while all was quiet everywhere else. The desperate attack of the Turks was repulsed. Another attack was made and another repulse, and this continued all day long, until the Turks had attacked and been beaten five successive times.

The Russian losses were becoming fearful. General Skobeleff had lost, he thinks, 2,000 men in attacking the redoubt. By the afternoon he had lost 3,000 more in holding it, while his battalions shrivelled up and shrank away as if by magic. One battalion of sharpshooters had been reduced to 160 men. A company which had been 150 was now forty. An immense proportion of officers were killed, or wounded only. Only one commander of a regiment is alive; scarcely a head of a battalion is left. Two officers of the staff are killed, one of whom was Verestchagine, brother of the great artist. Another brother was wounded. General Dobrovolsky, commander of sharpshooters, was killed. One officer was blown to pieces by the explosion of a caisson. Colonel Kurapatkin, chief of the staff, standing beside this officer, had his hair singed and suffered a severe contusion. Only General Skobeleff himself remained untouched. He seems to bear a charmed life. He visited the redoubt three or four times during the day, encouraging the soldiers, telling them help would soon arrive; Plevna would soon be taken; victory would soon crown their efforts; telling them it was the final decisive blow struck for their country; for the honour and glory of the Russian arms; and they always replied with the same cheery shouts, while their numbers were dwindling away by hundreds. He again and again sent for reinforcements, and again and again informed the Commander-in-Chief that the position was untenable. The afternoon wore away and no reinforcements came. . . .

General Levitzky, as I have been informed, formally refused reinforcements, either because he thought the position, in spite of General Skobeleff's representations, was tenable, or because he had no reinforcements to give. General Kriloff, on his own responsibility, sent the remnant of a regiment which had attacked the redoubt, which I saw rush forward and then back through the Indian cornfield. Of the 2,500 there were barely 1,000 left, so it was utterly incapable of going into action that day, and even this regiment arrived too late. General Skobeleff had left the redoubt at four o'clock to go to his tent on a woody hill opposite. He had been there scarcely an hour when he was informed that the Turks were again attacking the right flank on the Loftcha road immediately above Plevna. He galloped forward to see, and was met by an orderly with the news that the Turks were also attacking the redoubt a sixth time. He dashed forward towards the redoubt in hopes of reaching it in time, but was met by a stream of his own men flying back. They were exhausted by forty-eight hours' incessant fighting, and were worn out, hungry, and dying of thirst and fatigue. Owing to the inactivity of the Russians during the day, the Turks had been able to collect an overwhelming force which had made one last desperate effort and had succeeded in driving Skobeleff's force out. One bastion was held till the last by a young officer, whose name I regret I have forgotten, with a handful of men. They refused to fly, and were slaughtered to the last man.

It was just after this that I met General Skobeleff, the first time that day. He was in a fearful state of excitement and fury. His uniform was covered with mud and filth: his sword broken; his cross of St. George twisted round on his shoulder: his face black with powder and smoke; his eyes haggard and blood-shot, and his voice quite gone. He spoke in a hoarse whisper. I never before saw such a picture of battle as he presented. I saw him again in his tent at night. He was quite calm and collected. He said, 'I have done my best; I could do no more. My detachment is half destroyed; my regiments do not exist; I have no officers left; they sent me no reinforcements, and I have lost three guns.' They were three of the four guns which he placed in the redoubt upon taking it, only one of which his retreating troops had been able to carry off. 'Why did they refuse you reinforcements?' I asked. 'Who was to blame?' 'I blame nobody,' he replied. 'It is the will of God.'

Mr. MacGahan's account contains no description of the capture of the eastern redoubt, but Lieut. Greene describes it as follows. I begin his narrative at the critical point of the attack on the middle redoubt. He says:—

The arrival of the 7th regiment gave new courage to the men already so hotly engaged, and they made a renewed effort to advance up the slope, but found it impossible, and again they lay down and open fire. But it was evident that they could not long remain in such a position, only 200 yards from the redoubts; the Turks behind trenches and the Russians in the open and exposed not only to the infantry fire in front, but to artillery fire on both flanks—on the left from the Krishin redoubt and on the right from the redoubts of the 'middle group.' The critical moment had therefore arrived, and Skobeleff sent forward the rest of his troops, viz. the 6th regiment and the two remaining rifle battalions; and he himself, leaving the second knoll, whence he had been directing the attack, rode forward rapidly, caught up the two rifle battalions, and went forward with them. He was well known to his men as being the only general officer who always rode a white horse, and wore a white coat in battle, and there is no doubt that his personal presence encouraged the men: he had the good luck not to be hit, though nearly all his staff fell, and he entered (on foot, his horse being killed) the redoubt with his men. As these reinforcements came forward there was a tremendous enthusiasm and 'hurrah' among the men; one more final effort was made to get up the slope; the Turks were driven out of the trenches in front of the redoubt, then for a few minutes, just as at redoubt No. 10, the affair hung in the balance, but here it succeeded: the Turks began to weaken, a portion of the Russians entered the trenches between the two redoubts, then turned to the left, and finally, at half-past four, the middle redoubt was in the hands of the Russians. The Turks, still firing, retreated to a camp surrounded by a light trench, about 600 yards in rear of the line of redoubts.

The Russians had lost 3,000 men in the assault, which lasted little less than an hour.

But the fight did not now in the least abate. The middle redoubt, which the Russians had taken, as well as the eastern one, which was still in the hands of the Turks, were, properly speaking, not redoubts at all, since they were only built up on three sides: the front side of each was simply an increased height to the strong line of trench connecting the two and extending to the west (left) of the middle one; the other two sides were properly mere traverses to this line: and the fourth side—the rear—was wholly open and exposed to the fire from the trench of the camp only 600 yards off. The ground was hard and rocky, and there were no spades at hand for digging. While the Turks, therefore, kept up an incessant fire from this camp and from the eastern redoubt, which was still in their possession, a force of one or two battalions sortied from the redoubt (No. 13 of plan) on the left of the Russians, and advanced to the attack of the left flank. Seeing this, Colonel Kurapatkin, Chief of the Staff to Skobeleff, and the only one of his staff not killed or wounded, took about 300 men and went forward to meet these Turks in the open. A desperate fight at short range took place, in which the Russians lost the greater part of this little force, but drove the Turks back to their redoubt (No. 13). Just at this time some of the artillery which remained in front of Brestovetz increased their fire upon the Krishin redoubt from the other side, and a portion of the Cossacks on the left flank dismounted and advanced on foot against the same redoubt. This created a diversion upon the Russian left flank, and relieved them for a time from further attacks in that quarter. Meanwhile a small force of a few hundred volunteers came out of the middle redoubt, and made an effort to get into the eastern one, but they all, or nearly all, perished. Then Colonel Shestakoff, of Imérétinsky's staff, came across the valley from the third knoll to the line of redoubts with three companies of the 6th regiment and portions of the other regiments which had been left in reserve, and, picking up on the way the stragglers and scattered detachments in the valley, made a force of about 1,000 or 1,200 men, with which he made a desperate effort against the front of the eastern redoubt at the same time that a fresh lot of volunteers sortied from the middle redoubt against its left flank. The attack succeeded, and at 5.30 P.M. the eastern redoubt was also in the hands of the Russians. Soon afterwards darkness set in, and the fight slackened down to desultory picket-firing, with an occasional shell from the Krishin redoubt.

Skobeleff's position was precarious. He occupied, with the 6th, 7th, 61st, and 62nd regiments and the Rifle Brigade, the line of trench and redoubt shown on this plan just south-west of the town. In his front, at 600 yards, was the entrenched camp of the Turks; on his left flank, at 800 yards, was redoubt No. 13; and on his left rear, at 2,300 yards, was the Krishin redoubt (No. 14). On his right flank was the middle group of redoubts, and on his right rear was redoubt No. 10, where the Russians had been repulsed during the afternoon. He was entered like a wedge into the midst of the Turkish lines, and on three sides of him were strong works against which either no attack had been made at all or the attack had failed. In his rear, at about 1,800 yards, were still the 24 9-pounders, supported by two battalions of the 8th and two very weak battalions of the 5th regiment, which had lost 700 men in the affair of September 8. The other battalion of the 8th was at Brestovetz, and that of the 5th regiment was keeping up the connection between the two portions of his command. If the Turks in the Krishin redoubt were strong enough to come down upon his rear, there was a good chance that his whole force would be lost. He sent word to Zotoff explaining his position, and saying that it was untenable unless he were strongly reinforced, at the same time that other reinforcements were sent against the Krishin redoubt: saying also that he would hold on as long as he could, and asking for further instructions.

Not only was his position most critical, but his men were exhausted and their ammunition was running very short. Skobeleff was indefatigable. He himself posted the battalion of the 8th regiment between the two positions, with one company facing east across the little valley between the redoubt line and the third knoll, another company facing west towards the Krishin redoubt, and the other three companies in the centre. Some Cossacks who arrived during the night, he employed to bring up cartridges, and himself personally visited the left flank of the redoubt line, and set the men to work with their bayonets, soup dishes, and whatever they had, in throwing up a sort of traverse or trench against the fire from the redoubt No. 13. Twice during the night he was attacked, once from Krishin and once from the valley on the side of Plevna. The troops making the latter attack were in the darkness mistaken for Russians, supposing that they might be a portion of the IV. Corps coming to their aid from that direction. The Turks thus got within 100 yards of the Russians before it was discovered; the latter fell back upon the three remaining companies of the battalion (8th regiment), and then fired by volleys on the Turks, and thus drove them back. This was about midnight. About the same time arrived an aide-de-camp (Colonel Orloff) of the Grand Duke, who had been riding since six o'clock in the darkness and absence of roads (it was nearly fifteen miles round through the Russian lines from the Grand Duke's head-quarters to Skobeleff's position); the critical condition of affairs was explained to him, and he returned to head-quarters. A little before daybreak Skobeleff brought four 9-pounders forward and established them in the middle redoubt to open fire against No. 13.

The morning of September 12 dawned bright and

clear, after forty hours of continuous rain and fog. At six o'clock the Turks opened fire with their artillery from the redoubts surrounding Skobeleff's position, and with musketry from the camp in his front; and not long after appeared a strong column of infantry from the direction of the Krishin redoubt, which advanced to within 300 yards of the Russian position before it was arrested by their fire; it then fell back to redoubt No. 13. At eight o'clock they made their second attack in the same direction, but with no better success. Skobeleff had meanwhile brought up eight 4-pounders to the third knoll, which did good service with shrapnel against the advancing Turks. At 10.30 A.M. they made a third desperate assault, still upon the left flank of the Russian position; it was repulsed, but now the men in that part of the line, worn out and discouraged with thirty hours' continuous firing, began to drop out one by one and make their way to the rear. Seeing this, Skobeleff, who was on the third knoll, rode over and expostulated, threatened, ordered, and encouraged the men, and got them back into the redoubt again.

Meanwhile Skobeleff had received two orders from Zotoff, the first about 7 A.M., and the second at 10.30 A.M. They were as follows:—

'1. To General Prince Imérétinsky: By direction of the Commander-in-Chief, I give you and General Skobeleff the order to fortify yourselves in the position which you have taken to-day, and to hold out to the last extremity. We can send you no reinforcements, for we have none.

'(Signed)   ZOTOFF, Lieutenant-General.'

'2. To General Skobeleff: By order of the Commander-in-Chief, if you cannot hold the positions which you have taken, then you must retreat slowly—but, *if such a thing is possible*, not before evening to Tutchenitza, covering your retreat by the cavalry of General Leontieff. Send a copy of this order—which otherwise keep secret—to General Prince Imérétinsky. The Grivitza redoubt is in our hands, but in spite of this the attack cannot be continued; but the retreat must be slowly begun: 8.30 A.M.

'(Signed)   ZOTOFF, Lieutenant-General.'

This latter order was brought by the same Colonel Orloff who had visited Skobeleff during the night, and thence returned to the Grand Duke and Zotoff to explain the condition of things in Skobeleff's front.

Skobeleff did what he could to obey these orders—to hold on till evening; but from the very first his case was hopeless. He always kept hoping, in spite of Zotoff's first order, that a portion of the IV. Corps would be sent to help him, or at least that the attack would recommence on some other part of the line, and thus relieve the pressure on him. But this did not happen. There was hardly a shot fired from any other part of the line throughout this day. Zotoff and Levitzky were at the Grand Duke's headquarters all the morning, over on the hills east of Grivitza, about six and a-half miles in a straight line from Skobeleff's position, watching the fight with their glasses, but unable, of course, at that distance to make anything out of it. The distance over the route which messengers had to take through the Russian lines was about twelve miles. As to the question of reinforcements, the Roumanians and the 1st brigade, 5th division, were fully occupied in holding the Grivitza redoubt: from the Grivitza village to the Tutchenitza creek the line was held by five regiments of the IX. Corps and six regiments of the IV. Corps, and of these eleven regiments, five had not been engaged the previous day at all, viz. the 121st, 122nd, 119th, 120th, and 20th. Whether two or three of these regiments might not safely have been sent to Skobeleff—as there was no intention of attacking in any other part of the line—is of course a matter about which opinions will differ. The fact was, however, that at the Russian headquarters it had been determined not to continue the attack (on the ground that their force was not strong enough) and the Chief of the Staff had *no realisation* of what a desperate position Skobeleff was in. Hence the orders cited above.

Skobeleff's position, however, was most desperate. As the morning wore on and there was no sign of a renewal of the attack on the other parts of the line, Osman began to mass a strong force in Plevna to drive Skobeleff out. Whether these troops were drawn from the reserve camp in the valley between the town and the river, or from the Bukova position, or from the middle redoubts, is not known; but it is certain that Osman reinforced the troops in front of Skobeleff to the extent of not less than 12,000 men. Part of them went over the hill and round into the Krishin redoubt, and thence against Skobeleff's left flank, and part of them came out of the town and followed up the Tutchenitza brook for about three-quarters of a mile, and then climbing up its bank, endeavoured to get possession of the third knoll from the rear, and thus cut off Skobeleff's retreat. This latter movement began to make itself apparent at about 1 P.M., and to meet it Skobeleff brought up the two battalions of the 5th regiment, which up till now had remained with the batteries on the second knoll. Meanwhile, of the four guns which he had placed in the middle redoubt, two had been dismounted and the other two had lost all their horses and gunners; to replace these guns Skobeleff sent three of the eight guns which he had kept on the third knoll; they had been in the redoubt but a short time before they were dismounted, and about this time a caisson, which had been brought under the shelter of the side of the redoubt for protection, was, nevertheless, found by a shell from the Krishin redoubt, and exploded in the midst of the men, not only creating a fearful loss, but carrying dismay to those who were not hurt. Skobeleff again rushed forward in person to the redoubt, and endeavoured to reassure his men; and he was barely in time, for a few minutes later, between 2 and 2.30 P.M., the Turks from the direction of the Krishin redoubt and from No. 13, reinforced by fresh troops, made their fourth assault. The Russians let them approach to within 400 yards, and then opened on them with well-aimed volley firing, and with deadly effect. The Turkish line halted, and sought shelter, and returned the fire; but every time they endeavoured to move forward they met with such terrible losses, that they finally gave it up and returned to No. 13.

As Skobeleff was returning from the redoubt to the third knoll, he learned that the 118th regiment was arriving; it had been sent to him as reinforcement by General Kriloff, commanding IV. Corps, *on his own responsibility*, on account of the heavy firing which he had heard so long on Skobeleff's front. The regiment numbered 1,300 men. At 4.30 P.M. the Turks, greatly reinforced in numbers, began their fifth assault from the direction of Krishin, and simultaneously from the camp. They kept advancing in spite of the murderous fire of the Russians, and as they neared the redoubt, the majority of the latter, worn out with thirty-six hours' continuous fighting with no appreciable result, began to make off to the rear in small groups; the little band of 200 or more brave men who remained behind under Major Gortaloff were cut down to the last man in a fierce hand-to-hand fight.

The middle redoubt was thus lost, but still the men in the eastern redoubt and a part of the trenches between the two remained in their places and kept up the fight. To prevent their being massacred, Skobeleff hastily sent them an order to fall back to the third knoll; and in order that this might be possible, he himself took the 118th regiment (which had recently arrived as just stated) and led them to the assault of the line between the two redoubts. Under cover of this they returned (what was left of them) to the third knoll. The retreat was then continued under the protection of the twenty-four guns and two battalions (8th regiment) on the second knoll. Except those who fell in the last affair in front of the redoubts, nearly all the wounded were carried off; the dead were left upon the field.

Skobeleff retreated to the 'first knoll' and remained there all night and all of the 13th. The Turks were too much used up to follow or attack him. At night of the 13th he returned to Bogot. His losses were 160 officers and over 8,000 men. About 18,000 men had been engaged.

That is the American account of the third battle of Plevna, to which I only need to add that Mr. Mac Gahan subsequently states that, in a conversation which he had with Skobeleff before the assault began, he had declared that the plan of a general assault was a mistake, and a terrible mistake it proved.

Here is the Russian description of the events of the fatal day.

On the evening of $_{\text{Sept. 10}}^{\text{Aug. 29}}$ the clouds obscured the horizon and dissolved in heavy rain. At midnight all the troops received the dispositions signed by General Zotoff. They were as follows :—

To-morrow, $_{\text{Sept. 11}}^{\text{Aug. 30}}$, will take place the general attack on the fortified camp of Plevna.

1. At daybreak all the batteries will open a heavy fire

against all the enemy's entrenchments, and continue it until nine o'clock, and then stop at the same time everywhere. Resume firing at eleven and keep up till one. Afterwards cease firing till half-past two. At half-past two resume the bombardment from all guns, excepting those which would interfere with the assault.

2. At three will begin the attack.

The Roumanians and Baron Krüdner were to attack Grivitza, General Kriloff commanded the centre, and General Skobeleff the left wing; while the cavalry, under General Leontieff and General Lachkaroff, were to operate against any Turkish troops which might show themselves to the left bank of the Vid.

The object of the assailants was to determine the key of the enemy's position, and to strike so as to sever their line of operations and to weaken their resistance. We thought that the Grivitza redoubt was the vital point in Osman's defence. It was the largest and the highest, and against it we sent sixty-four battalions, while Skobeleff was given twenty-two battalions to attack the Green Hills. When the battle was over it was found that the key of the position was in front of Skobeleff, and that the Grivitza redoubt only represented the extreme front of the enemy's line.

The morning of $\frac{\text{Aug. 30}}{\text{Sept. 11}}$ began with a fine rain, which grew heavier as the hour of assault drew near. At nine o'clock, seeing that the reserves on the left flank were moving, we began to reply with shell.

On the other side of the deep isolated ravine

of Tutchenitza, Skobeleff had pitched his tent in a valley between two hillocks, and immediately in front of the Loftcha road.

Skobeleff knew that if he began to attack at three he should fail to take the redoubts. It was necessary to begin soon, he said, and without waiting for three o'clock he started the first battalions towards the Green Hills.

The Turks began by firing at intervals a few rounds. Skobeleff's took up a position among the vines; but the Turkish fire increasing in volume in proportion as the vanguard advanced, it became necessary to fall back towards the tents in the valley.

At three o'clock the general attack began. It was impossible for anyone to see all that was going on. They noticed that with Kriloff things did not go well; only on the two wings was there any success. The rain increased towards evening The night came: the bombardment died away. Kriloff had been beaten back with enormous loss. On the right the Grivitza redoubt had been captured, and on the left Skobeleff had chased the Turks out of two redoubts which defended the town of Plevna.

Before the battle began, Skobeleff, followed by his aides-de-camp, rode through the ranks of his detachment.

'Good day, my friends,' cried the General as he rode up smiling to the front of the regiment.

The troops returned his greeting with pleasure.

'I am very happy, my friends, to serve with you.'

'We will do all we can, Excellency.'

'Are you not brave fellows, then?' he asked, smiling.

'We will do all we can, Excellency.'

'And it will be necessary to do it, my friends. You know well that all Russia is watching us. But I know you—what you are worth. . . . We shall meet under fire,' and then, with a friendly nod, Skobeleff would ride off from the regiment. These simple words of his sank deep into the heart of every soldier. He did not trust them in vain.

Skobeleff led into battle against the Turkish redoubts, the regiments Vladimiri, the Suzdal, the 9th and 10th Tirailleurs. In the second line he placed the 1st and 12th battalions of Tirailleurs, and his infantry regiments. The Turkish redoubts were placed thus: one great redoubt rose at the summit of a gently sloping hill; half-a-mile to the right of this redoubt stood another smaller redoubt, and a mile and a-half further was the principal fortified camp. To the left of the central redoubt was another, also at a mile and a-half distance, which took the assailants in the rear as soon as they seized the central fort.

Before reaching the latter redoubt, our brave troops had to cross about a mile of country, entirely without cover, under the terrible fire from the Turks. On they went cheering, with flags flying, bands playing, and drums beating, as they marched. Skobeleff rode at their head on his white horse, and was one of the first to enter the redoubt. The Turks fled, but from the other redoubts they opened a deadly fire upon our troops. The redoubt was open to the rear, and every shell was dropped into our midst. The Turks had the range exactly; not a shot was wasted. Our soldiers found shelter as best they could in the redoubt, and then an attack was made on the neighbouring redoubt on the right. The first assault was beaten back, but at night they chased the Turks out of the second redoubt. The Turks attempted to retake it during the night, but they were driven back at the point of the bayonet. Next day the Turks attacked on both flanks. Twice our outnumbered garrisons were on the point of giving way, when Skobeleff appeared as if suddenly rising out of the ground, reanimated his men by his presence, and drove back the Turks. We had held them for twenty-four hours—under a deadly cross fire—counting upon the success of the general attack. But our hopes vanished. Our troops dwindled, not by the hour, but by the minute. Five Turkish attacks, the most persistent and desperate, had been repelled; the redoubts were literally drenched with Russian blood; but in the end Skobeleff's force failed him, and he was compelled to give way.

The failure of their five attacks did not dismay the Turks. Although the fire ceased along all the rest of the line, it never stopped for one minute on the left flank. There was a moment very propitious for us to attack the last redoubt on the right, but attack was out of the question ; it was more than we could do to hold our own. Towards four o'clock in the afternoon, after the fifth attack had been driven back, the Turks were so weakened that, if Skobeleff had only received a few fresh troops, he could have captured the third redoubt ; and, the position on the left flank being thus secured, the affair of Plevna would have been brilliantly concluded. Skobeleff thrice demanded reinforcements : but none were sent, and the opportunity passed.

The Turkish general, profiting by the general lull, brought together all his reserves, and launched them against Skobeleff's position. The Turkish column fell upon the small redoubt on the right, and of the handful of heroes who had defended it from the first, some were shot, others bayonetted. Only a few contrived to escape to the larger redoubt. That shared the same fate. The Turks, in overwhelming numbers, crushed all resistance. The remnant of Skobeleff's detachment in the redoubt was bayonetted, and Skobeleff brought back two companies alone of all the troops with which, but twenty-four hours before, he had captured the three redoubts.

The Turks were victorious. They had regained their redoubts, and their impregnable line once more confronted our positions. At seven o'clock Skobeleff fell back, according to orders, on Bogot, and the great assault had finally failed. But, if Skobeleff had

THE INVESTMENT OF PLEVNA. 83

only received the reinforcements which he had vainly demanded, Plevna would that day have fallen into our hands.

After the repulse of $\frac{\text{August 30}}{\text{September 11}}$ our forces remained almost inactive.

On September $\frac{10}{22}$ General Kriloff, at Teliche, allowed the Turks to reinforce Plevna with 12,000 men and 2,000 wagons of munitions of war; on $\frac{\text{September 23}}{\text{October 5}}$ Chefket reinforced Osman from Orkhanie. The day before this misfortune General Todtleben was appointed to the command of the army of the West, and the siege of Plevna was begun. Had the Sebastopol hero, so well appreciated and so brilliantly described by Mr. Kinglake, been appointed some few months sooner, our Plevna disaster would probably never have taken place. We had about 250 guns in position: 20 24-pounders and 230 9-pounders. The Turks had only 80 field guns. From his base at Orkhanie Chefket kept pouring supplies into Plevna by the Sophia road; for, strange though it appears, Osman's communications with Sophia were never cut until October $\frac{12}{24}$, when the Guard, which had just arrived from Russia, defeated, at severe sacrifice of precious lives, the Turks at Gorni Doubniak. Around Plevna nothing but trench-making and occasional firing went on, except at Grivitza, where the Roumanians, on October $\frac{7}{19}$ made two unsuccessful attempts to take the second Grivitza redoubt. The investment of Plevna was not completed until $\frac{\text{October 21}}{\text{November 2}}$, when General Gourko occupied Dolni Doubniak and threw a ring of steel around the Turkish fortress.

Skobeleff soon after recommenced active operations. On October 27 his troops, having gradually worked their way up to the Green Hill by trenches, captured the famous position by a sudden night assault. His division before the assault numbered 11,000 men. The Turks, taking advantage of his repulse on $\frac{\text{August 31}}{\text{September 12}}$, when he was ordered to fall back beyond the Loftcha road to Tutchenitza, constructed four other redoubts, so that, instead of three between him and Plevna, there were seven, or six, if we deduct that captured on November 8. The soldiers around Plevna now numbered 120,000, and the line of investment was forty-six miles long. Osman's line extended twenty-four miles.

The following is Mr. MacGahan's account of the successful surprise of the Turkish redoubt and the heavy fighting which followed for the next ten days:—

The Brestovetz redoubt is just opposite the Turkish Krishin redoubt, from which it is distant about 1,300 yards. But this Brestovetz redoubt forms a kind of angle projecting into the Turkish lines, and is somewhat exposed and dangerous. It became necessary to strengthen the Russian line. This could be done by seizing the small wooded hill immediately in front of the right wing between the Loftcha road and the parallel ravine.

It was most unfortunate for the Russians that these positions were ever abandoned, for they are about as high as the Krishin redoubt; they completely command Plevna, and the two redoubts captured by Skobeleff in the last affair, and fortified, would have rendered the Russian positions here much stronger than they can now be made. The Turks have now constructed a strong redoubt on the summit of the hill between the Krishin redoubt and the Loftcha road, the very spot where Skobeleff planted two batteries during the last affair. It was not the hill with the redoubt which Skobeleff resolved to capture, but one between the Loftcha road and the ravine. It was defended by trenches, and held by about fourteen tabors, perhaps 7,000 men, though Todtleben believed there were a great many more, as the position was most important. The combined movement was arranged with General Gourko, who was to open fire all along the line, and likewise advance and occupy the position in front of him towards the bridge over the Vid, in order to shorten his line likewise. The weather was so foggy one could not see more than fifty feet.

The attack was fixed for five o'clock. By that time it was so dark that nothing could be seen more than five feet off. Skobeleff reviewed his troops that were destined for the attack—the battalion of sharpshooters. He then got down from his horse, went about among the men, talked to them, told them, especially the under-officers, just what they were to do, and finished by informing them he would lead the assault in person. This regiment, I may remark, was one which attacked and carried the same heights during the last affair of Plevna on the second day of the bombardment. The regiment, having taken these heights, slipped out of the hands of its officers, and pursued the Turks to the foot of the glacis of the redoubt afterwards captured by Skobeleff, with the result that two-thirds of the regiment were destroyed. The regiment is now full again with reserves that have come up. It was the recollection of this event that decided Skobeleff to lead the attack himself. It was important that the men should be stopped at the right moment and at the right place, and that the intrenchments which he intended to throw up should be properly laid, as a little mistake easily made might end disastrously. It was not, therefore, mere bravado which made him decide to lead the assault himself.

At half-past four he mounted his horse, put himself at the head of his troops, and disappeared in the fog. At five o'clock the fog began to turn dark, showing the approach of night. The Turks must have thought there would be little call for further vigilance that day. On the approach of darkness the roar of eighty guns was heard that vomited splashes of flame upon the murky fog, and then were silent. Then came the scream of eighty shells seeking their destination in the obscurity. Then there was the crash of the infantry fire along the whole line, except on the point of the attack, for it was Skobeleff's design to use the fog for cover and take the Turks by surprise. The infantry fire rolled along in front of Brestovetz, where I had taken my station, and soon the bullets began singing overhead, telling that the Turks were replying; but we could hear as yet little firing on the right wing, where the attack was to take place. Finally, after about a quarter of an hour, there were two or three volleys in this direction, followed by a Russian shout, and we knew the position was carried.

As it turned out, the Turks were surprised, and did not discover the approach of the Russians until they were within one hundred yards. By the time they had seized their arms and fired two rounds, the Russians were on them with the bayonet, and it was all over. In a moment those who did not fly were bayoneted. The attack was led by two companies of sharpshooters, followed closely by the 9th Battalion and the Vladimirsky regiment. Every man was provided with a shovel, and immediately began making trenches, as indicated by Skobeleff. In a very few minutes they were under cover from a heavy but ill-directed fire poured into them from the next hill, not distant more than 250 yards. Skobeleff stayed until about ten o'clock, when he thought the men had made the place secure, and returned to Brestovetz to supper. He had scarcely washed when the fire broke out again with fury on the right flank. Skobeleff mounted again, disappeared in the darkness and fog, and did not return till this morning. He found the Turks making a desperate attempt to recapture the position, and arrived on the ground in the nick of time, as some confusion had ensued, for the reserves, who lost their way in the fog, coming in the wrong direction, got fired into from their own side. There was also a report that Skobeleff was killed, which discouraged the troops. He arrived in the middle of the Turkish assault, one fellow having leaped into the trench with the cry of 'Allah!' where he was bayoneted. The attack was repulsed, but the Turks made a second and third one, and each time were driven back with ease. The Russian loss was comparatively small, only 250 killed and wounded, among whom were two or three officers.

The new position of General Skobeleff not only brings him nearer to the Turks, but shortens the line of investment materially. There is a certain green hill to the north of the line, thinly wooded, and not over five hundred paces from the battery on the Loftcha road; on the slope of this hill has been stationed the advanced picquets of the Turks, who have made it at times decidedly uncomfortable for passers between the battery and this village, and have sent a multitude of compliments in this direction. General Skobeleff has been meditating for some days the capture of this territory, and it was decided to attempt the advance on November 9, in conjunction with a forward movement of General Gourko on the left.

At three o'clock the ragged red and yellow flag was taken from its place by the side of the door of the low mud hovel occupied by General Skobeleff, and the staff assembled to inspect the troops and to accompany the General, who was to conduct the attack in person. It was a most picturesque and romantic cavalcade that filed out of the yard and followed the young leader out to certain danger and possible death. General Skobeleff, alike heedless of cold and damp and whizzing missiles, was the only one who was not bundled up in overcoat and capuchin. He led the way through the narrow alleys of the village, mounted on a white horse—the soldiers look for the white horse as much as for their beloved commander—confident, cheerful, inspiriting to look upon. Behind him a motley retinue; Circassians with long surtout and silver-mounted harness and weapons; blond youths already scarred and covered with decorations, correspondents in civil dress, Cossacks half hidden in their grey coats and hoods, and in the middle of the group a picturesque Circassian on a white horse, bearing the tattered banner, quite like an old crusader, with his quaint arms and curious dress. The flag, too, is quite mediæval in appearance, and completed the illusion to perfection. It is a square silk banner, fastened to a Cossack's lance, and has on the one side the white cross of St. George, and on the other the letters M.C. (Michael Skobeleff), and the date 1875, in yellow on a red ground. The tattered silk was carried through the Khokand campaign, and has fluttered in all the hard fights which have made the young General so famous. We went on losing our way a dozen times, and at last reached the spot where the troops were massed near an encampment of straw huts, all drawn up in order, with arms in hands, and with spades to intrench the ground they were about to take; stretcher-bearers in a group at the rear, a suggestive but unpleasant sight; a battery of mitrailleuses bundled up like so many human beings to keep out the damp, and in front of the troops, the little body of picked men, each with his shovel, his rations, and plenty of ammunition, who were to make the first rush across, use the bayonet, and then throw it aside for the spade, and endeavour to cover in time to resist the attack of the returning Turks.

It was a dramatic and intensely impressive scene, these square masses of earnest men, every one with his eyes fixed on the face of the General, who passed before them all with the customary greeting, which was answered with a will like one voice from the battalion, in turn. Against the background of grey mists which had now settled down so thick that objects were not visible the length of a company front, came out the forms of men and horses in exaggerated relief and made wonderfully picturesque the groups and masses of expectant soldiers. General Skobeleff dismounted and told the men just what he expected of them—that they were not to storm the works of Plevna, but only to run forward and take the piece of ground they knew perfectly well in front of the road, and to hold it until they had works thrown up. He cautioned them, as many were young soldiers sent out from the reserves to fill the great gaps in the ranks, not to advance too far, but to mind exactly what the officers told them. He would be with them himself, and would direct the movements personally. Surely a finer lot of men never went into a fight; young, healthy, devoted, and confident, every face wore an expression that was a proof of courage and earnestness and even religious zeal. As we stood there the darkness rapidly increased, and it was nearly five o'clock as the troops moved forward at quick pace in front of the General and staff. As the men passed they all received encouraging words, and they went by smiling at the good-natured chaff from the General, who called to them by name, remarked on their new boots, which he said were like those of a Spanish don, and told the musicians they would play a waltz in the new redoubts on the morrow.

The perfect confidence of the soldiers, inspired by the presence of the man whom they regard as a protector, infallible leader, and beloved friend at the same time, made the success of the undertaking assured. The hot breath of sixteen field-pieces scorched our faces as the opening salvo shook the heavy air, then came a cheer on the right, just down in the hollow, and the singing of bullets filled the air over our heads. The musketry rattled and roared in the hollow, and off on the green hill on the right, and sounded like the surging of a storm. The fog began to condense and gather on the ground, and the cold increased, and still the battle roared, and rose and fell, ceased and began again. At last it was evident from the firing that the position was taken, and we retired to the village. At a quarter-past ten it broke out again, and the same fiendish noise and rattle went on as before, and the bullets and shells kept singing about our ears for a long half-hour, and all was silent, with an occasional cannon report, until daybreak, when we were awakened by a new peal of artillery, and had the same continuous rattle of bullets among the twigs. Then we learned the details of the occupation of the ridge. . . .

I have given the notes of one day at Skobeleff's camp and head-quarters. This is the treat he generally gives his visitors. The General himself is asleep on a stretcher in the trenches, and will not come up again until the occupation of the ridge is a settled fact, and there is no more danger of the Turks retaking it. It is no wonder that the soldiers of such a general fight well.

Writing on November $\frac{4}{16}$, Mr. MacGahan says:

The position here remains unchanged. Since the seizure of the Green Hill by Skobeleff, no important movement has been undertaken by the Russians. The Turks have made three attacks upon Skobeleff's position on three successive nights, but were each time repulsed with heavy loss. The defence of this new position is most successful and brilliant, and the position itself is of more importance than I was at first disposed to acknowledge. Skobeleff remains night after night in the trenches, and has succeeded in pushing his lines up to within one hundred yards of the Turks. They are indeed so close to each other that scarcely a night passes without heavy firing. Fire is opened all along the line upon the slightest alarm.

The Turks attacked on the 10th, 11th, 15th, and 19th of November (new style), but were always driven back. Skobeleff drove his trenches within 150 yards of the Turkish lines, and there he used to spend days and nights, encouraging his men, watching the enemy and pressing ever closer on Plevna.

His life in the trenches is described at some length by M. Némirovitch Dantchenko, extracts from whose reminiscences I venture to translate.

'Skobeleff,' says M. Dantchenko, 'was a constant puzzle to me. Is it possible, I used to ask myself, that in that iron heart there was no room for fear, dread, and the sadness which seizes everyone before going into battle? I once asked him the question point blank. "It is difficult to feel at one's ease, certainly," he replied; "never believe anyone who tells you the contrary; but," he continued, "it is not a time now to discuss, to criticise, to despair. You have said that men of talent ought to take care of themselves. It is better to die; and we would gladly die if thereby we brought no shame upon Russia and held high the banner of our country. It is good to die for one's country. There is no better death."

'While he spoke, we were confronted by a platoon of volunteers, under Lieutenant Tarashenko. They asked that they might be the first to assault the Turkish position. I glanced at the figures of these determined fellows. There was nothing remarkable about them. They were simply ordinary grey-coated soldiers, some smiling naïvely, all confident. Skobeleff caressed one, talked to another. There was no oration, no rhetoric. He chatted as a man with men. " Remember, my friends," he said, " to-day we are not going to take Plevna; we are only going to turn the Turks out of their trenches, and to occupy them ourselves; but, understand, once that you are in the trenches, you will stop there." " We will do our best." " And, look you, remember that it is not a question of courage, but of obedience. When your chief says ' halt,' stop where you are standing, no matter how you may be tempted to pursue the enemy. As for the Turks, there is no reason to fear them." " We don't fear them, Excellency." " All right. Do you remember how we fought at Loftcha?" " We do indeed, Excellency," they answered without hesitation. "You remember how we chased them?" "They ran altogether," said a soldier, smiling. "You were there with me then?" said Skobeleff; "you are probably one of the veterans?" "I took three redoubts also with your Excellency before Plevna." Skobeleff sighed. "Ah! well, my friends, you see the affair is not difficult; we have captured this hill once before. It has already belonged to us." "And we will take it again, Excellency," they reply; and Skobeleff passes on to hold a similar conversation with every battalion. Skobeleff came up to us and began talking. Sir Henry Havelock was there with his curious gutta-percha hat, Mr. MacGahan, and others. "Do you know," said he, "I am rather afraid about the young soldiers. It is a very risky affair. In a night attack during fog, even veterans might lose themselves. I will not remain with the reserve as I intended. I must lead them myself. Ah! if I only had my Turkestanis. You remember Makhram and Andijan," he said to Kurapatkin. The two comrades in Central Asian warfare gazed for a moment in silence into the stormy past. Then Skobeleff continued, "Do you remember how they derided my Turkestanis at the beginning of the campaign? They declared that they could not even trust me with a battalion, and they despised my officers, who, nevertheless, were the first to die. Where are they now? Some lie at Eski Saghra; others in the Balkans; most of them are dead."

'Skobeleff was right. When the war broke out the term Tashkentian was a word of reproach. But when the campaign progressed, and things began to be looked into, it was found that the Tashkentians were the best men in the army. It was they who created the Bulgarian Militia, and converted it into a compact body; it is they who have furnished the best chiefs of detachments, the best chiefs of staff, the best fighting officers.

'Skobeleff halted before the regiment. He took off his cap and crossed himself. As if a breath passed through the air, officers and men all made the sign of the cross, and each one silently offered up a prayer, and communed for a moment with himself; for who knew whether as they fell they would be able to cast a last upward glance to heaven? All uncovered; and even foreigners shared the solemn feeling of that moment—when, we know not why, there returns to our minds the memories of a distant past, the home of our childhood, our loved ones. It is but for an instant.

'"To your ranks!" At that word the long line of tirailleurs spread out like a fan, and the advance began.

'On their countenances there is neither sadness nor preoccupation. The eyes of some officers gleam with enthusiasm as they repeat their orders. Skobeleff is already well in front; we see his handsome figure in advance of the line. The line pushes on quietly, the figure of the General fades away in the distance.

The tirailleurs are but black specks hardly visible in the misty twilight. Night is coming on.

'Thank God the Turks do not notice our advance! "I begin to believe that the affair will be settled without great loss," murmurs a voice near me; but at that moment the sharp crack of a Turkish rifle rings through the air. The sentinel has given the alarm. Another shot follows and then another. The heart almost ceases to beat. Our men do not answer. The Turks do not yet realise their danger. They fire occasionally, but their dropping shots gave no alarm. Our fellows should now be near enough to attack. The suspense is painful.

'"Follow me, my friends!" suddenly sounds out of the fog, and in a moment the hurrahs of the assailants mingle with the roll of the Turkish drums and the fusillade of the first Turkish trenches. We can see nothing, but soon the balls come pouring thick and fast over our heads.

'The tirailleurs had done their work. They cleared the Turks out of several entrenchments, which they could hardly distinguish in the thick fog of that autumnal night. Then from all our batteries on the left flank our artillery opened on the Turkish position; the night air is alive with shells and the flame of cannon.

'The enemy flies. We can hear the tramp of flying men as they run through the maize fields. Where was Skobeleff? At his accustomed place. He led the volunteers into the trenches, and springing upon the breastwork stood round the powder smoke in the midst of the hottest fire from both sides, reanimating the courage of his men, and encouraging them to complete their task. When the fire lulled the Turks fled. Skobeleff strolled along the line chatting with his men, noting the construction of the work done by the reserves, and strengthening the weak points in his position. "Listen, my friends!" he exclaimed to the troops on the right; " the enemy is about to attack us again immediately. I shall be on the left flank. Hold your ground, my brave fellows! Die in your place rather than yield the position to the enemy."

'" Yes, Excellency. Do not disquiet yourself."

"' We are with Maneffsky," cried the soldiers. Skobeleff grasped the hand of Maneffsky and went off.

' There ensued a moment of stillness, and Skobeleff hastened to Brestovetz to send a report of the operations to the Commander-in-Chief. Hardly had he written the words when the firing recommenced. Skobeleff seized the first horse he could find, and rode back beneath a shower of shot and shell to the newly-captured positions.

' As they were beginning to climb up the steep slope of the Green Hill, they came upon a troop retreating in disorder. " Good day, my brave fellows," said Skobeleff. The soldiers instinctively fell into line. " What!" cried Skobeleff. " Are you running away? Dress. Follow me. March!"

' Sending Kurapatkin to the trench to announce

his immediate return, Skobeleff himself led the troop back to its work. Like a simple company officer, the General led the soldiers under fire, distributed their places, and after giving strict orders to the officers, he returned to the advanced trenches.

'Morning dawned grey and foggy. All night the men had had no rest. The moment the fight ceased, digging began.

On the trenches of his foremost outpost line, only 150 yards distant from the trenches of the enemy, they dug out a square shallow pit for the General, in which Skobeleff, Kurapatkin, and Melnitzky snatched a little sleep on the straw.

'The day passed, night again came on, and as the light faded from the sky, the vigilance of the officers increased. Orders were given to the sentinels to keep a strict look-out. The sous-officiers were ordered to remain awake in order to keep the sentinels perpetually under inspection.

'Skobeleff went round the trenches several times, urging the sentries to be vigilant, and commanding them, whatever they did, not to fire.

'" When you see the Turks," he said, "do not fire; but call out at once, 'The Turks are coming; make ready!' The nearer they come the better it will be; keep the muzzle of your gun low down; and when the order is given to fire you will not hit the crows up in the sky, but will fire directly on the enemy. Let no one fire a shot without orders. As soon as the Turks leap upon the breastwork receive them at the point of the bayonet. It will not be the first time we have beaten them, my friends."

'It became darker and darker. The Turks fired less frequently. It seemed as if they also were wearied. I heard some officers muttering in their sleep. "Stand firm!" murmured one; and then all was silence. I was alone as if in the kingdom of the dead. The fires went out. You could not even hear the rustle of a dry leaf. The sentries gazed more and more steadily into the darkness. It seemed as if something fell on the breastwork, then once more all was still. But then again there is a sound. It was the tread of stealthy footsteps. The sentry excitedly turns the muzzle of his rifle on the place where he heard the sound, and gazes with straining eyes and throbbing heart into the fog.

'"Do not fire," whispers some one behind the breastwork; "I am one of yours. I bring news from the front. Do not fire. Wake the General. The Turks are going to make a sortie; they are drawn up in line."

'Then behind me I heard the cry, "To arms!" I turned. It was Skobeleff already at the breastwork. "To arms, friends! Up to the front!"

'Skobeleff had heard the whispering in his sleep, and roused himself in time to hear the last words of the scout announcing the coming of the Turks.

'"I knew they would attack to-day," said he. "Friends, see now that you act as brave men. Let the enemy approach quite close ; do not fire a shot without an order. Officers, to your places!"

'"We shall beat them," he said to Kurapatkin, "but for half an hour they will give us some trouble."

'As the Turks advanced, they opened fire and continued firing. Judging by the flame jets of the rifle, their front was at least a verst in length. The Turks advanced not in skirmishing order, but in a dense mass. Thousands of bullets whistled overhead.

'"Don't let them get cool," said Skobeleff. "Fire along the whole line."

'Then our mitrailleuses began to speak. Our batteries at Brestovetz opened fire. The Turks replied from Krishin. One Turkish shell burst in the middle of their own men.

'"Again a volley," cried Skobeleff.

'It seemed as if the ground reeled beneath our feet. The Turks to-day were extraordinarily tenacious. Death was in their ranks, but they kept on advancing. The situation was becoming serious. Skobeleff mounted the breastwork and directed the defence of the breach. The opposing fires blazed like an aureole around him, and then everything was hidden in dense smoke. The air was thick with bullets, which splashed along the breastwork. The attack was directed against both sides simultaneously. Through the incessant roll of the rifles you could hear the cries of the officers. Then a kind of chaos seemed to come over everything, my head reeled, and I could no longer take count of anything.

"God be praised!" says some one near me, "they have been driven back."

"Stop firing; enough!" cries some one in the darkness.... "Why enough?" cried Skobeleff, "the Turks fire as they fly. Fire into their backs." Some more volleys were fired, and then all was still, but for the groaning of the wounded on the breastwork and the animated conversation of the soldiers.

During the night, the opposing trenches blazed away at each other, without exactly knowing why, for half an hour; then the Turkish outposts, climbing trees, began firing over our breastwork into the trenches. Their balls buried themselves in the earthwork all round the sleeping soldiers.

Skobeleff determined to place the scouts himself. Leaping over the breastwork he disappeared out of sight. The next half-hour was one of extreme anxiety. A stray bullet might strike him, and there would end at once that brilliant career and all hope of holding the position. Our men ceased firing. He should not fall by a Russian bullet.

"God keep him safe!" cried a soldier.

"None can harm him," said another. "God watches over him, and he will come back safe and sound."

"He is enchanted," said another, "nothing can harm him."

"At Khiva, he was nine days and nine nights under a Khivan spell. During all that time he neither ate nor drank, the incantations never ceased, and at the end he became proof against bullets. A ball can pass through him without hurting him in the least." [1] So ran the talk in the trenches when Skobeleff was away.

'This time he returned safely and our anxiety was at an end.'

So passed November. In December, at last, thanks chiefly to General Todtleben's skill and perseverance, Plevna fell. Skobeleff had no share in the fighting in the last struggle, when Osman tried to cut his way through the enemy's lines. His part in the affair is described by Mr. MacGahan, who was by his side during the whole of that eventful day. Here is his description of what happened, written on $\frac{\text{November 28}}{\text{December 10}}$, the night of the day on which Plevna fell:—

On Sunday night occurred the first snowstorm of the season. It was quite dark, and the lights of Brestovetz were barely discernible through the gloom when I found my way through the storm and the obscurity to Uzendol, Skobeleff's headquarters. Here I found everybody keenly on the alert. A spy had just come in with the news that Osman had issued three days' rations to the troops, one hundred and fifty cartridges, a new pair of sandals to each man, and that, to all appearances, the concentration would begin at once. At ten o'clock another spy came in, who reported that Osman was concentrating near the bridge over the Vid. A few minutes later there was a telegram stating that from the other side a great many

---

[1] The belief in Skobeleff's invulnerability was very general, but it was usually ascribed not to Khivan witchcraft, but to the direct interposition of the saints. Wounded men declared in hospital that they had been struck by bullets or shells which, before reaching them, had passed through the body of their General.

lights were seen moving about in Plevna, an unusual thing. Evidently there was some movement on foot, and the spies were right. The night wore slowly away. The snowstorm ceased, and was followed by dark clouds scudding swiftly across the sky, with now and then a blast of sleet. At three o'clock another spy brought news that the men of Skobeleff's command had a position on the side of the Green Hill, and that the Krishin redoubts were being abandoned. He was very sure, he said, that all the positions along our side would shortly be abandoned. Would he go along and lead the way into the Krishin redoubts at the risk of being bayoneted if his words should not prove true? Yes, he would, and orders were given by Skobeleff for the troops to begin to move cautiously forward, and feel their way with care. This was done, and the positions were taken. At last now it was certain that the Turks were moving, and that the final decisive moment had come. Skobeleff ordered the captured positions to be instantly placed in a state of defence, in case the Turks, repulsed and not yet ready to surrender, should attempt to recapture them. The grey light of morning came. It was cloudy, and threatened more snow. Suddenly there was the booming of thirty or forty guns speaking almost together, followed instantly by that steady, crashing roll we have learned to know so well. The battle had begun. We mounted our horses and rode towards the battle. It was in the direction of the bridge over the Vid, on the Sophia road, and half an hour's ride brought us in sight of the conflict.

A terrible and sublime spectacle presented itself to our view. Osman Pasha had during the night abandoned all his positions from Grivitza to the Green Hill, and concentrated the greater part of his army across the Vid, over which he passed on two bridges, one the old, and the other the new one lately constructed. He took part of his artillery, some three batteries, and a train of about five or six hundred carriages drawn by bullocks. He succeeded in getting his army, the artillery, and part of the train over by daybreak. The attack was directed against the positions held by the Grenadiers, north of the Sophia road, whose lines extended from the road to a point opposite Opanes, where they were joined by the Roumanian curving line through Susurla. The Turks advanced as far as they could under cover of their waggons, while the Russians poured in a terrible fire on them from their Berdan breechloaders, scarcely less destructive than the Peabody, and opened on the advancing line with shell and shrapnel. The Turks then dashed forward with a shout upon the line of trenches held by the Sibirsky or Siberian Regiment, swept over them like a tornado, poured into the battery, bayoneted the artillerymen, officers and men, who, with desperate heroism, stood to their pieces to nearly a man, and seized the whole battery. The Sibirsky Regiment had been overthrown and nearly annihilated. The Turks had broken the first circle that held them in. Had they gone on they would have found two more; but they did not have time to go on. The Russians rallied almost immediately.

General Strukoff, of the Emperor's staff, brought up the first brigade of Grenadiers, who, led by their general, flung themselves on the Turks with fury. A hand-to-hand fight ensued, man to man, bayonet to bayonet, which is said to have lasted several minutes, for the Turks clung to the captured guns with dogged obstinacy, and nearly all of them were killed. The others began a retreat which, under the murderous fire sent after them, instantly became a flight. The majority made for the deep banks of the Vid, where they found ample shelter from the Russian shells and bullets. They formed here behind the banks, and instantly began to return the Russian fire. It was now about half-past eight, and the Turkish sortie was virtually repulsed, but for four hours the storm of lead swept on, as 100 guns sent forth flame and smoke and iron.

About twelve o'clock the firing began to diminish on both sides, as if by mutual agreement. Then it stopped entirely. The firing had not ceased more than half an hour when a white flag was seen waving from the road leading around the cliffs beyond the bridge. Plevna had fallen, and Osman Pasha was going to surrender.

A long, loud shout went up from the Russian army when the white flag was seen, and its significance was understood.

A moment later, a Turkish officer was seen riding over the bridge with a white flag in his hand. He was an officer of inferior rank, and General Ganetsky, Commander of the Grenadiers, sent him back to send an officer with the rank of pasha to negotiate the terms of capitulation. Then thirty or forty of us, headed by General Skobeleff, who had been this morning placed on the Sophia road, rode down the road towards the bridge, within point blank range of the Turkish rifles, if the Turkish soldiers grouped in masses on the road behind the bridge on the cliffs overlooking the Vid had chosen to open on us. About fifty yards from the bridge, and seventy-five from some masses of Turks on the other side, we halted. General Skobeleff and two or three other officers waved white handkerchiefs. This signal of amity was answered by the waving of a piece of white muslin, about two yards square, attached to a flag-staff. Then two horsemen came forward, each carrying a white flag. They rode across the bridge and approached us. There was a moment's conversation with Skobeleff's interpreter, and then it was announced that Osman himself was coming out, and the two horsemen galloped back.

'Osman himself coming out!' exclaimed all of us with surprise.

'At any rate we will give him a respectful reception,'

exclaimed one Russian officer, in the spirit of true chivalry.

'He has saved the honour of his country,' said General Skobeleff. 'I will proffer him my hand and tell him so.'

All were unanimous in his praise, and the butcheries of Russian wounded committed by the Turkish army of Plevna were forgotten.

Two horsemen then were seen approaching with a white flag, the bearer of which was apparently merely a common soldier. The other horseman was not Osman Pasha, but Tefik Bey, his chief of staff. Tefik Bey rode up. He halted for a moment and was silent. He then spoke in French with good accent, but slowly, as if choosing his words.

He said 'Osman Pasha'—then stopped fully ten seconds before he proceeded—'is wounded.'

'Not severely, we all hope?' exclaimed General Skobeleff.

'I do not know,' was the answer, with a pause of a second between every word. Then there was a pause, which became embarrassing. The Turk showed no hurry to speak. Finally, General Skobeleff stammered out, 'Is there anybody you would like to see?—[pause]—With whom did you wish to speak?—Is there anything——?—[pause]—What the devil is the matter with the man? Why don't he speak?' blurted out the General, in English, turning to me. Tefik Bey remained impassive.

'General Ganetsky is in command here. He will be here presently, in case you should like to speak to him,' General Skobeleff finally observed. Tefik Bey simply nodded.

'Osman Ghazi has made a most brilliant and glorious defence,' said an officer. 'We esteem highly his soldierly character.'

The Turk gazed steadily before him, and gave no sign that he had heard.

'We look upon him as a very great general,' said another. No answer. The Turk's eyes were bent in the direction of Sophia, as though looking for Mehemet Ali Pasha. There was evidently no use trying to converse with this obstinately silent man, and they gave it up. Fortunately, General Strukoff, of the Emperor's staff, soon arrived, with powers to treat. He asked Tefik if he had authority from Osman Pasha to negotiate. It appeared not. I did not catch all that was said; but the final result was that Tefik bowed to us and galloped away back across the bridge.

We waited awhile longer. Then we thread our way cautiously over the bridge, through broken carriages and dead bodies of horses and cattle, and find ourselves among the Turks.

The terms of capitulation were easily arranged. The surrender is unconditional. Osman consented at once. He could do nothing else. In order to attempt a sortie, he had to abandon all the positions in which he had defied the Russians so long, and to concentrate his army down on the Vid. These positions once lost were lost for ever, because the Russians occupied them almost as soon as he left them.

We turned back over the bridge, and Osman Pasha got into a carriage and drove to Plevna. The Grand Duke Nicholas, with his staff, arrived a few minutes afterwards, and passed the troops in review. Then we pass again slowly across the bridge.

The scene had now changed. No more armed Turks were to be seen. The interview with Osman Pasha had taken place about two o'clock. It was now three, and the Turks had all laid down their arms.

We rode slowly on towards Plevna.

There was another halt in our slow onward progress, and the cry was heard, 'Osman.' I pushed forward to find that it was indeed Osman Pasha, who, having heard that the Grand Duke was coming in this direction, had turned back in his carriage to meet him. The Grand Duke rode up to the carriage, and, for some seconds, the two chiefs gazed into each other's faces without the utterance of a word. Then the Grand Duke stretched out his hand, and shook the hand of Osman Pasha heartily and said :—

'I compliment you on your defence of Plevna. It is one of the most splendid military feats in history.' Osman Pasha smiled sadly, rose painfully to his feet in spite of his wound, said something which I could not hear, and then re-seated himself. The Russian officers all cried, 'Bravo!' 'Bravo!' repeatedly, and all saluted respectfully. There was not one among them who did not gaze on the Hero of Plevna with the greatest admiration and sympathy.

'It is a grand figure,' exclaimed Colonel Gaillard, the French military attaché. 'I was almost afraid of seeing him, lest my expectation should be disappointed, but he more than fulfils my ideal.'

'It is the face of a great military chieftain,' said young Skobeleff. 'I am glad to have seen him. Osman Ghazi he is, and Osman the Victorious he will remain, in spite of his surrender.'

When Skobeleff was introduced to Osman Pasha by the Grand Duke, the inscrutable countenance of the Turk relaxed, and he heartily grasped the hand of the heroic conqueror of the Green Hills.

Osman remarked afterwards that one day Skobeleff would be Commander-in-Chief of the whole Russian army.

On the evening of the surrender of Plevna, Skobeleff invited Tefik Bey to dine with him at his headquarters at Usendol.

Mr. MacGahan says :—

A warm fire burning gaily in General Skobeleff's mud hut, a glass of vodka, and some hot soup at once thawed out our benumbed hands and feet, and we were soon enjoying a hot dinner, with the appetites of men who had been in the saddle since daylight, with not a morsel to eat. Tefik Bey seemed much depressed and downcast. He spoke little, and was at first almost as taciturn as he had been on the bridge. He brightened up, however, as the meal progressed, drank a glass of red wine, a glass of sherry, and a couple of glasses of champagne, when General Skobeleff proposed the health of Osman Ghazi, and drank to the brave defenders of Plevna. A merry smile broke over his face when Skobeleff asked him who had commanded the Turks on the Green Hill, and I think it must have occurred to him now for the first time that his entertainer was Skobeleff, the indefatigable, restless, daring spirit with whom he had exchanged so many hard blows on the Loftcha road and Green Hill. Nobody had mentioned Skobeleff's name in his presence, nor had Skobeleff told him who he was, but the fact that we had come out of the Loftcha road, together with Skobeleff's question about the Green Hill, was quite enough to enlighten him. So he said, with a smile, 'Ah, it is you who gave such tough work on the Green Hill all this time. You are General Skobeleff?' Skobeleff laughed, and said, 'Yes.' 'That was a very good attack of yours that evening in the fog and darkness. Very well done. But you did not get it all.' 'No,' said Skobeleff, 'I did not want it all.' And they both laughed. But, after this momentary fit of sunshine, Tefik Bey soon again relapsed into melancholy and gloom. We had hardly swallowed our coffee when Skobeleff, taking pity on him, turned us all out, gave up his bed to Tefik, had another hastily made up for Colonel Gaillard, and then retired and passed the night in a hut of one of his officers; and so ended this eventful day on our side of Plevna.

So ended the famous siege of Plevna. It began on July $\frac{8}{20}$, and ended on $\frac{\text{November 28}}{\text{December 10}}$, having lasted 142 days. The Turks lost 30,000 men during the siege, and when they surrendered we made 44,000 prisoners. A great sigh of relief went up from every Russian heart. Plevna had fallen at last, chiefly thanks to Todtleben. But when we talked of Plevna in Russia, somehow or other the name of Skobeleff was always on the tongue. Todtleben was in command, and the greatest victory belonged to him, but Plevna was also Skobeleff's glory.

CHAPTER V.

IN CAMP AND IN FIELD.

English testimonies—The superlative of eulogy—Mr. Forbes—Skobeleff's genius—Personal traits - Skobeleff as a linguist—Mr. Marvin's testimony—Lieutenant Greene's estimate of Skobeleff—An ideal commander—His relations with his officers—'A stupendous military genius'—Skobeleff's preference for young soldiers—His estimate of the Sepoys—Mr. Boyle's story—Verestchagine on Skobeleff's 'superstition'—Mr. Rose on 'the Russian Bayard'—His iron discipline—Care for his men—Popularity among the soldiers—Generosity—A practical joke—Skobeleff-worship—Punishes cruelty—The peasant's cow—Capacity for work and for sleep—Teaching by example—His life in the trenches—His legendary bravery.

It was the singular good fortune of Skobeleff to have been accompanied throughout his great campaign in the Balkans by English and American correspondents, who have left on record what they saw of that most remarkable soldier. To describe him in camp and in the field, I need only collect some of the testimonies which have appeared in the English press. 'By all means,' wrote me my brother the other day, 'give as many English testimonies as possible. The more, the better. They cannot then say that Skobeleff only owes his renown to partial judges.' This task is a pleasant one. In all the contributions to the English press I cannot find one disrespectful, one disparaging remark. Not one.

This, in itself, is no slight tribute to our hero, and surely it also is creditable to the generosity of England. If ever there was a time when English newspapers—some English newspapers, at least—were in a mood to find everything wrong with everything and everybody in Russia, it was when Skobeleff was at the height of his glory.

There were representatives of all kinds of papers in Bulgaria, many of them violently prejudiced against Russia and ardent advocates of an Anglo-Russian war. Yet, not even these Russophobists had a word to say against Skobeleff, although for Russia and Russia's cause they might only have unkind words. Of course, Skobeleff, as every other Russian, would have much preferred being attacked and calumniated himself rather than see that systematic hatred for a country which certainly was dearer to him than his life. But that was not a matter of choice. If all the other prejudices could not be overcome, one was—it is, perhaps, a good beginning. . . . Perhaps!

Mr. Forbes, for instance, is not exactly a gentle soul, subject to the enthusiastic impulses of a schoolboy, nor can he be reproached with partiality for Russians; but when the news of Skobeleff"s death reached this rough and hostile witness in far Australia, he declared: 'It was impossible to know Skobeleff, to have him smile on you, and not to love him.' There was another correspondent, Mr. Boyle, of the 'Standard,' who was, I cannot imagine why, expelled from the Russian camp, and who after his expulsion wrote a book which did not overflow with honey for Russian generals; but in his 'Diary of an Expelled Correspondent' he speaks of Skobeleff with almost as much enthusiasm as if he had been a Russian. But so it was always. English officers like Colonel Brackenbury, distinguished Anglo-Indians like Sir Henry Havelock, American officers like General Grant and Lieutenant Greene, all agree in praise of Skobeleff.

There is one very curious trait about Englishmen. Whenever they wish to exhaust the language of compliment and outdo all the superlatives of praise which they have bestowed upon a foreigner, they say 'he might be taken for an Englishman.' I like that complacency. There is something so simple, so charming, in the confident assumption that an Englishman is the finest work of God, and that to be like an Englishman is the utmost that poor foreigners can aspire to. The correspondents unanimously agree that Skobeleff might anywhere have been mistaken for an Englishman. 'He looked to me,' said Mr. Forbes, 'like an English country gentleman of the best type.' 'He would pass anywhere,' said Mr. Boyle, 'for a brilliant officer of the English service.'

Higher praise, of course, is impossible from Englishmen.

But I have not heard of anyone in the English service for whom the army and the nation feel anything of the almost idolatrous regard with which Skobeleff was regarded in Russia. England has brave generals and heroic soldiers, no doubt, as have other nations; but Skobeleff stands alone. To repeat a phrase used by an English lady, who had just been reading Sir Henry Havelock's description of Skobeleff in the field, 'He recalled the ages of heroism and romance.' There was something about him that reminded you at once of the Paladin and the Crusader, as well as of the heroic warriors of classical antiquity. He not only commanded admiration, he fascinated the imagination, he enchained the heart. 'It was impossible not to love him,' has been said not by Mr. Forbes alone.

Of the personal appearance of Skobeleff many descriptions have been given, but, like his portraits, they leave him undescribed.

Speaking of his first meeting with Skobeleff, Mr. Forbes wrote:—

I thought then, as I have never ceased to think, that I never looked on a finer man. Six feet high, straight as a pine; the head carried high with a gallant *débonnaire* fearlessness; square across the shoulders, deepened chest, slender of waist, clean; of frank, graceful, supple figure, set off to perfection by the white frockcoat with decorations and gold lace on it, Skobeleff, with his high frank bearing, looked a genial king of men.[1] As I write, I see before me that lofty forehead, shaded with the chestnut curls, the clear, frank, manly blue eyes, that met yours so

[1] *Melbourne Argus*, July 10, 1882, Mr. Rose uses the same expression. 'One felt instinctively that he was face to face with a king among men.'

staunchly, the long, straight decisive nose—the kind of nose Napoleon said he looked for among his officers when he wanted to find a general—the beautiful mouth, with its wonderful mobility of expression, the well-turned compact chin with the deep dimple in the centre. At this time he wore only whiskers and moustache, later in the campaign a silky chestnut beard grew over his broad chest, he looked to me like an English country gentleman of the best type.

Almost all who have attempted to describe Skobeleff noticed the nicety, the elegance of his dress. 'His hands were shaped like those of a cavalier in Vandyke's portraits.'

Skobeleff was sensitively sympathetic in his intercourse with others. His smile was full of raillery, and there was what Mr. Boyle calls 'a reckless frankness in his speech,' but he shrank instinctively from wounding anyone. He was transparency itself, but for the sake of others he put a curb upon his tongue.

Perhaps what attached casual acquaintances and strangers as much as anything else, was his boundless flow of high spirits and the universality of the interest which he took in everything, from the loftiest idealism down to the gossip of the theatres and the clubs. Of this Mr. Forbes gives a very good idea when he says:—

It seemed to me that this young man had been everywhere, seen everything, and read everything. He was familiar with episodes of my own professional career. He had carried a flying reconnaissance from Khokand, over the Pamir steppes, round Lake Uclona, unto the banks of the Hindoo Koosh. He quoted Balzac and Hamley's 'Operations of War'; he had no belief in the first favourite for the then approaching Derby. He thought Madame Chaumont very *chic*, and he imparted the information that the upper parts of the Oxus were dangerous because of quicksands. We dined together, and after dinner went to the music saloon, where Skobeleff, to his own pianoforte accompaniment, sang songs in French, German, Russian, Kirghiz, Italian, English, and wound up with 'Auld Lang Syne' in admirable vernacular. He impressed me with the belief that he was out of sight the most muscular thinker of any Russian I had met, and that altogether he was a Muscovite, or rather, indeed, a cosmopolitan 'Admirable Crichton.'

A Correspondent of the 'New York Tribune,' who seems to have known him well, writing of him after his death, describes one of his characteristics which some people overlooked, viz. a love of order and method which strangely conflicts with the impression prevailing in some quarters that he was nothing but an impetuous hot-head :—

Skobeleff had a strong mental digestion for science and literature. If he had not been a soldier, he would have probably been a great geographical explorer and historian. There were few more able strategists. It was a great error to think he was a mere dare-devil warrior, like the theatrical Murat. The lamented general was no less a man of study than of action, and extremely methodic. Apple-pie order reigned in his lodgings. He travelled about with a small library of books of instruction, reference and amusement, or rather, recreative entertainment. It contained neatly-bound diamond editions of the British,

German and French classic authors, the margins of which were covered with annotations written in small, distinct characters. When he bought a standard work unbound he had several blank pages added between the chapters in the binding for critical and other observations that might suggest themselves.

One day in Paris I was about to take notes at his dictation. He handed me some English copybook paper, and a varied assortment of pencils, neatly cut, and steel and quill pens to choose from. 'That paper,' he said, 'I bought in Spain of a stationer who wanted to get out of the way of the Carlists. It was with me in Central Asia. I hate waste as much as any skinflint; as if I were living on board a war ship. I am particular about my pens. For military work I like a hard and finely pointed one, that lets down the ink sparingly; for reports I take a freer one; and for writing letters into which my heart overflows I prefer the goose-quill. There is no better medium with which to express the feelings and sensations. People call me headlong. So I am, but not in the sense they imagine. I have never in my life butted against a stone wall. In daring much I have nearly always succeeded.'

These little details are not so trivial as perhaps they may appear to some. Nothing is trivial, not even a shoe-lace, if it enables one to realise more vividly the character of a man.

Skobeleff had learned English in childhood from an English nurse, and his familiarity with the language was a constant source of astonishment to Englishmen.[1]

[1] Skobeleff was a remarkable linguist. Mr. Rose says: 'Skobeleff spoke English without the slightest foreign accent. French, German, and Italian he read, but did not love Greek. He spoke modern Greek. He was well versed in the classical works of England, France, and Ger-

His high spirits were well under control. His vitality, though vigorous, was never rude, and his suavity, urbanity, and high-bred courtesy gave an additional brilliancy to his conversation.

Of course when a man is so universally praised, it is natural that some may have been disappointed when they met him, and that was Mr. Marvin's expectation when he went to St. Petersburg to see Skobeleff, with whom, as the latter told me shortly afterwards at Moscow, 'he had held very interesting conversations.' But Mr. Marvin was agreeably disappointed. He says:—

As a rule, I have found that important personages are best regarded at a distance, through the medium of portraits and biographies. Skobeleff is the only great personage I have met who has become enhanced in my estimation by personal acquaintance, and I have never come in contact with any man who has left so charming an impression upon me. An interview with Skobeleff would have revived the extinct fires of Carlyle's hero-worship; as for Thackeray, I think, if he had known Skobeleff, he would have made him his ideal of a perfect gentleman.[1]

many, and his favourite authors seemed Horace—whom he was never tired of citing—Schiller in German, and Byron in English, though he was quite apt in quotations from Shakespeare. The other languages which he spoke were Wallach, Bulgarian, Serb, Kirghiz, and I believe one or two other Central Asian dialects. In peculiarly military matters he had read a great deal; and while his head-quarters were at Slivno during the Russian occupation of Bulgaria following the war, the walls of his private office were surrounded with bookcases filled with volumes all bearing on the art of war. He did most of his reading early in the morning, before receiving the members of his staff. A large proportion of his collection, I noticed, were in English and French, many of the former being records of British Indian campaigns, with at least half a dozen on the great American civil war.'

[1] *The Russian Advance*, p. 97.

The most detailed account of Skobeleff, alike in camp and in the field, which I have seen in English, is Lieutenant Greene's beautiful description in his 'Sketches of Army Life in Russia,' from which I take the liberty of making a lengthy extract :—

The third attack on Plevna was faulty in principle, and with the force which Skobeleff had, was doomed to failure from the beginning—but this was no fault of his; he simply obeyed his orders, and did his utmost to accomplish the impossible. And, although nearly fifty per cent. of his command perished under him, yet from that day his name was spoken of among the soldiers of the entire army, in words of fables, as a man whose bravery could not be described. I have heard them speak of him as a general under whom they would rather fight and die, than fight and live under another; for with him they knew they could never come to disgrace, but were sure they would achieve the fame of military heroes, whether they gained or lost the day, whether they lived or were killed.

On the following day Skobeleff was made Lieutenant-General, being then not quite thirty-three years old, and was appointed to the command of the Sixteenth Division, which command he retained, in addition, at times, to the command of other divisions, till the close of the war. He then set to work to make that the most famous division in the army, and he succeeded. It is commonly spoken of to-day as 'the famous Sixteenth Division.' He won the unalterable affection of the men by his ceaseless care for their wants. They were the best-clothed and the best-fed troops in the army: they were never short of ammunition: they were never needlessly moved or exposed. If he was without public funds, he never hesitated to advance, or give outright, whatever private funds he had, if it could in any way contribute to their comfort. At Constantinople, for instance, when there was considerable delay in transporting the sick to Russia, Skobeleff advanced over 15,000 roubles out of his own pocket, and succeeded in chartering an English steamer then in port, and obtained permission to ship the sick of his own division in it to Odessa. They thus reached home several weeks in advance of their regular turn. When his friends expressed their admiration at his generosity, he replied, 'I owe everything in the world to these men, and the least I can do is to spend a few thousand roubles to help them in their sickness.' He passed his whole time in the midst of his men, tasting their food, inspecting their arms, learning their every want with his own eyes, and supplying it with orders based on his own knowledge. He was always with them in their most exposed positions, and when he was slightly wounded he refused to go to the rear; but had a cot brought up and placed in the trenches, and remained on it there until he was able to mount his horse again. At the instant of going into a fight he called as many officers as possible about him, to explain the exact purpose and object of it, and the manner in which this object was to be gained; and then he always made a short speech to his men, telling them what he expected them to do, and that he felt sure they would do it. In a word, he made himself and his division one—he representing the brains and they the body, and the heart being in common. He succeeded so thoroughly in accomplishing this union, that his men responded to his thoughts as readily as the muscles obey the will. I have listened in wonder at the enthusiastic admiration with which they spoke of him and the no less enthusiastic way in which they obeyed him, and I doubt if a more thoroughly ideal relation between a general and his men has existed since the days of Cromwell.

In return for his care of his men he demanded of them, first of all, unhesitating, unflinching, unquestioning obedience to his orders. If he ordered a man to do anything, where immediate death was as certain as the sun in heaven, he expected to be instantly obeyed without so much as even a look of question or surprise. Himself a man of wide reading, speaking many languages, and having travelled in many lands, he gathered about him, in his personal staff, as rough and uncultured a lot of men as I ever saw in officers' uniform; but they answered his purpose to carry orders, and, as he said, if he ordered one of them to ride his horse against the muzzle of a discharging cannon, he would do it instantly. One morning that I was with him on a reconnaissance we came to a small brook. An officer of his staff, with whom he had had some cause of dissatisfaction just before, rode forward to try its depth. While he was cautiously feeling its depth, another officer—a Cossack—rode toward it, and, as his horse drew back, plied both spurs and the whip with all his force; the horse sprang forward into the middle of the little stream, and as it was very deep, though very narrow, both horse and rider disappeared under the water.

'There,' cried Skobeleff to the other, 'that's the way I want my officers to do things.'

The first officer, greatly nettled, then put spurs to his horse, and, though Skobeleff, seeing his purpose, yelled at him to stop, in an instant he and his horse disappeared under the water. Both men were then dragged out, dripping from their cold bath. Everyone laughed, and Skobeleff was in the best of humour.

'Now go home and dry your clothes. You're both fine fellows.' 'But,' turning to the first one, 'after this *never hesitate* in what you have to do.'

On another occasion Skobeleff heard one of his colonels, just as he was going into action, trying to make a speech to his men, but hesitating, and stammering, and breaking down in it. He relieved him instantly. 'If at such a moment,' he said, 'a man can't find a few simple words to tell his men what he expects them to do, then he don't know it himself. At that moment a man can't lie; his heart will speak if he have a heart for fight; and if he can't find words, it is either because he is a coward, or because he has no notion in his head of what he is going to do.'

Again, he punished his men without mercy for the slightest depredation on unarmed inhabitants or their property.

These little episodes read queerly; they seem to be almost like the doings and talk of a madman; but it was madness with a direct method—the pleasantry which is merely another name for intense concentration of thought and energy in a single purpose.

Of new officers he required that they should know their own business; not that they should be cultured, should present a fine appearance, should be gentlemanly in their speech. He demanded none of these things, but that they should combine unflinching bravery and obedience, with a thorough knowledge of the way to handle the number of men each commanded, so as to obtain the greatest results with them. If they answered these requirements there was nothing he would not do for them; he continually praised them, he secured them rewards and promotions, he shared with them whatever he had. If they failed in these qualities, he pursued them relentlessly, abused them in unmeasured terms, and sought the first opportunity to get them out of his division.

His personal bravery was not only of the most reckless character, but at times it seemed to partake of the merest bravado, in which only extraordinary luck prevented him from reaping in death the well-earned reward of his foolishness. He always wore a white coat, a white hat, and rode a white horse in battle, simply because other generals usually avoided these target marks. He was perpetually riding at breakneck speed the same fence or ditch, leaving half his staff sprawling in it. He never lost an opportunity of displaying courage. He went into battle in his cleanest uniform and fresh underclothing, covered with perfume, and wearing a diamond-hilted sword, in order, as he said, that he might die with his best clothes on.[1] For a long time he wore with evident affectation a coat in which he had been wounded, and which had a conspicuous patch on the shoulder. Yet all this was not mere bravado and nonsense, but was the result of thought and almost cold-blooded calculation. It was intended to impress his men, and it did so. They firmly believed he could not be hit. Whenever they saw a white horse, coat, and cap among them, they knew that was Skobeleff, and seeing he was there they felt sure that everything was going well. At the beginning of the war he made up his mind firmly that he would never come out of it alive. After reading over the telegram announcing the armistice, one of the first things he said was, 'Well, perhaps, I won't get killed after all.' With this idea firmly fixed in his mind, that his death was only a question of a few weeks or months, his one thought was how to best use his life so as to make an impression on his men, and gain such a control over them that they would follow him anywhere. In everything that he did he tried to eliminate the idea of danger from their minds, and to make the most dangerous exploit appear as an ordinary everyday affair. His bandsmen were kept up to their full strength, and their musical instruments as carefully inspected as the men's arms; when they went into battle, it was with colours flying and the bands in their parade positions, with orders to play till they had not a gasp of breath in their bodies. At the battle of Shenova, he moved over the snowy ground in this order and got over

---

[1] According to M. Némirovitch Dantchenko, he used to don the best of his clothes on going to a battle. 'We must all be prepared for death, and go to meet it dressed as we are when going to take the Holy Communion.'

thirty per cent. of his musicians killed and wounded. But this device of giving to a bloody assault the air of a customary afternoon parade, helped not a little to encourage the men to do their usual part in it.

All these little affectations were merely superficially calculated and employed for their effect on his men; but behind and below all this, forming the solid structure on which these airy trifles rested, was his stupendous military genius. I use these words advisedly, and firmly believe that, should he live twenty years more, he will be commander-in-chief in the next war about the Eastern Question, and history will then speak of him as one of the five great soldiers of this century, side by side with Napoleon, Wellington, Grant, and Moltke.

Napoleon defined the requisite qualities of a great general to be, first, greatness of character or moral courage, which produces resolution; second, coolness or physical courage, which masters danger; third, a well-grounded knowledge of the guiding principles of his profession; and fourth, and above all, the capacity to see things as they are, and not to make pictures in his mind. Although all these men have differed widely in their personal character, and in the bent of their minds, yet they have all possessed these qualities in an eminent degree, and Skobeleff possesses them all no less eminently. . . . He already belongs to history, though he has lived but thirty-five years; he has commanded twenty thousand men in battle, he has received the surrender of an entire army of nearly forty thousand, he has led more assaults than any living man but Grant, and in not one of them has he failed to carry the line he assaulted, though in one case he was subsequently overwhelmed with numbers and driven out.

Such was the estimate of an American observer writing two years before Skobeleff died. It may seem high, but it is no higher than that of an

English soldier and war correspondent who declared Skobeleff to be the very incarnation of the genius of war, and who once predicted that, if ever Europe were to be overwhelmed by an invasion from the East, as she was eighty years ago invaded from the West, Skobeleff would prove himself to be in no degree inferior to Napoleon.'

[1] Mr. Marvin, in the course of the 'interesting conversation' before alluded to, elicited from Skobeleff some criticisms of the English army, which perhaps may not be without interest to some English readers. 'Skobeleff said that he had followed the whole of our operations in Afghanistan.' 'For General Roberts,' he continued, 'I have a great admiration. He seems to me to possess all the qualities of a great general. His was a splendid march from Cabul to Candahar. I think more highly of him than I do of Sir Garnet Wolseley, but there is this to be said of all your generals—they have only fought against Asiatic and savage foes. They have not commanded an army against a European enemy, and we cannot tell, therefore, what they are really made of.' On my describing the controversy between Roberts and Wolseley in regard to the Long and Short Service Systems he said: 'I myself prefer young soldiers to fight with. We take our soldiers at twenty-one, and I think two years or three at the outside is quite sufficient to fit them for war.' It is noteworthy that Skobeleff likes to surround himself with young officers. The recent brilliant campaign against the Turcomans was essentially a war conducted by young men. There was hardly a grey head in the force.

Mentioning Sir Garnet Wolseley's objections to the Tunnel, he said: 'If I were an Englishman, I do not think I should like to see the tunnel constructed. The possibility of 2,000 or 3,000 of the enemy treacherously seizing the English end deserves to be seriously considered.' He went on to say, in regard to the English army, that he thought we ought to have compulsory conscription in our country. I pointed out the impossibility of carrying this into effect, and observed that we had a vast reserve of military power in India, which a Government like Russia would know better how to make use of than our own. 'I do not think much of the native army in India,' he replied. 'We have also a vast native reserve—Tartars, Circassians, and so forth—but we do not draw upon them beyond a certain point. Asiatics cannot be trusted against European troops.' I referred to the Indian troops brought to Malta during the Turkish War, and said it would have been interesting to have seen how they would have com-

Mr. Boyle, in his 'Diary of an Expelled Correspondent,' gives some details which I have not met with elsewhere, and which are worth quoting:—

A more recent history I may mention—one that is told around camp fires, and contributes to raise still higher the pedestal upon which Skobeleff already stands in the soldier's simple view. In one of the forays or reconnaissances, or what you please to call them, around Plevna, his Cossacks suffered much from thirst. They breasted a high ridge—I know it well—and saw below them a delicious spring, stone-faced and cisterned, as are all springs near the highway in that Turkish land, which they tell us is so brutal and so far behind the age. The General cried for water, but his Cossacks pointed out how thick the Turkish bullets were pitting the slope below, and how they pattered round the spring. Skobeleff leapt down and slowly talking over his shoulder with the trusty captain who has followed him for love from Turkestan—his name I am sorry to forget at this moment—very slowly he walked to the cistern, took a long drink, and then another, washed his face and hands, shouting to his officers how sweet and cool was the water. I know this sounds like fanfaronade, though of the best sort; yet I think that, if everything could be told that bears upon the subject, even such acts would be recognised as neither injudicious nor uncalled for at present. However that be, the story goes on to tell that Skobeleff's Cossacks were mad to see their idol thus run into danger which they seemed to shirk. They clambered out of their forked saddles as swiftly as men can disengage themselves from

ported themselves in the presence of a European army. 'It would have been interesting,' he replied, 'but you did not use them, and we therefore do not know what they would have done. The best criterion of the quality of the native troops of India is the fact that India should allow itself to be dominated by only 60,000 European soldiers.'

such a clumsy apparatus, and pressed forward. In the tones of real anger, which are perfectly recognised by the followers of this good-humoured General, Skobeleff ordered them back, and put under arrest—not a nominal punishment—those who had ventured to risk their lives a few feet in the direction which he had traversed.

This is the camp story; another is told in the 'upper circles.' I could not myself doubt which represents the truth. The General's knowledge of English speech, and liking of things English—saving our policy alone—have brought him into close relationship with correspondents here. We know him well, and I regard him as the one soldier whom Russia has visibly at command.[1]

Our famous painter, Verestchagine, gives some traits of Skobeleff in a letter which the English correspondents appear to have missed:—

As a man Skobeleff, although sympathetic, was too capricious, but he was brave. As a soldier Skobeleff was beyond comparison. I do not speak of his valour, which was surprising, extraordinary, but of his military sagacity, which is so much more valuable. He was not merely a swordsman as many pretend. He was also widely read. He knew the military history of all nations by heart. Very often in the middle of a battle, on march, or in the bivouac, he would say to me, 'Do you remember what such and such a captain said on such a battle?' As I was not so well versed in the annals of war I was much embarrassed, and had to reply, 'Do leave me alone; I don't know.'

His reports on the actual condition of the Russian soldiers and officers, reports which did not please everybody, are full of good sense and of just observations. The number of his writings, such as observations, narra-

[1] *Diary of an Expelled Correspondent*, Boyle, pp. 321, 322.

lives of campaigns, is very great, and for a Russian officer almost unprecedented. Our officers love better to fight than to write.

To me Skobeleff appeared the incarnation of military genius. One of my friends called him the god of war. This may appear to you exaggerated, but not to those who, like me, have seen him prepare for and command in battle, address the soldiers, inspire with his spirit, and superintend the provisioning of his troops and the supply of all their wants, even to the greased cloths with which, in severe frost, they enwrapped their feet.

Skobeleff was superstitious.[1] Once we made an exchange of flags. He had given me his famous old banner, torn and pierced in twenty battles. I had made him a new and very beautiful one of Chinese and Indian stuffs; but he often demanded the old flag, which I refused to give up. When before Geok Tepé, he ascribed every little reverse to the ill-luck which my banner brought him, and every failure led to a fresh demand for his old flag. Not until he had taken Geok Tepé and ended the campaign was he a little more satisfied with my banner.

Contrary to what has been said, he wept easily; not only at the death of his father and mother, but at that of the Emperor he shed many tears.

In one word, to sum up my impression of my departed

[1] Mr. Rose was of a different opinion, and it is probable that Skobeleff's 'superstition' was confined to the banner. Mr. Rose says: 'Nothing could be further from the truth than the allegation that so robust-minded a man was superstitious, taking that word either in its grosser or its more spiritual acceptation. But, like every other generous or high-minded man, he regarded the superstitions of a simple and ignorant people more with compassion than with contempt, and on more than one occasion, touching on this very subject, he expressed to me the hope that superstitious observances, which he wisely insisted degraded both individuals and nations, would by-and-by be eradicated by the spread of education.

friend, if I were not sure of the rapid forgetfulness of man, I would be the first to raise a subscription for a monument 'to the memory of the bravest Russian soldier.'

The war correspondence of 1877-8, both English and Russian, teems with anecdotes illustrating his care for his men, his indifference to danger, and his attention to every detail of a soldier's life. After his death, two of these correspondents recorded their recollections of Skobeleff. Mr. W. K. Rose wrote in the 'Fortnightly Review' in London, and Mr. Forbes in the 'Melbourne Argus' in Australia, and both, although at the opposite end of the world, agreed entirely about his military genius. Mr. Rose, after saying that it would be impertinence on his part to speak of what has already been said by the highest military critics in Europe, gives the following details, which are very interesting :—

Like all great commanders, Skobeleff inspired in the officers and men under him the warmest attachment and devotion. To use an old phrase, 'they would go through fire and water for him.' Skobeleff was naturally the object of much jealous irritation on the part of the older generals in the service of the Czar. I remember him referring to this unpleasant state of matters, and stating that with him honours brought additional labour and greater weight of cares, and enforced the most unwearied vigilance against the slightest mistake.

With the officers of his own command he was frank and friendly, but he never lost his dignity or proper reserve even in moments when his natural geniality led him to unbend. His keen glance took in all the details of an action, and he never failed to note, commend, and reward any display of gallantry. The fall of a comrade, however humble, he sincerely mourned.

It has been well said that Skobeleff had 'an almost magic power of identifying himself on occasions with the humblest of his men.' It was a proud day for a private to be selected for even the slightest notice by the general, and, mayhap, to have his ears gently pulled—a favourite and peculiarly caressing habit of Skobeleff's when he was in good humour. In a campaign he shared the privations and the food of the meanest soldier in the ranks, he shirked no hardship which his men were compelled to bear: if they were in want, no luxury was spread on his board. On their part, the men admired his intrepidity and his brilliant dash. Under such a nature even the faint-hearted became brave warriors. When, after a three days' struggle with the snows, the ravines, the precipices of the pass of Hemedli, during which guns, waggons, tents, even much ammunition, had to be abandoned—Skobeleff's tired column emerged on the valley of Tundja and came face to face with Vessel Pasha's army, which had just victoriously driven back Radetzky's and Mirsky's columns—General Skobeleff rode along the line, informing his men that there was no retreat: all that was left to them was death, glory, or—after a pause—shame. 'Death or glory!' was the cry, with loud huzzas for their loved and devoted leader, and right nobly did they vindicate their choice. Many instances of his consummate courage and coolness in danger are already well known to readers in Western Europe. Let me add one or two. On the day before the assault on the Green Hill redoubt at Plevna, I was with him on a vine-covered ridge which commanded a view of the Turkish position. Skobeleff was making preparations for the assault. He had from personal inspection made a plan of the surrounding ground, and was, quite in view of the enemy, making a series of sketches of the exact points and the ground leading to them which were to be the objects of attack by each of his battalions. The Turks opened fire; at first the shells were short, then they flew overhead, but suddenly two shrieked unpleasantly near. One burst within a few yards of where Skobeleff was sitting on a camp stool, drawing, and he and his paper were covered with the friable soil of the vineyard. Without a word or a wince, he simply shook the soil off the paper and finished the preparation of his plans, ordering his staff, when he observed that the fire continued exact, to find cover under a sloping bank some twenty yards off. At the battle of Shenova—and I refer to this engagement frequently because the details of it are almost wholly unknown in England—Skobeleff, mounted on his white charger, went out alone to reconnoitre the Turkish position. Of course he was the mark for a pretty hot fusillade from both infantry and artillery. Suddenly a shell appeared to strike the ground right beneath his charger and exploded. Thousands thought his temerity had at last brought the death he seemed to court. But when the smoke cleared away the white charger was observed plunging gallantly onward, and his rider, unharmed, soon afterwards rejoined his own troops. Skobeleff told me that when the shell exploded he was almost suffocated with the sulphurous smoke, and that for a moment he actually believed his hour was come. The plunging of his horse, as it were, awoke him from the shock, and he was able to finish his survey unnerved. It would be wearisome to multiply instances of his escapes or of his daring.

As a disciplinarian he was firm and strict. No point was too minute to be overlooked. Skobeleff's vedettes were never caught napping. His knowledge of the detail of military duty was universal—even to sounding all the bugle calls. An illustration of the discipline of his corps occurs to me. I had been talking with him of military breech-loaders and discussing the merits of various systems. Taking a 'Berdan,' with which the troops were latterly armed, from a soldier, he undid the breech and lock and explained the mechanism with the precision of a gunsmith. Returning the rifle to the soldier, he turned, and walking up to a sentry a few paces distant, he said, 'Let me see your rifle'—extending his hand as he spoke. The man saluted and replied, 'I cannot, your Excellency.' 'But I want to see if it is clean,' persisted the General. 'I cannot, your Excellency,' again said the sentry, as firm as a rock. Skobeleff smiled, pulled his ears, and walked on. I asked an explanation, whereupon he said that a rule of war with him was that no sentry on duty was on any account to give up possession of his arms —not even to the Tzar himself. 'But, said I, 'suppose the sentry had given up his rifle when you were seemingly so serious in asking it. What then?' 'He would have been shot,' quietly replied the General, 'for disobedience to orders in time of war.'[1]

That is a grim little trait of the discipline which he maintains in all his campaigns.

Mr. Forbes's testimony, although not so detailed, is no less effective. 'Skobeleff,' he says, 'told him that he wore white in battle that "my fellows can see where I am and know, therefore, whither to follow."' It was but the nineteenth century reproducing the white plume of Henri Quatre at the battle of Ivry. Speaking of his generalship, Mr. Forbes says :—

Skobeleff, the evening before the successful assault, promulgated detailed instructions to the officers, with some words of soldierly advice to the men. The 'scheme of attack' has become a standard in all the war schools in

[1] *Fortnightly Review*, Oct. 1882.

Europe as a model of tactical conception, of lucid clearness, of careful prevision for any and every contingency. I am content to stand by it alone in my contention that Skobeleff is to be ranked as one of the greatest generals of modern times. He alone was a practical sanitarian.¹ He kept his camps clean, he made his men wash themselves, he gave them exercise, he saw to the baking of bread for them, and bought them vegetables out of his own pocket, and abolished nostalgia by instituting amusements. . . . Skobeleff was the most brilliant man I ever knew, and incomparably the finest fighting-man.

Skobeleff was the soldier's hero. His fame has already become legendary in our army, and not in our army only, but wherever Slavs are found. To understand the love, the adoration with which the soldiers speak of Skobeleff, it is only necessary to listen to the stories which they tell round their camp fires of their young and idolized hero. In their eyes he was more than mortal. One of his soldiers, coming unexpectedly on the crowd which blocked the street opposite the *chapelle ardente* where Skobeleff lay dead, on asking ' Why this crowd ? ' received answer, ' Skobeleff is dead ! ' ' Nonsense,' replied the simple veteran. ' Skobeleff is not dead. He

---

¹ Here is Sir Henry Havelock's account of Skobeleff's care for his men. At Brestovetz, before Plevna, his division, the 16th, up to its full number, is all ensconced in excellent huts, a mile and a half further back, prepared for any cold, and with a fireplace and chimney to every hut. His is the only Russian camp I ever saw that is clean in the English sense of the word. All others are pigstyes or worse, polluting the streams and breeding disease regardless of consequences. His is clean. Being a rich man, Skobeleff keeps open table, and all his Brigadiers and Colonels sit down with him twice daily, quite unlike Gourko, of whom it is said that 'he never dines,' but takes tea occasionally, writing and working all the rest of the day.

would not consent to die. It is impossible.' And so he unconcernedly went his way, confident that his beloved General was still alive.

'Ah! he knew the soul of every soldier, as if he were himself a private,' was the common remark of the men who had fought under him in so many battles and camped with him on so many fields. 'He was so simple, so unassuming; he was indeed one of ourselves.' He used to eat with them with the common spoon out of the camp-kettles, and no one was ever more careful to see that the camp-kettle was in its place. It was not only the superb military genius which they admired, but his sympathy, his affection, his homely brotherliness. There was no pride in him: with the poorest he was as friendly as with the most powerful.

'Well, are you going to be a general?' he would say familiarly to a private whom he met on his round. 'Never, Excellency,' would be the reply. 'What, never? That is a bad sign. My old grandfather was a peasant like you. Yet he became a general, and so may you if you are brave.' All had their chance; at least, as much chance as his grandfather, one of the heroes of 1812.

Skobeleff's generosity was lavish. He gave away every penny of his pay to his men. He repeatedly provided for their wants out of his own purse. No father could be more careful of his children than Skobeleff was of his soldiers. He was careful to spare their feelings, and if by chance he offended, his reparation was prompt. When in Constantinople after the war, he met a Russian prisoner in a Turkish uniform. 'What a shame!' he cried impulsively; 'how can you wear an enemy's uniform? it is too bad!'

No sooner had the words escaped him than he reflected and exclaimed, 'I am vexed with myself. Perhaps the poor wretch had nothing to put on his back. MacGahan, lend me some money; we have only twenty pounds—that is so little; you go at once and find him, and give him some money.'

MacGahan got some fifty pounds. 'Now go,' said Skobeleff; 'there are three Russian prisoners at the Seraskeriate; find them and apologise—apologise for me heartily. Say how sorry I am. I should have gone myself, but I cannot go to the Seraskeriate.'

When I returned, after having fulfilled my mission, I found Skobeleff impatient and fidgetty. 'Well, well, how is he? Has he accepted your help? What a disgrace to leave our prisoners so long with the enemy! Write me an official paper about what you saw and found. Though, of course, I cannot approve.'

'Approve what?'

'Why, of course I cannot approve of an officer who allowed himself to be made a prisoner.'

'But what could he do?'

'What so many Russians did on the Shipka; a revolver has six shots; five to the enemy, the sixth to oneself. What is the life of one man? The principle is the great point.'

Somebody wanted to warn Skobeleff—'One of your officers is spreading scandalous lies about you. I may give you his name?' Skobeleff seized his interlocutor by the hand. 'No, no, not a word, man. My officers fought like heroes. I love them. One word of mine was sufficient for their going willingly to death.'

When the interview was over and the guest left the room, Skobeleff called his servant. 'Have you well remarked that face?' asked he.

'Yes, General.'

'*If so, for this man henceforth I am never at home, never!* Do not forget my order!'

Skobeleff was not a saint, and he was too young and too witty not to be fond of jokes. A beautiful young Bucharest lady, very eccentric and foolish, having heard no end of stories of Skobeleff's heroic deeds and his extraordinary fascinations, sent him a very enthusiastic letter, announcing at the same time her intention to visit him the next day. The letter, hardly read, was thrown to the fire and the whole thing forgotten. At the appointed time, Skobeleff was deep in conversation with an old, decrepid General, who was rather tiresome and wordy. A servant brought in a card; it was the eccentric Roumanian. 'Dear General! Do help me! I am in great trouble!' exclaimed Skobeleff.

'What can I do?'

'There is a lady—I dare say a very nice one; but I am really too busy. Go and receive her; tell her you are Skobeleff, and are anxious to know what you can do for her!'

The old veteran went and soon returned with an angry face. 'I do not know what she wanted. She stared at me, exclaimed, " What! you are the young hero?" burst out laughing and rushed away. She must be mad.'

Soon after that the Roumanian lady met one of Skobeleff's aides-de-camp. 'Do you know that Russians have a very funny notion of youth?' said she, wondering.

'And why do you say so?' he asked.

'Well, I saw your young General Skobeleff. What a monkey, what a horrid monkey!'

But Skobeleff, although full of fun, was also full of generosity to all who needed his help.

Soon after the taking of Plevna he was walking in Bucharest, and saw an officer looking very pale and half-starving. 'What regiment are you in?' asked he. 'Have you dined?'

'Well, I tried to get a dinner, but prices are tremendously high at Bucharest; I am trying to find something more in accordance with my pocket.'

'Come with me; be my guest,' interrupted the commander. The dinner was over, and the poor officer went home. On his table he found an envelope containing ten pounds and a note from Skobeleff. 'You forgot your money on my table. You should not do so again!'

An eye-witness relates a scene which deeply impressed him. Skobeleff went to visit a transport of soldiers badly wounded. One of the moribunds recognised him. 'Oh,' said he, 'there is our own one, our Skobeleff.' The others heard the name. 'Hurrah, hurrah!' they tried to cry out; so weak and wavering were their voices it reminded one of death more than of life. One of the wounded soldiers who had to be operated on had both legs and an arm to be amputated. Chloroform was offered. He refused. 'Why do you object?' exclaimed the doctor. 'I cannot,' replied the man; 'rather let me smoke a pipe during the operation. I cannot take any chloroform, I tell you. I am a "Skobelevets—"' belonging to Skobeleff's division.

Another case: they bring in an officer. 'I am dying,' said he; 'no use concealing it from me,' said he. 'Where is Skobeleff? I want to see him, if possible.' They sent for Skobeleff, who was about a mile off. 'I am here,' said the General, as he hastened to his side. 'What can I do for you?'

'Just shake my hand, General, before I leave this world. I want nothing more. Thank you so much for coming.' He fell dead as he uttered the last word.

His example even in small details was followed by his men. When a reconnaissance was ordered, one of the soldiers began putting on his new uniform. 'Why is this?' he was asked; 'you will spoil your uniform.'

'I must; Skobeleff says that on going to meet

one's death one has to be dressed as when going to take the holy communion. Skobeleff himself is smartly dressed when he goes to a battle.'

Though insisting on the strictest discipline and obedience, Skobeleff was not a formalist, and no believer in red-tape. In the trenches soldiers were allowed to sit even in the presence of their commander. A soldier must have as much rest as possible; he must economise his strength. Had he to jump up at every appearance of his chief, the latter would be obliged to avoid going to his trenches.

After one of the attacks—the Turks already quite defeated—the Russians by mistake were continuing to shoot. 'What are you doing?' cried Skobeleff, with a voice of thunder. 'Are you mad? Are you Turks? Are you blind? The enemy is taking away his wounded and his dead, and you are firing at him! Stop immediately!'

The Turks called Skobeleff 'the just one.'

He once summoned all his officers. 'Gentlemen,' said he, 'I insist upon one important fact which you ought to keep always in mind. I cannot tolerate cruelty or injustice amongst my troops. We must pay for every trifle we take, and not plunder shops and villages, as brigands. If you or anybody does any harm to any child or woman, such an infamy as that shall be punished, mercilessly punished. Keep that well in mind, I tell you.'

He never treated his soldiers as machines. 'It is not enough,' he used to say, 'for soldiers to be brave;

they must also be intelligent.' And he constantly tried, with very great success, to make every infantryman in his division understand all the details of the battle in which he took part.

There was a dangerous skirmish once at night, a very dark night indeed it was. The troops could not see their chief, but they heard his commanding voice. They needed no better guidance.

When any young fellow in another division distinguished himself, Skobeleff used to give himself no rest till he had secured his transfer to his own division. To be chosen by Skobeleff, to be a Skobelevets, was an honour indeed. Another thing that endeared him to his troops was the gaiety of his heart, joined with deepest sympathy, which sometimes, as we have seen, even found expression in tears. Skobeleff never was other than gay with his men, although sometimes when alone, the injustice and stupid hatred of some of the Petersburgers nearly drove him mad. He soon got over that, and his spirits used to rise with danger, until he never seemed so much himself as when he was leading a charge upon the enemy's batteries. As he once said when asked why he dressed for a battle as if for a ball, 'Is not every battle a ball for a soldier?'

There was something fascinating about the way in which this splendidly gifted man absolutely ignored himself and lived only for his country and for his brethren. Why should not men be proud to die for him who seemed only to covet the privilege of dying for them? He only prized his life in order that he might give it away for Russia and the Slavs. Who would not be glad to follow such a chief? And his troops followed him with an absolute devotion. His presence was enough to induce them to confront any number of foes. It was sufficient if Skobeleff was there. Once, in the Tekke campaign, a fierce skirmish took place in the night. It was so dark the troops could not see the white coat of their General, but they heard his voice through the black night, and it was enough. With him, even though unseen, they could not be defeated.

And now, after giving so many English, Scotch, and American testimonies, let me add a few details from a Russian author, M. Némirovitch Dantchenko, who gives some charming specimens of his ways and manners with his soldiers.

The General, though he was the chief, at the same time was the beloved comrade of all.

Once, M. Dantchenko says, when the heat was intolerable, Skobeleff was driving in an open carriage. He saw a soldier hardly able to move a step, perfectly exhausted. He cried. 'Well, poor fellow! it is hard to walk.'

'Yes, your Excellency,' he replied.

'I daresay you think it rather unjust that a general, lighter and better dressed than you, should be driving, and you should have to trot. Is it not so?'

The soldier, not knowing what to answer, was silent.

'Well, come, sit down with me and drive.'

The soldier, thinking the General was joking, hesitated.

'I tell you, sit down.'

The soldier looks amazed and delighted, and takes his place.

'Are you well?' continues Skobeleff.

'Admirably, your Excellency.'

'Well, earn your general's epaulettes, then, as my grandfather did—he also was at first a private —and you will drive in your own carriage as I do.'

On another day, at Giurgevo, Skobeleff meets a soldier crying. 'What a shame!' he exclaimed. 'What is the matter? Why are you weeping like a woman?'

The soldier tried as well as he could to look brave and self-controlled.

'What is the matter, I ask? Speak to me without fear.'

It turned out the poor fellow had just received a letter from home. The cow was dead; arrears had to be paid; the harvest was bad. There was no help. . . .

'You should begin by telling me what has happened,' said Skobeleff, 'and not go on weeping. Can you read and write?'

'Yes, Excellency.'

'Here are fifty roubles; send that home, and bring me the receipt from the post-office.'

The sum was more than sufficient, and made the soldier very happy.

Skobeleff was kindness itself. He never touched a farthing of his pay. It all went for good deeds. The numbers of applications of every sort he got daily was enormous.

Skobeleff's physical powers were very great.

'When do you sleep?' somebody asked him.

'Oh, I can easily pass three days and three nights without shutting my eyes, as I can also sleep uninterruptedly for twenty-four hours.'

He never trusted any report or description of the positions, and always at daybreak was studying everything himself, with his own eyes. Riding full speed, sometimes fifty versts, he would immediately resume his other work, reading and receiving official reports, making annotations, and giving orders. He would go to the kitchen, taste the soldiers' food, and then begin to read again. It was curious to see how he never failed getting books, and always serious works, newly-published. He used to discuss their contents with his friend General Kurapatkin or others, showing on these occasions the profusion of such an arsenal of facts, such a knowledge, that he looked like a military professor in his pulpit.

'Skobeleff is quite one of us,' declared the troops. 'He is a thorough Russian, he knows and loves us.

He is a regular eagle, flying in the air,' added some, admiringly.

'You must explain to the soldiers,' he used to tell his officers, 'what you want them to do. A soldier who realises his duty is worth a thousand times more than a man who is marching with closed eyes.'

Skobeleff liked to be himself always in the most dangerous place, though he did all he could to spare others. Once he went to the front, and turning round perceived a group of his officers. 'Why are you here?' he cried; 'you are not necessary.'

'We will not let you die alone,' answered they.

He understood their stratagem, smiled, and returned to another spot. But he yielded thus very seldom. 'A general who is a coward ought not to be tolerated.'

'My dear fellow,' he once said to a diplomatist, 'you have the right to be a coward. A young, unexperienced officer may understand fear; but a chief, a commander, has no right to think of his precious life.'

M. Némirovitch Dantchenko's sketch of Skobeleff, although somewhat flippant, abounds with anecdotes of the General's influence over his men. Sometimes, although very rarely, he had to use threats. Once a wood-cutting party, assailed by a murderous fire from the Turks, fell back upon the trenches. 'What are you coming here for?' he asked. 'We are leaving our work,' they replied. 'Have you finished it?'

'No, the Turks are firing; it is impossible; their numbers are incalculable;' and, in a panic, the men jumped down into the trenches. 'You are frightened!' cried Skobeleff, in tones of thunder. 'Your comrades are working, and you are frightened. Form in rank!'

They obeyed.

'March back to your work, and that at once. If not, God be witness if I do not make you go through your drill before the Turkish trenches. You know me. It is enough.'

They resumed their work without hesitation. It was seldom that they needed such exhortation. His horses sometimes refused to go further; his men never. Their devotion for him was boundless. As he never spared himself, neither would they. Their greatest ambition was to be like him. His example was ever before them. At the beginning of the campaign, when he had swum his horse across the Danube, he said, 'I never propose to do anything without first doing it myself as an example. What one man can do, can be done by hundreds and thousands of others.'

A striking illustration of his method of teaching by example is told by Doukonin, Chief of Staff of the Fourth Corps. 'The cavalry having fallen much behind the infantry in effectiveness, Skobeleff undertook to bring the former into better condition. After having put them through manœuvres on land, he ordered them to swim a river. He explained how the operation should be effected. Then he selected the worst and most obstinate horse in the troop to show them how it should be done. Undressing, he mounted the horse and forced it into the water. The animal yielding to the stream landed on the same side further down the river. He plunged in again and then again. The regiment left on the river bank shuddered as they saw their general persisting in compelling the unwilling horse to take the direction he had indicated at first. The persistence of the man overcame the obstinacy of the horse, and it at last swam across the stream and landed its wilful rider on the other side.' Skobeleff then re-entered the river and swam back to the place of starting. 'Now, my brave fellows,' said he, ' follow the example of your commander.' In a moment the whole regiment, officers and men, plunged in the stream, each anxious to prove himself more bold and more skilful than his comrade.

Skobeleff was far more careful of others than he was of himself.[1] When in the trenches before Plevna,

---

[1] Prince Léon Schahofsky, in his vivid and brilliant book, *Two Campaigns beyond the Balkans*, gives the following illustration of this in a description of a meeting between General Gourko and General Skobeleff.

Having fixed an interview at the Mirkovitch redoubt, in order to decide together upon the elevation of new fortifications, near Plevna, they both came in the redoubt with their numerous suite of officers and chiefs of their different regiments. The redoubt was some 800 or 1,000 sagènes distant from the Turkish forces. Turkish shells reached it so easily, that almost every shot hit the mark. The Turks seemed quite sure of their safety, and some of them were calmly working, others walking or riding on their fortifications. Gourko seemed vexed at that apparent *sans-gêne*, and drew Skobeleff's attention to it; then, turning himself to the chief of the battery : ' Send them some bullets,' his staff one day discussed how they could prevent him from so recklessly exposing himself. The only expedient they could devise was that they should accompany him whenever he went outside the breastwork into the enemy's fire. Immediately afterwards Skobeleff stood upon the breastwork against which the Turks were firing heavily. In a moment all his staff got up beside him. 'What are you doing here, gentlemen?' he asked. 'Are you coming to court the enemy's balls?' One of the officers saluted him gravely and replied, 'We have the honour to belong to the staff of your Excellency.' Skobeleff saw the trick. He burst out laughing, and finding they persisted, he returned to the trench.

His life in the trenches was spent among the soldiers. He slept on a stretcher in the straw, beneath an awning of thatch which was often pierced by Turkish bullets. In the bitter cold nights he used to make a little fire in a frying-pan to keep him warm. He slept very little. In the trenches, as in the drawing-rooms of fine ladies, or at the dinner-table

he cried, hardly interrupting his debates with Skobeleff. All the Turks suddenly disappeared, then some few of them came back. 'Some more bullets,' again ordered Gourko, and resumed his conversation. Again the Turks disappear, and this time they remained below for a longer period of time. After which a light smoke is beginning to be seen from their side. 'Lie down all of you,' cried the Russian canonnier de service. Everybody immediately obeyed, except Skobeleff and Gourko, who remained standing and talking. A Turkish shell, howling and whistling in the air, fell near one of the officers without bursting. Another cry of 'Lie down!' is heard, another Turkish shell traverses the air; the two generals, both looking calm, continue their conversation. A third Turkish shell followed the second, and also fell unburst.

of boon companions, he was continually drawing maps and plans, jotting down ideas and suggestions. When the Turks were not troublesome, he spent the time in reading and writing. He was never idle. 'We have no time for rest,' he used to say. 'Russia cannot wait. We shall find rest in our graves.'

He carried the same spirit into the campaign against the Tekkes. A doctor who accompanied the expedition and who recently published some reminiscences of Skobeleff in the *Russ*, says: 'I once ventured to give advice to Skobeleff, urging him not to expose his life so recklessly. "Doctor," answered he, "if I am wounded I am in your hands, and you have to order. Till then pray give me no lessons." The intonation of the voice gave me to understand that my *rôle* of voluntary mentor had to cease once for all.'

'Soldiers when they perceived their chief in the trenches rendered him military honours. "Don't do that," said he, "don't bow to me when I pass, and also never bow to the enemies' bullets." All that is related about Skobeleff's legendary bravery, all that seems hyperbolical, is only strictly true.'[1]

[1] For some of Skobeleff's orders of the day, see Appendix A.

CHAPTER VI.

THE PASSAGE OF THE BALKANS.

After the fall of Plevna—The position of the Turks—Gourko crosses the Balkans—Skobeleff's advance—Camp kettles and boots—The position at Shipka—Across the Balkans by a sheep track—The plan of the attack—Ascending the hills—The descent—Turkish resistance--Sviatopolk-Mirsky's attack — Occupation of Imetli—The battle of Shenova—Surrender of Vessel Pasha—Capture of the army of the Shipka—Advance on Adrianople—Occupation of the Tchataldja lines — The armistice — The English fleet in the Bosphorus Advance to San Stefano—End of the war.

WHEN Plevna surrendered there still remained 175,000 Turkish soldiers in the Balkan Peninsula. Of these, more than one-half were in the quadrilateral. Against them some general is said to have proposed to lead our armies. But a bolder policy found favour at headquarters. Instead of a war of sieges, it was decided to march at once across the Balkans. It was a very adventurous undertaking. Bulgaria in December is no Paradise. The broad Danube behind us; the snowclad Balkans in front. The roads were terrible. Northern Bulgaria was stripped of food and forage. But Skobeleff and Gourko insisted upon an immediate advance, and the Grand Duke approved. General Gourko, with 65,000 infantry, 6,000 cavalry, and 280 guns, was ordered to cross by the Arab Konak Pass, and then to advance by Philippopolis on Adrianople. Radetzky, with Skobeleff and Mirsky, with 56,000 infantry, 2,000 horse, and 252 guns, had to cross by the Shipka, and also make for Adrianople.

Suleiman Pasha, who was then commanding the Turkish army south of the Balkans, distributed 35,000 infantry, 2,000 cavalry, and 114 guns in various positions opposite Gourko. Vessel Pasha, with 36,000 men and 93 guns, held the southern end of the Shipka Pass, the northern end of which never passed out of the hands of the Russians since Skobeleff made his way into the abandoned position in July.

As it is not my duty to tell the story of the campaign,[1] I may briefly dismiss the heroic exploits of Gourko's column, as they may by themselves form a brilliant separate *épopée*.

[1] Beginning with the fall of Plevna on December 10, and ended with the conclusion of the armistice of Adrianople on January 31. In these fifty-one days the Russian armies had marched over 400 miles; had crossed a lofty range of mountains, where the snow was from three to ten feet thick and the temperature as low as 10° Fahr.; had fought three series of battles, lasting from two to four days each, resulting in the complete capture of nearly 40,000 men and the dispersion of another army of over 50,000; had captured 213 guns, and small-arms, baggage tents, and supplies of all kinds, including cartridges and rations by the millions; and, finally, had been able to dictate such terms of peace to the conquered as to remove them permanently from the list of independent military nations: and this the Russians had accomplished with the loss of less than 20,000 men, of whom about half fell in battle and the other half succumbed to the rigour of the season and the climate. The natural difficulties of the winter campaign were overcome by the extraordinary patience and physical endurance of the men, and by the untiring energy of their commanders, Gourko and Skobeleff.—Greene's *Russian Army and its Campaign in Turkey*, 1877-78, pp. 367-374.

Gourko reached Orkhanie on December $\frac{11}{23}$ from Plevna. Two days later the advance began. On the $\frac{18\text{th}}{30\text{th}}$ his column was safely across the mountain. On $\frac{\text{December 22}}{\text{January 3}}$ Gourko occupied Sophia, having lost in action 1,000 men in eleven days, not including 53 men who were frozen to death, and 810 who were utterly disabled by frost in General Dandeville's column, which had to retire upon Etropol. Gourko advanced on $\frac{\text{December 23}}{\text{January 9}}$ from Sophia.

Nine days later he occupied Philippopolis, after having destroyed a strong and well-provided Turkish army and captured 114 guns, together with an immense store of provision and munitions of war. His total loss was only 1,250 men.

Harder fighting, but even more signal success, attended the Radetzky column, which advanced through the Shipka Pass. That story, however, must be told with more details.

The following account of the passage of the Balkans by Skobeleff is taken from the narrative of M. Imchenetzky, who was himself an eye-witness of that remarkable feat of arms:—

Plevna, the fatal Plevna, still detained the Russian army, but a full month before its fall Skobeleff had established sources of supply, of food and forage, for the whole 16th Division, at Gabrova, Tirnova, Selvi, and in other places. Even then he was preoccupied with the thought of crossing the Balkans. Yet after Plevna fell we remained inactive for two whole weeks. Plevna had wearied us during the siege, but it was now more insupportable than ever. Impatient to advance, we were doomed to complete idleness; and, as day after day passed, we began to lose all hope.[1]

The only consolation we had was the assurance Skobeleff used to give us that we should soon be off again. 'Take care of your horses, gentlemen,' he used to say, ' you will soon have need of them for a long and difficult march. Buy all the horses the Turkish officers have for sale. You will want to buy soon, and you will find none.' Soon afterwards he told us that we were to march on Shipka.

It was not till December $\frac{10}{22}$, 1877, that we started. The march from Plevna was by no means easy. The snow had fallen heavily, but sledging was not yet established; and the road over heaps of frozen earth was terrible, especially for the baggage wagons and the artillery. It took us two stages to reach Loftcha, a distance of thirty versts (twenty miles). The third stage—to Selvi—was twenty-five versts. We could not take all our artillery; two cannon in every battery were left at Plevna. Not only was a battery reduced from eight to six pieces, but each cannon, even the small four-pounders, needed eight horses instead of six. The forage and the mass of the baggage of infantry was transported upon sledges dragged by oxen and mules. The reserve baggage, and part of that of the artillery, which could not by any possibility cross the Balkans, were left at Plevna; and only rejoined the army six months later, long after peace had been signed.

The detachment was divided into two echelons. The weather was propitious. The frost was steady, without wind or thaw. The detachment before crossing the Balkans had always been lodged day and night, and had never bivouacked. The camp kettles were always despatched with great care in advance to the place where

---

[1] The delay was caused, first by the necessity of waiting for reinforcements, and secondly by a severe snowstorm and the horrible state of the roads.

the troops were to sleep, and when the men arrived their food was ready cooked. Skobeleff always tasted it, and recorded whether it was good or bad. The order of the day next morning praised the good cooks, and pilloried the careless.

After the detachment had defiled past him, Skobeleff severely reprimanded all who remained behind, insisting that they should always advance with perfect regularity. It was necessary to be very strict about this. A soldier when left behind takes to plundering, and often is frozen to death.

When the detachment began the march, it defiled before its beloved chief singing gaily as it marched by. He was accustomed to greet them with great geniality, recalling the battles in which they had taken part, and talking sometimes of the soldier's position, and sometimes of subjects far removed from the scenes of the campaign. The privates, instead of being, as usually is the case, awkward in the presence of their chief, were put perfectly at their ease, and showed themselves at their best whenever they had the kind and hearty greeting of Skobeleff. It is needless to add that he treated the officers with the greatest humanity as comrades. But why say more? Ask any officer who has ever been in direct communication with Skobeleff, and he will speak with enthusiasm of that man, the charm of whose sympathetic manner was irresistible to all who surrounded him. What was not less remarkable was the popularity which Skobeleff enjoyed among the Bulgarians. They crowded around him, and testified warmly their affection for him and for his troops.

Skobeleff never forgot the saying of Marshal de Saxe, that the strength of an army lay in its feet. He was most rigorous in seeing that there were no damaged boots in his division. He spared no efforts to secure new boots for his men, and it fared ill with the soldier and with his

officer if the boots were not well and regularly greased.
Every man received a pair of warm stockings. Skobeleff
insisted strongly on the excessive importance of clean
feet; and he used to recall the fact that when the French
before Sebastopol were so badly off for fuel as to have to
dig the vine roots out of the ground, the officers kept
part of that scanty allowance for heating water in which
the soldiers could wash their feet.

On arriving at Selvi on December $\frac{12}{25}$, we remained
there a week. (Gourko had already begun the passage
of the Balkans near Sophia.) During this period Skobeleff
repaired to Shipka,[1] where he received instructions from
Radetzky as to the advance southward. Radetzky added
some regiments of Bulgarian Militia to Skobeleff's command, and ordered him to cross the Balkans by the track
of Imetli.[2]

[1] Radetzky commanded the troops with which he had held Mount
St. Nicholas, since it was seized by Skobeleff in the early days of the
war. The Turks occupied the village of Shipka, to the south of Mount
St. Nicholas. The cold at Shipka that winter was so intense that
Radetzky had no fewer than 6,000 men *hors-de-combat* by frostbite and
exposure on December $\frac{13}{25}$.

[2] Lieut. Greene writes thus of Radetzky's plan of campaign :—' The
arrival of General Skobeleff with the 16th and 30th divisions and the
3rd and 4th rifle brigades at Gabrova, in the first days of January,
placed a force of 74 battalions, or about 56,000 infantry, besides artillery and cavalry, at Radetzky's disposition ; but of these troops, the
24th division had to be sent to Gabrova to refit, and was for the
moment practically *hors-de-combat*. The rest of his troops, however,
were in good order. Radetzky's plan for forcing the passage was to
divide his troops into three columns, one of which, under his own
orders, was to remain in the works at the summit of the pass, while
the other two were to pass on either flank, cross the mountain, and attack
the pass from the rear (south) simultaneously with the attack from the
north. Radetzky's detachment consisted of the 14th infantry division
and the 35th regiment of the 9th division. The column of the right,
under Skobeleff, consisted of the 16th division, the 3rd rifle brigade
(3 battalions), 7 Bulgarian battalions, the 9th Don Cossacks, 6 mountain guns, and 6 4-pounders,—in all, 22 battalions, 6 squadrons, and
12 guns. It was to pass over the trail which leads from the village

It was no easy matter. The snow lay in some places ten feet deep. The track—for it was a mere track among the hills—was not a road which even in summer-time the natives of the hills cared to traverse. Only when there was great urgency would a Bulgarian peasant, even in summer, drive his ass along the mountain track over which Skobeleff had to force an army in the depth of winter. The artillery officers protested that it was impossible. At last Lieut.-Colonel Kurapatkin, commanding the 4th Battery of the 16th Brigade of Artillery, a young man of thirty years, who had done good service in Turkestan, volunteered to take six of his four-pounders. All the rest were left behind, with the exception of a mountain battery of eight guns.

On December $\frac{19}{31}$ we sent our cannon back to Selvi, and started for Gabrova, which we reached in safety. From there Skobeleff again went to Shipka, where he secured a prize, in the shape of 800 pairs of boots, from the chief of a tirailleur battalion. Skobeleff was very uneasy about the march. His letter to Kurapatkin of $\frac{\text{December 21}}{\text{January 2}}$ showed a minute attention to every detail—

of Zelenodrevo to the top of the mountains (only about two miles and a half from the left flank of the Turks on the Bald Mountain), and thence descends to the village of Imetli in the Tundja Valley; here the detachment was to turn to the left and attack the works defending the village of Shipka. The column of the left, under Prince Mirsky, consisted of the 33rd, 34th, and 36th regiments of the 9th division, the 30th division, the 4th rifle brigade, 1 Bulgarian battalion, the 23rd Don Cossack regiment, 6 mountain guns, 8 4-pounders, and 8 9-pounders.—in all, 26 battalions, 6 squadrons, and 22 guns. It was to leave the village of Travna, and follow the trail over the Selky hill, debouching in the Tundja Valley, at the village of Gusevo, then turn to the right, and, joining hands with Skobeleff, attack the works defending the village of Shipka. The movement was fixed to begin on the morning of the 5th of January, and it was calculated that the columns would arrive in the valley on the evening of the 7th, and attack on the morning of the 8th.'—Greene's *Russian Army in Turkey*, pp. 349-350.

forage, cartridges, the distribution of troops, the preservation of the shells from damp, nothing was forgotten. The sappers were then sent on in advance into the mountains to clear a path through the snow.

The chief strategic difficulty in the way of successfully executing the operation was the distance which separated the columns. It was impossible to keep open communications between three divisions operating from Shipka in the centre, Kazanlyk, and Imetli. Everything depended upon the simultaneous attack of Mirsky, Skobeleff, and Radetzky; but beyond a calculation as to the distance to be traversed, there was no guide to the commanders, and distance was but only one factor in the problem. A shorter road often takes more time to travel than a longer; and this Skobeleff found to his cost. His detachment consisted of the following troops :—The 16th division of infantry, the 9th, 11th, and 12th battalions of Tirailleurs, two companies of the 4th battalion of Sappers, seven cohorts of the Bulgarian Militia, the 4th battery of the 16th Brigade of Artillery (six guns), the 2nd mountain battery (eight guns), the 9th Cossack regiment of Naguibine, one sotnia of Kersloff's Cossacks of the Ural. Towards the end of the march they sent three regiments of the 1st Cavalry Division, Cossacks, Dragoons, and Lancers. Neither battalions nor squadrons were up to their normal strength. The sotnia of the Naguibine Cossacks only numbered forty men, and their horses were little better than skeletons.

The first echelon of the main body marched southward on the Shipka road on $\frac{\text{December 24}}{\text{January 6}}$. After marching eight miles they turned to the right near the Devil bridge along the bed of a stream. The line of march was very serpentine, and they had repeatedly to cross and recross the bed of the stream. The weather was good, a slight frost and no wind. After marching along the stream for five or six miles, the road turned to the left, at a village named Topliche. There they halted, pitched their camp-kettles, and boiled their rations. It was almost the last warm meal they had until they crossed the Balkans; it was impossible to carry the camp-kettles any further.

During the night a welcome reinforcement arrived in the shape of a transport of medicines, warm clothes, &c., come from the Countess Adlerberg. Each regiment received twelve bottles of brandy and nine of wine.

Skobeleff, with his chief of staff, installed himself at Topliche, from whence began the dolorous road to Imetli, a mere mountain track in summer, in winter not even that. Little by little the Bulgarian Militia began to come in. The night was dark. Immediately before us stood a dense forest; between the trees the snow lay soft and deep. They were compelled to march in single file. It was terrible work getting the mountain battery over the ground. The guns were light, weighing six pouds, about two English hundredweight, but the feeble half-starved horses could with the utmost difficulty drag them through the snow. The soldiers had to help them at every step. The difficulties with the mountain battery foreshadowed no good to Kurapatkin's six-pounders, which were more than three times as heavy. If a single false step was made, the horse and his driver plunged overhead in the snow.

Skobeleff determined to stop after marching seven miles. The troops were exhausted. At six o'clock only a few regiments had arrived, including the sappers, tirailleurs, and the mountain battery. The snow was cleared off the ground, and fires were kindled, and the soldiers with their little frying-pans set about cooking their rations. The only water was melted snow, which had a detestable taste. At seven o'clock the scene was striking in the extreme. All the fires were burning brightly, and the glowing flames lit up the depths of the forest. The soldiers grouped round the camp fires were full of life and gaiety. Skobeleff, Kurapatkin, Verestchagine, and some others sat around a bonfire and enjoyed their supper. The horses alone seemed miserable. Those only of the mountain battery received hay; the others were perforce content with the twigs of trees.

Skobeleff formed a detachment under the command of Colonel Laskoffsky, composed of twenty Cossacks, two companies of engineers, and one battalion of the regiment of Kazan. Two Bulgarian guides led the way. The vanguard toiled slowly up the heights. The culminating point of the ascent was reached near the Kardam Mount, a perfectly regular cone, which it passes on the right by a steep and narrow ledge, which wound round the hill. On the right of the ledge towered the rock, on the left was a precipice of incalculable depth. The day before the sun had shone warmly, and the snow had melted. In the night it froze, forming a crust of ice over the snow, on which it was very difficult to walk. We advanced very slowly after we had passed the crown of the Balkans. The descent was almost as difficult as the ascent. We laboured on, however, and at seven o'clock in the morning came upon a declivity not more than 100 fathoms deep, but excessively steep, the angle not being less than 45 degrees. We hoped that at the bottom of this slope we should find the village of Imetli. Volunteers were called for, and they slid down the slope. An hour and a half passed, and it became evident that we were not yet at Imetli. The vanguard therefore scrambled, half sliding, down the hill, catching a distant glimpse of the valley of the Tundja between the mountains, and began their march onward. The track wormed its way amid great stones and rocks, on the edge of a great ravine thickly strewn with boulders, at the bottom of which the Tundja made its way to Imetli at the foot of the hills.

Far below, so far below that their horsemen appeared no larger than grasshoppers, we could see the fortified position of the Turks, between Shenova and Shipka. An indescribable confusion was visible in the camp as they caught sight of our troops. Two pieces of artillery were sent out to oppose our advance, and presently the first sharp sound of rifle-shots rang through the ravine.

The Turks attempted to surround us, and very soon their bullets were whistling overhead along the whole line. Their fire on our right and in front did not matter much, for we were sheltered by rocks; but on the left they had us at a great disadvantage. Lying themselves hidden behind boulders in the ravine, we could not hit them, whereas we were without cover. They approached within two to three hundred yards, and the number of casualties became formidable. All round us were heard the groans of the wounded. The fire of the Turks was not returned. Cartridges were dearer than life. The contest might last all day, and not a shot could be wasted. The Turks were continually reinforced. Their fire became hotter as they drew closer. Our ranks were thinning fast. The Turkish bullets, ricochetting among the rocks, wounded those whose cover seemed the safest. There was no sign of succour. Our little band began to lose heart. From break of day till one o'clock in the afternoon we had kept the road. The Circassians were mounting the ravine behind us. In a short time we should be completely cut off.

'I was sent,' says Imchenetzky, 'with a couple of Cossacks as escort, to inform Skobeleff of our desperate position. The scene was terrible. The Circassians were gaining ground every minute. Our wounded, pale and despairing, were writhing on every side, their groaning mingling horribly with the hiss of the bullets. It was two o'clock, and still there was no sign of succour. Another hour, and it might be too late, and the Turks would be able to fortify and hold against Skobeleff and all his troops the position we had seized.

'With unspeakable joy I saw, even when almost despairing, the appearance of the head of one column. The Kazantzi, and part of the regiment of Ouglitch, fell upon the Circassians, who were on the point of occupying the road, and drove them back. Our vanguard was saved. At the foot of the steep declivity down which we had to slide I found the officer in command of the Ouglitch regiment. While I was describing the position Skobeleff himself arrived. All the others were on foot. He alone was riding, although the foot soldiers were falling under the enemies' fire. Providence shielded the solitary horseman.'

Skobeleff at once threw upon the heights on the right flank a platoon and a half of Cossacks, under Doukmassoff. The Cossacks threw themselves with ardour upon the Turks. They pushed their way without firing through a hailstorm of bullets until they were close to their foes. Then they poured in a volley at such short range that the Turks turned and fled towards the village of Imetli. The affair ended at four o'clock.

Before night set in Skobeleff ordered that great fires should be kindled upon the surrounding heights to deceive the enemy as to the numbers of our detachment. As soon as the regiments of Kazan and Ouglitch were all got together, Skobeleff ordered them to advance upon Imetli. They marched in silence in the darkness of night. Skobeleff himself accompanied them. The Turks had fled. Imetli was evacuated, and immediately occupied by our troops.

At daybreak the mountain battery, the Tirailleurs, and the Bulgarian Militia began the descent. On $\frac{\text{December 27}}{\text{January 8}}$ the Kazan and Ouglitch regiments occupied the valley, driving out a few insignificant Turkish bands. Our mountain guns fired a few rounds to advertise their presence. Skobeleff, who was very anxious about his weakness in cavalry, sent at once for the 9th Cossack regiment, which at 11 o'clock began at once to skirmish with the Turkish cavalry. The tournament looked well from the

mountain; but, although the Turks outnumbered the
Cossacks by two to one, they never came to close quarters,
though many were hit on both sides with rifle-balls.

Far away in the east we could distinguish the roll of
musketry, and the cries of men in deadly combat.

'It is Sviatopolk-Mirsky,' said Skobeleff. 'How an-
noying it is that we can do nothing to help him!'¹

¹ The following is Lieut. Greene's narrative of the fighting which
Skobeleff heard in the east, which, as it also mentions some details as
to Skobeleff's march not given by Imchenetzky, I give at some length:
'On the morning of the 8th, the day calculated for the attack,
Radetzky watched eagerly on Mount St. Nicholas for the appearance
of the other two columns in the valley. About 10 A.M. Mirsky's
troops were seen coming out of the mountains near Gusevo; and de-
ploying about noon, they moved forward to the attack in the direction
of the Shipka village. Skobeleff's troops were not in sight, but a
cannonade was heard in the mountains in his direction, where he was,
in fact, still fighting with the Turks in the position half way down the
slope. About noon also arrived a messenger from Skobeleff, explaining the difficulties that he had met. Radetzky sent word back to him
to concentrate his column in the valley and attack Shipka from the
rear on the morning of the 9th, and, if possible, to open communications with Mirsky and attack in conjunction with him. He also informed Skobeleff, that the 1st cavalry division had been sent over his
trail to assist him. Mirsky, meanwhile, heard the cannonade off on
his left, but saw no Russian troops. Finally the cannonade died
away, and still no troops were in sight. He was evidently in a bad
position to attack alone, with his left flank out in the air; but, during
the previous night, he had received a precise order from Radetzky to
attack on this morning. He therefore moved forward with the 4th
rifle brigade deployed as skirmishers, supported by the little mountain
battery and the 33rd regiment. In his second line were the 34th,
36th, and 117th regiments. The 120th remained with the baggage at
Gusevo, and the 118th and 119th, which had occupied Maglis on
his left flank the previous night, were ordered to move forward to
Kazanlyk.

'After a short but hot fight, his troops carried the villages of
Janina and Haskioi, but beyond Haskioi was a small range of hills
stretching across the road, covered with several tiers of rifle pits.
Here Mirsky's troops were brought to a halt by a very hot fire, and,
the colonel of the 33rd regiment being severely wounded about this
time, the line began to waver.

The troops which had been in bivouac began to descend into the valley. By night most of the detachment had arrived, including the mountain battery, Kurapatkin's cannon, which subsequently had to be left behind; the regiment of Sousdal, the Lancers, and a few infantry were still in the hills.

It was impossible to attack that day. Our troops were still scattered. Our position was not fortified, we had no *point d'appui*, and Radetzky's orders were precise —that no attack was to be made till the whole of the detachment had been got together.

'The 36th regiment was then sent forward to the support of the 33rd, which held the right of the line, and the 34th to the support of the rifle brigade, on its left. One battalion of the 117th was sent off in the direction of Kazanlyk to guard the left flank, and only the other two battalions of the regiment remained in reserve. The little mountain battery advanced to within about 700 yards of the Turkish position, and sent a lucky shot which exploded one of the Turkish caissons. The Russians then moved forward with a rush, in spite of the fire of the Turks, and carried the line of the trenches, capturing 3 guns and about 100 prisoners.

'They thus came in front of the last line of defence of the Turks, a series of redoubts on the hills just south of Shipka village; but darkness was coming on, the troops were tired out, and their ammunition was almost exhausted. It was impossible to try to carry these redoubts that night. The Turks, however, pressed to the attack, and rushed forward upon the Russians with considerable impetuosity, but were driven back by the deliberate volley-firing of the latter.

'Although Mirsky was informed early in the evening that the 118th and 119th regiments had entered Kazanlyk without finding any enemy, yet his position was anything but comfortable. His left flank was in the air, at his back was a high range of mountains, over which it would be almost impossible to retreat, and in his front, only 200 yards off, was the enemy, in a position which he felt he could not carry. He sent a report to Radetzky explaining his critical situation, stating that he had fought all day with superior numbers, had sustained very great losses, was nearly at the end of his ammunition, and, unless he could be reinforced, he must begin to retreat. Radetzky sent word back to him to hold on for another twenty-four hours; that Skobeleff would come to his relief on his left flank; and that he, Radetzky, would try to operate a diversion by attacking the Turks in front the next morning.'

M

That night around Imetli bonfires were blazing, as if we had an army of 100,000 men. Two bands of music were ordered to play. The Turks hurled a few shells into our camp. We answer by firing a salvo into Shenova. The tableau was splendid.

The troops were ordered to rest. The Cossack patrols kept the fires blazing, while most of the men went to sleep in Imetli. Before the village Skobeleff met them, praised them for their fortitude, and explained to them briefly what should be done in case of a night attack by the Turks. In Imetli we found an enormous store of forage and provisions, very welcome to our horses and our men.

Weary and worn with the excessive fatigues of the march across the hills, the men slept as if they could never awaken. The night was tranquil. It was the lull before the storm. Only in one house sleepless eyes kept watch through the night, where Skobeleff and his chief of staff, Count Keller, drew up the plan of attack for the morrow's battle. The dispositions for attack were drawn up with difficulty. They had hardly any ink, and had no clerk. The following is an extract from the plan then drawn up:—

'The object of the battle is the capture of the fortified camp of Shenova.

'The advance will be made by the escarpments of the right flank.

'I shall be found near the vanguard at the beginning of the battle; later I shall be near the general reserve.

'The wounded will be taken to Imetli.

'The positions which will be held by the infantry will be indicated on the spot by Count Keller.

'The Bulgarian Militia and the engineers will defend the village of Imetli from an attack coming from Kalofer.

'(Signed) General-Lieutenant SKOBELEFF.'

It was indispensable to take Shenova before attacking

Shipka, otherwise he would have exposed his flank to the enemy's attack. Shenova was the strategic key of the position. If the enemy were cleared out of it, he could extend his hand to Sviatopolk-Mirsky, and unite for the final attack on the Turkish position.

It was at nine o'clock on the morning of $\frac{\text{December 29}}{\text{January 10}}$ that the famous battle of Shenova began.[1]

[1] M. Imchenetzky only describes the fight which he saw. Here is Lieut. Greene's narrative of the fighting on the day of Shenova, under Radetzky and Sviatopolk-Mirsky:—

'On the 10th of January, unfortunately, there was a tempest of wind, filling the air with blinding snow and a dense fog of particles of frozen mist. Radetzky could see nothing of what was going on in the valley, but through the fog came the sounds of heavy artillery and infantry fire, indicating that the Turks had begun to attack Mirsky. Radetzky at once made his preparations for attack, in the hope of relieving the pressure on Mirsky. He sent forward the 55th and 56th regiments, and part of the 35th, along the high road and on its right, against the Turkish trenches in front of Mount St. Nicholas. The ground was extremely unfavourable for attack, and in the dense fog it was impossible to see what was going on at a distance of ten yards away. Still these troops, between noon and 2 P.M., carried the first two lines of Turkish trenches in open assault, but with enormous losses—over 1,700 men. Having gained these positions, the troops remained there, unable to advance, until news arrived from Skobeleff during the afternoon announcing the surrender of the whole Turkish army.

'Meanwhile, in the valley, the fog was not so dense. The Turks had early in the morning opened an attack on Mirsky's right flank, but had not made any impression upon it. They then made an attack upon his left flank without any better success. Mirsky then riposted with his left and carried a second Turkish redoubt (capturing two guns in it), and also the village of Shipka. This cut off this portion of the Turks from the Kazanlyk road, but they still held a line of redoubts behind Shipka village. While Mirsky's troops were halted in front of this and a lull had succeeded in the battle in their front, they heard loud cheering off on their left at the village of Shenova. It was the attack of Skobeleff's troops, the most brilliant assault of the whole war, deciding the day and the fate of the entire Turkish army at Shipka.'

The Turkish army which thus surrendered numbered 41 battalions, containing 36,000 men in all, of whom about 6,000 were sick

The Turks, like the excellent engineers that they were, had carefully fortified their position. They had strengthened their earthworks, and mounted them with artillery of long range.

Skobeleff's first care had been to attempt to open communications with Sviatopolk-Mirsky. With that end and wounded, and with it were captured 93 guns (including 12 mortars) and 10 flags, but the Russian losses were not slight, being as follows:—

	Officers	Men
Killed	19	1,103
Wounded	116	4,246
Total	135	5,349

Of this loss, 1,700 men were in Radetzky's, 1,500 in Skobeleff's, and 2,100 in Mirsky's detachment. Only 37 battalions, or about 25,000 men, had been brought under fire; so that the proportion of losses was about 22 per cent.

The capture of this Shipka army surpasses in boldness and brilliancy the advance of Gourko over the Balkans at Arab Konak. Although Radetzky's attack in front caused him terrible losses and apparently gained no result, yet without this it is possible that the Turks might have withdrawn from the mountains under cover of the fog, and, concentrating about Shipka village, have broken through between Mirsky and Skobeleff, and escaped to the south; and, although Mirsky may be blamed for opening his attack before he had established communication with Skobeleff, according to the plan of battle, yet it is possible that, had he remained idle at Gusevo during the 8th, the Turks might have discovered him, and begun to retreat. Finally, Skobeleff's energetic attack, as soon as he had got all his men together in the valley, was one of the most splendid assaults ever made, and renders more than doubtful the conclusion which has been hastily drawn from this war (from Plevna particularly) that successful assaults of earthworks defended by modern breechloaders are impossible.

The Turks seem to have relied, here as at Arab Konak, upon their conviction that the intense cold, the deep snow, and the impassable nature of the mountains, except over the road which they held, would render any such movements on the part of the Russians *wholly* impossible.

One of the remarkable features of this battle is the fact that Mirsky and Skobeleff both had to leave all their artillery behind (except the little mountain guns, which amounted to nothing), and that both of them carried the enemy's works without any preparation of the attack by artillery.

in view, and also in order to cut off the retreat of the Turks to the Little Balkans, he sent off all his disposable cavalry to turn the left flank of the Turks. He then selected a position advantageously situated for seeing the progress of the fight. It was the first time since the war began that he had not taken his position in the hottest of the fight. He was surrounded by a few sotnias of Cossacks, and the clump of horsemen attracted the fire of the Turks. A shell burst under Skobeleff. He disappeared in the smoke and upheaved soil. 'He's lost this time!' cried everyone; but to our amazement he was unhurt.

The combat deepened. The fire on the side of the Turks was really infernal. The companies of the Ouglitchani and Kazantzi, taking advantage of every bit of cover, went forward in rushes from one shelter to another without firing a shot. The bands went into action playing as if on parade. The Bulgarians flung themselves upon their hated foe with less order certainly than the Russians, but with equal courage, and even more fury. The wounded grudged to die before at least slaying one abhorred Turk.

No Turkish fire, however infernal, could stay the charge of the Russian soldiers. They flung themselves upon the Turkish lines, and cleared them at the point of the bayonet. The Bulgarians gave no quarter. After finishing with the fortifications, they all attacked the town. The Bulgarians attacked on the right, the Kazantzi on the left, the Ouglitchani in front. It was difficult to drive the Turks out of Shenova. They fired from every house, they clung to every garden. At last, however, the bayonets convinced them that they could no longer hold the village, and they fled *en masse* to their principal redoubt. The Kazantzi followed them at the run, firing without ceasing. They hastened to finish the affair and seize the central redoubt.

This redoubt, properly speaking, was not a redoubt at all. It was a hillock surrounded by a spiral trench. On the highest point stood the cannon. The whole hill was covered with a multitudinous mass of Turks. The variety of their costumes gave an extraordinarily chequered appearance to the hill. It looked like a kind of fantastic bouquet. Imagine the infernal flames which such a bouquet could produce when every man of the bouquet fired not less than ten shots a minute.

'Hurrah, hurrah!' cried the regiment of Ouglitch as it flung itself against the monster! But behold a thing altogether extraordinary and unexpected. The fire begins to diminish along the whole Turkish line.

'The white flag! the white flag! they surrender!' is the cry in all our ranks.

It is true. The white flag is floating on the hillock; and thus, after a fight lasting five hours, from nine in the morning till two in the afternoon, the battle is over and Shenova is ours.

Skobeleff went forward to receive the army which he had captured. He found that he had only taken half the army of Shipka, and that 15,000 more were opposing Radetzky.

Skobeleff insisted that Vessel Pasha should send the Pasha who commanded these men the order to surrender. Vessel at first demurred. Skobeleff pointed out that he would at once attack them in rear, while Radetzky attacked in front; and that as resistance was useless, it would be well to prevent a useless effusion of blood. Vessel gave way, and sent an officer with Colonel Stolétoff to order his troops to lay down their arms. They obeyed at once; and Stolétoff set off to announce the glad news to Radetzky.

Radetzky's attack had been repulsed. The nature of the locality was such that there was no room to manœuvre. The dead lay piled up in two heaps like logs of wood. The Russians were downcast. What then was their astonishment to see a Russian general leaning on some Turks—for Stolétoff was exhausted with the toils of the day—suddenly appear in the Turkish lines, and wave his handkerchief as a signal to stop firing! They ceased, and then an exultant hurrah rang through the hills. The struggle was over, the battle was won!

The troops established themselves in the Turkish fortified camp at Shenova, and Skobeleff and his staff in Turkish barracks close by.

It was evident that the Turks had intended to retreat. Carts, filled with the property of officers, had already taken the road. Their drivers lay dead, and the death-rattle sounded in the throats of the wounded horses. What a mass of corpses lay everywhere!

The victor exulted. It was a gigantic success surpassing all expectation. 32,000 men, 93 cannon, and 6 standards were in our hands. We feared to ride over the field, so thickly was it strewn with rifles. Trenches were filled with boxes of cartridges, of the best English manufacture, and cartridges were scattered everywhere in the mud; rations had been issued, and everything made ready for flight.

We seized at Shenova the hospital of the Red Crescent, with seven doctors—one English, one Prussian, two Swiss, and two Greeks. They told us that the Turks never expected any attack from the west. The pass of Imetli they regarded as absolutely impracticable. All their attention had been devoted to Radetzky and Sviatopolk-Mirsky. It was only on seeing the blaze of our fires that they had fortified their position on that side.

The victory of Shenova only cost Skobeleff 1,500 men.

Very little is known in England of that great rush across the Balkans. The Russian army, under Gourko, was accompanied by English correspondents, but Skobeleff fought unattended by his friends. The most brilliant action of the war has thus been least appreciated. But the victory of Shenova is one of the brightest laurels any general ever won.

Little time was wasted after the capture of Vessel Pasha on January $\frac{1}{3}$. Orders were issued for an immediate advance on Adrianople. General Gourko commanded the right and General Radetzky the left wing of the Russian army, while Skobeleff took command of the centre. General Stronkoff, commanding Skobeleff's advance guard, left Kazanlyk on New Year's day, old style. Skobeleff himself followed two days after, crossing the railway junction of Tyrnova, and marching directly on Adrianople. The programme was executed to the letter. Tyrnova was seized on June $\frac{3}{15}$, after a smart engagement. Skobeleff reached the place on the night of the $\frac{4}{16}$. He had marched his men fifty-five miles in forty hours. He then started for Hermanli. It was here that occurred one of the saddest incidents of the war. The great train of Turkish fugitives, several miles in length, moving eastward under a strong escort, was almost simultaneously overtaken by the advancing forces of General Gourko, and intercepted by the cavalry of Skobeleff. The escort fled, but the peasants fired on the Cossacks. At the moment when Gourko's troops were preparing to attack in the rear, Skobeleff's horse appeared in front. A wild panic seized the fugitives. They left their 20,000 carts in the snow, deserted their children and their old people, and fled to the mountains. The Bulgarians plundered the deserted encampment, and scenes ensued among the most horrible of the war. Skobeleff resumed his march, and the ghastly camp at Hermanli was left to its fate. The next day, Skobeleff's advanced guard, under General Stroukoff, occupied Adrianople. The Turkish garrison had evacuated it after blowing up the powder-magazine, and were then in full retreat on Constantinople. The second city in the Empire, girdled with earthworks and intended as a bulwark of Constantinople, fell without a blow. Two days later, $\frac{1}{2}\frac{9}{2}$, Skobeleff entered Adrianople, having marched 100 miles in four days.

The rapidity of the advance was not slackened for a moment. Skobeleff assumed the command of the advance guard, and marched off along the line of the railway, to attack the Turkish lines at Buyuk Tchekmedje. His troops left their baggage and artillery to follow by rail, living partly on the country and partly on rations sent after them from Adrianople by the railway. At Tchorlu General Stroukoff, who was still commanding Skobeleff's cavalry, overtook the Turkish rearguard, and the last shots fired in the war were exchanged between Skobeleff's Cossacks and the retreating Turks. That was on January $\frac{1}{2}\frac{7}{9}$. On January $\frac{1}{3}\frac{9}{1}$ the armistice was signed at Adrianople and the war was at an end.

On the way to Adrianople, Skobeleff repeatedly declared that we should enter Constantinople. 'This,' he said, 'is absolutely necessary. Russia expects it. We can only stop at the Bosphorus.' Russian troops did reach the Bosphorus; but alas! they abstained from going to Constantinople. No one regretted this more than Skobeleff. 'However improbable it may seem,' says M. Dantchenko, 'I can positively declare the truth, that I saw even Skobeleff sob with patriotic anguish when, in the neighbourhood of Byzantium, he learned that we were not going to enter Constantinople, and were losing thus the result of all our sacrifices.'

If the war was ended the advance was not. By the terms of the armistice the troops had to garrison the lines of Tchataldja, while the Turks had to go back behind the lines of Buyuk Tchekmedje. They said they would go, but they delayed so long that once it seemed as if Skobeleff would have to eject them by force. The evacuation was completed on $\frac{\text{January 30}}{\text{February 11}}$, and the great march southward was over.[1]

It was a memorable march. Victories succeeded each other so rapidly that we ceased to take count of them. Every day brought a new success, and each order and despatch brought more and more prominently forward the name of Skobeleff. General Gourko and General Radetzky did admirably, but the hero of the march on Constantinople was again the favourite of the Russian people. It may indeed be said

[1] Lieut. Greene says: 'In both columns the guns were unlimbered and arranged to be drawn on sledges; but it was soon found impossible to get them up the mountain even in this manner, and they were all left behind, except the little mountain guns, one battery of which was with each column.'— *Russian Army in Turkey*, p. 350.

that Skobeleff and the Russian soldier shared equally the highest place in the national admiration, and Skobeleff was the very beau ideal of the Russian soldier. None of their leaders did they love as they loved him; none was so absolutely devoted to their welfare, so enthusiastic in their praise. And after all the Russian private soldier deserves more than I have said of him in my attempt to pay homage to his chief. Well does Lieutenant Greene say in speaking of the winter campaign—

The great and permanent cause of their success lay in the almost boundless patience and endurance of the Russian soldier. From the time the movement was well under way the men never saw their knapsacks, which remained north of the Balkans till some time after the armistice. They marched and fought and slept in snow and ice, and forded rivers with the thermometer at zero. They had no blankets, and the frozen ground precluded all idea of tents; the half worn-out shelter tents which the men had used during the summer were now cut up to tie around their boots, which were approaching dissolution. Always half of them had to sleep in the open air without shelter. Their clothing at night was the same as in the day, and it differed from that of the summer only in the addition of an overcoat, woollen jacket, and bashlik. Their food was a pound of hard bread, and a pound and a half of tough stringy beef driven along the road; they were forced to carry six and even eight days' rations on their backs—in addition to which a supply of cartridges in their pockets. There was more than one instance where the men fought, and fought well, not only without breakfast, but without having taken food in twenty-four hours. Yet in the face of these unusual privations and hardships, there was not a single case of insubordination; the men were usually in good spirits, and the number of stragglers on the march was far less than during the heat of the preceding summer.

Even when badly led the Russian soldier has never disgraced his country. When led by Skobeleff he was irresistible.

After the two armies had taken up the positions appointed to them by the armistice, they were again put in motion—this time by Lord Beaconsfield—and again Skobeleff played the most conspicuous part.

Before the armistice was signed, when it was believed that at any moment the English fleet might enter the Bosphorus, it was decided that, until the war was ended, Russia had no option but to treat every ally of the Turk as her own enemy. Dispositions were taken for the occupation of Gallipoli, and the immediate entry of Russian troops into Constantinople. The fleet very nearly precipitated a collision. It steamed up to the mouth of the Dardanelles, and was only counter-ordered at the last moment. If it had not been recalled there would have been war. Possibly a knowledge of that fact explains its recall. But even after that narrow escape, Lord Beaconsfield very nearly made war inevitable.

What a comedy of errors it seems now we look back upon it all, and see how two great Empires were almost plunged into war by the merest trifles! The 'Nous sommes dedans' of Count Schouvaloff, misinterpreted by journalists to whom French seems like an unknown tongue, provoked an intervention from which war would have been inevitable but for a curious delay which arose in the transmission of a telegram. As the facts appear to be but imperfectly known in England, I will venture to repeat them, although they will be found at much greater length in a paper written by the body physician of the Grand Duke Nicholas in the *Nouvelle Revue*.[1]

When the English fleet anchored at Prince's Island, that is to say, within less than an hour's sail of the Bosphorus, the Grand Duke telegraphed to St. Petersburg, asking what should be done if the English, who were at the entrance of the Bosphorus, should attempt to enter. This telegram, like all that passed between Adrianople and St. Petersburg, passed through Constantinople, owing to the breakdown of the wires across the Balkans. The day after he had telegraphed he received from the Emperor a reply, couched as follows: 'I understand neither your questions nor your hesitations, for I have already sent you detailed instructions as to what you should do in case the English enter the Bosphorus.'

Great was the consternation at headquarters on receipt of this telegram. The detailed instructions to which the Emperor referred had never been received. Meanwhile time was progressing. The English were within an hour of the Bosphorus, while the Russian army was three days' march distant.

Pending the arrival of the Imperial instructions, which although despatched had never arrived, the Grand Duke made all necessary preparations for a forced march on Constantinople, in order that he might close the Bosphorus.

After a period of great suspense the famous instructions arrived at last. They had been three or four days

[1] June 15, 1880.

en route. Turkish personages absolutely to be depended upon subsequently told us that the telegram had purposely been detained at Constantinople in order to avoid a collision between Russia and England. The Imperial orders were to the effect that while Gallipoli was not to be occupied, the entry of the English into the Bosphorus was to be the signal for the immediate occupation of Constantinople. While we were wondering whether Prince's Islands should be regarded as the Bosphorus, a telegram arrived from Constantinople announcing that the English fleet had withdrawn to Ismid. The cause of this strange manœuvre, suspected at the time, was confessed frankly afterwards.

When the Turks deciphered our telegram, and discovered that the orders of the Emperor were precise and categorical for the immediate occupation of Constantinople if the English entered the Bosphorus, they communicated the contents of the despatch to the English ambassador, and begged him to send the fleet away. He intervened, and in order to save the capital from a Russian occupation, he sent the ironclads to Ismid. This being effected, the Turks then transmitted the Imperial telegram to the Grand Duke, as there was no longer any cause for keeping it back.

So it was not the heroic advance, but the discreet retreat, of the English fleet which 'saved' Constantinople. But the fleet being in the Dardanelles, it was necessary for us to be within the lines of Buyuk Tchekmedje against a renewed surprise or act of bad faith. The Grand Duke therefore told the Turks that he must occupy San Stefano, and Skobeleff was ordered to prepare the 4th Corps for immediate advance. The Turks protested, but gave way, and in February $\frac{1}{2}\frac{1}{3}$ our head-quarters were installed at San

Stefano. Thus what would have been known as the Peace of Adrianople became the Peace of San Stefano, thanks entirely to the interfering of the English fleet.

On $\frac{\text{February 19}}{\text{March 3}}$ the famous treaty was signed. With the exception of the defence of the Shipka and General Gourko's two passages of the Balkans, there was hardly one successful enterprise undertaken in the whole war in which Skobeleff had not taken a prominent part. He shared the honours of the passage of the Danube at the beginning, and it was he who led the Russian troops from Tchataldja to the walls of Constantinople. It was he who first occupied the forts of the Shipka, who, along with Prince Imérétinsky, won the first victory at Loftcha, and whose valour made heroic the second and third assault on Plevna. In the winter campaign it was Skobeleff who captured the army of the Balkans at Shenova—Skobeleff who occupied Adrianople, and Skobeleff who pursued the flying Turks to the lines of Tchataldja. Wherever he had held sole command he never sustained a reverse, and wherever he held a subordinate place it was his division which preserved the honour of our arms in the midst of the disasters of the campaign.

'To an army which has accomplished what you have, my friends,' said the Grand Duke to the troops at San Stefano, 'nothing is impossible.' That it accomplished so much is partly due to Skobeleff, who inspired every private with a sense of responsibility, and set the whole army so brilliant an example of absolute devotion to the service of his country.

CHAPTER VII.

IN SOUTHERN BULGARIA.

Expected war with England—Drilling the Bulgarian Militia Skobeleff and the Turks—An excursion to Shenova—Bulgarian gratitude—The battle-field revisited—Impressive service for the dead—The pass of Hemedli—The Turks and the Balkan Passes—Russia prepared for war—Skobeleff at Slivno.

PEACE was signed, but Russia had to keep her armour on, and prepare for war with England, which Lord Beaconsfield seemed to be meditating. The time was not lost. Skobeleff spoke quite truly when he said:—

We were quite ready for England in May; we were as well armed as you were, and we had received new artillery for the army. If there had been an attempt to sever our communications, we had two years' supplies in the country. Austria was watched by 400,000 troops, and I do not think that even if she had joined England we should have been beaten. All depended, however, upon the attitude of Germany, whether she would adopt a policy of neutrality—of honest neutrality—or not.

That was apparently the opinion of the English Government, for on May $\frac{18}{30}$ Lord Salisbury signed the secret memorandum with which a few days later Mr. Marvin astonished the world.[1]

---

[1] The secret memorandum was the record of a private surrender by Lord Salisbury to Count Schouvaloff of most of the points pressed in the English Circular of April 1, 1878.

After that typhus broke out, and we lost no fewer than 60,000 men in a single month; but the immediate danger of war had passed. Skobeleff was placed in command of the 4th Division of the army of occupation in Southern Bulgaria, and he did not waste his time. From his head-quarters at Slivno he co-operated in what was the practical creation of Eastern Roumelia, so far as Eastern Roumelia possesses any ability to defend its own independence. Europe drew up the organic statute, no doubt. The Porte appointed Aleko Pasha; but the foundations of Bulgarian liberty south of the Balkans were laid by Russia, when, by the aid of Skobeleff and others, she organised and drilled the Bulgarian Militia.

During the eighteen months which he spent south of the Balkans, Skobeleff won the love not merely of the Bulgarians, but, strange though it may seem, of the Turks.

The excellent Bulgarian paper 'Rabota,' which has recently published a series of reminiscences of Skobeleff, says that 'Ak Pasha' was a great favourite amongst the Turks. Here is an example of his ways with the vanquished enemy, taken from an October number of the 'Rabota.' The Russian troops were staying at Adrianople. During the Ramadan, when the Turks generally light up their mosques, Skobeleff having given strict orders to his men to be kind to the Turks, the latter were grateful and seemed pleased to see 'Ak Pasha.' He observed once, how

N

ever, that they looked very gloomy and sorrowful. Faithful to his habit, he investigated thoroughly the cause of their grievance, and learnt that the 'faithful' Mussulmans were distressed at having no means of lighting up their mosques. Skobeleff used all his influence with the Russian authorities and got three thousand roubles for 'his Turks.' It is easy to understand their gratitude and delight.

This was no isolated instance. In the midst of the great struggle, even when the Turks were mutilating our dead and torturing our wounded, Skobeleff was kindness itself to his conquered enemy. 'Take care, my children,' he used to say to his soldiers after the peace was signed; 'the Turks are now your friends. Be kind to them. There is no greater shame than to attack those who cannot defend themselves.'

During the war a young Turkish officer was made prisoner, and his captors began asking him of the position of the enemy. 'Let him alone,' cried Skobeleff; 'an officer must not be a spy.' The young Turk, however, offered help to our troops, and when the campaign was over Némirovitch asked him 'how he, a Turk, could serve the enemies of his country?' 'Because,' replied the young officer with enthusiasm, 'to serve Ak Pasha is an honour to anyone. There are no other generals like him.'

The Turks used to express their admiration and astonishment at Skobeleff. 'Your Ak Pasha,' they said, 'is better than our Osman. Yours visits even the Turks his enemy and their churches. Osman never saw us near at hand.'

'Ak Pasha,' said an old Ulema, 'could be a good Mussulman. He knows the Koran so well.' Not only did he know it well, but he was very fond of quoting it.

He always maintained the most friendly relations with the Ulemas. He wished them to come to him. 'We are obliged to obey our conqueror,' they replied. 'But if we give up Adrianople to the Bulgarians, what then?' he asked. They answered, 'The Russians, not the Bulgarians, have conquered us. But if they are as just as you, we will praise God for his punishment. Life with the Russians is easy. Our property, our wives and children are safe—thanks to them.' When he revisited Kazanlyk, the Turkish women sent him a beautiful bouquet. 'What is this for?' he asked. 'To express their gratitude for the good treatment they have received,' was the reply. 'Quite unnecessary,' exclaimed he; 'the Russians are not fighting with women.'

There was such a pleasant picture of the closing scenes of his administration south of the Balkans given by Mr. Rose, more than three years ago, that I venture to give part of it [1] here :—

'Will you accompany me in an excursion to Shenova and Shipka?' said General Skobeleff to me one day in the second week in May. 'We are about to leave the country,'

[1] The full description is in a paper called 'Shenova and Shipka Revisited,' in the *Gentleman's Magazine*, July 1879, p. 87.

continued General Skobeleff, 'and I wish once more to look upon the scenes of our greatest struggles and our bloodiest triumphs.' The invitation so heartily given was as heartily accepted, for I too desired to revisit the Tundja valley. On the following morning I breakfasted with General Skobeleff and Prince Tzérteleff.

It was an hour and a half after midday before a start was effected. The mode of travelling was a calèche drawn by four horses harnessed abreast, and as we rattled over the streets of Philippopolis and across the new iron girder bridge which spans the Maritza, and which the Russians have built as a parting gift to the capital of Eastern Roumelia, the General informed me that we should require to go at a very stiff pace, as we had to accomplish a hundred versts ere nightfall. We spun along with astonishing smoothness, the road considered, at a mad gallop. The small but hardy horses of the Ukraine breed never seemed to tire, and maintained the gallop for two hours at a stretch. At a village called Karatoprak we changed horses, and in a few minutes were continuing our onward way at the same headlong speed. Following the bed of the Giopsu river, we cut through the Lower Balkans, and entered the valley of Karlova. Passing the village of Cukurli, we observed the gymnastic society at their afternoon drill, and while the horses were being changed the General and I walked on a short distance. A turn in the road brought us face to face with the National Guard, as these volunteers now delight to call themselves. They had seen the General, and had marched rapidly round the village so as to salute him as he passed. A fine body of fellows they were, with good-natured expression, intelligent features, and considerable aptitude for drill. Twelve months' experience of absolute freedom from Turkish oppression, and safety for life, honour, and property, have created a wonderful change in the poor

Bulgarian peasants. Their bearing is totally different from what I remember it two years ago. The cringing obsequiousness which was their characteristic while the overbearing Turk was still their master has disappeared, and they carry themselves as men who feel something at any rate of the dignity of manhood. 'Now,' said General Skobeleff, 'I will show you what we have made of these lads in a few months.' Thereupon the hero of a score of battles took command of this village band. At the word they formed line admirably, broke into column, and marched and counter-marched, re-formed line, and fired a volley at 400 yards. We examined the rifles of nearly every man to see that he understood what he was about, and found without exception the 'sights' properly adjusted. Then, in obedience to the bugle calls, which the General sung out, skirmishers extended and advanced in front of half the company, which acted as supports. At another rat-ta-ta-ta from the General, the latter also extended as skirmishers, and the whole advanced. Ta-ta-ta tum sang out the General, and down the fellows lay and commenced firing. So went on the drill, and the manœuvres ended in a grand bayonet charge. Before taking our leave of these interesting young volunteers, whose determination it is never to permit a Turkish soldier again to enter their country, General Skobeleff made them a short speech, in which he complimented alike their intelligence and their new-born patriotism.

When fairly in the Karlova valley we skirt the northern slopes of the Lower Balkans, which, for the most part, are covered with oak scrub, with here and there patches of forest.

The necessity for having a broken spring of the carriage repaired gave me the opportunity of a closer inspection of the ruins of Kalofer, and of conversing with many of the inhabitants who have returned to their desolated homes. Some of the houses are being rebuilt with money granted by the Russian administration, but the work of reconstruction progresses slowly. Among the charred remains of the houses human bones are still to be found —indestructible testimony to the truth of the tale heard on every side of the cruelty of the Turkish soldiery. During our promenade, melancholy though it was, a bright incident occurred. Half a score of little children, very scantily clad, but with pleasant features and beaming faces, came and offered flowers, testifying alike to the domestic qualities of the Bulgarians and their gratitude to their deliverers. That the Russians are loved by the children no less than by the adults is proof positive that all the tales spread by interested persons of Russian oppression being greater than that of the Turks are baseless falsehoods. Were the Muscovites the Huns some people would have Western Europe believe, they would not command and retain the love of old and young which is manifested on all hands and in every district. This was only a specimen of the stories which we heard at every step. One woman with tears in her eyes said:—'Thank God that the Christians have remembered that we, too, are Christians; that we were suffering, and that they have brought us relief. We are very poor, God knows, for our all was stolen from us or destroyed; but we will work and trust in God and help each other.' This woman had also taken to her home two orphans, and, commenting on the fact, General Skobeleff told her that it was the duty as well as the privilege of the poor to help each other at a time when God sent misfortune upon them. 'True,' replied the woman; 'and we do what we can for each other. We are happy now that we are free and shall never see the Turks again.'

Time pressed; and, our carriage having been repaired, we bade the women be of good cheer, while the General comforted the hearts of the children by a free distribution of sugar bought from a primitive store in a half-ruined house, and we took our departure from ill-fated Kalofer. Clearing the mountain retreat, we descended by a steep path to the plain of the Tundja. After fording a stream called the Ak Dere, we leave the great chaussée which leads to Kazanlyk, and strike northwards and eastwards towards the base of the Greater Balkans. At last, in the fast-approaching twilight, we reach the village of Becerli, embosomed among trees and surrounded by rose gardens. The General now stood up in the carriage scanning the country on either side, and consulting a map in his hand. At last the General said, 'I come to Shenova to pray for the dead, and to take my last look at a battle-field which, if it brought us some glory, cost us so much blood. I have not seen it,' he continued, 'since the eventful 28th December, 1877—five days before Gourko's battles at Philippopolis.' Again he stood up in the carriage, and eagerly scanned the contour of the ground. A few minutes afterwards he raised his cap, and, looking round and upwards, began to recite in his sonorous but musical voice a Russian poem. Turning suddenly to me, the General said, 'Here in this wood I posted nine regiments of Cossacks to cover my right flank; and there is the plain over which my devoted men, without a single gun, advanced against an enemy which outnumbered them, and which moreover had 120 pieces of artillery.' 'It is with great emotion,' he went on, 'that I look again upon this battle-field. Many thousands of lives were lost there upon my responsibility as a general.' Again he took off his cap, sighed, and in solemn accents recited a Russian poem by Aksakoff about death, in which the poet pictured the entrance to the tomb as terrible to the imagination at a distance, but that when face to face with it in a holy cause it lost all its terrors and became the entrance to heaven itself. His voice rang with emotion, and his gestures, as he continued to repeat the lines, were characterised by a tremulous yet graceful animation, which told of the deep feeling that stirred his heart. 'It was,' he said, 'the bloodiest battle of the war.' With a quick turn of thought, pointing to a spot on our left, he said, 'There, when reconnoitring the enemy's position before the attack, a shell burst literally under my horse, and the smoke coming up almost suffocated me. My steed reared, and I thought for a moment that the end had come; but God was good—my work was not yet done —and, strange to say, neither my horse nor myself was harmed.' Onwards we went towards a wood. At every step the General pointed out the dispositions which the troops had taken during the progress of the battle. In the darkening night a Cossack met the carriage, and led the way into the wood, where twinkling lights discovered a small encampment. Descending from the carriage at the outskirts of the wood, the General, pointing to several mounds, quoting Byron, said, 'There Slaughter heap'd on high his weltering ranks,' and, for the time throwing aside the melancholy gloom which had sat upon him during the last hour, he advanced with cheerful stride to General Schnitnikoff and the members of his staff, who had come to the Shenova wood to meet him, and had formed the encampment.

The manner in which General Skobeleff was surrounded by all his officers, young and old, the greetings with which he was received, and the earnest inquiries made as to news, told of two things—the love and admiration with which the young but brilliant soldier is regarded by all.

Next morning our little camp was early astir, and a universal demand was made for coffee, which was speedily brought by some soldiers. Very soon General Skobeleff came out of his tent, and being joined by the whole staff, we commenced, under his direction, an inspection in detail of the positions. We had only gone a few steps when we came upon a wooden cross erected under the shadow of a group of four spreading beeches. The General at once uncovered, an example which all followed, and stood for a few minutes in silence. Turning away, the General said to me, 'That is the grave of a hero, and on the day of the battle I especially ordered that cross to be planted over his grave so as to mark his last resting-place. He was a mere boy of between fifteen and sixteen, of good family in Russia. During the war, fired by military ardour, and the righteousness of the cause for which the armies of Holy Russia were fighting, he escaped from school and home and made his way to the seat of war. Turning up at Plevna, I accepted him as a volunteer, and he fought gallantly and well at the great assault and subsequent capture of Osman Pasha's stronghold. At Shenova he led a company of the 32nd regiment, and their duty it was to make the attack on the central redoubt. Carried away by his enthusiasm and utter disregard of danger, the brave boy speedily left his men a considerable way behind, and escaped the shower of bullets only to be bayonetted as he entered the redoubt. His was a brief but heroic life!'

Crossing the stream, we entered the centre redoubt on the little peninsula, and what a sight was presented! All around the door of the redoubt were scattered broken canisters, fragments of shell, rags of uniforms, as if the battle had only taken place a few days ago. But I was hardly prepared for the ghastly scene within. Several hundred men had been hastily buried here; but the rain and the snow had beaten aside the loose earth, wolves and dogs had done the rest, and all over the floor of the redoubt was scattered a vast mélange of human bones. Vertebræ, arm and leg bones commingled in the strangest fashion with skulls bleached by sun and rain. General Skobeleff said to me, as we gazed on this charnel-house,

'And this is glory!' 'Yes,' I responded, 'after all, General,

> The drying up a single tear has more
> Of honest fame than shedding seas of gore.'

'You are right,' he replied, 'and yet I am nothing but a soldier.' Leaving the redoubt, he called out two small detachments of soldiers representing the infantry and cavalry who had taken part in storming these positions, and desired them to accompany us. 'Every one of these men,' he said to me, 'was wounded in the battle, and they have a right, as representing their comrades, to take a last look of the field where they shed their blood.' As we crossed into a large entrenchment, which had offered a stout resistance to the Muscovite assault, and which also bore marks of being the burial-place of many a brave soldier, we encountered a small flock of sheep, the leader's bell tinkling softly in the morning air. 'Is there not,' said General Skobeleff, 'something extremely poetical in the idea of these sheep so peacefully browsing on the grass enriched with human blood?' Onwards we strolled from position to position, stopping every few moments, when the General, with his staff around him, would discourse on their strength relative to other positions, on the method adopted by him in arranging his attack, and on the reasons why he made such and such dispositions. In fact, the staff throughout the day received on the spot practical demonstrations of the science of war and the value of well-conceived tactics. By-and-by we came out in the open plain, where a monument had been erected commemorative of the battle. It is situated on the extreme right of the Russian position, and consists of a small marble column, surmounted by a cross and surrounded by pilasters crowned with large cannon-balls. A Russian priest here donned his robes, lighted his censer, and, with a simple dragoon for a clerk, began a solemn service for the repose of the souls of the dead. Every head was uncovered, the party stood in respectful groups around the column with its cross—the General to the right of the priest. The sun shone in unclouded splendour, nature seemed hushed for the moment, and the white mists floated hazily around the head of St. Nicholas. I have witnessed the gorgeous ceremonial of Continental Catholic cathedrals,—have taken part in the rich ritual of Anglican churches,—have listened to the sonorous mass in a Greek cathedral,—have worshipped in the simple chapels of Presbyterian Scotland,—but have never been present at a more impressive religious service than that on the battle-field of Shenova. Creeds and forms were forgotten in the solemnity of the act and the earnestness and devotion of the worshippers; and as the trembling accents of the priest, with the deep but sweet responses of the dragoon-clerk, were borne on the still morning air, one could not but hope that 'all was well' with the thousands of brave men who had perished in the discharge of their duty as soldiers. As the service progressed, the General wept like a child, and among the small but deeply moved congregation there were few dry eyes, albeit these hardy and sometimes rough warriors are seldom used to the melting mood. One and all advanced and reverently kissed the cross extended to them by the priest, and thus was brought to a close a service touching in its inception and the simple manner in which it was carried out.

But with a soldier weeping may only endure for a moment, and the General gave the signal 'to horse.' All were speedily mounted, one of Skobeleff's celebrated white chargers being provided for me. The brief emotion of the hour appeared to be dissipated in a smart gallop to the south-west, where we came to the great redoubt stormed by the 61st regiment. We rode to the crest of the tumulus, and surveyed the field with astonishment that such a seemingly impregnable position should be taken by an army inferior in numbers, and without artillery.

Then we turned into the wood, and inspected the masked redoubts and the theatre of the bayonet fights, where corpses had at the end of the day been piled on each other four and five deep. In shady glades were long lines of trenches, where the brave fellows had found hasty burial, and it was without regret that we left the deeply interesting but melancholy spot. A brief examination having been made of the trenches, by means of which his right flank had been secured in the early part of the day, and which looked as fresh as if only raised a week ago, we rode up to the village of Hemedli, which commanded a front view of the whole battle-field. A halt was called, and the General once more proceeded to deliver a discourse on the strategy and tactics he had adopted, and the manner in which all such positions should be attacked. An ascent was now made into the pass of Hemedli, in order that we might observe the difficulties which General Skobeleff and his troops had to encounter in their passage of the Balkans in mid-winter. I said to the General, 'How was it possible for infantry, much less for cavalry, to overcome that obstacle?'—pointing to the cliff. 'All things are possible to determined men,' replied he. 'The men crept down round by the sides on hands and knees, as we will do presently, and I will show you how we got our cavalry down.' Dismounting from our horses, we tied the reins over their necks, and drove them up the precipitous slope. Sometimes the fore legs doubled under, and back they would roll down the slope till, mayhap, caught by some tree-trunk. It was every man for himself. Scrambling on hands and knees, seeking the shelter of a tree as a horse threatened to roll down upon you, taking breath every few steps, and renewing the laborious ascent, at length a dozen of us gained the summit of the cliff, which we had circumvented; and I must confess that I bowed before the genius and daring of a General who could successfully conduct an expedition through such places, and over such, to ordinary human judgment, insurmountable obstacles. Horses and men alike were permitted to enjoy half an hour's well-earned rest—the horses in cropping the grass, and the men in discussing the situation. When we had been sufficiently rested, a commencement was made with the descent. First of all, the horses were collected and one by one driven to the side of the cliff, where the ground slopes somewhat. Planting their four feet together, the wise brutes allowed themselves to slide down, guiding themselves with wonderful instinct, and taking advantage of any little shelving places to stop for a minute. Without accident, all reached the bottom of the defile, and began to walk quietly along the track. 'It was thus that twenty squadrons of cavalry were able to accompany me to Shenova,' said General Skobeleff. We made for Kazanlyk at a gallop and reached it at six o'clock. Next day was one of unclouded splendour, and early in the morning a move was made to the meadows west of the town, where a triumphal arch had been erected, around which had congregated the whole people of the district in their picturesque national costume. The *raison d'être* of the assembly was the reading of the Proclamation of the Czar of Russia, counselling peaceful behaviour to the Bulgarians. General Obroutcheff, the Imperial Commissioner, on his arrival at the spot, was literally bespattered with flowers. After General Obroutcheff had read the Czar's address, he made a short speech on the same lines of peaceful policy; and then there ensued a mass performed by the Bulgarian clergy. Adieus were said, the General continued his way into the Bulgarian principality, and we returned to Kazanlyk.

Soon afterwards Bulgaria was evacuated and Skobeleff returned home. Russian influence is no doubt great both in the principality of Bulgaria and in so-called Eastern Roumelia, but it is not maintained by the presence of an army of occupation, or even by the appointment of Russian residents. But before England can venture to trust to a similar influence in Egypt, let her make for the Egyptian nationality one-fourth, or say even one-tenth, of the sacrifices which Russia has made for the Bulgarians.

After the war was over, Skobeleff was placed in command of the army south of the Balkans. His headquarters were at Slivno, and he made it his duty to organise the Bulgarian militia into a formidable force, which would not have been left alone if the Turks had attempted to occupy once more the Balkan passes.

That clause of the Berlin Treaty, to secure which Lord Beaconsfield was on the point of declaring war, and even ordered his express train from Berlin, was made a dead letter from the first—thanks largely to Russia and Skobeleff. This was very simple. The Turks—most interested in the upholding of that famous Berlin verdict—have not fulfilled to this hour its most important clauses; for instance, those relating to Armenia, Macedonia, Crete, and their other provinces in Europe. If they had insisted on reoccupying Shipka, we should not have made that a *casus belli*, for that was their treaty right. But half-a-dozen legitimate causes for war were supplied us by the Turks' neglect to execute other clauses of the same treaty, and a declaration of war for the violation of the Berlin arrangement about Armenia and

Macedonia would have left our hands free to help the Bulgarians against the common foe. Mr. Rose was perfectly right when he said :—

I believe that, had the English Government persisted in 1879 in demanding the literal fulfilment of this part of the treaty, war would have been declared once more by Russia. The whole of the male population of Eastern Roumelia had been organised by General Skobeleff into a well-drilled, fully-equipped militia, and in view of such a contingency as a new war, Skobeleff had prepared the most elaborate plans of the campaign. He himself had ridden over almost every mile of Turkey from Constantinople to the Danube, had surveyed every position capable of defence or attack, and a new military map had been constructed. I have no doubt that the plan of the campaign is now in the archives of the Russian War Ministry ready for future eventualities.[1]

Mr. Rose's account of Skobeleff at Slivno, although brief, is so suggestive of his relations with the Bulgarians, that I make no apology for quoting it here :—

Genial good-nature and a remarkable warmth of heart were eminently characteristic of this chivalrous soldier.

When the 16th Division, of which he then held command, was quartered in and around Slivno, I accompanied him one day in his round of inspection. And here is an exact report of the visit written at the time to a little friend in England. 'General Skobeleff carefully goes over the soldiers' quarters to see that the men are comfortable and that their food is good. He tastes their broth, and millet porridge, and bread and meat, and woe be to the contractor who supplies bad stuff! When we made our

[1] *Fortnightly Review*, Oct. 1882, p. 417.

unexpected entrance into the yard which constituted the kitchen of the regiment, we found a lot of hungry little boys and girls whose parents had been killed by the Turks. They were hanging about quietly watching the soldier-cooks with hungry eyes, and hoping that they might come in for a little bit of the dinner. The soldiers, when they saw the General, whom they all love and admire, were not very sure that they were doing what would be approved of in giving a share of their dinner to the poor starving orphans. So they tried to screen them when they drew themselves up to salute the General. General Skobeleff, however, observed the urchins, and at once surmised what they had come into the yard for. And he said to the soldiers, "Do you give some of your dinner to these ragged children?" They saluted, and said, "Yes, your Excellency." "Do they come every day?" again asked the General. "Yes, your Excellency," was the answer of the soldiers. Then the General, quite moved, dropped his angry tone and said, "That is right, my men; a brave soldier is always a kind comrade; and a kind man is always a brave soldier. Never forget," he added, "to share your little with the poor and the starving." The soldiers thereupon gave a hurrah, and Skobeleff instructed his aide-de-camp to distribute some money among the little things.'

Some time before the last recorded incident I was travelling with General Skobeleff from Philippopolis to Kazanlyk, when our carriage broke down at Kalofer. During our enforced stay the General, as was his wont, went in and out among the inhabitants, making kindly inquiries as to their lot in life. A woman who had taken to her home two children, orphaned during the massacre at that place by the retreating Turks on Gourko's first advance across the Balkans, was earnestly commended for her disinterested behaviour by the General, who added that 'it was the duty as well as the privilege of the poor to help each other at a time when God sent misfortunes upon them.' I wished to offer a little money to the woman, but the General, speaking in English, forbade it, stating that it might take the edge off the very proper feeling which had manifestly prompted her good action, and blunt the spirit of independence which he was glad to observe was the rule among the peasants of Bulgaria. But the General himself comforted the hearts of a crowd of children who had collected by a free distribution of sugar—the whole stock of which he had purchased from a little store in a half-ruined house.

Naturally conforming to the orthodox Greek Church, which he thought, with his friend Aksakoff and the majority of Russian Slavophils, peculiarly suited to the genius of the Slav people, he was not theoretically only religious. His lofty conception of duty always endeavoured to take a practical shape, which he discharged as earnestly as the strength of the hour permitted. The motto of his life seemed often to be: 'Fais ce que dois, advienne que pourra.'

CHAPTER VIII.

GEOK TEPÉ.

Commander of the Fourth Army Corps—The Akhal Oasis—Expedition against the Tekkes—Skobeleff in command—The advance to Bami—The siege begun—Skobeleff on Asiatic tactics—Parallels opened—Tekke sorties—Skobeleff in the trenches—The mine—The final assault—Pursuit and slaughter of fugitives—Skobeleff's theory of dealing with Asiatics—Proclamation to the Tekkes—The Akhal Oasis annexed—Skobeleff on the campaign.

AFTER the war in the Balkans was over, Skobeleff was named Commander of the Fourth Army Corps, and appointed Aide-de-Camp General.[1] After he returned from Bulgaria for nearly six months he remained in Russia, but at the end of the year he was again in the field.

Along the northern frontier of Persia, south of the great sandy desert which stretches northward to the Oxus, stands the long narrow oasis of Akhal. Its entire population is only 1,200,000. Its length from Kizil Arvat to Gyaoors is only about 190 miles; its breadth is sometimes not more than five miles. But this narrow ribbon of land, studded with only fifty villages, cost Russia more to conquer than the great Khanates of Turkestan. There was none of our

[1] $\frac{\text{August 30}}{\text{September 11}}$, 1878.

campaigns so long, so costly, so deadly as that which was needed to reduce these borderers to order. The greatest siege of Central Asian history in the nineteenth century was that which Skobeleff conducted against Geok Tepé. Our first attempt under General Lomakine failed completely. The defeat was serious. It might have been disastrous, for the reverse severely injured Russian prestige throughout Central Asia. England was believed to have taken means to profit by our misfortune. The Tekkes were led to believe that English troops would be sent to their assistance, and pressure was brought to bear upon the Court of Teheran to induce the Shah to place himself in opposition to her Russian neighbour.

Skobeleff was sent to retrieve the position in the Akhal oasis, while M. Zinovieff, one of the ablest and most active of our diplomatists, undertook the defence of Russian interests at Teheran. Working together they achieved a complete success. But it was not easily won.

The Tekkes, of all the Turkoman tribes, are the most formidable. The brigands of the border, no race exceeds them in cruelty and in courage. The pest of both Khiva and Persia, they have pillaged impartially both. They were not mere marauders; they were slave-traders. Their raids were made for capturing slaves. No caravan was safe within a long distance of their kibitkas; every village on the frontier lamented some of its people carried off to slavery and torture by the Tekkes. The Persians in vain attempted to extirpate this nest of hornets. They defied Persia and even inflicted a defeat on Russian troops. But it was intolerable that a horde of man-stealers should seize their prey on the borders of Russia and Persia, and Skobeleff was sent to punish them and reduce them to order. It was rough work. Skobeleff was almost as long about getting it done as the army of the Balkans was in making its way to the lines of Tchataldja. But it was done at last, and done thoroughly. There are no slaves in the Akhal oasis to-day; nor any slave-dealers to carry on the practice of manstealing. Russia answers for order along the Persian border. It is the latest addition to the police duty of the world which Russia has undertaken for mankind.

The Tekkes, according to a very interesting communication made to the Russian Imperial Geographical Society, although barbarians, are remarkable for the position which they accord their women. With them the woman is the equal of man. She is not the slave of her husband. Her property is her own after marriage as it is before. She can vote in all the national assemblies, and if her husband treats her badly she can demand a divorce. Another curious detail is that the social and political equality of the sexes is accompanied by an almost exact identity of dress.

When Skobeleff was appointed to command the expedition against the Tekkes at the beginning of

1880, some people shook their heads. They imagined that Skobeleff was too reckless. He soon undeceived them. Nothing could be more cautious, more skilful than his operations. He arrived at Tchikishlar early in May. It was not till the middle of July that he made a reconnaissance up to the walls of Geok Tepé. He began the siege on December $\frac{4}{16}$, 1880, and he did not storm it until January $\frac{12}{24}$, 1881. Everything was throughout most methodically and carefully carried out, and Skobeleff showed a prudence and foresight quite as remarkable as the more brilliant qualities by which he is most widely known.

It is not my intention to give more than the briefest outline of the campaign. The limits of my work forbid it, even if I were competent to describe operations which are only interesting from a military point of view. Neither is it necessary, for the Intelligence Department of the War Office has published in English an excellent translation of Skobeleff's own report on the siege of Geok Tepé, and before very long another and more detailed account of the campaign will be written by Mr. Marvin, who, whatever his political prejudices, will not intentionally misrepresent the actions of Skobeleff.

As in all Central Asian campaigns, the most serious enemy with which we had to contend was not the inhabitants, but the country which they inhabited. Mr. O'Donovan's book on his adventures on his way to Merv gives a lively account of some of the features of the region in which our expedition had to campaign. Transport and commissariat were our great difficulties, as they were those of England in Afghanistan. 'To subjugate Akhal,' said Skobeleff to Mr. Marvin, 'we had only 5,000 men, and needed 20,000 camels. To get that transport we had to send to Orenburg, to Khiva, to Bokhara, and to Mangishlak for animals.' When the campaign began, Skobeleff used to tell his officers that the Akhal-Tekke expedition ought to be divided into two parts: the first might be considered as terminated when the troops and the provisions were concentrated at Bami. According to Skobeleff, that first part of the expedition was more difficult than the second, viz. the final blow at Geok Tepé and its capture. Bami is nearly 200 miles from Tchikishlar, and the work of conveying all the stores from the Caspian to his base at Bami was indeed no child's play.

Bami was occupied on June $\frac{11}{23}$, and three weeks were spent in strengthening it against a hostile attack. On $\frac{\text{June 21}}{\text{July 3}}$ Skobeleff started on a reconnaissance for Geok Tepé.

He took with him 800 men, a few guns, and the musicians. The distance was about 100 versts, or 66 miles. In crossing the oasis, the expedition met with almost no obstacles except a few skirmishes with some village inhabitants. At Geok Tepé the Tekkes heard of the approach of the Russians, and a severe resistance was prepared. When the Russians came within sight a gun was fired at Geok Tepé as a signal of the enemy's approach. The Russians were now at a distance of four versts from Geok Tepé, and the topographers were busily engaged in taking sketch plans of the land and the fortress. The Tekkes seemed greatly surprised at the small number of the Russian troops, and hastened to take the initiative of the attack. In the meantime, the survey being terminated, our detachment began to retreat. The Tekkes almost surrounded the Russians. Skobeleff perceived that there was no order and no shadow of discipline among the Tekke troops; the Russian guns fired; the music, without which Skobeleff never made any attack, played continually and produced a superstitious fear upon the assailants. The Russians escaped the danger and reached Bami with very slight loss. Skobeleff thus gained the conviction, which he communicated to his troops, that the Tekkes were not so terrible as they had been described.

They were, however, much too formidable a foe to be trifled with. Skobeleff set to work to fortify the lines of his communication with the Caspian at Tchikishlar and Krasnovodsk, which for the next four months were exposed to the constant raids of the Tekke horsemen. Even after the siege began, they seized a convoy of 2,000 camels on the road between Kizil Arvat and the Caspian. It was retaken, but the attack cost us the lives of twenty-five soldiers. Early in December, sufficient munitions of war having been stored at Bami, and the transport being ready for further advance, Skobeleff began his march on Geok

Tepé. On December $\frac{12}{24}$ he reached Samur, six miles from Geok Tepé, and made it the new base of his operations against the Tekke stronghold. Next day he conducted another reconnaissance against Geok Tepé, and there remained throwing up intrenchments and bringing up supplies of food and gunpowder from Bami. The troops were regularly drilled in camp, and they frequently rehearsed the assault and accustomed themselves to the use of dynamite, an explosive which it was intended to use against the fortifications of the enemy.

An abortive reconnaissance was made on December $\frac{14}{26}$, but the next day the attempt was renewed with better results. The heliograph which accompanied the reconnoitring party was used with signal success to order up reinforcements which saved Skobeleff from being surrounded and cut off by the Tekkes, who came out in great force. Three days after Colonel Kurapatkin, Skobeleff's chief of staff in the Turkish war, arrived with some Turkestan troops, after a long and difficult march from Petro-Alexandrovsk.

On December $\frac{18}{30}$ Skobeleff had under his orders 3,520 bayonets and 650 sabres. A reconnaissance was made towards the Kishlak of Yanghi Kala, a fort lying to the south of Geok Tepé, commanding the roads to Astrabad and Persia, and occupying a position from which Skobeleff intended to attack Geok Tepé. On December $\frac{19}{31}$ Skobeleff issued the following instructions for the officers of the troops on the field:—

The circumstances under which we have to fight are peculiar, and a series of hard struggles for localities lie before us. The enemy is brave and skilful in hand-to-hand fighting; he shoots well and has good *armes blanches*, but he fights in masses or in small bodies which obey the will of no one leader, and are therefore unable to co-operate towards the attainment of a common end.

The various peculiarities of the theatre of war and other circumstances compel us to employ few troops, and at the same time to act on the offensive. The recognised European method of fighting is therefore inadmissible with our small forces. In the open field, the enemy's cavalry, which is brave, well-mounted, and skilled in the use of its arms, would be a source of the greatest danger to long, thin fighting lines, and his infantry masses, although badly organised, are composed of brave, strong, and skilful men, and would of course seek to turn the fight to their own advantage by rushing to close quarters.

The main principle of Asiatic tactics is to preserve close formations.

In combats, such as we shall shortly have, against an enemy who holds a position covered by gardens, buildings, and walls, previously carefully prepared, we must expect an obstinate defence, and this species of position will be preferred by the enemy; firstly, because it was against such a one that we failed last year; and secondly, because it also protects the families and property of the defenders. We shall have to enter on a life-and-death struggle against knives and yatagans. Long, thin lines, in which troops easily get out of hand and separated into small groups which cannot obey the will of their common leader, prevent the latter from opposing strong formations, in which the superior discipline and mobility of our troops tell most, to sudden or unexpected hostile attacks. The observance of the principle of close formations is the secret of good Asiatic tactics, and will enable us to look forward with confidence to the result of a struggle, however superior the enemy be in number.

We shall defeat the enemy by means of those attributes which he does not possess. We shall take advantage of our superior discipline and quick-firing arms. We shall conquer by means of close, mobile, and pliable formations, by careful, well-aimed volley firing, and by the bayonet, which, in the hands of men who by discipline and the soldier-like feeling have been made into a united body—the column of operations—is always to be feared.

The attack of the enemy's cavalry is to be met by corresponding change of front, if necessary, and by volleys at short ranges. I recommend even squares (battalion or other) when circumstances permit.

Volleys are to be used against an attacking force, cavalry or infantry, when it arrives at 600 paces from our line; but it must also be remarked that volleys at long ranges on close masses, whether under cover of walls, &c., or in the open, are very effective. In such cases volley fire may be opened at 3,000 paces, the sight being varied, and an aim being taken at the top of the wall or even over it. Such indirect firing at 3,000 paces is, however, only to be carried out by parties of the strength of a company or under: it requires careful control by the commander of the party.

Mitrailleuses are to be used exclusively in close connection with infantry or dismounted cavalry, like the former regimental guns; all other guns are at first to be kept in reserve, so that they may be used in masses where required; and so good results will be obtained by a few dozen guns working under one man's will. Artillery is only to be brought up from the reserve on my express order, but its taking up position and the choice of the object to be fired at is the business of the commander of the artillery. Souvoroff's well-known saying—'The artillery follows its own sweet will'—must constantly be kept in mind by artillery commanders and also the commanders of the detachments to which they are attached. But all this holds good only till the signal for the attack is given. In this solemn moment the artillery must devote itself to closely supporting its comrades without the slightest regard for itself; it must come up in line with the attacking party, and shatter the enemy by its fire at close ranges, which has always a depressing moral effect on him. All purely technical (artillery) maxims must then be set aside. In the decisive moment the artillery must have a soul, for the gunner is not a mere machine. The artillery must, if necessary, sacrifice itself that the attack may succeed and expose itself as the infantry do in an attack. Its escort provides for its safety, and the shame of losing a gun is not borne by the artillery, but by the other troops.

The cavalry is to be kept in reserve till circumstances permit of its action in masses, and our cavalry must not let itself be drawn into isolated fights with a numerous enemy possessed of splendid horses, and accustomed from childhood to the use of *l'arme blanche*. As long as the enemy's cavalry is unshaken and is not in an unfavourable position, *e.g.* with an obstacle in rear, in a hollow, &c., our cavalry must not enter on a combat with it. Pursuit of a retreating Turkoman cavalry is useless, as it only breaks up the tactical formations—our one strong point and sheet-anchor. Cavalry must attack in close formation, which even infers no intervals being left between regiments, squadrons, or sotnias.

In attacks so much importance is not to be attached to the pace as to the keeping knee to knee; and attacks, only to be made under favourable conditions, must therefore be short, so that the troops may not get out of hand. The shock must be carried out in close order and with decision; in a word, caution and care must be the fundamental principles of our cavalry tactics in action.

On the contrary, attacks against disordered masses of infantry, as all Asiatic militias are, must be made with *élan*, although dash must be tempered by order and caution, and sufficient reserves must be kept.

I must refer to the extreme importance of careful performance of outpost duty while in camp before Geok Tepé. The commanders of outposts must realise the importance of the roads which lead from our camp to the points where the enemy can assemble for sorties. Each commander must study and carefully watch the ground in his front, and take all measures for supporting the parties on each flank; for I repeat that co-operation is the key of victory. Ranges are to be measured. This last point must be carefully attended to, as experience has shown how difficult is the conduct of a fight by night. Any deviating from certain lines of fire may lead to firing on friendly troops, and thence to confusion and disaster. I also draw attention to the utility of putting up marks by which the men may recognise the various ranges. Large heaps of wood, which can be kept burning all night, and behind which the picquets or even sentries are placed, are of great use. No large fires must, however, be lighted in camp without permission of the officer commanding, and in the event of an attack all fires in camp must at once be extinguished.

While by day a combat is decided by carefully utilising the ground and the means at one's disposal; by night everything becomes more complicated, and more energetic action is required. Therefore by night volley firing alone is allowed. It must be remembered that distances are judged with difficulty by night, and soldiers should therefore be impressed with the necessity of aiming low.

On $\frac{\text{December 20}}{\text{January 1}}$ after a vigorous bombardment, Yanghi Kala was carried by storm. The siege had now begun in earnest, but the first parallel was not opened until dawn on $\frac{\text{December 23}}{\text{January 4}}$ at a distance of 700 yards from the south-eastern angle of the mud-walls of Geok Tepé; 1,250 workmen were set to work at the trenches, while a demonstration in force was made on the other side of the fortress. The attack, although not intended to divert attention from our works, cost us the life of Major-General Petrushévitch. 'My extremely energetic and brave assistant,' as Skobeleff describes him, under whose command the demonstration took place. It was but poor consolation for such a loss to know that several hundred Tekkes fell in the fight.

At midnight on $\frac{\text{December 24}}{\text{January 5}}$ a volley was fired from all the guns at the fortress of Geok Tepé, and afterwards all the bands played the national anthem. Work in the trenches was continued without intermission. The troops even when relieved from work and resting in the camp had often to go on forage duty, escort transport trains, to go to the assistance of the troops in the trenches when suddenly atttacked. On the night of $\frac{\text{December 26}}{\text{January 7}}$ the first parallel was completed, and an approach driven forward towards the second parallel, which was opened on the next night. On the night of $\frac{\text{December 28}}{\text{January 9}}$ the Tekkes, in overwhelming force, made so sudden and determined an onslaught on the right of our lines that they swept across our second parallel, captured the colours of the 4th battalion of the 81st Apsheron regiment, and carried off one mountain gun and two boxes of ammunition. Two staff and three regimental officers were killed;

and ninety-one non-commissioned officers and men; more than thirty were wounded. The sortie was very spirited, and was only driven back after very severe fighting. In order to remove the impression it had produced, Colonel Kurapatkin was ordered to take by storm, the very next day, the Grand Duke Kalas, a group of forts only 116 yards in front of the moat of Geok Tepé. After three hours' bombardment the storming column issued from the trenches and advanced to the assault of the position with bands playing, drums beating, and colours flying. The Tekkes resisted bravely, but in the end the forts were taken. The newly-captured fortress was at once connected with the parallels, and we were now brought into very close quarters with the garrison of defence. On the next night another sortie took place, this time against our left flank. Although we had warning of their approach, the vigour of the onslaught was such that they swept our troops out of No. 3 redoubt, captured a mountain gun and carried it off into Geok Tepé. Our losses were fifty-three killed and ninety-eight wounded. The camp was next day brought nearer to the fortress. Our line was shortened and strengthened. It was also determined to push forward the siege works exclusively from the Grand Duke position to the ditch and the wall of the fortress. The third parallel was begun on the night of $\frac{\text{December 30}}{\text{January 11}}$. The resistance of the Tekkes was so determined that the situation began to look serious. All the cavalry were detailed for duty.

'The state of affairs was so serious,' Skobeleff reported, 'that for the protection of the camp and flanks of the siege works it was necessary to violate for the first time the fundamental rule of warfare in Central Asia, not to send small cavalry detachments into the zone of operations of the enemy, especially at night.' On the night of the $\frac{3}{15}$, an enclosure with earthen walls seventy yards from the wall of the fortress was occupied. On the same night the following instructions were sent to the commander of the flanks and centre:—

In case of an attack by the enemy, and in anticipation of it, detachments are to be posted behind the trenches, aiming as low as possible should the enemy escalade the trench. The best shots and sentries are to line the parapet of the trenches. This, it is of course understood, is only at night in view of the absence of hostile fire, especially before and after an attack. The troops may sleep, covering themselves with a blanket.

There was not very much sleep for the besiegers. Firing went on every day. Skobeleff had 69 guns from which he fired 100 to 500 shots into Geok Tepé, and from 10,000 to 70,000 rounds were fired daily by the infantry. Every night there were alarms of sorties, not always unfounded. A determined sortie was made on January $\frac{4}{16}$, but it was driven back before it reached our line. 'Trenches,' said Skobeleff, in this struggle with such very brave opponents had not the same importance that they have in warfare with European armies. By day they served as a covered road of communication, and the troops could meet the enemy firing and concealed behind the parapet. At night, when the enemy crept up within very close range without firing, the troops behind the parapets of the trenches at the time of a determined attack, would have to fight under very unfavourable conditions at the decisive moment when the enemy was on the crest of the trenches.

On the night of the $\frac{5}{17}$th a volunteer went up to the wall and measured the ditch. Our advanced trench had been driven to within 68 yards of the ditch; the ditch, which was dry, was 4 ft. 8 in. deep and 16 ft. broad. From that day it was made the custom to relieve the troops at night before it was quite dark, so as to enable commanders of companies and troops an opportunity to see how the ground lay, and how these neighbouring detachments were distributed.

The following description of Skobeleff in his last campaign is taken from the account given by one who was with him at the taking of the Tekke stronghold:—

'Without paying any attention to the misgivings of some, Skobeleff was never absent from his appointed post. Pale and nervous, but sustained by an energy like iron, he worked without relaxation, sometimes receiving reports, then drawing up dispositions and plans of attack. At night he either wrote or examined books describing former sieges, searching in history for examples resembling the task he had in hand. He only ate and slept by snatches. Working in this fashion he exacted from everyone the strict discharge of all his duties.

Notwithstanding the anguish which he must have suffered in those bitter moments when the Tekkes swept down like an avalanche in the night upon our lines, he never showed the least discouragement. His troops always saw him wearing the same gay and smiling countenance which the 16th Division used to see at Plevna and Shenova.

When the soldiers saw him, they felt a true leader of men was in their midst. The force of his inspiration was felt in every trench. Every soldier felt that the eye of his General was upon him. 'Skobeleff is coming!' said the soldiers. 'Good-day, my brave fellows,' rang out that sonorous voice, and an electric flash would leap through the harassed and dust-covered ranks of officers and men, and ringing cheers would salute the General. He went through the ranks, the balls whistling round his tall, upright figure, clad in a white uniform, with the Cross of St. George, and at his word the soldiers were ready to live without resting, and to die without a murmur.

During the whole of the time of the siege, Skobeleff was constantly on foot superintending everything, and seeing that his orders were carried out in every detail. Thanks to this unceasing solicitude, the mine which played so decisive a part in the issue of the siege was got ready in an incredibly short time, at a period when, owing to the difficulty of securing fresh supplies of food or of munitions of war, hours were worth days. Skobeleff was adored by his soldiers, who were devoted to him without reserve. He was as careful of their blood as he was prodigal of his own, and he always made it a point to explain to them both the object and the development of the operations which they were to accomplish under his orders.

On the morning of January $\frac{6}{18}$ a mining shaft was sunk and mining operations commenced. A mining gallery was driven with a vaulted roof and without boring at the rate of four feet per hour. A column with 82 packhorses attached was despatched to cut reeds for fascines in the gorge of Djermab. Two ventilating shafts were made in the mining gallery and the breaching battery was enlarged. On January $\frac{7}{19}$ an armistice was offered to the Tekkes during which they could bury their dead. The decomposing bodies around our works filled the air with the worst of odours. They refused our offer and the firing was resumed. A breach was knocked in the wall 23 yards broad, but it was quickly repaired by the Tekkes. On January $\frac{9}{21}$ the ventilating apparatus went wrong in the mine, and the assault, which had been fixed for the next day, was postponed till the $\frac{12}{24}$. Every night rockets were thrown into the fortress, the garrison of which was beginning to show signs of losing courage. On the $\frac{11}{23}$ 72 pouds or 1 ton 3 cwt. of powder was placed in the mine under the wall of Geok Tepé.

Next day, January $\frac{12}{24}$, everything was made ready for the assault. Geok Tepé was to be attacked on three sides simultaneously. Colonel Haidaroff, on the left, began by attacking and occupying Mill Kala at seven. He then advanced to the eastern front of the walls, and opened fire for three hours. On the right Colonel Kurapatkin was told off to storm the breach that was to be made by springing the mine, while Colonel Kozelkoff in the centre was to storm the breach made by artillery in the extreme southern point of the fortress. In addition to the fire from the heavy batteries, a heavy fire of common shell and shrapnel was kept up on the fortress, to which the enemy replied vigorously. They were also seen throwing earth on to the breach made by artillery in the midst of the fire. At 11.20 a high column of earth and smoke rising from the eastern face of the fortress, a great concussion, and a deafening roar told both besiegers and besieged that the mine had been fired. Large lumps of earth fell like rain on all the advanced troops, half a company of volunteers were nearly buried alive. When the smoke cleared away it was seen that nearly 40 yards—140 ft.—of the wall had disappeared, and in its place there was a yawning smoking crater, into which, notwithstanding all the defenders on the wall had been blown to pieces, the brave Tekkes had rushed to resist the besiegers. Colonel Kurapatkin's column, or rather the first section of his column under Major Sivinis, flung themselves into the breach. Simultaneously, Colonel Haidaroff, on the other side of the fortress, advanced to the attack, planting scaling-ladders against the walls, while Colonel Kozelkoff's column, between the other two columns, attempted to storm the breach made by the artillery. The Tekkes met Colonel Kurapatkin's column on the right with a heavy and well-directed fire. Our men pressed on, and a fierce fight with bayonets, lances, and swords ensued. So energetic was the resistance that Colonel Kurapatkin ordered the second party of his column, under Staff Captain Fok, to support Major Sivinis. After a 'fearful resistance,' the besiegers succeeded in forcing their way in, and at once began extending to the right and left. On the left they had to effect a junction with Colonel Kozelkoff's column, but at first that column met with little success. It had rushed into the breach shouting hurrah! but it was met by thick masses of the enemy, who overwhelmed it with bullets and stones, and finding the breach not easily practicable, it lay down at the foot of the breach and commenced an obstinate engagement with the enemy. A reserve was ordered up, and when it arrived with bands playing, colours flying, and drums beating, the column sprang up and this time successfully stormed the breach. At half-past twelve Colonel Kozelkoff's column formed hands with Colonel Kurapatkin and Lieut.-Colonel Haidaroff, who had effected an entry with little difficulty, and the fortress was practically in our hands. At four o'clock the enemy began to retreat in two large masses in a northerly direction. They were hotly pursued. 'The pursuit,' says Skobeleff in his official report, 'was continued by the infantry for $6\frac{2}{3}$ miles (10 versts), by the cavalry for four miles further, when complete darkness and the thorough depression of the enemy caused the pursuit to be abandoned and the troops to return to camp. In this pursuit by the dragoons and the Cossacks, supported by a division of a horse-artillery mountain battery, the killed amounted to 8,000 persons.' This number included some women who took a part in the fighting and could not be distinguished by the Russians. After the capture of the fortress 6,500 bodies were buried outside. When Mr. Marvin was at St. Petersburg he asked Skobeleff about the slaughter. This is his account of the conversation :—

'Do you know Mr. Marvin,' said Skobeleff, 'but you must not publish this, or I shall be called a barbarian by the Peace Society—that I hold it as a principle in Asia that the duration of peace is in direct proportion to the slaughter you inflict upon the enemy. The harder you hit them the longer they will be quiet afterwards. We killed nearly 20,000 Turcomans at Geok Tepé. The survivors will not soon forget the lesson.' 'I hope you will let me publish this opinion,' I said, 'and for this reason. In your official report of the siege you say that, during the pursuit after the assault, you killed 8,000 *of both sexes*.' 'That is true. I had them counted. The number was 8,000.' 'This statement,' I continued, 'provoked great comment in England, for you admit that your troops killed women as well.'

Skobeleff replied : 'It is quite true. When the dead were counted, women were found among them. It is my nature to conceal nothing. I therefore wrote, in making the report, of both sexes.'

'Were any dishonoured?'

'None at all. The troops did not outrage a woman. I must tell you I was deceived by the Persian agent, Zulfagar Khan. He came to me and said that there were many Persian women among the prisoners, and asked to be allowed to take them and send them home. I gave him permission, and gave him money. He thereupon chose the most beautiful women, and sent a number to Meshed, where he sold them into harems. Directly I was told of this, I stopped the permission at once.'

On my remarking that it was the great defect of our last Afghan war that we entered the country without a policy, and never applied his principle (or Wellington's) of hitting the enemy as hard as possible, he said: 'Those executions at Cabul were a mistake. I would never execute an Asiatic to strike terror into his countrymen, because you are sure to fail. Whatever punishments you resort to, they can never be so terrible as those inflicted by a Nasrullah, or any other despotic native ruler; and to these crueller punishments the natives are so accustomed, that your milder ones produce no effect. Then, worse than this, the execution of a Mussulman by an Infidel provokes hatred. I would sooner the whole country revolted than execute a man. If you take a place by storm and strike a terrible blow, it is the will of God, they say, and they submit without that hatred which executions provoke. My system is this—to strike hard and keep on hitting till resistance is completely over, then at once to form ranks, cease slaughter, and be kind and humane to the prostrate enemy. Immediately submission is made, the troops must be subjected to the strictest discipline: not one of the enemy must be touched.'

Mr. Marvin also mentions that General Grodekoff says that, although 'many women were killed,' Skobeleff gave orders to his troops to spare the women and the children, and none were killed intentionally. I cannot, of course, answer for the accuracy of Mr. Marvin's reports, nor am I responsible for Skobeleff's system, which, terrible as it seems, may in the long run be more merciful than its alternative; but it is evident that when a mountain battery is playing upon a mass of fugitives, and when the cavalry is pursuing in the shades of night a crowd of both sexes, both dressed almost alike, the result could hardly fail to be such as Skobeleff reports. War is horrible at the best, and the Tekkes, who themselves have been so ruthless in torturing, massacring, and enslaving their neighbours for generation after generation, would probably be the last to complain that upon them in turn had fallen a frightful retribution.

In the assault and in the subsequent pursuit the infantry fired 273,804 rounds; the cavalry 12,510, and the artillery 5,864; 224 military rockets were also expended.

We retook our captured cannon and mountain guns. We only took 1,500 weapons, a proof that the pursuit was as necessary as the capture of the fortress to break the resistance of the Tekkes.

The system, bloody though it was, seems to have provoked no resentment among the Tekkes. Their chief soon afterwards came in and did homage to the representative of the White Tzar. Our troops advanced almost without a protest through Askabad to Annoo and Gyaoors. Soon after the fall of Geok Tepé

Skobeleff was out riding with his escort when he met 700 Tekkes. He asked who they were? They answered, 'Friendly Tekkes.' 'How can I believe your word?' asked the General. 'Tekkes never lie,' answered they. 'Well,' said Skobeleff, 'if such is the case, I send my escort home, and will return accompanied by you.' Which he actually did. Nor was his confidence misplaced. General Tchernayeff displayed a similar confidence in Asiatic magnanimity when, on the evening after he captured Tashkend, he rode through the streets and accepted a dish of tea from the hands of a native.

After the fall of Geok Tepé the following proclamation was issued.

To the Akhal People.

I declare to the whole Akhal Tekke population that your fortress of Geok Tepé has been taken by the might of the troops of my Great Sovereign. The defenders have been annihilated, and their families and the families of those who have fled from the fortress are the captives of the victorious troops under my command. I therefore invoke the whole remaining population of Akhal Tekke to place its destiny at the unconditional mercy of the Emperor, in which case I hereby make it known that the lives, families, and property of those who declare submission will be in complete security like those of His Majesty, the White Tzar.

On the contrary, all those who oppose his victorious troops, and continue to persist in a useless opposition, will be destroyed as are robbers and criminals.

Adjutant-Gen. SKOBELEFF.

The summons was obeyed. The Tekkes laid

down their arms. The submission was complete. Our garrison was reduced. Skobeleff returned to St. Petersburg, and almost immediately after his return the Akhal oasis was formally annexed to the Empire. Skobeleff's own account of the matter is brief and simple. He said:—

I was recalled because the operations were finished, and because the army, having already been reduced, the troops were too few to warrant a general of my position retaining the command. It was impossible for us to relinquish Akhal. The English could retire from Afghanistan, because there was a King they could leave behind. But there was no form of government among the Turcomans. We had, therefore, to impose one of our own. Had we retired, they would have recommenced their raids as soon as the effect of the defeat had worn off.

One year after the capture of Geok Tepé a banquet took place at St. Petersburg in honour of the event. At that banquet Skobeleff naturally was present. His speech, which made a great sensation throughout Europe, referred to the campaign in the Akhal oasis in the following terms:—

If mutual distrust in private affairs is naturally opposed to our sympathies, it should be remembered, gentlemen, that, on the other hand, an extreme mistrust of everything foreign and capable of disturbing the legal historical ideas of the Fatherland is an obligation of patriotism, because it cannot possibly be admitted that the newly-propounded theory of triumphant and illegal might over physically weaker right is the privilege of some one particular race. It follows, as I imagine, from what I have observed, that patriotic hearts must experience a sensation of great delight when the course of events leads into error a sagacious and talented enemy of the Fatherland. This feeling is one of peculiar pleasure when one finds oneself in the midst of those who, by their labours and gallantry, and with their blood, aided in drawing that enemy into the committing of a mistake.

You all know that our highly talented enemy, Sir Henry Rawlinson, predicted so long ago as in the year 1875 that the animosity of the Tekkes of Akhal would involve Russia for many years in enormous expenditure of men and money, and in a war with Persia; that it would render it obligatory on Russia to establish a cordon of forts from the mouth of the Attrek, through the entire oasis, and from the Attrek to Merv; and that finally, and to crown all, it would undermine the political power of Russia in Central Asia.

It is pleasant, gentlemen, to look back to that precious confine on this auspicious day, and assure ourselves of the fact that, thanks to the Almighty, Sir Henry Rawlinson's prophecy has been in no way justified. We all know the condition of affairs too well for me to enter into details, but I may say that our troublesome Asiatic confine has never enjoyed such perfect tranquillity as it does now. Never since the time of Mahomed Shah's march to Herat, coupled with the memorable services of Count Simonitch, has the influence of the Russian Minister at Teheran been more predominant. In one word, the spell of the Russian standard is powerful far away to the East, even to the conquered region; and this will doubtless be confirmed by the engineers who have just returned from Saraklis.

Gentlemen, let me ask to whom is our country indebted for the favourable issue of this great work? First and foremost let us respectfully give honour to the instrumentality of our late Sovereign the Martyr Tzar. Having firmly taken the Akhal Tekke business in hand, the late

Emperor fully realised the immense importance of a *place-d'armes* at the gates of Herat and Afghanistan at a given period in history. In the second place the success of the enterprise was in principle insured from the very beginning by the efforts of his Imperial Highness the then Viceroy of the Caucasus, whose heart was ever with the brave troops under his command; and here I have to express my thanks to all the military authorities in the Caucasus for the assistance which was so largely given me, to our various military departments, and, not least, to our Minister for Foreign Affairs.

M. Zinovieff, our Minister at Teheran, not alone facilitated the execution of our task, but what is much more important, he has secured the durability of the results.

I need not enlarge on the gallantry of our Caucasian troops, with whom our glorious Turkestan forces have fraternised in battle. Our Caucasian standards came to the Akhal field direct from the fields of Asiatic Turkey covered with glory, and the commander of the Akhal expedition was too heavily charged with the fame of Russian arms for his heart to be below the level of the spirit of the troops which he led to Geok Tepé; and when the heart is in its right place on the field of battle, victory is three-quarters ensured. It is with deep feeling that I call to mind all those who co-operated with me, the brave soldiers and my brilliant staff of officers; and among those who fell, General Petrushévitch, conspicuous by his sense of duty, modest courage, and learning, and all the other officers who died for the faith, such as Prince Magolof, Count Orlof, Mamatsef, Bulygin, Zubof, Studitski, Yablotchkof, Merkhilef, Grek, Ivanof, Kunakofski, Moritz, Nelepof, Yurenef.

Gentlemen, so long as we have in our ranks such officers as those I have named, we may boldly look any enemy in the face, remembering those who fell at Geok

Tepé, and emulating their deeds when the day of trial by battle should come.

With these words of Skobeleff's concerning the last of his campaigns, I close this very inadequate account of Skobeleff as a soldier.

PART II.

SKOBELEFF IN POLITICS.

1. THE SLAVONIC CAUSE.
2. THE ST. PETERSBURG SPEECH.
3. SKOBELEFF IN PARIS.
4. RUSSIA AND GERMANY.
5. RUSSIA AND AUSTRIA.
6. RUSSIA AND ENGLAND.
7. SKOBELEFF AND CONSTITUTIONALISM.
8. DEATH.

CHAPTER I.

THE SLAVONIC CAUSE.

Skobeleff on politics—Panslavism—Pan-Germanism—Skobeleff's detestation of war—The Slavonic idea—The brotherhood of the Slavs—Slavonic solidarity—M. Louis Leger—Origin of the idea—George Krijanitch—Philology and politics—Panslavism and Slavophilism—Krijanitch in Russia—Banished to Siberia—His 'policy'—Fascination of the Slav idea—The Slavonic Congress at St. Petersburg—Count Tolstoy and Count Ignatieff—The Kremlin Declaration, 1876—Slavonic disunion—England and the Slavs—Russian disinterestedness—The San Stefano Treaty—What Russia seeks.

SKOBELEFF in politics, like Skobeleff in war, was a great force. 'Ak-Pasha,' as the Turks used to call him—or the 'White General,' as he was designated often by his troops—was more terrible to his enemy in the Bulgarian campaign than a whole *corps d'armée*.

He fought many battles, he made few speeches; but his most brilliant victory produced less impression abroad than the least of speeches he made, or was supposed to have made. A simple conversation, a passing utterance, was reported by greedy newspapers and gravely discussed by foreign statesmen. Europe not only listened, but indulged in endless comments, perverted every word, misrepresented every sentence. It amused Skobeleff; it amused many Russians. Nothing diverts us more than 'frightening the foreigner.' I am not defending this —certainly not, but I am stating a simple fact. Last winter a man occupying an official position, cultivated and intelligent, and far from young, called upon me in Moscow. We talked of all sorts of things, when they announced an English traveller. I introduced my two visitors to each other; but fancy my surprise when I heard my compatriot say, 'Have you not just arrived from our future possession—India?' I thought he had lost his senses. 'But,' continued he, 'perhaps you come from our other possession, Constantinople?' I interrupted; for, although his eyes were laughing, the tone was as solemn as that of a bishop. 'It is much better,' continued he, 'to designate beforehand what we are determined to take.' Then he added, in Russian, 'Pray let me go on; it is delightful.' I, of course, tried to stop him, knowing the danger there was in such jokes; but he was determined to have his way. If my English visitor is a literary man, I can well imagine the dreadful correspondence he may write about that meeting!

Skobeleff, like my mischievous guest, dearly loved a joke; but, clever and ingenious as he was, he always managed to impress his listeners. His words went deeper than those of many statesmen both in Russia and other countries. Skobeleff was no firebrand; he spoke not to provoke but to avert a conflagration. He knew, however, that there were limits beyond which oppression would provoke an explosion.

Russia wanted, and wants, peace; she has plenty of work to do at home, but 'peace at any price' has never been her motto, and never can be, as long as there remains one single Russian in the world.

Besides, Skobeleff's views as a politician should be distinguished from those which he held as a soldier.

When considering a military problem Skobeleff was before all things a soldier. Hence, when discussing the situation in 1878, it was as a matter of military strategy he advocated the prolonged occupation of Adrianople; and it was when weighing the chances of an invasion that he declared the Russian frontier could never be regarded as secure until she held the Bosphorus. From a purely military point of view he may have been right. Russia might be safer from attack if she held the Bosphorus, just as the position of France would be more secure if she held the English end of the Channel tunnel. But these questions are not settled by military experts, and Skobeleff himself, as a politician, would have been the first to acknowledge that certain problems cannot be settled from the standpoint of military science alone. I do not think it is wise to attach any political value to the expositions, however ingenious, of the strategic importance of different positions which Skobeleff published during his eventful career. His views are important when endorsed by Russia; and in order to understand the spirit of the whole nation, its real and powerful aspirations, people have to study her carefully, and this can be done only when the usual preconceived ideas and obstinate prejudices are honestly put aside. The great merit of Skobeleff consisted in his perpetual efforts to identify himself with his country, to serve her highest interests, to keep them alone perpetually in view, and to devote to them alone his whole life. Such an identification is not easily achieved, and it was only in the last years of his eventful life that he thoroughly realised how impossible it was to be a Russian without at the same time earnestly and thoroughly espousing the Slavonic cause. One without the other is shallow and incomplete. One is the necessary, the logical development of the other.

Slavs sympathise, and ought to sympathise, all over the world. 'Slavophilism' is only a substitute of that 'circuitous paraphrase.' In other races such a feeling is regarded not only as legitimate but admirable. I wish somebody would be kind enough to explain why it should only be detestable and criminal when those who share it use the Cyrillian alphabet and belong to the Slavonic stock. If any race in Europe should be able to understand the feelings of Slavs for Slavs, it is the great race which has found in the sentiment of German brotherhood a lever for revolutionising the Continent. Perhaps they understand it too well, and therefore they fear it. But their fears are needless. Panslavism seeks merely the independence of all the Slav races, and is a very different thing from Pan-Germanism, which seeks the political unity of the German fatherland. This difference should never be forgotten. Yet there is a Pan-Germanism which excites no indignation even amongst those who are directly concerned in it.

The other day some German residents in Odessa sent Prince Bismarck a present in commemoration of the twentieth anniversary of his appointment as Prime Minister of Prussia. In acknowledging the gift, the Imperial Chancellor used a form of words which, if employed by a Russian minister in a similar position, would have been regarded as an unpardonable offence. Prince Bismarck wrote: 'I rejoice to accept the expression of the recognition of my fellow-countrymen abroad, as a token that the tie of a common devotion to the Emperor and the Fatherland mutually unites all Germans abroad and at home.' Now there are so very many thousands of 'Germans abroad' in the Russian empire, and, notwithstanding all the delusions prevailing in the West concerning my country, thousands flock across our borders every year, that Russians might take alarm at this frank recognition of a 'common devotion' on the part of all Germans to the Emperor William and the Fatherland. But, of course, Russians have too much sense to get easily alarmed, and too much honesty to pretend to be alarmed when they are not. Pity our neighbours do not sometimes follow our example in this respect.

Skobeleff's efforts were all directed in a defensive not an offensive direction. Although a soldier, he never was a mere swordsman. 'Why should we attack

Germany,' I asked him once, rather impatiently, 'if she is not attacking us?' 'If!' retorted he—'all the power of the argument lies in that word "if." I only assure you,' continued he, 'we are not so weak nor so unprepared as some people imagine both at St. Petersburg and abroad. I know our forces, having studied them very accurately. We have nothing to fear ; absolutely nothing.' I shall never forget the expression of Skobeleff's face when he uttered these words. Never! There was no boasting, no humbug, nothing for the galleries ; but there was such a firmness, such a hard and determined look, that I thought I saw before me quite a different man from the one who was talking so mildly, so courteously, just a few seconds before. Skobeleff's face was remarkably attractive, not only by its regular features, but by its combination of extreme kindness and extreme energy. His pale grey eyes flashed with ever-varying intensity, reminding me of the gleaming of bright swordblades. There was also a depth in his look, as if his very soul were trying to manifest itself through his eyes. But Skobeleff distinctly and repeatedly said that to him war was only a means to an end, not, as with many soldiers, an end in itself. From Count Moltke's views as to the beneficence of war no one dissented more vehemently than the Slavonic hero whom his countrymen described as 'the poet of the sword.' Not even our great painter, Verestchagine, so aptly called 'the Apostle of Peace,' because his pictures of war are purposely made most disheartening, could detest more the terrible business of warfare. Again and again Skobeleff used to declare: 'I hate war; it is all that is sickening, odious, and atrocious. No more monstrous, no more loathsome, no more terrible crime can be imagined than to make war without absolute necessity. It is only as the last means, the very last argument, that a step like this can be justified. It can only be pardoned when made with a noble and generous end in view, as, for instance, when I defend myself or those who stand near to me by their faith or nationality.'

Skobeleff was a man of ideas, and some of them those of a statesman, taking that word not in its narrow sense, as sometimes represented in the chanceleries of Europe, which rather illustrate the maxim of Oxenstiern—' With how little wisdom the world is governed.' At the same time, he was the very last man in the world to claim for his views any originality. His great merit was, that he was chiefly receptive; for his utterances represented not the views of an individual, but those of a race. His greatness gave a glimpse of the greatness of the Slavonic idea, which, in other words, means Brotherhood of the Slavs. To some this may seem a craze; to Slavs it is a simple fact, from which flow other facts equally simple. The Slavs ask to be governed by the Slavs; that is all. The bed of Procrustes is not a Slavonic institution. The Slav lays down no shibboleth as to forms of government. He is contented with autocracy in one country; and constitutionalism in another. The form does not matter. All he asks is to be left alone to develop his own destinies in his own way. Leave the Slavs to the Slavs, each Slavonic people to itself, and the Slavonic ideal will have been realised.

Its watchword is 'Hands off,' and its formula self-government.

Unfortunately, millions of Slavs are governed not by Slavs, but by Turks, Hungarians, and Germans. These subjugated Slavs, as long as they are not left to themselves, will naturally look for help from their self-governed, eldest brother. 'Fraternité oblige;' help—at a great cost indeed to the helper—has been often granted. Not long ago the heroic little Montenegro was the only Slavonic country, except Russia, which had a Slavonic ruler; to-day, the Kingdom of Serbia and the Principality of Bulgaria are, thanks to Russia, and in spite of Europe, free from the yoke of the oppressor. The history of the Eastern Question for the most part is the narrative of the progressive emancipation of the Slavs. A great deal has been done, much remains yet to be achieved; but, like one of our Russian rivers, although its progress is slow, not the less will it reach the sea. 'To liberate, not to annex,' has been Russia's grand motto when she fought for the Slavs. She neither wishes to occupy Slavonic lands, as England occupies Cyprus, nor 'administer' them, as Austria administers Bosnia, nor absorb them, as France has absorbed Tunis.

Mr. John Aksakoff, who is justly considered as one

of our best leaders, wrote long ago : 'It is not a question of territorial conquest for Russia. It is a question of calling to an independent existence, political and social, all the different Slav groups. The Slavonic countries must belong to the Slavs.'

This doctrine is neither new nor Russian in its origin. As Russia received through Bulgaria her Evangel and her alphabet, she received the Slavonic idea from Croatia. M. Louis Leger's most excellent book, 'Nouvelles Études Slaves,' gives a very interesting sketch of the whole question. Anybody who wants to know the Slavonic world ought to study M. Louis Leger's works. He is a trustworthy and most valuable authority, and, without even attempting to compete with him, I will briefly indicate some few points in M. Leger's work, as I am afraid his book has not been translated into English as yet.

'The idea of a moral, intellectual, and political solidarity between all the members of the Slavonic race was born not in the empire of the Tzars, too strong to have need of theories, but in the little peoples of the East, among the Slovenes, the Croats, the Tchèques, menaced without ceasing by their redoubtable neighbours, the Hungarians, the Turks, and the Germans. The hatred of the oppression, the deep consciousness of a profound humiliation, woke the national conscience among the poets, the philosophers, and the philologers. In the midst of the miseries of the present, they found a consolation in the memory of the former unity of their race, and an encouragement in the hope of reconstituting it in the future.'

The noblest promoter of the Slavonic ideas was a Croat who lived in the seventeenth century.

What have the Slavs done for the world? is often scornfully asked.

They produced Huss, a century before Germany gave birth to Luther; and they formulated the doctrine of nationality two centuries before Mazzini popularised it in Italy. I take but these examples amongst many others. The precursor of the doctrine of nationality was George Krijanitch.

Two very interesting facts deserve to be noted here. The Roman Catholic Church, which now-a-days is trying to interfere in family ties, and to separate brethren from each other in more senses than one, in the seventeenth century held quite a different position; so much so, that George Krijanitch, who went to Russia with his heart full of confidence and love to his Eastern brethren, was a Roman Catholic priest.

I regret to blame our Government, but truth has to be spoken. Although some of our Emperors, such as Peter the Great, Catherine II., Nicholas I., and Alexander II., have served the Slavonic cause as true Russians should, other rulers have shown a wonderful short-sightedness and egotism in dealing with the Slavonic cause; the part of a generous helper or that of a reckless donor did not tempt them.

Like every other government, the Russian sometimes shrank from a disinterested, 'foolish' policy—which is only desired and insisted upon by real servants of the Slavonic idea. Governments often either consider themselves mere money-lenders, only careful of their percentage, or they resemble those parents who fancy that nothing is so good for their children as a money match, or so terrible as one made for love. The Slavophil party in Russia—up to the last few years—has been calumniated, vilified, described as treacherous to its oath, to its country, and its Emperor, and found anything but support in official St. Petersburg circles.

Poor Krijanitch, in return for his effusive sympathies, met with a sad reception in Russia. His services might have been most useful. Though a Roman Catholic, he was a thorough theologian; he studied at Vienna and Bologna; but, not contented with that, he went in 1640 to Rome to study, for polemical purposes, the language and the doctrines of the Greek Church. He discovered the great truth so sneered at by so many shallow observers, that the life of a nationality lay in its language and religion.

'Among the lesser nations,' says M. Louis Leger, 'philology and politics are "solidaires." It is the grammarians and the poets who have renewed the face of the Slavonic world.'

With all respect to the talented inventor of Professor Craniocracs, a great historical fact is not disposed of by a jest.

Luther's translation of the Bible, perhaps, did more to unify Germany than even the needle-gun.

Huss was almost as anxious to preserve the purity of the Tchèque language as to rid the Church of abuses, and it is impossible to sever the Slavonic movement from philological studies, the importance of which Krijanitch was the first to discern. Not that the Croatian priest was the first to recognise the fraternity of the Slavonic peoples, the unity of the Slav race.

The theories of philology but revive the memories of the Slavonic family. One of our earliest historians, Nestor, who wrote soon after England was overrun by the Normans, maintained that 'the Slavs were one of the seventy races, sprung from Japhet, who afterwards took different names,' but whether they called themselves Tchèques, Croats, Serbs, Poles, or Russians, they all belonged to the Slavonic race. A later historian was careful to trace the scattered members of the Slavonic family back to the building of the Tower of Babel. Thrice, at least, before the time of Nestor, Slavonic princes had endeavoured to unite the Slavonic peoples against their oppressors, and each time the champion of our race arose further to the east. Samo the Wend, who vanquished King Dagobert, assisted for a time the independence of the Slavs; but his kingdom did not survive, and the short dream of Slav freedom departed with his life. The next was Sviatopolk, of Moravia, the defender of our race. In the tenth century Boleslav the Great, of Poland, assumed the title of King of the Slavs, and reigned from the Elbe to the Dnieper, from the Baltic to the Danube. I only mention these few facts in proof that the idea of the unity of the Slavonic races is by no means new.[1]

I will quote another instance :—In an old book about Bosnia, entitled 'Spicilegium observationum historico-geographicarum de Bosniae Regno,'[2] Ivarko III., of Bosnia, who succeeded to the throne in 1396, had to struggle against the Magyars and the Neapolitan factions in Dalmatia, trusting himself on national, Panslavist support. In accordance with his 'Panslavistic' policy, he sent a messenger to Vladislav Jagellon, of Poland, appealing for his aid on the ground of the common origin of the Poles and Bosnians.

'Panslavism' is of an old origin, and its tendency was external and political; Panslavists dreamed of a moral, and some among them dreamed also of a political, union amongst all the Slavonic peoples. The Slavophils are also well-wishers of the Slavs, but their first and chief interest is domestic, and aims at restoration of primitive ideas, customs and institutions, the great majority of which were rudely interfered with by Peter the Great. Slavophilism is of modern growth; in fact, it is some fifty years old altogether. Its best representatives were, the

[1] Vide Louis Leger, *Les Origines du Panslavisme*, *Le Monde Slave*, p. 329. Paris, 1873.
[2] Lugd. Bat. 1837, p. 7.

poet and theologian Chomiakoff, George Samarine, the three Aksakoffs (one of whom is the editor of the 'Russ'), the brothers Kiréefsky, Hilferding, and others. They stood all on a high moral level and great intellectual culture.

But to return to George Krijanitch.

When England was fighting her King, the Croatian student was compiling, from ancient and modern Greek, a great work, summarising all the differences between the Greek Church and the Roman. The book is lost. The motto survives: 'They shall be no more two nations, neither shall they be divided into two kingdoms, but they shall be one fold and one shepherd.' It was the cry of the devout soul for the spiritual unity of Christendom, but it was also the yearning of a Slav for the reunion of all his brother Slavs; for only in union was there hope of deliverance. Thus from a cloister of a Roman monastery came forth the first articulate expression of what is now troubling all our enemies. But a man with such aspirations could not remain in Italy. He must visit the scattered races of the Slavonic fatherland; above all, he must make a pilgrimage to the greatest of the Slavonic races. Poland he saw with sorrow destroyed by her anarchy. In visiting Little Russia, he urged the inhabitants to throw in their lot with the Tzar. Alas! poor Krijanitch! His fate foreshadowed the difficulties the later Slavophils had to encounter. He also thought it his sacred duty to serve fearlessly the interests of the Tzar, and therefore, though a newcomer, a stranger, he began to denounce with singular freedom the abuses of the Courts of Russia. Croat though he was, he grasped with the Slavonic instinct the Russian conception of the Tzar. 'The duty and honour of a sovereign is to make his people happy, and to be the father of his subjects,' said he. Unfortunately he went much further, and thought, singularly enough, that he was obliged to lecture everybody he disapproved of for any reason. Now, any foreigner, coming to an unknown—or only superficially known—country, and expressing his frank views upon everything and everybody, is seldom thanked for his frankness, even in our ultra-liberal times, and even in most liberal parts of the world. I abstain from giving instances, very eloquent instances indeed, in support of my assertion, as I have to deal yet with Russia of the seventeenth century. So it happened that the poor lecturer was listened to at first; then in 1661—banished to Tobolsk; a dreary place, no doubt. He was allowed books, money, and free communication by correspondence; but, still, to be exiled for having simply spoken too much was hard and might have disheartened anybody. But Krijanitch, like a true enthusiast, lived more in the future than in the present: he dreamed apocalyptic visions of the coming grandeur and unity of the Slavonic world, and, I daresay, was happy in spite of his exile. How little could he imagine that up to the year 1876 the Slavonic cause would hardly be tolerated by the official circles in Russia; that the era he foresaw would actually only begin with the Emperor Alexander's speech at the Kremlin!

For fifteen years he lived and wrote at Tobolsk. His great work on 'Policy' pleaded the unity of the Slavs, and defined the principles by which a Slav State could become strong, great, and honoured. His watchword to the Slavs was the same as Skobeleff's. 'Rely upon thyself,' said Krijanitch, in addressing the Slav world, 'and beware of foreigners.' 'The more we study the work of Krijanitch,' says M. Leger, 'the more we are astonished to find under the most diverse forms the reveries and the aspirations of the men of his race, which were never really made known until the nineteenth century.' The reason is simple. These reveries, these aspirations, have never been absent from the Slav mind; but it is only recently that the Slavs have attracted attention beyond their frontiers, save as Slavs, to be crushed and plundered. 'We are plundered by the Germans, the Jews,' wrote Krijanitch, in the seventeenth century, 'the gipsies, the Armenians, and the Greeks. No people under the sun,' exclaims he, 'has been so insulted, so injured, as the Slavs by the Germans.'

Skobeleff's expression of distrust and hostility to Germans—not to Germany, but to the intruding, aggressive German who endeavours to transform the Slav into a German—has excited some surprise in the ill-informed West. It was even imagined that the General referred solely to Russia's oldest and firmest ally, the empire whose seat is at Berlin. That is pure fiction. I possess a letter he wrote to me a few weeks before his death, in which he positively repudiates his hatred of Germany. Slavophils are no lunatics. They gladly admit that there are Germans and Germans; those who identify themselves entirely with the life, the hopes, the joys, and the sorrows of their adopted country deserve to be trusted and treated accordingly. A man is not answerable for what he is born, but for what he has made of himself. Surely no Englishman would be base enough to consider Lord Wolseley as a stranger because he was born in Ireland! We have now in Moscow one of our principal military chiefs. His name is half German, half Swedish. Todtleben is another instance of Germans being as good Russians as the best. Examples of this kind are numerous.

Looking in another direction, that of science, we find the same patriotic devotion: one of our best Slavophil scholars—Hilferding—was of half German, half Jewish descent, but his death has been much lamented by his Moscow friends, and his works are studied with love and veneration by every Russian studying the Slavonic history and literature. The only difference lies in the natural obligation which the newcomers generally feel to give obvious proofs of their union, whilst, as for the original natives, their motives are supposed to be what they ought to be, what is sometimes a 'courtesy confidence' only.

Krijanitch seems to have been born again in the

shape of Skobeleff. 'It is for thee, oh great Tzar,' said the banished idealist of Tobolsk, 'to watch over the Slav peoples, and, like a good father, take care of thy dispersed children. Rouse them to be aware of their shameful condition; give them assistance in throwing off their foreign yoke. Extend to the Slavs of the Balkans that exterior force which they need to regain their feet, and once more to be numbered amongst the nations.' He lamented the fatal discord sown by foreign intrigues between Poland and Russia, countries which could have no greater happiness than in a brotherly concord, and he insisted earnestly upon the importance of literary propaganda.

Krijanitch spoke in vain. He was before his time, and when in 1676 he was allowed to leave Tobolsk, his career seems to have been closed. 'Regenerated Slavonia,' says M. Louis Leger, 'will one day raise a monument to the man who first understood all the miseries of his race and sought to remedy them.' George Krijanitch did more: he not only sought, but he found. And if 'Slavonia' is not quite regenerated, and no marble monument erected, still the time is already come to build a monument of gratitude by those who share the views and aspirations of their neglected leader.

It is beyond my power to give a detailed history of the Slavonic movement during two whole centuries. Besides, there were epochs when that vital movement seemed to shortsighted observers almost extinct.

It continued, however, though from the first it

was primarily literary and philological, the dream of unity of language never ceasing to fascinate the imagination of our race. For many years its chief exponents were the Tchèques of Bohemia. It is only in comparatively recent times that my countrymen took the lead in the development of the Slav idea. It has now passed into the political stage, and is a legitimate and recognised force, animating millions of souls and bringing into close alliance many throbbing hearts.

Mazzini, who certainly had nothing in common with Slavophils, and whose very name is disliked in Russia, where he is known only as a Revolutionist, recognised repeatedly the justice of the claims of the Slavonic family, 'covering,' as he said, 'a zone extending from the North Sea to the Adriatic;' and before he died he expressed a deep conviction that 'no permanent peace was possible in Europe while the Slavonic question remained unsettled; that is to say, while the legitimate claims of the Slavonic peoples to manage their own affairs remained unrecognised.' It struck Kossuth, that Slav renegade whose despairing execrations only testify to the vigour and vitality of the movement which he dreads. Poets, philosophers, novelists, prelates, historians, have all surrendered themselves to the charm of the great Ideal. Most wonderful of all, it has even thawed occasionally the habitual chill of diplomatists by profession.

But even a hurried sketch of Panslavism would

be incomplete without the description of the great Slavonic Congress which was held at Moscow in 1867. Seventy-five deputies from the various Slav countries assembled in May, to exchange fraternal greetings and consult as to the welfare of their common race. They were graciously received by the Emperor, the Grand Duke Constantine, the Grand Duchess Helena, and many great personages of the State. The Prince Gortchakoff, our chancellor, remarked, 'The Russians welcomed you so heartily to their country that there remained nothing for the Government to do.' And, in truth, the Government did nothing.

A banquet was offered them at St. Petersburg; speeches delivered by Tchèques, Croats, Servians, and Russians. The Bohemian leader, Dr. Rieger, welcomed 'the day, at last arrived, when the Slavonian races unite for the common welfare. If it were impossible to effect a political reunion, let us at least strive for the establishment of an intellectual alliance. What we want is harmony, the rest will follow in its train.' M. Polit, a Croat of Agram, expressed, with burning eloquence, the sense of brotherhood which united the emancipated Slavs to their powerful kinsmen in Russia. 'In the Servian heart,' he exclaimed, 'love to the Russian is innate. In our very cradles our mothers sing as lullabies songs of Russian magnificence. Upon her we have reckoned, even when she had not risen to the height of a great Slavonic power. The creative task of Russia lies not only in

Asia, but on what may be called the threshold of her house—the European East. Races must be henceforth independent. The Slavonian question must be solved by the Slavonians themselves, and chiefly by Russia. Russia is no longer Russia. It is Slavonia; nay, " Pan-Slavonia." The resources at her disposal are not only material, but moral. Slavonic Russia is no menace to civilisation, but only prepares Europe for witnessing the reunion of the Slavonic family. The first blow in the great struggle must be the cutting through the Eastern knot.'

But the spirit of the gathering was best interpreted by one of our first poets, Tutcheff, in a poem, of which this is only a poor translation :

'Welcome, twice welcome, oh brothers of the four quarters of the Slavonic world! The family feast is offered to all. Not as strangers, not as guests are you here. You are at home. In Russia every Slav is at home. More at home often than in his own country, where, alas! he is often ruled by a foreigner, and where it is a crime to be a Slav. Severed long by envious fate, we have never ceased to be one nation ; the sons of one mother. For this the world cannot pardon us. But as you will never desert Russia, Russia will never desert you. The world dreads the thoughts of all Slavs standing together, and addressing it as one. It has injured and insulted us so long, the memory of our wrongs will never be effaced from our hearts. At the awaking of Slavonic self-consciousness it trembles and dreads the judgment of God. The treatment accorded us for centuries has not ceased. Our brethren assembled here still bear traces of their ancient wrongs. Unavenged is the field of Kossova and the fatal battle of the White Hill. Belief in Divine justice will never be extinguished in our hearts, whatever may be the sacrifices demanded of us. God lives, and the cry " All hail the Tzar liberator! " will some day be heard far beyond the Russian frontier.'

Poets, they say, are prophets. Have these words not been already realised in Bulgaria?

The present Minister of the Interior, Count Tolstoy, was then Minister of Public Instruction. In spite of his official position, he made a very remarkable speech at the Slavonic banquet. He said, ' We have simply come together as Northern, Eastern, Southern, and Western Slavonians. You have been led here by the impulse of your hearts, by the consciousness of the brotherly ties binding us together. The ties of the history of a thousand years; the ties of blood, language, and the Panslavonic idea have asserted their rights. Let us strengthen those ties by the unity of speech and the creation of a common science. The scientific study of the Russian language is impossible without the study of the Slavonic dialects, just as the study of Russian history is incomplete without the insight into the simultaneous development of related nations. The ties between you and us, therefore, are not alone physical, but also moral and spiritual. Is there anybody sceptical enough to doubt the durability of these ties, to doubt that Providence has a grand future in store for the great Slavonic race?'

By one of the curious coincidences of history, General Ignatieff was almost at that very moment giving practical effect at Constantinople to the declarations which his future successor was making at St. Petersburg. He had just been raised to the rank of ambassador, and in presenting his new credentials to the Sultan, he reminded Abdul Aziz significantly that the welfare of Turkey depended upon the execution of the benevolent promises which he had made so often, and warned him, that while Russia harboured no selfish design, she was so closely bound by a common religion, tradition, and nationality to the Slavs of the Balkans, that she was bound to take a most earnest interest in everything that was really calculated to promote their welfare. The warning fell on deaf ears. Before eleven years had passed, General Ignatieff dictated at San Stefano the famous charter of Bulgarian freedom which emancipated the Slavs from the Danube to the Ægean.

M. Lamansky, one of our best authors, could well boast that the Slavonic idea from a mere phantasm had risen to be a solid and substantial fact. It had left the privacy of the scholar's study, and appeared in the church, in the street, in the theatre. It had become a Russian, nay a European question.

What has happened since then certainly has not lessened its importance. The 10th of November,

1876, when the Emperor-Liberator declared his resolve to defend alone the Slavonic cause, marked the advent of a new epoch in the Slavonic world. 'The historical conscience of all Russia,' said M. Aksakoff, 'spoke from the lips of the Tzar, and his word thundered forth as one having authority. On that memorable day he spoke as the successor of the Orthodox Grand Dukes, as the descendant of Ivan III., who received from the Palæologi the Byzantine arms, and combined them with the arms of Moscow, as the descendant of Peter and Catherine, the crowned protector of ancient traditions. From these words there can be no drawing back. The Emperor's words are a great event in the history of the present time. In the grey joyless twilight which surrounds us, in that chaos of contradictory aspirations and activity, in that lassitude of expectation from which all Russia is labouring, these words shine through the darkness as a star to encourage and guide us. They contain a whole programme of action. These words, and the unanimous, spontaneous, popular expression of fraternal love for the oppressed Slavs, form such historical landmarks, that if we only let ourselves be guided by them, we cannot lose our way, and cannot fail to fulfil our mission, whatever obstacles we may have to encounter. The slumbering East is now awakened, and not only the Slavs of the Balkans, but the whole Slavonic world, awaits its regeneration.'

To those who share the popular delusion, that the characteristic of the Slavs, especially of the

Russian Slav, is despotism, such words may seem ominous. Besides those who know that the inborn, besetting sin of the Slav race is not deference to authority, but a tendency to anarchy, which has been the source of untold disasters to our several tribes, will not wonder at the desire of the philo-Slavs to promote the unity of the Slavonic world. For a thousand years disunion has been our bane. We are now divided among four States. There are several groups of Slav nationalities, each with its own grammar, its own idiom; fortunately they at least are content with only two alphabets. We are again divided between three different religions—the Orthodox, the Roman, and the Lutheran.

It is nearly a thousand years since Sviatopolk, the great Slav sovereign of Moravia, repeated to his son, as he lay on his deathbed, the familiar fable of Æsop. Presenting him with a bundle of darts, he asked him to break them, to illustrate the importance of concord. The lesson, alas! was thrown away, and down to the present day we suffer from the result. Only in Russia, thanks to the autocracy, which has been the salvation of our country, have these fatal elements of division been effectively opposed. To unite Slavs, even of a single race, under one head is no easy matter. In Poland the attempt failed. In Russia we only learnt the lesson after terrible trials, the like of which, it is to be hoped, Europe will never see again. But to imagine that Russians dream of establishing a universal empire over all the Slav peoples is to impute to us a degree of madness of which, really, we are quite incapable. Slavonic unity in that sense is impossible, even if it were desirable. The unity of the Slavonic world, for which we hope, is such a unity as the English-speaking world already enjoys. Nowhere in the whole universe are any populations of English-speaking men under laws not of their own making, under rulers not of their own choosing. 'Blood is thicker than water' all the world over, as the American admiral said when he attacked the Chinese enemies of England; but no one on that account dreams of an English conquest of the United States, or an American annexation of England. Such a moral union as the friendship, the alliance of the great nations on each side of the Atlantic, that, and nothing more than that, is all we seek for ourselves. Is it so impossible, so impracticable, so wicked an ideal? But, after all, that, and nothing else, is the great Slavonic idea.

That the oppressors of the Slavs do not like it is natural enough. But is it regarded with alarm in England? She sympathises with all the nationalities in Europe; even in Egypt, she only suppressed a national leader in the name of 'the real national party.' Why are the Slavs regarded as beyond the pale of England's sympathies? Not that the Slavs expect anything from Great Britain, or from any foreign race. 'Help yourselves' was the cry of George Krijanitch, and it was also the watchword of Skobeleff. Russia has, as if carried away by a divine impulse, sometimes also as if against all her 'practical considerations,' helped the weaker members of the Slav race. The stronger must help themselves. The utmost that we ask from England is that she may leave us alone. At present her influence is felt in Slavonian lands only for evil, except since 1880, in Montenegro. She has redelivered Macedonia to the Turk, and constituted Austria—to use Sir W. Harcourt's own phrase—'the gaoler of Slav nationalities.' These things were done before the Liberals entered office; but how many Liberals there are who make it a point of honour to repudiate, as if it were a crime, all suspicion of sympathy with the Slavonic cause! Even some English 'philanthropists'—those declared friends of humanity—object to the Slavonic race being treated as the others. Capital specimen of justice and impartiality, indeed!

As to the favourite remarks, that 'the Slavonic cause is only a blind behind which lies Russian aggression,' 'To sympathise is to steal,' &c. &c., I hardly need notice them. Have our polite and courteous assailants ever asked themselves what Slavonic land Russia has liberated in order to annex? Poland was not partitioned in the name of the Slavonic cause. But we have fought for the Serbians. Have we annexed Serbia? For the Montenegrins. Have we taken a single stone of the Black Mountain? We poured out our blood in torrents for the Bulgarians, but we refrained from taking an inch of their soil, or a stone of their fortresses. Those who actually wish to learn something, to speak with a semblance of knowledge, let them read the San Stefano Treaty; they will see there what Russia desired to do, and gave up solely thanks to the intervention of Europe. At that time the latest fashion was to talk of 'Europe': what it meant in reality was not very clear; but people never mentioned that cabalistic word without putting on a solemn face.

Well, I was at Moscow at that time, and the day when the San Stefano Treaty was published there was such a joy, such a delight, that few Russians, I dare say, will ever forget it.

The articles of that treaty, relating to Bulgaria, embody the policy Russia would like to see adopted in relation to every other Slavonic race under Turkish or Austrian rule.

What are these articles?

Art. 6. Bulgaria is constituted an autonomous tributary principality, with a Christian government and a national militia. The definite frontiers will be laid down on the principle of the nationality of the majority of the inhabitants, conformably to the topographical necessities and the practical interests of locomotion for the local populations.

Art. 7. The Prince of Bulgaria shall be freely elected by the population and confirmed by the Sublime Porte with the assent of the Powers. Before the election of the Prince, an assembly of Bulgarian Notables shall draw up the organisation of the future administration. In the localities where the populations are mixed, account will be taken of the rights and interests of these populations in the elections and in the preparation of the organic law.

That is all Russia asks.

All the other stipulations are mere detail, consequent on the war which was brought to a close by the treaty. Russia does not want another war. All that the Slavs ask could be granted without war and would be granted to-morrow if their rulers were wise. Free local government; a prince elected by the population; a constitution drawn up by their representatives, and the frontiers and the organisation arranged in strict conformity with the nationality and the interests of the mixed populations. What is there in that which constitutes a menace to the peace of Europe, except so far as that peace is based upon the denial of human rights to the Slavs?

It is very odd how widely different is the estimate of the Slavonic character prevailing among the Slavs, and those who know nothing about them except the fictions of their neighbours.

'We Slavs,' said Palacky, the famous Tchèque historian, in 1848, 'repudiate all domination which rests only on force. We demand equality before the law without conditions, not only for individuals but for all nations. Nature has destined no nation to be the mere servile instrument of the views of its neighbours; all nations have an equal right to advance to the highest stage of human development, nor can they transgress this law with impunity.'

Once more, and once for all: Russia repudiates

all desire to annex a single part of Slavonic soil; she seeks to found no great Panslavonic empire. She helps her weaker brethren, and she is their only helper. This gives her a prestige which would be lost if she were supporting in order to devour. Our strength lies not in annexing or occupying the territory of our kinsmen, but in the conviction which the Montenegrian Vladyka Peter so eloquently expressed to Marshal Marmont in 1807: 'You detest and calumniate the Russians, and you flatter the other Slav peoples, in order that your Emperor may attain his ends. But we, the Slavs, know nothing of hope or of glory save through our powerful brothers of Russia. If they perish, all the other Slavs will perish, and who is against the Russians is against the Slavs.'

CHAPTER II.

THE ST. PETERSBURG SPEECH.

Why Skobeleff spoke—A warning to Austria—The conscription in Bosnia—The rising in the Herzegovina—Russia and the Crivoscie—What Skobeleff said—Good result of his speech.

SKOBELEFF, although particularly gifted with the faculty of expression, seldom spoke in public. Russia is not governed by talkers, and men with us are not made Cabinet Ministers because they can make phrases. We go even further: we, strangely enough, feel a certain mistrust of those who speak too well. With us, 'an embellisher of fine phrases,' *un beau parleur*, is not a complimentary expression at all. Besides, Russians are rather impatient, and unless you tell them at once what you want, they simply leave you alone with your eloquence. So, whether you like it or not, you have to come to the point. Skobeleff seldom allowed himself to discuss publicly even the political questions in which he was most interested. But at the beginning of 1882 he felt that the time had come when it was necessary to call attention to the rising clouds on the political horizon. He fancied it was his duty to speak, and he spoke clearly the thoughts which were burning in the Russian heart.

I was in England at the time when he delivered his first speech—his only speech, I may say; for what is called 'his speech at Paris' was merely an inaccurate collection of disjointed remarks, uttered in conversation without any system or plan. Without any communication with him at that time, without even knowing that he was about to raise so potent a voice in defence of the Slavonic cause, I was endeavouring to explain, as well as I could, to Englishmen, in the pages of the 'Contemporary Review,' the feelings with which Russia regarded the alarming development of Austrian policy in the Balkan peninsula. My little sketch on the crisis in Serbia appeared almost the same day that General Skobeleff was delivering the speech which shook the ground beneath the feet of the intriguers of Vienna. Skobeleff was in the capital of his country, I a thousand miles away; but each, without knowing what the other was about, explained and defended the same great principle, which was equally apparent to superior as to commonplace observers. Both expounded the common faith, the master passion of the Slavonic heart. Both sounded a warning note, of which Austria did well to take heed.

The occasion which led Skobeleff to speak was a banquet given at the anniversary of the taking of Geok Tepé—of his references to England and the Central Asian question I may speak later. Here I mention only his reference to the Slavonic question.

Before reproducing the chief passages of this

memorable speech, it is necessary briefly to recount the state of things in the East. It was loudly asserted in Austria-Hungary and elsewhere, that the hour had come for the complete realisation of the programme of 'crushing the head of the Slavonic serpent,' to use the eloquent metaphor of a Hungarian 'statesman.' The process began in the occupation of Bosnia and the Herzegovina. Lord Beaconsfield had urged that step in order that the predominance of the Slavonic race might not reappear, as he naturally concluded it must do, if the two provinces were permitted to enjoy any kind of local self-government. It had been begun in bloodshed. It was being persisted in in despair. Austria, in cynical defiance of the treaty which sanctioned the occupation and administration of the north-west provinces of Turkey, began to enforce the conscription. To levy the blood-tax on a hostile people can hardly be described as either occupation or administration. The Porte protested. Turkish opinion denounced the conscription as a flagrant violation of treaty-faith, an usurpation of the essential attributes of sovereignty.

For once Russians did not differ from their traditional foe. To them, as to every one else in Europe, Austria was exceeding her rights. But they did not interfere. Russia desired peace. When in November the conscription began to be enforced, the Russian Government neither interfered nor even protested. We were busy, as we still are, with our internal reforms. Russia wanted peace, as she wants it still;

and with heavy hearts we stood silent by, whilst the Austrian set about dragooning the Bosnian Slavs into the ranks of the Royal and Imperial army. Nor was this all. Encouraged by our apparent apathy, the Austrian stretched out its hand over Serbia. Prince Milan—he is a kinglet now—was Austrianized. His Cabinet was filled with Austrian sympathisers. The Serbian constitution was put aside; the Serbian revenue was mortgaged to the swindler Bontoux, an Austrian protégé. Worst of all, the Archbishop Michel was deposed, and an attempt was made to create a schism in the Serbian Church. On the Danube Austria was grasping at supremacy. She was extending her influence in Roumania, and the press, both of England and the Continent, was full of letters from well-informed correspondents describing the preparations for the advance on Salonica.

But all these things were conducted in silence. Russia's silence was misunderstood. It was taken for indifference, even for impotence. The Austrian press exulted in our fancied helplessness. Austria was to settle the Eastern question as she pleased: Serbia was to be annexed; Montenegro occupied; even Bulgaria was to become the vassal of the Hapsburg. If Russia objected—and in justice even to these defamers, let me say that they admitted Russia could object—Austrian armies would drive her back beyond the Dnieper. The air was full of threats, all of which we bore in complete silence. But when the brave peasants of the Herzegovina and the Bocche drew the sword against the Austrian oppressor, then indeed the Russian heart was stirred to its depths, and the feelings which throbbed there were bitterly hostile to Austria.

It is a mistake to suppose that Russia officially, or unofficially, encouraged the rising of the Herzegovina. Even the Ministers of the Hapsburg admitted that the conduct of Russia was most pacific, and that no one was authorised to doubt the loyalty of our Government. The revolt was, as M. Tisza admitted, caused by the attempt to force the conscription. He blamed the party of cosmopolitan revolution for fomenting it, just as Lord Beaconsfield blamed the non-existing 'secret societies' for making the Serbian war. Indeed, so far were we from being friendly to the rebellion, that the first impression in Russia was that the insurrection was purposely got up by the Austrian Government in order to afford a colourable pretext for seizing Serbia and Montenegro. But, although we did not assist, we could not avoid sympathising, and our sympathy was all the more intense because we saw that it would be too great a sacrifice to have plunged Europe into a gigantic war to save a handful of peasants from conscription.

In Herzegovina Austria merely broke a European treaty—the Treaty of Berlin—a precedent which is not likely to be forgotten. But in the Crivoscie she did much worse. The Bocchesi were surrendered to

Austria by Montenegro in 1814, in obedience to the advice of our Emperor, Alexander I., who, in giving this counsel, guaranteed the inhabitants, in the name of the Emperor of Austria, the full enjoyment of all their ancient rights and privileges. By degrees every one of these rights and privileges was withdrawn, until the exemption from the conscription alone remained. In 1869 that last relic of their guaranteed freedom was assailed. The attempt was defeated by the Bocchesi, who remained exempt until the beginning of this year. When the attempt was renewed, Russia saw with indignation and shame the ruin of a brave race who, at the counsel of a Tzar, had made the mistake of trusting the guarantee of an Austrian Emperor.

It is easy, I suppose, to imagine the bitterness with which were read the telegrams from Vienna and Cettigne describing the successive changes in that campaign, and to understand something of the universal relief which many Russians felt when Skobeleff broke the oppressive silence, and dared to say, in the hearing of all the world, what was burning in so many hearts. The Herzegovina was being crushed; Serbia was stupefied. At any moment, we were insultingly told, Montenegro might be invaded. Then, while a paralysed diplomacy silently surveyed the crime of the strong, Skobeleff stood up to assert the rights of the weak. Here are some of his burning words, which fell like shells in the enemy's camp, and destroyed in a moment the delusion, not less dangerous than absurd, that Russia could not be provoked too far:—

We are in our generation living through a significant period, unexampled in history. Some ages ago brute force governed all international relations; since then has followed an epoch of treaty obligations, the observance of which in form, with their repudiation in the spirit, has been considered as a feat of the greatest statesmanship.

In this age it has been our lot to experience the fact that the stronger, to all appearance, of two Powers, has established relations based on blood and iron, and that might governs right. Gentlemen, it is most significant that such an official recognition of illegality, actually committed, had never occurred in earlier history.

Our iron times impose on our generation great patriotic obligations. It is all the more sad to find in our midst so many unhealthy-minded Utopians forgetting that at such a period as the present the first duty of everyone is to make every sacrifice for the development of the powers of his mother-country.

If mutual distrust in private affairs is naturally opposed to our sympathies, it should be remembered, gentlemen, that, on the other hand, an extreme mistrust of everything foreign and capable of disturbing the legal historical ideals of the Fatherland, is an obligation of patriotism, because it cannot possibly be admitted that the newly propounded theory of triumphant and illegal might over physically weaker right is the privilege of some one particular race.

. . . .

I have one thing more to say to you, gentlemen; but allow me here to exchange my beaker with wine for a tumbler with water, and I call upon you all to bear witness that neither I nor any one of us is or can be speaking on this occasion under any abnormal influence.

We live at a time when even Cabinet secrets are badly kept, and what is spoken on this occasion will of a certainty be divulged, so that extra caution would not be amiss.

The experience of late years has taught us that when a Russian accidentally remembers (thanks to the history of his race) that he is one of a great and powerful people, and when—the Lord preserve him!—he happens to remember that the Russian people are a member of the great Slavonic race, some of whose families are now being persecuted and oppressed, then certain home-bred foreigners raise a cry against him, and say that he is labouring under abnormal bacchanalian influences. That is why, I repeat, I beg leave to put down my beaker with wine, and raise to my lips a glass filled with water.

It seems strange to me that any individual Russian, or that our society, should display a timidity when we touch on any question near to the Russian heart—a question legitimately arising from our thousand years of historical existence. There are many reasons for this, but I cannot enter into them; the principal one, however, is that lamentable difference which exists between certain sections of Russian society, between the intellectual classes and the Russian people. Gentlemen, whensoever the Sovereign of the country has called upon the people, that people has risen to the occasion of the historical necessity of the time; it has not always been so with our intellectual classes, and if anyone has ever failed to respond to the Tzar, it has been those intellectual classes. I perfectly understand this; cosmopolitan Europeanism is not a source of strength, but an indication of weakness. There can be no strength independent of the nation, and the intellectual classes are a power only when in combination with the people.

On this anniversary of the fall of Geok Tepé it is only our best feelings that are uppermost. Frederick II. used to say that 'Russians not only had to be killed, but they had to be thrown down even after life is extinguished.' My soldier's heart and my experience tell me that I am in an assembly of such people as those referred to by the Marshal. This is why, in the midst of soldiers, I utter words which are to be understood in a military sense, and not as having anything in common with politics of a given time.

Referring to the struggle for faith and nationality then going on on the shores of the Adriatic, General Skobeleff concluded with the following words :—

I will not express all my meaning, gentlemen. My heart aches. But our faith in the historical mission of Russia is our consolation and our strength. Long live the Emperor!

How can I describe the tumult of emotion which this speech called forth in Russia. The few who at every great crisis have played the coward's part, lifted their voices in horror. No calumny was too base for them to heap on the head of the fearless general. 'He was mad;' 'he has lost his senses'—I know not what! But Russia was not deceived by these lies. Russia heard in her hero's words the utterance of her deepest thought. Skobeleff had spoken, and Europe had heard. Austria was warned. It was something already achieved. The diplomatists, as usual, were alarmed. Presently newspapers announced that Skobeleff was going abroad on a lengthened leave of absence. 'Banished!' 'exiled!' exclaimed with delight his enemies, and the enemies of Russia, who, within a few days were asserting as positively that he had been despatched on a confidential political mission. In reality, Skobeleff, consulting his own convenience, went to Paris, and there, by a curious accident, a few sentences, dropped in the course of a simple conversation, made so much stir as to cause his St. Petersburg speech to be quite forgotten. But that remains the only political speech Skobeleff ever made.

CHAPTER III.

SKOBELEFF IN PARIS.

<small>A soldier's right to speak—Skobeleff's alarm—German menaces—His visit to Paris—Desires to avert war—The conditions of peace—What Skobeleff said—His political ideal—The address of the Serbian students—The scare—A Bulgarian deputation—His recall—Speech at Warsaw—Russia, Prussia, and the Poles—Received by the Emperor—The forgery of the 'France'—M. Gambetta and Skobeleff.</small>

I WELL remember talking to Skobeleff at Moscow a few weeks before his death. 'It amused me greatly,' said he, in his frank and charming way, ' to see what people said about my speech at St. Petersburg. " A soldier," they cried ; " and to talk politics ! 'Tis monstrous." But they never seem to remember that I was in Russia, where relations between the sovereign and his subjects are quite different from those prevailing in constitutional countries. There really exists a paternal feeling between our Emperor and ourselves. Why should we not let him know what we think ; what we suffer from ; what we long for ? You know very well that everything can be said and written when put in a proper shape. I thought it my duty to speak, and I spoke.'

That was his theory, not shared by everybody to be sure ; but in countries where the talking apparatus is not so highly developed as in England, where they talk six weeks before deciding whether a debate ought ever to be closed, it is well not to be too pedantic in limiting the right to speak where there is both the ability and the will. Skobeleff had both, and his speech did good. I really think it did. It cleared the air. It reminded the world that Russia existed. It reminded Russians that their historical mission was not forgotten, and it made an end once for all of all schemes for invading Montenegro. The Crivoscie it could not save.[1] But it threw the shadow of the Russian sword across the path of the aggressor and bade him beware. I am not the only one to think that the warning sufficed.

[1] Mr. Arthur Evans writes to the *Pall Mall Gazette* as follows:—
'The state of Crivoscia is still such as those who like myself knew the determination of its heroic sons, from the first predicted it would be if Austro-Hungarian cannon succeeded in dislodging them from their mountain eyries. "Order" there reigns with a vengeance, for the country is a desert. The results of the Hapsburg attempt to enforce the violation of their oaths, by introducing the conscription in the chartered Bocchesi districts, are thus described by the *Pester Lloyd*: "The Crivoscians and Ubliani show no inclination to return to their homes. Over 4,000 human beings, young and old, women and children, have been now for the last ten months exiles from their hearths and homes, seeking scanty shelter and subsistence among their kinsmen of the Black Mountain, who themselves have nothing. With the exception of soldiers and a few hundred workmen engaged from a distance to execute the new works of fortification, *not a single living soul is to be found in the whole Crivoscian country* [the italics are the *Pester Lloyd's*]. Every village is deserted. From the mighty rock wall of the Pazua, the Bora (the icy nor'-nor'-easter of the Dinaric Alps) sweeps down with all the terrors of the elements on the devastated shells of villages and habitations. Not a shepherd pastures his sheep among the rocks; not a plough for the last year past has furrowed the fields of the upland plains of Ubli and Dragail, Knezlac and Unirine."'—Dec. 14, 1882.

But along with this good his speech brought some evil. Skobeleff was no diplomatist. He spoke straight out what his heart was full of, and the result of this was that he provoked a storm of indignation in Germany, which was entirely without warrant. Skobeleff, in turn, took alarm. He believed that Austria backed by Germany meditated an attack upon the western frontier of Russia. A defensive war, such as broke the power of Napoleon, was by no means to his taste. 'If we are to be attacked,' he said, over and over again, 'let us at least be ready to carry the war into the enemy's country.' Beyond that he never went. Of an aggressive war with Germany he never even dreamt. Of this he assured me several times. Now I cannot conceive why he should say to me things which he did not think. Whatever he told me always bore such a character of complete frankness that I could guarantee his sincerity.[1] In Moscow nobody

[1] Skobeleff was singularly truthful. Since writing the above I have come upon the following anecdote of him in an English newspaper. The writer says:—

'Skobeleff has had in his life to tell diplomatic falsehoods, but they stuck in his throat and nearly choked him. On one great occasion he boldly told a lie, or rather a bundle of lies. His mendacity was to veil the scheme of a campaign on which tremendous issues depended. When the person whom he was deceiving rose to quit him he insisted on seeing him to his carriage. On his way out, the General stopped short and said, "You look very honest, and you are a person of breeding. If you suspected the importance of some questions you have been asking, you would have cut your hand off rather than put them." He then recapitulated them, and added, "All my answers on these points were lies. I can't bear the feeling of lying to you. You may guess the truth from this. I place my secret at your mercy, and am sure you will not give me cause to regret doing so."'

shared his alarms; but I suppose a readiness to take the offensive if attack is threatened is not incompatible with a purely defensive policy. Fortunately, at the present moment we have no ground for picking a quarrel with an old ally and friend like Germany, and Germany has no serious ground for attacking us.

I must beg the permission, however, to say, in justice to Skobeleff, that the remarks of some of the German newspapers were not much calculated to allay his suspicions of the intentions of the party whose watchword is 'Drang nach Osten.' The press in all the world is doing no end of mischief. One could less expect to find it in that of Germany, because in no country is the general level of culture and information so high as in the native land of Kant and Hegel; but, unfortunately, men are not guided only by their faculty for judging and weighing the real facts. The press is losing its ground every day more and more, but it has not lost it entirely yet. The 'Voss Gazette,' for instance, declared that 'Germany had an absolute necessity to extend herself on her eastern frontier. The material and intellectual position of the Polish, Lettish, and Lithuanian populations would be considerably ameliorated if they were placed under the rule of Germany. The history of the last ten centuries shows how easily it is to Germanise the Slavonic populations. The Slavonic races of Pomerania, Silesia, and Lusatia, and of the March, are illustrations of this. In order to Germanise all Slavs, as well to protect the German

Empire, the German frontier has to be pushed far eastward.' How far was not stated, but possibly it was on the west of Moscow. Such menaces as these were ringing in the air when Skobeleff crossed Germany and found himself at Paris.

Everybody goes to Paris. Parisians are neither afraid nor suspicious of foreigners who have a liking for their country. Nobody dreams of asking a newcomer, ' How on earth are you again with us ? What is your object ? ' If anything surprises a Frenchman it is the fact that people are foolish enough to live anywhere except in Paris. Skobeleff's mother used to live there, and he very often visited France. But his previous visits had attracted no attention. This time short-sighted people congratulated each other on the belief that ' they should hear no more of that hot-head Skobeleff.' He was supposed to be under a cloud. Diplomacy had extinguished him. He dared make no more speeches, and so on. But Skobeleff was not so easily snuffed out. He went to Paris dominated by two feelings. The first, sympathy for the Slavs of the Adriatic, and second, a terrible conviction that war was inevitable if Austria persisted in carrying out the programme proclaimed by her journals.

If Austria invaded Montenegro, Russia would be compelled to intervene. To keep the peace, Austria must be prevented from crossing the frontier. If Austria mediatised Serbia, and annexed the country up to the Ægean, the danger of a collision would again be very great. But, if common report were true, that is exactly what Austria proposed to do. To prevent war, Austria must be reminded of the limits of the Treaty of Berlin; and as no one else seemed disposed to bell the cat, Skobeleff determined to do the work himself.

It may have been presumptuous, but it was not a foolish ambition which prompted him to speak. As a patriot and as a man, he wished to prevent a war which he thought might become inevitable, and if his warnings proved in vain, he wished to see how far the Powers which had signed the Treaty of Berlin could assist Russia in preventing its violation. Let people call it a madcap quixotism, or what they will, I do not defend it. I do not ask anybody to refrain from condemning it. I only ask them to look at it, only for a moment, from Skobeleff's own standpoint, and not to judge our impulsive hero until the real motive of his expedition is thoroughly understood.

When Skobeleff came to Paris he saw many Frenchmen. To all he spoke with the utmost unreserve. With that engaging candour which gave so great a charm to all he said, he told all his visitors exactly what was his position. 'He held no mission,' he said, 'from the Government; he was merely a Russian who knew a catastrophe impended immediately ahead; if Austria executed the aforesaid programme, no power on earth in that case could keep Russia from defending the Southern Slavs from Austrian aggression. It might be deplored, but the fact could not be ignored. Austria must stop her threatened advance. Peace might be secured, if the Powers assisted in maintaining the treaty they signed.' That, and much more to the same effect, Skobeleff said to all who met him, to friends as to foes. Over and over again he repeated that he had come not to raise a storm, but to avoid it. The means he used were, perhaps, not correct; but surely the motive was not a bad one?

Suppose an Englishman had gone to Paris after the fall of M. Gambetta, and had said exactly what Skobeleff had said, only with relation to Egypt, instead of the Balkan, is it not possible that it might have cleared the air? He could have said quite truly that, unless Arabi desisted from the policy on which he had entered, he would inevitably force England to draw the sword. Arabi might have been warned in time, and England might have been spared the painful duty of supporting her word by drastic measures.

Of course Skobeleff spoke only as any other Russian could speak; his official position had nothing to do in the matter. Such at least was his conviction, though many Russian generals would never dare to separate in that way their private character from their official uniform. I saw Skobeleff several times this last spring, and each time he denied having made any speech at all in Paris, in the ordinary sense of the term, and he never uttered the wild and mischievous words put into his mouth by the French press. His

mistake was that he allowed his French friends to spread the wrong report, which they wanted as a feeler for their own purposes, and contradicted it only to the 'Daily News' Correspondent, and to the Correspondent of the 'Kölnische Zeitung.' He not only admitted, but insisted upon the accuracy of these two accounts, and I therefore reproduce their substance as testimony to my own explanation. He said :—
'Europe is in imminent danger of a great war. It is inevitable ; the provisions of the Berlin Treaty are to be trampled under foot by Austria. Russia has no reason to love that treaty. It was a bad treaty, for her and for the Southern Slavs; but it at least secured the latter from being crushed by foreign despots. If not, there will be war. It would be a mad war, a war of suicide, you say—perhaps. But there are some circumstances where even suicide is unavoidable. But there is no need for war.'

(Skobeleff often used to say that in war, instead of being made prisoner, it is better to kill oneself on the spot. Such were his views—not mine. I only explain what his theory of suicide meant.)

'Peace can be maintained,' continued he, 'if the facts are recognised in time. I wish to remind you of these facts, which the diplomatists, who are always for ignoring the truth until it is too late, have obscured.

'I have no hostility to Germany. But why does she not restrain Austria from aggression? If Berlin were to say "Hands off," the word would be respected at Vienna. The Slavs only wish to remain Slavs. They object to be either Magyarised, Germanised, or Jesuit-ridden. Austria was only authorised to occupy, and to administer, to restore order in the two provinces. She was exceeding her commission. She was enforcing the conscription and promoting a Jesuit propaganda amongst the people. Russia had not delivered the Slavs from the Turk to have them trampled on by the Austrian. Even under the Turk the Slavs had more independence than under the oppressive yoke of the bureaucrats of Vienna. Why cannot she let them develop in their own way, and live their own life? It may be rough and rude; but such as it is, it must be the basis of their own social and political evolution. But they are prevented from doing it ; they must set all their clocks by Vienna time. The Austrian machine works like a clock. It is regular, but it is inflexible and unfeeling. The Slavs of the Adriatic would be content with almost any kind of social autonomy. It is denied them, and they revolt. In Serbia also the foreign element is constantly encroaching. That element is the enemy against which we have always to be on guard. The Slavs have to struggle without ceasing. It is a long and arduous contest between the two civilisations ; it is going on in every Slavonic land, but if we are true to ourselves, in the end we shall be victors.

'The West is deluded about Russia. It thinks that we are so crippled by the late war as to be helpless. It is a mistake. A nation of ninety millions, capable of sacrificing itself with enthusiasm for an ideal, is not so easily effaced.

'Our provinces are disordered; we are weakened by the war, and the Nihilists, these deformed children of the German philosophy, are giving trouble. But Russia is still living, and if certain lines were overpassed, she would fight. In such a war all the risks would not be on our side. Most of the Austrian troops are Slavs, and they would not be very enthusiastic in opposing the power that sought the liberation of their brethren.'[1]

---

[1] In this Skobeleff agreed with Lord Derby. In the speech which the former Foreign Secretary delivered after leaving the Beaconsfield Cabinet, he said:—

'I think it is fully open to doubt whether you can rely much on Austrian co-operation. Without disclosing anything that is not before us, I say only what is known to everybody when I assert that Austria cannot take the bold policy of coming to a rupture with Russia unless personally assured of the support or the neutrality of Germany. There are so many different races in Austria that a single unsuccessful campaign might very possibly break up the Empire. No doubt the Magyars, who have attracted and deserved so much sympathy in this country, are vehemently and intensely anti-Russian. But you have a not insignificant Slav population which takes exactly the opposite view, and portions of the Austrian army distinguished by their Slav nationality could not be trusted to fight the Russians. You have the Slav-Germans, who only want peace. In addition to this, we know that the finances are in such a state that the Austrian Government had some difficulty in raising the 5,000,000*l.* or 6,000,000*l.* necessary for the first organisation. I say, that with all these elements of weakness and confusion, Austria is not a power on whose support we can rely.'—*Speech in the House of Lords*, April 8, 1878.

The spontaneous recognition of Slavonic and Orthodox unity on the part of Austrian Slavs has sometimes proved somewhat embarrassing for Russia. Of this the following extract from Palmer's *Notes on a Visit to the Russian Church*, 1840-41, may serve as an illustration:—

Skobeleff continued : 'And the delusion is that Russia wants to seize the Slavonic lands. The more real freedom you give to the Slavs of the Adriatic and the Balkan, the less likelihood is there of their seeking new masters elsewhere. What we want to see is a Slav federation, founded on the fraternity of the race, and the liberty of all its members. We fought to emancipate, not to enslave our brothers. Russia wants nothing for herself. She is the only State in Europe sufficiently idealistic to go to war for a sentiment. Her people shrink from no sacrifice in the cause of religion and of race. Beware lest you provoke them too far!

'I am not here to foment war. On my honour and conscience, I detest it. No one who has seen the sickening horrors of war through which I have passed could be otherwise. But war can only be prevented if we drop the masks of diplomacy; and,

'When the Emperor Alexander was at Laibach, the Austrian Slavonic soldiers attending the Liturgy at his tent-church, and seeing all the same as in their own worship, and hearing the Church Slavonic, from which their vernacular Slavonic differs less than does the Russ, exclaimed publicly, according to Sir James Wylie, "This is our Emperor!" at which the Emperor Alexander was much annoyed, and he and the Austrian Ministers had some difficulty in preventing a still greater excitement. And it appears that any Russian Emperor might have them all with him—20,000,000 of Slavonians—Sir James says (besides those which he has already), if he were to proclaim himself Emperor of the Slavs. There are fine roads within the Austrian territory, which end suddenly before they reach the frontier, and all communication is strictly interdicted. It is even felony to possess a Russian book. So Austria has another source of weakness besides the Magyars and Hungary.' (Page 236.)

T

like Prince Bismarck, talk as business men of what we want. We want peace.'

That is the substance of what Skobeleff said, and what he often referred to in his conversations at home as well as abroad. What he was supposed to have said no one knows. Who can sum up the absurdities of which the press can be guilty? We have a vulgar but graphic proverb in Russia : ' The tongue has no bones, it can say what it likes.' A free press is no doubt a great thing, but it has the same privilege. When a free press means the free dissemination of calumnies and slanders, its benefits are hardly so obvious. Skobeleff was disgusted beyond degree at the sensational falsehoods they spread abroad about him and about Russia. All the mischief resulting from his visit to Paris was due, not to what he said, but what foreign newspapers pretended that he had said. The occasion which they took for creating a sensation was an interview which Skobeleff had with a band of Serbian students who came to present him with an address. This document, which was published by ' La France,' was dated January 30, and ran as follows :—

General,—Deeply impressed by the energetic and noble words which you have addressed to our brothers who gather to-day in the mountains of Bosnia, the Herzegovina, and Dalmatia, around the flag of Liberty and national independence, and who baptize it with their blood and their tears, the Serbian youth in Paris feel themselves bound to express their gratitude in presenting you with this address.

The undersigned, General, are fully convinced that they have heard, not only the salutation of a Russian soldier, whose sword has flashed on many battlefields both of Europe and Asia, but that through your fraternal and heroic heart there has reached them the true and powerful voice of Slavonic Russia herself. They beg you to believe that this humble manifest alone is only a testimony of the aspirations of the whole Serbian people from the Danube to the Adriatic.

Animated by sentiments of admiration for the fraternal enthusiasm to which you have abandoned yourself, the undersigned cannot conceal their joy at seeing the hand of these great sister-nations extended, in spite of all obstacles, towards one another, to dress the wounds which the strong of this world have inflicted and are still inflicting on the Southern Slavs in general, and on the Serbians in particular. They cherish the hope that the day is not far distant when that same hand will be offered against their civilised oppressors, as it has aided them against their savage conquerors, and that upon the classic ground of the Serbian and Slavonic East, Russia will erect monuments of her history and of her mission of which the most lasting foundation is the equality and independence of the people, and whose crown is the ideal of the human race—Justice and Liberty.

Finally, General, the Serbian youth will not cease to regard you as the heroic interpreter of their race, so nearly related to your own, alike in its unequal struggle for independence, its secular trials, and its legitimate aspirations.

Paris, January 30, 1882.

After the address had been presented, Skobeleff, in his free and unrestrained fashion, talked to the young fellows about the Slavonic cause, thanked them for their fraternal feelings, and encouraged them to preserve their nationality and their religion against foreign influences. It was merely an informal conversation, such as passes between would-be friends. No reporter was present. There was no speech, and nothing was further from Skobeleff's mind than that any of his observations would be published as a manifesto against our allies at Berlin.

A painful fact has to be recognised—a very painful one indeed, especially to Russians—who have sustained terrible losses during the Serbian war; losses which no time, no efforts can make them forget. All Serbians are not friendly to Russia. Some of them think themselves less well treated than the Bulgarians, and in return for Russian help are even hostile to us. Some go still further, and pretend having become 'too' civilised not to sympathise with constitutional or even with Socialistic views. Have such Serbians been in that meeting in Skobeleff's room? and if they have, can their testimony be implicitly accepted? I prefer not answering these questions. The undoubted fact is, that Skobeleff, immediately after he saw his pretended 'speech' in the 'France,' spoke to the Correspondents of the 'Kölnische Zeitung' and of the 'Daily News,' and though these papers, as a rule, are hostile to Russia, on that occasion they acted fairly. Skobeleff urged them to give a true version of his remarks to the world, and they both acquiesced in his request.

Those who did not know Skobeleff, or who had

some hidden motive for preferring the version of the
'France,' of course clung to that authority. What
Skobeleff ought to have done, according to my impression, would have been to insist upon the 'France'
denying its first version; but he thought the
'Daily News' and the 'Kölnische Zeitung' were
more read and listened to than that Paris paper, and
did not go further in his contradiction. The sensation produced by all this was enormous. In
Russia we were half-amused, half-amazed. We
knew Skobeleff could never have said the nonsense
imputed to him, but for a few moments it was as
bad as if it were true. The Russian funds fell, and
all the people—for we have some of those also in
Russia—who regard the rise and fall of stocks and
shares as the barometer of heaven, set up a cry, a
very loud and angry cry, against Skobeleff. He was
'a madman,' 'a criminal,' 'a traitor;' I know not
what else. There was such a commotion in all
Europe; there was such anxiety at St. Petersburg,
that it was decided Skobeleff should be summoned
home to explain what he had really said and done.

The newspapers reported that, whilst in Paris,
Skobeleff received a Bulgarian as well as a Serbian
deputation. According to a Bulgarian correspondence, which appeared in the 'Neue Freie Presse,' the
deputation presented him with an address, which
contained the following passage :—' Your oppressed
Slavonic brothers only await your frank and manly
words to throw themselves into the unequal conflict

with the enemy of the Slavs. The light of your speech has shone on the heights of the Balkans, as well as the valleys of the Danube, the Tundscha, and the Maritza. It is upon you that we count to realise the Treaty of San Stefano, and to found the great Bulgaria.' Whether such an address was presented or not, I do not know; but it is worth notice that the report says the presentation was only followed by a conversation, as I know was the case after the Serbian address was presented. Skobeleff did not formally deliver an oration to a handful of youths. He entered into a friendly chat with them individually. All that is reported of his conversation with the Bulgarians is, that he advised them to fortify without delay the line of Karadja Dagh and of the Balkans. 'The town of Slivno,' he said, 'could be made a Slav Saragossa if its inhabitants shared the bravery of Spaniards.'

Before he left Paris, he had an interview with the Correspondent of the 'Daily News,' whom he greatly impressed, as he generally did everyone, by his winning manners, his lofty idealism, his chivalrous devotion to the cause of the oppressed. 'He is the Godfrey de Bouillon of the Slavonic race,' summed up the Correspondent. The account given in the 'Daily News' of his parting conversation, although brief, is yet so true, and so like Skobeleff, that it delights me much. It is accepted too often as a positive truth that Englishmen are egotistical, cold-hearted, that they have no enthusiasm. Nothing seems to me less founded. English people are capable of generosity and enthusiasm, perhaps not less than any other nation ; but these feelings in England manifest themselves in their own way, and to my mind in a very attractive, though unconventional, way. If an Englishman gets positive proofs of an error he was under, there is no man more ready to confess it, and no man more eager to declare it openly and courageously. The way in which Skobeleff has been judged and appreciated by some English people will always constitute a strong tie, a real sympathy between the two nations.

Immediately after he left Paris—never, alas! to return to the Western world—Skobeleff was in a state of no small uncertainty about the result of his self-imposed mission. His words had been misrepresented, misunderstood. What had been intended to be a warning had been changed into a defiance, almost a manifesto. His attempt to preserve the peace seemed as if it were likely to bring about an immediate collision ; and as a reward for all this, he was now recalled to St. Petersburg to be reprimanded, perhaps dismissed, perhaps banished. But Skobeleff had a brave heart. He was not afraid of sacrificing his great position, his career, if in so doing he could help the Slavonic cause. Had he not over and over again exposed his life, and what can a man do more than that?

He had given a warning to Austria. His voice had been heard. If it was not all, it was something.

The newspapers, with their usual truthfulness, reported some sayings of Skobeleff's during his stay at Vienna. In reality he made there no stay at all, having gone home full speed.

At Warsaw he stayed but a few hours, and availed himself of that short space of time for addressing, at a banquet offered to him, a few friendly words to the Poles. But, *entendons nous*! Friendly feelings, in order to bring positive results, have to be sincere on both sides. It is hopeless to expect a real harmony if all Russia's overtures remain unanswered.

To most English people Poland is still the same Poland as that for which Kosciusko fought. She has changed, and is changing still more. There is a new Poland of which the West knows little. This new Polish party begins to understand the policy of reconciliation, inaugurated by the Marquis of Wielopolski, between the Poles and their Slavonic brethren. The material prosperity of the present Poland has gained for her the name of the 'Belgium of Russia.' It will be no slight triumph for 'the Slavonic idea if it should prove the means of the reunion of two races, whose feuds have dyed crimson so many pages of our common history.'

'I wish the Poles,' he said, 'all the good in the world, and sincerely wish they were at one with us, as all the Slavs should be. Are we not brethren? It is true there is a Russian garrison here; but if it were removed, you would have a German garrison in its place. During the last war, the 16th regiment was under my command. It was officered by Poles, who were amongst the bravest of the brave. From that time I have learned to respect the Poles.'

These were good words bravely spoken. Skobeleff but expressed a sentiment which two hundred years ago had been enlarged upon by a Polish ambassador to the Russian Court. But, of course, this was a new offence. To say a good word to a Pole is held by some as a bad word to the Germans.

According to the 'Czas,' an eminent member of the Polish conservatives recently expressed himself thus to Prince Bismarck:—' If Prussia were to seize any part of Poland, the sympathies of the Poles for the Russians would at once be awakened ; for these sympathies are founded on history, psychology, and political economy. On history, for the Prussians have always been considered as the most violent enemies of our nationality. Upon psychology, for of two evils, one always endures more easily that which is old ; and upon political economy, for everyone knows that of all parts of ancient Poland, those who found themselves in the best economic condition are those which have fallen to the lot of Russia. Polish industry and commerce would be undoubtedly injured by a Prussian annexation and perhaps destroyed.'

But let us return to Skobeleff. Ever since the calumnies published by the French newspapers, Skobeleff had been the mark for innumerable assaults from German sources. His name was mixed in popular rhymes with contemptuous epithets, no attempt was spared to injure his position and his reputation. After leaving Warsaw he immediately went to the Minister of War, the Minister of the Interior, and thus was received by the Emperor. His Majesty is all for peace, but the Russian Emperor understands Russian feelings. Skobeleff was heard and was not banished. Since this, however, officers and generals in service have been forbidden to make political speeches.

M. Aksakoff published in the New Year's number of the 'Russ' an account of Skobeleff's 'speech' at Paris which entirely confirms all that I have said. Skobeleff wrote to M. Aksakoff telling him that the 'speech' was in reality never delivered, but was concocted by Camille Farcy,[1] from the statements of

---

[1] Here is the famous forgery which at first I was very loth to reproduce even as such; but as Skobeleff has declared it to be a tissue of fabrication, I give it in a footnote:—

'I need hardly tell you, my friends, how deeply I am moved by the warm manifestations you have indulged in. I assure you that it is true happiness to me to see around me the youthful representatives of Serbia—of that nation which was the first to raise the standard of Slav liberties in the East, which is the birthright of the Slavs. It is my duty to speak to you frankly. I shall not shrink from that duty. I am bound to tell you the reason why Russia is not always equal to the discharge of her patriotic duties in general, and to the fulfilment of her mission as a Slav Power in particular. It is because at home as well as abroad Russia has foreign influences to contend against. We are not the masters in our own house. Yes, the foreigner is everywhere and everything in Russia. His hand is in all our affairs. We are dupes of his policy, victims to his intrigues, slaves to his strength; and from his baneful influence we can only be delivered by the sword. And shall I tell you the name of that intriguing intruder —of that oppressor of Russians and Slavs? You all know him. It is the author of the "Drang nach Osten." It is the German. I repeat

the students, pieced out by all the ingenuity and talent at the command of the 'French press.' It contained much that General Skobeleff said, but in a greatly exaggerated form, and with considerable additions. When the General, on reading this production in the paper, went down to one of the best offices to remonstrate, he was entreated not to deny the words attributed to him—words which had already spread like wildfire, and awakened the dormant patriotism of France. General Skobeleff allowed himself to be persuaded, and afterwards received the thanks of M. Gambetta himself, who said:—'The speech has already done great good; it has filled all hearts with patriotic ardour, and rouses hopes of a Franco-Russian alliance. *Cela a pris comme une trainée de poudre.* Look at these telegrams I have just received from Havre and Marseilles! The fleet and army are wild with enthusiasm; but I warn you that in my paper I shall have to condemn the want of tact shown by General Skobeleff, out of political caution, and so as not to appear a party to its utterance.' M. Gambetta further spoke of his efforts to

it, and entreat you never to forget it—the German is the enemy. A struggle is inevitable between the Teuton and the Slav. It cannot be long deferred. It will be long, sanguinary, and terrible, but I entertain the faith that it will culminate in the victory of the Slav. It is quite natural that you should be anxious to know how matters stand, since your kith and kin are even now shedding their blood. I will not say much, but I can assure you that if any one ventures to touch the States recognised by European treaties, such as Serbia and Montenegro, you shall not be left to fight alone. Once more I thank you, and if fate wills it, may we meet again on the battle-field, shoulder to shoulder against the common enemy!'

obtain a revision of the Constitution, to raise up a strong power in France, and of the value of the Franco-Russian alliance, saying, amongst other things, 'Thank God that you have no Parliament; if you had one, you would go on talking for over a hundred years without doing anything.'

M. Aksakoff says: 'If Gambetta's enemy was "the German"—the cause of the fall of France—Skobeleff's actual enemy was, not the German, but the Austrian; only the German of the Berlin Congress, the supporter of Austrian aggression upon Slavonic liberties, and the enemy of Russian nationalism was disliked. The Austro-German alliance at that time was represented by the press infinitely more close than it proves to be.'

CHAPTER IV.

RUSSIA AND GERMANY.

Lord Beaconsfield on the Berlin Treaty—His declaration repeated by Skobeleff—His sentiments towards Germany—Russian distrust of Republican France—'We cannot go hand in hand'—Panslavism not hostile to Germany—Identity of Russian and English policy—'Hands off,' and no entangling alliances—Russia's foreign policy—Circular of M. de Giers—The Dantzig interview—Moscow—The German alliance—M. Katkoff on German policy at the Berlin Congress.

IT is odd what a difference it makes whether the same sentiment is uttered by one man or by another. Lord Beaconsfield, when the laurels of peace with honour had not yet withered on his brow, used language almost the same as Skobeleff, and was applauded in Austria as if he were the guardian angel of the peace of Europe. 'I can say,' the noble Lord declared, ' that it is the policy and determination of Her Majesty's Government that the Treaty of Berlin shall be carried out in spirit and to the letter, and believing that the settlement of Berlin expressed in the treaty is one that will advance the progress and civilisation of the world, and that it includes provisions admirably adapted to secure peace and the maintenance of peace, Her Majesty's Government, if necessary, will appeal with confidence to the people of this country to support them in maintaining to the letter, and the complete spirit, the Treaty of Berlin with all their energy and all their resources.'[1]

Now what was the crime committed in Paris by Skobeleff? All that he meant to say, and indeed all that he said, was that, unless that very treaty, so emphatically praised by Lord Beaconsfield, was observed in letter and in spirit, Russia would be forced to draw her sword.

'So there was actually no aggressive attack on Germany?' asked I of the General, soon after his return to Russia. 'Certainly not,' replied he. 'It is surely no great offence to Germany to demand that the treaty drawn up under the presidency of Prince Bismark and signed at Berlin should not be treated as waste paper? It seemed at one time as if Germany intended to attack us, and only in that case would I ever recommend such a war.'

Without boasting of being a very sharp observer, I think I may say that I know my countrymen pretty well. They understand present Germany much better than present France. Russians, with their simple, untheatrical ways, have in their souls an altar to worship, a God to obey. There is a passionate tendency to self-sacrifice, to generous devotion, which, when wrongly directed, can be very dangerous, no doubt. But France, as she is now, is too 'advanced' for us; her crucifix is destroyed; her idols are too prosaic. Her absorbing care for the 'Bourse'; her indifference to foreign questions; her peculiar

[1] November 9, 1878.

way of understanding patriotism, and what constitutes the happiness of a country, are the very extremes of Russian views and feelings. In fact, knowing some Frenchmen as I do, and seeing how deeply they regret the reigning tendencies of their country, I feel sure that some day or other, in view of some great cataclysm, France will have to return to her past unpractical times, when she was actually one of the guides of civilisation, and then we both will use the same language. But what is our mutual position now? What can we expect from her? She would perhaps become our ally in case of a war with Germany; but is that all we want from a friendly ally? How does her sympathy to Russia manifest itself? The German Emperor, effusively and publicly, in black or white, spoke of his *gratitude* to our late Emperor, insisted upon friendship with Russia, and though it 'were only words,' some words will always have a meaning and an importance, especially when facts support them. Our alliance with Germany has lasted for more than a hundred years. That is a good, solid fact. Her policy, her Government are known. France yesterday meant M. Gambetta; to-day M. Grévy; to-morrow, perhaps, M. Clémenceau, if not M. Rochefort. . . . No! We cannot go hand in hand. The gulf is yet too great.

As to Germany, whose unity we assisted materially, as was recognised by the Emperor-King in his telegrams, what do we ask from her? Some Slavs of Prussia are Germanised too completely for us to designate their place in the brotherhood of the Slavonic race. Of the subjects of the German Emperor, excepting a hundred thousand Lusatians in Saxony and Silesia, the only Slavs are the Poles of Posen, who are almost as hostile to Russia as they are to their own Government. We can hardly for the sake of a mere handful, daily growing smaller as the process of Germanisation advances, quarrel with a staunch ally of 120 years' standing. Panslavism that defends the rights of the Slavs recognises the rights of non-Slavonic peoples to similar liberties. Look at Finland. The Fins have enjoyed, and still enjoy, the local independence and autonomy which we ask for the Slavs in other States. They have their own laws, their own institutions, their own customs; their own Church, their own Parliament, their own coinage, their own language. In the Baltic provinces the German element is stronger and has more power than it is entitled to by its numbers, for the lower classes do not belong to that nationality, which is the cause of the troubles the German nobility have with their peasants. But agrarian agitation does not mean Russification.

It was remarked the other day by somebody who evidently did not know much what he was writing about, that I was mistaken in remarking on the great similarity between the foreign policy of Russian Slavophils and English Liberals. I was, perhaps, wrong. Their policy is not similar, it is the same; although, perhaps, Russians are more altruistic than the English. We both strive for the independence and autonomy of subject races ;—the only subject races left in Europe are Slavonic. Italians, Magyars — partly Greeks are free. The Slavs alone await their deliverance. The Slavophils of Moscow adopt with fervour Mr. Gladstone's watchword, 'Hands off!' It is the motto of our policy in the East. The identity goes even further—it extends also to means. Everyone knows the familiar Liberal formula : 'Friendship with all ; alliance with none.' England departed from it in Egypt in 1879, with results not altogether satisfactory to anyone—least of all to the two allies. We share English views in respect of these entangling engagements. 'Russia,' said M. Katkoff, the editor of the 'Moscow Gazette,' 'has no need of alliances, not even though they be triple. The more she preserves her liberty of action the more powerful will be her international position, the more surely guaranteed will be the national character of her policy. A firm and exclusive alliance for a definite end has always resulted in the sacrifice of her own interests for the benefit of others. The national policy of Russia has never been, and can never be, of an aggressive character, menacing to the peace of Europe. Russia will enter into no coalition against any of her neighbours, and will preserve terms of friendship with all. Such a course will constitute the surest guarantee for the European equilibrium.'[1]

[1] Moscow $\frac{\text{July 30}}{\text{August 11}}$, 1881.

M. Katkoff is a man whose voice carries a great weight. But we have a still better authority. What has been the history of the present reign? I need not refer to the reign of the late Emperor. Of his attitude to Germany there never was any doubt. The actual Emperor is, as we are proud to say, the truest representative of his people, and of his race. But what has been his course since he ascended the throne? The principles of his foreign policy were laid down in the circular issued by M. de Giers immediately after his accession. The despatch is as follows:—

Despatch of M. de Giers, dated March $\frac{4}{16}$, 1881.

The foreign policy of the Emperor will be entirely pacific. Russia will remain faithful to her friends; she will unchangeably preserve the sentiments consecrated by tradition, and will at the same time reciprocate the friendliness of all States by a similar attitude, while maintaining the position to which she is entitled among the Powers, and assuring the maintenance of the political equilibrium. In accordance with her interests, Russia will not deviate from her mission, in common with other Governments, of protecting the general peace, based upon respect for rights and treaties. Above all, Russia has to care for herself, and only the duty of protecting her honour and security can divert her attention from the work of internal development. Our august monarch will endeavour to strengthen the power and advance the welfare of Russia, and secure her prosperity without detriment to others. These are the principles by which the policy of the Emperor will invariably be guided.

What was the first visit paid by the Emperor to any of his neighbours? That remarkable visit to Dantzig—to which Prince Bismarck was specially invited—surely cannot have been forgotten so soon, even in England, by those who pretend to follow political events.

There is no need to enter into speculations concerning that interview. To quote the official circular, 'The ties of near relationship and of traditional friendship which unite the two sovereigns suffice to explain the motive, and to define the character of this interview.' As the 'Journal de St. Pétersbourg' remarked, 'the meeting was significant indeed. The Emperor could not have given a greater proof of his fidelity to the traditional friendship of his Empire, and of his family, than by hastening to embrace the friend and ally of his august father.' 'The welcome,' again to quote the official circular, 'which our august master had received at Dantzig has entirely corresponded to the sentiments which animate his Majesty, and has testified once more to the stability of the relations happily established between the two countries in their reciprocal interests, as well as in that of the general peace.' Even the official papers of Vienna were good enough to remark that the interview entirely put an end to the groundless fears inspired by 'Panslavism.' The waste-paper basket of Pesth—for the 'Egyetertes,' unlike your 'Globe,' did not even stand in need of the friendly services of Mr. Marvin—revealed two despatches, the authenticity of which has never been seriously disputed. In the first, our Emperor telegraphed to the Emperor-King: 'I have been very happy to meet again the Emperor Wilhelm, the revered friend to whom we are attached by the common bond of the most intense affection.' The second is a despatch from Count Kalnoky, who had not then been promoted to the portfolio of Count Haymerle. In it the Austrian Ambassador records some conversation of M. de Giers, to the effect that 'The Emperor Alexander has returned from Dantzig with an increased sense of tranquillity and contentment. There was no question of foreign politics calculated to inspire any anxiety. By his journey the Tzar has manifested to all Russia his intention of following a conservative and peaceful policy.' That Dantzig interview indicated a policy from which Russia has not departed, and had no ground for departing. The conquests for which she longs are the triumphs of peace.

Skobeleff's declarations startled Europe, but although they gave every one a nervous shock, left the peace of the Continent on a firmer foundation. Skobeleff followed the national views; he incarnated them almost involuntarily, but he never was the chief of the Slavophil party, and his authority on questions of policy was but small compared with that of such men as M. Katkoff and M. Aksakoff. None of the recognised exponents of the Slavophil party have ever expressed any hostility to Germany, though both would protest in case of German encroachments upon Russian individuality or interests of any kind. In their frank, outspoken way they have objected to the Germanisation of Slavonic peoples, but to the German Empire they have expressed no hatred. In this they represent alike the policy of the Court and the sentiments of the nation. The extent to which the opposite belief has spread is really matter for surprise. But a belief is not necessarily true because many are deluded, and facts cannot be altered by the vote of a majority.

Almost immediately after Skobeleff's speech in Paris there appeared in a St. Petersburg paper, the 'Novoé Vrémya,' an interesting description of what happened to M. Souvorine, the editor of that paper. Desiring to recover his moral tone, says he, he went to Moscow, to the true centre of Russian life, where the national sentiment, strong and serene, contrasts so strangely with the feverish and vacillating views of the Petersburgers. When in the railway carriage he met a Moscovite, a man of influence and of importance, whose business kept him *en rapport* with the citizens of both capitals. When they were talking the Moscovite let fall the words 'German alliance.'

'What!' exclaimed the editor, 'are you not a Moscovite?'

'Certainly,' replied the other.

'And you are in favour of the alliance with the German?'

'Not with the German, but with Germany, which

has a different meaning. What disputes have we with the Empire, with the German nation? None. I am not speaking of a passionate devotion of one country to another; but we can testify for her respect and consideration, and we have a right to expect from her consideration and respect in return. We are equals in strength, and when equals in strength go to war with each other, they usually contend in vain, while their neighbours *exploit* the conflict to their own profit.'

Views of that kind are often expressed in Russia from persons belonging to all stages of life and position.

Shortly after the Skobeleff incident the birthday of the Emperor of Germany occurred, and, as usual, our Emperor telegraphed to his ally his cordial congratulations. I cannot illustrate better the real feelings of the much-abused national Moscow party at the very time when Skobeleff was supposed to have set the world on fire by his anti-German speeches, than by translating here the leading article on the Emperor William's birthday, which appeared in the 'Moscow Gazette' of March $\frac{11}{23}$, 1882, and which was written by M. Katkoff himself.

Moscow, March 11*th* (*O.S.*), 1882.

An event took place yesterday which ought to suffice to silence all rumours of a supposed coldness between Russia and Germany, and consequently of a danger which was supposed to imperil the peace of Europe. Yesterday, March $\frac{10}{22}$, was celebrated the eighty-fifth birthday of the Emperor William, and the congratulations offered to the old hero and Sovereign, the creator of a united and powerful Germany, tendered by Russia in the person of her ruler, witnessed to the fact that the ancient bonds of friendship existing between the two Powers were in no wise weakened, that the relations between them had undergone no change, and that no danger threatening the peace of Europe had arisen either on the part of Russia or on the part of Germany. Nothing but a spirit of downright falsehood could bring one to affirm that Russia stands in need of an active policy and has in contemplation warlike designs. For the same reason there is no ground for anxiety that a quarrel with Russia is a necessity for Germany. On the contrary, one and the other, as history testifies, stand in need of mutual goodwill, friendship, and union. It is only an inflammatory political want of good faith, amounting to absolute mendacity, which is capable of affirming, as was done not long ago in a Petersburg print, that Germany felt herself in some measure thwarted and confined by Russia and injured by her in view of its policy. Nowhere have Prussia and Germany in general met with good will and co-operation more sincere and advantageous than in the policy of Russia. We opine—we have reason to do so—that we on our side could look with confidence for hearty co-operation on the part of our neighbour, if we showed ourselves anxious to secure it. The fact is, that Prussia follows at all times, with wisdom and foresight, the exigencies of her national policy; she knows well what is to her advantage and detriment, she knows what she is desirous of. We ourselves, unfortunately, have not always known our own mind, and have sometimes wished for what did not coincide with our true interests. Just relations between individuals, and still more between states, demand on both sides a healthy and constraining conviction of mutual efforts and mutual aspirations.

In Russian circles there still remains a feeling of dissatisfaction grounded on the stand taken by Germany both before and after the recent war. How many envenomed reproaches aimed at the 'honest broker' have appeared in our papers, who has been accused of taking a side adverse to Russian interests. But history has not yet had her say on this matter, and justice demands that these reproaches should be referred, not to others, but to ourselves. We have no right to demand of the Minister of a foreign State, although in intimate alliance with ourselves, that he should feel, think, and act with a view to our interests, divine these interests, point the way to their fulfilment, and make his action chime in with our own. And yet—shall we be believed by the Russian public?—in point of fact the German Chancellor, while intent on the interests of his own country, was urging us at that very time to have an eye to our own. Prince Bismarck spared no pains to come to some understanding with us, such as should subserve mutual interests; but we, with no less persistency, with an obstinacy worthy of a better cause, turned a deaf ear to his offers, only giving way on the very eve of events of the greatest moment, in which our interests were so intimately bound up, and which were destined to cost us such losses and so much blood. Having allowed ourselves to be drawn into the Eastern war, which arose without our co-operation, and having entered upon a war of world-wide significance, it did not occur to us to take any measures to make our national interests harmonise with the policy of the only Power in alliance with ourselves. It were impossible to deny that our diplomacy on this occasion was a blind one, and could find no support in popular sentiment and feelings at home. From the very first moment, when the bloody banner of the Eastern Question unfolded itself on the horizon, the 'Moscow Gazette' instantly and unceasingly encouraged and exhorted our Government to enter into an understanding with Germany. The leader of German policy, both publicly and in private communications on this subject, addressed to our Foreign Minister, insisted that Germany had no interests in the East, and that here she was prepared to accord to Russia perfect freedom of action, provided only that German interests did not suffer. 'Donnant donnant,' such is the line of action followed by Powers in their mutual relations, and on which alone a friendly feeling can be established between them.

But if the German Chancellor found not so much as one German interest in Constantinople, we on our part—can it be believed?—before the outbreak of the war in the East imagined that we had an important Russian interest in Rome, in the Vatican! This is the literal truth. It was this circumstance which deterred us from coming to an understanding with Germany, at that time engaged in the 'Kulturkampf' with the Vatican. We found that that war interfered with freedom of conscience, and were not prepared on this account to side with Bismarck.

And thus, not the cunning machinations of the 'honest broker,' but our care for the Russian interests bound up with those of the Papal Curia, and our dread of disturbing the balance of power in Europe—this was why during the war we were obliged to look around on all sides; this was why our armies did not occupy Constantinople for a time; this is the reason why in Berlin we had to stand at the bar of the accused. . . .

Ergo no one but ourselves is to be accused if our affairs in the East did not take a regular turn in accordance with our interests. And if, at this present time, matters do not take such a turn as appears to ourselves to best subserve our own policy, we can take comfort in the thought that in the Vatican all goes well. . . .

Whatever turn things may take, we believe in Russia and in God. We do not doubt that, whatever may betide, circumstances will lead onwards either by a straight or circuitous route, on this side or on that, to the triumph of those interests in which lies hidden a power destined to play a leading part in the history of mankind.

I hardly think that justifies the accusation so frequently brought against the Moscovites, that we are Germanophobes. Fortunately, there is no reason why we should be enemies; on the contrary, all our reasons are in the other direction.

This is luckily also the conviction of Prince Bismarck, whose declaration in the Reichstag, that 'Germany, having been connected with Russia for many years, by the ties of a sincere and mutually profitable alliance, he for one would think twice before giving up the friendship of so great and powerful a State without real necessity.'

That 'real necessity' has not arisen, and is not likely to arise.

CHAPTER V.

RUSSIA AND AUSTRIA.

Austria 'only a Government'—Hostile to Slavs—Not necessarily an enemy—Possible alliance with Slavophils—Count Taafe's policy—Austria's only safety—Bad state of the occupied provinces—The Great Powers on trial in the East—Collective Europe found wanting—France in Tunis—England in Egypt—Austria in Bosnia—Russia in Bulgaria—Prince Alexander and the Constitution—The Russian secret—An anti-Slavonic policy treason to Austria.

PRINCE GORTCHAKOFF wittily observed one day, 'Austria is not a nation; she is not even a State; she is only a Government.' There is indeed no Austrian language, no Austrian literature, no Austrian Church. There are Hungarians, there are Germans, there are Slavs, there are Italians, there are Jews (the latter more numerous than supposed), who serve the House of Hapsburg, but there are no actual Austrians.

How is it then, that when you ask a patriot Slav living in that geographical combination called by courtesy 'Austria,' what his nationality is, he invariably says, 'I am a Slav belonging to Austria'? How is it, on the other hand, that when you ask a Slav who identifies himself with the highest spheres of Austrian government, he emphatically declares himself 'an Austrian'? I could give several names to support that statement. I remember a Slavonic

Count, a general, attending the Court, whose name was well connected with the history of one of the Slavonic countries. I asked him what nationality he belonged to, and, suggesting a possible thing, added, 'Are you not a Slav?' 'Oh, no,' he exclaimed, with an expression of horror which amused and rather disgusted me. ' I am an Austrian, and have nothing to do with that *engeance'* (with that brood). Now 'Austrians,' as a rule, are very well-mannered, having all the ways of men of the world. To utter such an expression, to speak with that vehemence to a Russian woman, at the Russian Embassy, was only possible in a state of excitement.

Another remark. How is it that Austria is so deeply detested in all the Slavonic countries, belonging and not belonging to her? The Austrian Emperor, the head of the Hapsburgs, is a very good, cultivated man; perhaps weak, perhaps unable to grasp once for all an energetic policy and follow it out; but whenever he is discussed as a separate character, he is rather liked. Still, there it is—'Austrians' were hated by all who came into contact with that Power. Turkish pashas were not more dreaded in Bosnia and in all Slavonic lands than, up to the other day, Austrian officials were. How is this? What constituted an Austrian official? First of all, and above all, hatred to all that was Slav; hatred to all who could sympathise with the Slavs; still more so to those who could help them. Therefore, all the Slavs had to become renegades to their country, to their traditions, to their language; and thus to do exactly what Turkish pashas of Christian origin have to do. The latter ones, though officially they are not obliged to give up their creed, do so in reality. During the last Turkish war, pashas of Christian communities were as cruel, if not worse, to their co-religionists than the actual Mussulmans.

What is it, then, that is '*hateful*' (yes, I maintain the expression, though I know I shall be blamed for it)? What is hateful in 'Austria'? It is *her* hatred, her injustice, her cruelty; the persecution of the Slavs who object to become renegades!

Take away that systematic persecution of the Slavonic countries, and that vast congregation of races which make up Austria and Hungary, and there will exist no more unfriendly feeling in any Slav, be he Russian or Bosniak, be he Eastern-Churchman or any other churchman you like. That hatred of the Austrian officials towards a race who were supposed to remain always 'ignored and oppressed' was a crime and a mistake. Now, since there seems to be a slight hope of improvement, a slight attempt to do justice to the Slavs, there may also spring up a friendliness between the Russian nation and the 'piebald conglomeration.'

And how absurd, how groundless, how impolitic was that systematic persecution of the Slavs! If, in the vast 'conglomeration' of races which make up Austro-Hungary, you subtract the Magyars and the Jews on one hand and the Slavs on the other, there will remain but a meagre residuum of Germans, with whom alone it might be supposed that Russians could have grounds for dislike.

But, as I tried to show in the previous chapter, there is no blood-feud between Germans and Slavs. To retain his own customs, his own views, his own civilisation, and his own language, is a desire just as legitimate in a German as in a Slav.

Not only Slavophilism, but even Panslavism—the latter in some points differing from the first—is no danger to Austro-Hungary, if Austrian statesmen were less guided by morbid feelings of hatred than by just, impartial statesmanship. And, at all events, it is not too late, fortunately, to transform Panslavism from a possible hostile force into a friendly ally. It is still easier for the Austrian Government to transform the Russian Slavophils into allies. What do we, the Russian Slavophils, ask from the Austrian Government? We wish to see our brethren happy, unpersecuted. We wish that they may have the opportunity to act according to their own ideas, that they may have their language, their own schools, their churches, even their parliaments if they should want them (which, however, according to Russian views, would be greatly to be regretted). In one word, that the Slavs should be allowed to live their own life without being molested in their rights either as Slavs or as Christians.

The Slavophils are the well-wishers of the Slavs;

but they reject Panslavism in the sense of aggressive Pangermanism. The difference between these two ideas is extremely well described by M. Louis Leger. M. Leger's works on the Slavs deserve to be studied not only by foreigners, but by Russians as well.

'The Slavs,' says M. Leger in his 'Études Slaves,' 'claim the attention and the sympathies of Russia.' Further on he accuses my countrymen of having been so slow in listening to the voice of their brethren. Russia never had the need of the Slavs which the Slavs had of her.

Now, if the House of Hapsburg consented to be just towards her Slavonic nationalities, it naturally would have all the Slavophils of Russia as allies. As long as Lord Beaconsfield's Government was in power, Austria was blind to her true rôle. When Lord Salisbury was playing the part of Herald Angel and announcing, as 'good tidings of great joy,' that Austria had accepted the post of gaoler of the Slav nationalities, it was not surprising that the Camarilla at Vienna and Pesth mistook the path of safety. The English elections first made her doubt the wisdom of this course. Skobeleff's speech and the rising in the Balkans deepened that doubt into a certainty. But it is a great thing that they should try to enter the right road.

On the day when Count Taafe proclaimed that it was necessary for Austria, even for Austria, to recognise the historic rights of nationalities, the Slavs began to hear a friendly and a rational voice—began to hope for a better future. The establishment of the Tchèque University at Prague gave point to Ministerial declarations, and, according to the comment of a passionate Germaniser, 'brought to a close the German period of the history of Austria'—if that measure does not remain, of course, an isolated fact; if it does not remain an exception proving the general rule.

Count Taafe—poor Count Taafe!—one sees he is embarrassed and afraid of everything, even the accomplishment of a duty. Count Taafe denies that the Government wished to make of Austria a Slavonic State. Just imagine such a denial being needed three years ago! According to him, Austria should neither be a Slavonic nor a German State, but a centre of action between different nationalities, all equal in law, and all of which accept no other limit for the exercise of its rights than those dictated by the necessities of the commonwealth. 'Austria,' said Hegel, 'is not a nation, it is an empire.' If it is a federated empire it may survive, but if it represents the ascendency of a minority it is doomed.

The reduction of the electoral franchise which has recently been effected secures the extinction of the unjust ascendency of the German element in the Cisleithanians of Austria. Hitherto the high suffrage has excluded largely the Slavonic majority from exercising its legal full share in the elections. Now that the lower middle class and the peasants have entered the pale of the constitution—to use the English phrase—German domination is dead and buried. Such, at least, is the opinion of acute observers at Vienna. I do not pretend to understand all these details. I only report that such is believed by people more versed in constitutional *chinoiseries* than I, to be the probable result of the new electoral law.

The occupation of Bosnia and Herzegovina was a touchstone of Austrian sincerity, or rather, as to how far she has opened her eyes to facts. Preparations were made to occupy these provinces in 1877, when Count Andrassy was solemnly protesting that such a step was never contemplated by the Austrian Government. They were occupied under a European mandate in 1878, and so far the results have not been brilliant. And why have they not been brilliant? Because Austria forgot that her only safety lay in conciliating the Slavs.

It is not unkindness to Austria to point this out. If she had recognised her provinces, not as a farm to be cropped, but as a state to be developed, she would have reaped a richer harvest. It is because she turned loose against the unhappy Slavs the dregs of her officials, the Jewish locusts and her Jesuit agents, that her military expenses in the occupied provinces amounted this year alone to 3,000,000*l*. A bad bargain, truly, for the wise men of Vienna. She might have saved that, to say nothing of many men and much hatred, if she had taken counsel with the majority of her subjects and left Slavs to govern Slavs.

The evil influence of the Beaconsfield period could not be so easily shaken off. Austria—we must not forget—went into Bosnia avowedly to 'crush the Slavonic serpent.' She tried to do so, by leaning first on the Turks and then on the Jesuits. What has been the result? I will not quote from a Russian or a Slavonic source. I will refer to the correspondent of the 'Times,' who, after travelling this autumn through the occupied province, thus describes the state of things which he found there:

Before the Austrians occupied Bosnia, there was a strong Austrian party here even among the Mahomedans. It is extremely doubtful whether an Austrian party now exists even among the natives. Whatever may be their religious differences, all creeds seem as one in their dislike of the Austrian occupation. The trade with Turkey is cut off, but Bosnian goods are still taxed on entering Austria. The commercial advantages derived from Austrian administration are not obvious. The same remark may be made about Austrian law, Austrian police, and Austrian officialism in Bosnia. Turkish law has become a byword in Europe, yet the Bosnians look back on it almost with regret. Few good officials come to Bosnia. This beautiful country is the Botany Bay of Austrian officials. Before the revolt of 1875 Bosnia was one of the safest countries in Europe to travel in. It is now one of the most unsafe. Travelling is more dangerous under Austrian than it was under Turkish rule.[1]

That is not a pleasant state of things, but Austria

[1] *Times*, letter from Serajevo, dated Sept. 29, 1882.

has only herself to blame, as indeed she seems to be slowly discovering. The appointment of M. de Kallay was a sign that the old policy is clearly untenable. There are indications that the statesmen of Austria recognise the impossibility of governing Bosnia from Vienna. The administration is to be localised. The provinces have to be governed from Serajevo. Events will show, however, whether Baron Nikolitch is a true Slav or a Slav renegade, as there are so many among Austrian officials. He is a relative of King Milan of Serbia that is true; but King Milan himself does not seem to be intelligent enough to understand his own interests. Baron Nikolitch may exercise a fatal influence over his Serbian Majesty, and not improve matters. A near future will show what the Baron is and what is to be hoped or dreaded of him.

The agrarian and judicial questions are to be dealt with. A promise is given to improve taxation. Now to promise is one thing, to perform another, especially in certain quarters. But that there should even be a promise of improvement is a step in a good direction, and a proof that the former state of things is becoming intolerable.

It is the truest friendship to call the attention of your friends to evils which may lead to disasters, and Austria's tardy reformation is a tribute to the services of her so-called foes.

Has it ever struck you that all the nations of Europe are on their trial in the East? The Ottoman Empire is being put in liquidation. To each Power has been allotted a portion of Turkish territory to deal with it in its own way. To none has any province been ceded. Nominally, everything is Turkish—in reality nothing. It has been allotted to Russia to shape the destinies of Bulgaria ; to Austria to occupy and administer Bosnia and Herzegovina ; to Europe to reform Macedonia and Armenia ; to France to absorb Tunis ; to England to establish order in Egypt. To each Power a portion, so that all methods may be tried and every experiment made on the Eastern field. It is a great arena, and the task is critical. Which Power is acting the least selfishly? Which is doing most for liberty ; which is working most for the development of self-government among the subject populations?

Let us look at the facts. What has Europe done? That is easily answered. Europe has done nothing. I beg pardon—the European Concert has made representations, has raised its powerful voice ; but nothing else. In Macedonia and Armenia, which Russia most mistakenly abandoned to Europe to be reformed, and protected by all the Powers, nothing has been done. Everything is as bad as ever, or worse. No autonomous institutions have been established. No reforms have been executed. The miserable populations are tortured by their oppressors, and Europe—the very image of impotence—does nothing.

In Tunis, France has absorbed everything. The Bardo Treaty made the Bey a vassal of the

Republic. French soldiers occupy the province, and French ministers, govern it. It is almost a French department. There is no semblance of popular government. Democratic principles, which once were supposed to have made the tour of the world with French soldiers have not crossed the Mediterranean. Instead of liberty, fraternity, and equality, France in Africa establishes usury, stockjobbing, and despotism.

And England? What does England do? She has gone to Egypt, to give Egypt to the Egyptians. Well and good. It is a noble programme, but not an easy one; especially as there are so many voices which suggest another solution.

Austria has occupied and administered Bosnia and Herzegovina. She has established no popular institutions. She has enforced the conscription at the cost of three millions sterling and much bloodshed. Austrian officials govern with the rigour of martinets and the folly of officials. The 'Schwab' has made himself as hated as the 'Tedeschi.' 'They would shoot us through the head,' said an Austrian officer, referring to the Bosnians, 'at the first opportunity.' And why? Because Austria, disregarding the wise counsel of Count Beust, acted on the sinister suggestions of Lord Beaconsfield, and endeavoured to destroy 'Slavonic preponderance in the occupied provinces.' 'The Serbs,' said one of their chief officials, 'are our mortal enemies.'

If they had not been so, they were not to lack reasons for such hostility. Even the national

alphabet was proscribed. The bayonet alone had
to elicit the love and equality of the Serbians, whose
province they were supposed to be administering.
They stamped upon the national sentiment, and there
sprang up thousands of armed men, whose only
thought was to rid themselves of the hated foreigner.
Why? Because the Austrians interfered with their
local institutions, and attempted to Germanise them
with the jackboot and the halter.[1]

Bosnia and the Herzegovina were, in short, to be
governed, not for the Bosnians, but for the Austrians;
that is to say, for the Germans, and Magyars, and
Jews, who were dispatched to stamp on the head of
the Slavonic serpent, and restore order by crushing
the strongest aspirations of the people.

There remains now the province which fell to
the lot of Russia to reorganise. To purchase that
privilege cost us thousands of the best of our sons.

---

[1] English people do not realise how strong, how intense is the love
of nationality among the Slavs. Mr. Arthur Evans, who knows these
lands, is an exception, and his words should not be forgotten. 'Among
the Serbs, the whole being of the people is concentrated in these
aspirations after national unity. The spirit of nationality has become
to them more than a political conviction. It is a religion, almost a
fanaticism. In these regions it has so far crushed religion itself as to
leave it only a secondary place as the humble handmaid of nationality.
. . . No diplomatic jugglery, no constitutional makeshift, no show of
military right, no laws, no police regulations can avail such a government (as that of Austro-Hungary) to crush out a nationality, which
finds the best propaganda, not in Jesuit intrigues, not in an anti-
national system of education and an inspired press, but in a thousand
heroic lays, and on the strings of the Serbian lyre.'—'The Austrian
Counter-Revolution in the Balkans,' *Fortnightly Review*, April, 1880.

Skobeleff alone had 21,000 gallant men killed under his command, and many other commanders sustained also heavy losses. The liberation of Bulgaria cost us sacrifices better worth the name than any entailed by the promenade to Cairo which the gallant General, Lord Wolseley, executed this year. Yet what has Russia taken for herself in Bulgaria? I confess, it is with not a little national pride that I see the difference between our policy in Bulgaria and that of all the other Powers in the East. Russia, yes, 'despotic,' autocratic, 'aggressive' Russia alone among all the other Powers dares to trust solely to moral influences in maintaining her ascendency in the province she has delivered.

I do not pretend that the Garden of Eden may be rediscovered between the Danube and the Balkans, nor is the Bulgarian Constitution destined to usher in the millennium. By no means. The experiment of Bulgaria for the Bulgarians was spoiled before it was fairly begun by the meddling diplomacy of Europe They deprived the principality of the most intelligent of its citizens, and diverted the attention of the Bulgarians from the pacific development of their autonomous institutions to the patriotic duty of working for the liberation of their re-enslaved brethren in Macedonia, and their reunion with their divided brothers in Eastern Roumelia.

It is not for the first time that English diplomacy has been the curse of the oppressed populations in the

East. If our experiment failed, it would be England's fault. Its success would be our own.

Russia asked from the Bulgarians nothing; not even gratitude itself, and there is not a single tie beyond that of gratitude on one side, and fraternal solicitude on the other, uniting the two countries. Russia did not even ask for any recognition of her position as protecting Power. That Bulgaria is under the Russian protectorate is true enough. We freed Bulgaria, and our shields are thrown above the nationality which we delivered. Every Bulgarian knows that in Russia, and Russia alone, can he find a helper, in case Turk or Austrian attempted to rob him of his independence, and that Russia, and Russia alone, will assist him when circumstances permit in re-establishing the unity of his divided country. From other nations he will only receive either abuse or empty compliments. We are his only friends. That establishes Russian influence upon the only solid foundation. If you want to secure the friendship of these little peoples, you cannot do better than leave them alone as much as you can. This is what Russia has done in the part of Turkey confided to her care, and we have no reason to regret the result.

Left to themselves, the Bulgarians drew up a Constitution chiefly modelled by American missionaries, which might have done for the American States, but which was sadly out of place in Bulgaria. However, such was the free will of the people—we respected it, though we thought it a dangerous mistake.

The Constitution did not work well. How could it? But the Prince Alexander, who, by the bye, is not a despotic Russian, but a constitutional German, suspended it for a time, and Russia of course was blamed for that. It was not Russia's doing, but so far as it was wise, it met with our approval.

The ex-Premier of Bulgaria, M. Karaveloff, declared most positively, in the midst of the crisis, that the real instigators of the Prince's action were not Russia, but Austria and Germany. The Prince himself said to the Correspondent of the 'Standard': 'I declare to you, and to Europe most emphatically, that Russia never sought to influence me. Read the constitutional history of Bulgaria for the last two years, and then you will know all.'

The exact facts concerning Russia's share in the late crisis were clearly explained by M. de Giers in a circular which is worth referring to, as showing how Russia acted in a very critical and trying position. M. de Giers recounts how Prince Alexander came to St. Petersburg, and protested that it was impossible to govern with the majority of the Chamber.

Prince Alexander wished to avoid a direct breach of the Constitution. He wished to remain in the path of legality. So he proposed to submit three conditions to the Chamber, which, if rejected, would justify a new appeal to the people. In compliance with the request of the Prince, M. de Giers instructed our Consul-General to use his personal influence with the deputies, to induce them to arrange a *modus vivendi*. If these efforts failed, as they did, and there was an appeal to the people, the position of the Russian Consul-General would become very delicate. 'Our attitude,' wrote he, 'ought to give no colour to the suspicion that we have concocted any anti-constitutional measures, and it is necessary to avoid giving the Radical party any pretext for saying that we are trying to treat Bulgaria as a Russian province. All that the representatives of Russia should do, therefore, was to give the people to understand that, if they were to range themselves at the side of the factious minority, they could no longer count upon the support of the Power whom they regarded as their liberator.'

Considering that England had just intervened in Egypt to establish the Khedive's right to rule independently of his Chamber of Notables, Russia's intervention in the matter was very modest indeed. Russian officials in the service of Bulgaria may have done more—as, for instance, General Ernroth, the Minister of War; but, if so, they acted, not as Russians, but as officers being in the service of the Prince. I do not suppose English officers acting as servants of the Khedive would desert their master because he took a short way of freeing himself from his Notables. English officials, indeed, recently took a leading part in quite another sense, and the rôle of M. Hitrovo was quite liberal compared with that of Sir E. Malet and Sir A. Colvin.

Even this platonic intervention was resented by some in Russia. The 'Novoé Vrémya,' which often supports the Slavophil views in St. Petersburg, wrote on the affairs of Bulgaria very shortly after Skobeleff"s speech : 'Russia ought to avoid interfering in the affairs of the Principality, while watching jealously that no one else shall interfere. She ought, once for all, to renounce a directing rôle with regard to the Bulgarian people, and only to represent the purely moral influence which springs from identity of race. Bulgaria ought to be fully persuaded that Russia desires the complete development of her national element, and will place no restraint on the independence of that development.'

This may seem inconsistent to some with the declaration of M. Katkoff, in the 'Moscow Gazette,' that 'Bulgaria is not a world in itself, but a part of that planetary system of which Russia is the centre of gravity, and the source of light and heat.' In reality the one is the key to the other. If we did not leave the Bulgarians free to develop their destinies in their own way, instead of being attracted to the sun of Russia, she would be repelled. To protect without interfering is the secret of our influence.

And we have not been without our reward. In Serbia, which we liberated long ago, and which for the moment is under an Austrian hand, and in Bulgaria, Russia is regarded as the head of the great

Fatherland. Go into the Slavonic countries, live with the Serbian or Bulgarian peoples, and I defy you to say that the people have any animosity to Russia—to say nothing of the intense hatred which is inspired in Bosnians by Austria, in Tunisians by France, or even, shall I say ? in Egyptians by England. Quite the contrary. You will find that their sentiments to their elder brother, as they call us, are most affectionate. These peoples, the Bulgarians especially, have not yet attained the degree of political development where the theory of ingratitude is become a dogma and a proof of independence and *savoir-faire*. Of this I have experienced a very touching proof in my own family, on the discovery and the burial of the remains of my brother Nicholas, killed in Serbia.[1] This, it may be said, was exceptional. In details, perhaps; but the spirit with which Bulgaria regards Russia is the same as that with which these humble peasants regard the memory of those who sacrificed their life for them.

But let us return to our 'Austrians.' The truth which Russia divined by her instinctive sympathy with the Slavonic heart has at last, however slowly, made its way into the high places of Vienna-Pesth. M. de Kallay, reporting the other day the result of his experience in Bosnia, informed the delegations that he had observed, in the course of his tour through the country, the strong local feeling and patriotism of the natives, which prompted them to desire an

[1] Vide Appendix C.

organisation by which every commune and village would be left as much as possible to manage, quite independently, its own affairs, and to do as it pleased. This was, indeed, not practicable; but the Minister thought this local patriotism, if allowed to develop itself within proper limits, was likely to be a safeguard against agitation prompted from without. That to develop local self-government is the best protection against revolutionising intrigue is the tardy discovery of statesmen. It will soon be patriotic, I suppose, in Austria to recognise that M. Tisza's anti-Slavonic policy was treason to Austria. If so, it will be a curious illustration of the heresy of to-day becoming the truism of to-morrow. Last year I ventured to say, in an English review, the substance of what M. de Kallay is saying to-day. The Government of Vienna-Pesth did me the honour of forbidding the review containing my article to cross the frontier. Scarcely any copies of it reached Serbia. The times have changed, and even Austria has learned to change with them. Skobeleff's noble outbursts of sympathy with his brother Slavs of the Herzegovina has at least done no harm. Nay, may we not say that it has done good, and has compelled this statesman to recognise truths which, until he spoke, were felt only by the Slavs?

I have no intention to pass in elaborate review all the domestic policy of Austria-Hungary. But the persecution of the Ruthenian peasants, the constant pressure brought to bear upon the Serbians, the cordon of forts which they are building around Montenegro, the restless propaganda of the Roman priests amongst Orthodox populations, the war against the Slavonic language, conducted in so many parts of the Dual Kingdom, all show how far Austria is from entering frankly into the path of safety and justice.[1] How slowly and unwillingly Austria is moving in that direction may be imagined by the fact that it is still regarded as treason to the State on the part of the Slavs even to correspond with the Philo-Slavs of the other countries.

The mania of Germanisation still lingers in many places, like snow-wreaths in spring-time, as if to

[1] On this subject I will again quote from Mr. Evans: 'Meanwhile, as if to show the Bosnians and Herzegovinians what they may expect if they find themselves handed over to the tender mercies of the Hungarian half of the Monarchy, the political and intellectual persecution of their kinsmen the Slovacks is being actively proceeded with. The suppression of the Slovack schools and their academy—the Matica Slovenská—and the confiscation, for Magyar propagandist objects, of their literary fund, together with some of the private money of the deprived professors: all this, high-handed and iniquitous as it was, was, it seems, only a foretaste of what the Hungarian "Cultus-Ministerium" had in store for this unfortunate people. Some recently published instructions to official subordinates, issued by Trefort, the Magyar "Minister of Culture" (the same who suppressed the Slovack schools and academy), enjoin the summary dismissal of any Slovack student or teacher in a Hungarian educational establishment who shall presume to join any Slovack club or be a member of the literary society "Zora," denounced by the "Cultus-Minister" as a "Panslavistic committee" (!) In the case of some dozen young men convicted of these heinous offences, and in consequence dismissed from their lyceums, the "Minister of Culture" (who in modern Hungary appears to occupy the place of the Chief Inquisitor) condescends to intervene, with the express object of ruining the young men's prospects for life by prohibiting them from either learning or teaching in any school or college in the kingdom.'—*Pall Mall Gazette*, December 14.

remind us of the winter from which we have just escaped. According to the 'Narodni Listy,' the Commander-in-Chief at Prague has issued an order to the effect that all the volunteers who serve for one year with the army are, in their private intercourse, as well as when on duty, to use the language of the army—namely, German. That is not an order which a Power 'frankly Slavonic' could have issued. Let us hope that such facts are only 'survivals' from bad old times, and will soon become extinct. No doubt Austria is timid. She is so artificial a creation that she shrinks from running any risks which might even endanger her existence. But is it no risk to have a hundred thousand men permanently neutralised by the Bosnian blunder, and to have acute observers like Skobeleff and Lord Derby calculating confidently that Austria need not be feared because most of her troops are Slavs? It was not a Russian but an 'Austrian' newspaper[1] which addressed our Emperor as the natural protector of all the Slavs, and implored him to intervene on behalf of the Slavs of Austria, as he intervened on behalf of the Slavs of the Balkans.

Russia has no intention of doing any such thing, for with Skobeleff's warning written in bold letters before her eyes the statesmen of Austria-Hungary will think twice, and even thrice, before provoking Slavonic sympathies too far.

[1] The *Narodni Listy* of Prague.

CHAPTER VI.

RUSSIA AND ENGLAND.

Skobeleff's admiration for England; but not of Lord Beaconsfield—Sir Henry Rawlinson's Russophobia—Geok Tepé as a *place-d'armes*—A Russian invasion of India—Russia and England in Central Asia—One drawback of party government—Skobeleff's prediction—Russian policy in Egypt.

SKOBELEFF was a great adherent of my favourite dream of the Anglo-Russian alliance. He greatly admired England. 'What a pity,' said he once to me, 'Russia and England know so little of each other! In Asia they could co-operate and work together.' As far as he himself was concerned, he spared no efforts to acquire that knowledge. He was thoroughly master of English classics, and was quite at home in English military works. He spoke English quite fluently, and wrote it also pretty well. One of his letters to me is written in English, and in in it he begged me to give some information on 'Slavophilism' to an American author. Skobeleff was very active, and overloaded with important work; but anybody showing an interest in Russia was sure to find him always ready to oblige, and render all possible service.

I think Mr. Marvin—who really deserves to be known for something else than his exploit with Lord

Salisbury's memorandum—would endorse my present statement. He was equally impressed with the sincerity of Skobeleff's friendliness when he interviewed him at St. Petersburg on the possibility of a Russian invasion of India. 'I consider the Central Asian question,' said he, 'all humbug.' He expressed an earnest desire that it might disappear altogether as a source of difference between the two nations. 'Throughout the whole conversation,' writes Mr. Marvin, 'which Skobeleff carried on with great animation and good-humour, there was no indication whatever at an attempt at plausibility or desire to make an impression. His manner was so simple, so straightforward, and so transparent that it would have carried conviction to an Urquhart or Ashmead Bartlett. I think Skobeleff's words should have a calming effect. The limit I should assign to them is this : that Skobeleff is not the Russian Government, and that his friendly feeling and prudence might not always prevail against that diplomacy which is the curse of every country.'

That Skobeleff spoke of England, at one time, as an enemy is true ; and he did so, as almost every Russian, because England at that time was our enemy. Skobeleff's great career was made in the years during which hostility to Russia was the keynote of English foreign policy. When Lord Beaconsfield was England, England was the enemy of Russia ; as Lord Beaconsfield seemed to distant observers to be England from the time Skobeleff conquered

Y

Khokand till the day when he was dispatched to reduce Geok Tepé, it is not surprising that he occasionally acted and spoke as if he accepted the English Conservative idea of the natural hostility between England and Russia. In the great campaign which established his renown it was England which cynically insisted on undoing Russian work and giving back the Southern Bulgarians for which so many Russians had died, to set them free. For months, while Skobeleff stood guard at the lines of Tchataldja, Russia was expecting at any moment to hear that Lord Beaconsfield had declared war. If France were to threaten to attack England in Egypt, in order to compel the latter to share with her the honours of the campaign, even the imperturbable Lord Wolseley might venture upon remarks anything but friendly to your allies in France. But, how unfair, how ungenerous it would be, to set down the outburst of impatience and of a national and justifiable indignation against the perfidy and baseness of such conduct as sufficient evidence that your general was 'an enemy of France'!

In Mr. Kinnaird Rose's charming paper in the 'Fortnightly Review,' on the 'Russian Bayard,' there occurs the following passage, which is greatly in accord with everything I ever heard him say on the subject:—

In many quarters in the course of the last few weeks it has been said that General Skobeleff was the enemy of England. In no sense do I think was this a truthful description of the man. He was an ardent admirer of England and of English institutions, though he did not believe that the latter were adapted for his own country. It is true that before and after the signature of the Berlin Treaty he bluntly expressed his hatred of the policy of the Beaconsfield Government. This is his exact language as noted at the time. 'Cannot you see how this policy should stir us so? For two years we have deluged this land (Bulgaria) with our blood. Our brothers are slain, our country has made enormous sacrifices, widows mourn, children weep, and fathers lament the loss of promising sons. All this we would have borne with the patience which God gives, had the full freedom which we had won for our brothers in race and religion, in language and faith, been accorded to them. But accursed diplomacy steps in and says, "No; only the smaller half of them shall be free, and the greater number shall be again handed over to the tender mercies of the Turks." You know yourself what the Turks have been, and are, and ever will be; and placing yourself in our position, would you not also be consumed with wrath that our sacrifices are to be in vain, and that the men over whose graves we are now treading should have died for nought?'

The passage in his speech at St. Petersburg, on the anniversary of the capture of Geok Tepé, may be said to conflict with his view. I say that, on the contrary, it confirms it. Skobeleff then refers to an enemy, but that enemy is not England. A Russian could not refer to England as a 'sagacious' and 'talented enemy of the Fatherland.' Sagacity and talent are qualities usually imputed not to nations but to individuals. The 'enemy' of Russia particularised by Skobeleff was Sir Henry Rawlinson;

that he is our enemy he would be the last to deny. Enmity to Russia is written on every page of his book, every line of his essays. It is with him a fixed principle, not an impatient, passing feeling, such as that expressed sometimes by Skobeleff.

The Russophobist theory of the universe is, that England is the Ormuzd and Russia the Ahriman of the Eastern Hemisphere. We have no counterpart to such creatures in Russia. But I must again quote English testimony. 'To speak plainly,' writes Mr. Marvin, after his visit to St. Petersburg, 'there is no Sir Henry Rawlinson, or even the ghost of Sir Henry Rawlinson, in Russia; there exists no Anglophobia in Russia to match the Russophobia in England. This of itself is a striking fact; for, as a Russian officer put it to me—England has certainly done its utmost to make us her bitter enemy; yet, you find us without feeling against her, and desirous of being her friend.'

It is a curious instance of the extent to which Russophobia blinds those who suffer from it, that such an able man as Sir Henry Rawlinson, who so ridiculously exaggerated the facility with which we can approach India in one direction, should by a strange perversity have imagined that our advance was impossible in the direction which Skobeleff proved to be comparatively easy. Seven years ago Sir Henry Rawlinson proved, to his own entire satisfaction, that, to quote Skobeleff's summary of his views, 'the animosity of the Tekkes of Akhal would involve

Russia for many years in enormous expenditure of men and money; and in a war which would render it obligatory on Russia to establish a cordon of forts from the south of Attrek and through the entire Oasis, and from the Attrek to Merv, and that finally, and to crown all, it would undermine the political power of Russia in Central Asia.' What an odd fatality it is that the only place where the Russophobist ventured to believe that he was safe has proved the least secure of all!

The Attrek frontier was the line along which your Central Asians and ours elected to fight out their battle. An English officer, Lieut. Butler, fortified Geok Tepé. Sir Henry Rawlinson declared that Persia must be detached from Russia *coûte qui coûte*. But Skóbeleff stormed the fortifications of Geok Tepé, and M. Zinovieff, our Minister at Teheran, belonging to the actually useful and energetic diplomatists who uphold the standard of Russia with a firm, unfaltering hand, by a very brilliant display of diplomatic ability secured Persia as a friend and ally. The Butlers and Rawlinsons, and *tutti quanti*, were discomfited all along the line. The very fact that the Tekkes, instead of being scattered all over the country, were concentrated in one spot, facilitated Skobeleff's victory. But to make the Russophobist prophecies really ridiculous, Russia did not go to Merv, much less to Herat, and settled the frontier dispute with such moderation as to leave the furthest limit of our territory two hundred miles distant from Sarakhs. We baffled their intrigues, we checkmated English diplomacy, and then we falsified their predictions as to our annexations.

Skobeleff said that the late Emperor, having taken the Akhal Tekke business in hand, fully realised the immense importance of a 'place-d'armes' at the gates of Herat and Afghanistan. No doubt he did. It was important, very important, and if unfortunately Russophobists should once more come into power in England, we shall be better able to hold our own in Central Asia by reason of the establishment of our garrisons in Akhal. On the other hand, if England should want our support for some united action, Russia could offer a more effective hand.

Do we not know—does not everybody know—that one great idea of the Russophobists five years ago was to attack *us* in Central Asia? It is not four years since Sir Henry Rawlinson told us 'Russia must not be left in any uncertainty as to our intentions. She might, indeed, be warned that, if necessary, we were prepared, in self-defence, to support the Turcomans with arms and money, or even to turn the tables on her by encouraging the efforts of the Uzbegs to recover their liberty.' That is to say, Russia was told in 1879 that England contemplated in certain circumstances the raising a rebellion amongst our Central Asian subjects in order to overturn our dominion in Turkestan. If such were England's intentions, openly expressed by a man occupying a high official position, who can blame us for desiring a *place-d'armes* at the gates of Herat and Afghanistan? Was it not a legitimate measure of self-defence? A *place-d'armes*! Was it not Lord Beaconsfield's phrase when he annexed — I beg pardon — occupied a certain island named Cyprus? Yet we never made him understand, in Sir Henry Rawlinson's fashion, that we proposed to invade Asiatic Turkey; but he deemed it necessary to seize that island in order to defend the Turkish frontier, distant I do not know how many hundreds of miles. Why should we not also have a shelter for our arms to defend our own frontier against a possible enemy coming from the gates of Herat and Afghanistan? Skobeleff, not being in the least mad, never really thought of attacking India from Geok Tepé. But he used to tease a little English Correspondents during the Bulgarian campaign by discussing plans of campaign against India. But when he talked seriously to Mr. Marvin about such a project, he expressed himself in exactly the same sense as all Russians generally do except when indulging in practical jokes. When discussing this question three years ago, I said that the invasion of India was barred by two words — transport and commissariat. In exactly the same sense spoke Skobeleff to his inquisitive interviewer.

'As to a Russian invasion of India' [General Skobeleff said], 'I do not think it would be feasible. I do not understand military men in England writing in the "Army and Navy Gazette," which I read, of a Russian invasion of

India. I should not like to be commander of such an expedition. The difficulties would be enormous. To subjugate Akhal we only had 5,000 men, and needed 20,000 camels. To get that transport we had to send to Orenburg, to Khiva, Bokhara, and to Mangishlak for camels. The trouble was enormous. To invade India we should need 150,000 troops; 60,000 to enter India with, and 90,000 to guard the communications. If 5,000 men needed 20,000 camels, what would 150,000 need? And where could we get the transport? We should require vast supplies, for Afghanistan is a poor country, and could not feed 60,000 men, and we should have to fight the Afghans as well as you.'

On my urging that the Afghans might be tempted by the bribe of the spoliation of India to side with the Russians, he said: 'I doubt it. To whom could we offer the bribe? If we bribed one Sirdar, you would bribe another. If we offered one rouble, you would offer two; if we offered two, you would offer five—you would beat us in this. No, the Afghans would fight us as readily as they fought you.'

'But if you occupied Khorassan beforehand and made it a second Caucasus?'

'Why should we occupy Khorassan? We should only get provisions from the province, and we could get them as it is. We derive a revenue from Khorassan now, by its trade with Nijni Novgorod; but we should lose this if we occupied it. I do not believe Russia would ever occupy Khorassan. I think the new frontier will be permanent. Do you know' [here he rose and spoke with vehemence, regarding me with a smile] 'I consider the Central Asia question all humbug.'

'But in regard to the possibility of invading India, General Soboloff expressed to me a clear opinion on Monday that Russia could march an army to India if she chose.'

'That was diplomacy,' replied Skobeleff; 'of course it is possible—all things are possible to a good general; but I should not like to undertake the task, and I do not think Russia would. Of course, if you enraged Russia: if, by your policy, you excited her, if you made her wild—that is the word—we might attempt it, even in spite of all the difficulties. For my part I would only make a demonstration against India, but I would fight you at Herat. I was very much interested during your war whether you would occupy Herat or not. It would have been a mistake if you had done so. It would be difficult to march an army from the Caspian to Herat to fight you there, but we should be tempted to do it in the event of a war.'

There ought not to be a war; but we have read and heard too much of Russophobia for Russia ever to be off her guard. We wish to be friends; with Mr. Gladstone's Ministry we rejoice to believe friendship is possible; but even Mr. Gladstone has been compelled (in 1874) to resign, and with England's constitutional machinery a Lord Beaconsfield or a Lord Salisbury is always possible. Russia has often been on friendly terms with the Conservative party in England; but since Conservatism has construed patriotism to mean Russophobia, that would seem to be somewhat difficult, at least until they change their minds.

The fear of a Russian invasion in India reminds me of the people, 'half-lunatic and half-designing,' who, as Mr. Bright says, 'got up in the year 1836 a panic about the invasion of the English shores from Russia, from the Baltic through the Sound. The Baltic is shut up for about half the year by frost. What happened during the Russian War when the English fleet went into the Baltic? The Russian fleet did not go out of it, because it could not, but took shelter behind the fortifications which had been erected at Sveaborg and Cronstadt. They did not come out to meet the English ships, and the English ships did not dare attack them within those formidable defences; and yet forty years ago we were told that we were to have an invasion of this country by Russia, and the government of that day actually added on the strength of this panic 5,000 men to the roll of the British navy. Wherever there is the slightest panic of any matter of this kind these absurd and extravagant acts are committed.'

Of course, if the imaginary Russian aggression in India is a good pretext for augmenting the roll of the British army—and for misleading once more the credulity of the English public—let it be used. It can do no harm to Russia, though it will not strengthen much the authority, either of the English press or the so-called 'public opinion,' however deified and worshipped it may be in this country.

'I consider the Central Asian question all humbug.' How I like that frank, outspoken word of Skobeleff's! 'Humbug,' indeed, it is; and it would have been well for us, as for Englishmen, and well for the world, if these great piles of blue-books relating to the Russian advance in Central Asia had never been printed—or, better still, if these despatches had never been written.

What right has England to say what we shall do or what we shall not do, in any part of the world outside her own dominions? We are the only judges of our own duties and interests, as England is the only judge of her own. If it pleases her to annex territory in Southern Asia, we make no remonstrances, utter no protests, demand no assurances. Why should the St. James's Cabinet do otherwise, when we make, voluntarily or involuntarily, annexations in Central Asia?

Is it not time to be done with all these absurd protestations that no war is to be made in Central Asia unless by the good pleasure of Downing Street? England is a great Power with great Asiatic possessions. Russia is a great Power, also with great Asiatic possessions. Why should either of them be perpetually giving explanations and assurances to the other? Countries as well as separate individuals speak and write too much, far too much. Is it because silence is too aristocratic for our democratic days? In good old times people exchanged ideas; now they generally only exchange sounds, and very shallow ones indeed.

But in this case, Russian diplomatists, somehow or other, went even further: instead of accepting shallow remarks for what they were worth, our officials, especially those belonging to the St. Petersburg school, deemed it necessary to give assurances, which dire necessity compelled Russia sometimes to put aside. How did the matter stand up to very late times ? England actually imagined that Russia was bound in duty to seek absolution for every step she undertook. It is too absurd. It is worse—it is humiliating, and it will not be continued.

Why should we give assurances, which, as the rulers of India know very well, circumstances over which there can be no control often render it impossible to keep ? Russia has been far too complaisant to the whims and caprices of England in those matters. The time has come for changing all that, and allowing affairs to be arranged on a simple and more rational basis. In the future let us each have a free hand. South of the Oxus you do as you please ; north of the Oxus we will have the same liberty. That is an arrangement about which there can be no doubt any longer, and it has now, I hope, superseded all the Penelope's webs of understandings that were always misunderstood, and of assurances which could not be fulfilled.

Skobeleff, so far from being an enemy of England, was quite notorious for his friendship for Englishmen, and his liking for all things English, except her policy in the East in Lord Beaconsfield's days. But Skobeleff was far too well read in the history of English politics to believe that the Russophobist fever of 1878 was likely to be permanent.

Englishmen do not fully appreciate the difficulty, the almost insuperable difficulty, which the English system of government by parties throws in the way of a cordial understanding with every foreign Power. At St. Petersburg, at Berlin, even at Vienna, it is possible to speak, it is possible even to treat, without reserve.

Whether these Governments are friendly or hostile, we know what they are, and can treat them accordingly. But in England, who can say what England's policy is ? Yesterday it was Lord Beaconsfield's ; to-day it is Mr. Gladstone's ; to-morrow it may be Lord Salisbury's. It has no stability. Parties holding diametrically opposed views come to power every five or six years, if not oftener. So far as Russia is concerned, the vicissitudes of parties in England make more difference than even a revolution in France. Monarchy, empire, and republic are to us alike indifferent. The form of the government is immaterial, the policy of all to Russia remains the same. But in English politics the distinguishing characteristic of parties is their antagonism on questions of foreign policy, and to one large section of English people, the only foreign policy is opposition to Russia.

We may be as friendly as you please to the existing government ; but how can you establish confidential relations with a Cabinet which may be bound to-morrow, by some sudden turn in the tide, to hand over all your secrets to your bitterest foe ? It cannot be done ; until the Conservative party lay aside its recently acquired hostility to Russia, it is impossible for Russia to regard England as other than a possible enemy. To those whose dream it was to see an Anglo-Russian alliance a well-established fact, that logical result of deeper reflections is a serious obstacle.

My hope—alas! it still only remains a hope!—is that both parties in England will come to understand that it does not always tend to the advantage of British interests to have the defence of those interests irrevocably bound up in the minds of one of the great parties in the State with virulent Russophobism. There would be much less anxiety in St. Petersburg about Egypt, for instance, if Mr. Gladstone's tenure of office did not depend upon the shifting foundation of popular support.

Representative governments and parliamentary institutions have their advantages, no doubt; but a firm consistent policy in foreign affairs is hardly to be included among their number.

Who knows, however, but the Conservatives may become as warm supporters of a Russian alliance as they used to be in the old days? Nothing, as I said, is fixed in English politics, not even the political sympathies of the Conservative party.

Skobeleff's knowledge of English politics was most remarkable. Immediately after the signature of the Treaty of Berlin—that is to say, in the autumn of 1878—two years before the general election, and when, as I well remember, English Liberals were almost in despair over the prospects of their party, Skobeleff penned a memoir upon the political situation. He was then commanding south of the Balkans. In this memoir he passed in review the changes which had from time to time taken place in the attitude of the different English parties towards Russia since 1840, and deduced from his historical epitome the remarkable, but accurate, conclusion that the Russophobist period in England was drawing to its close, and that, in accordance with the precedent of the past, the English nation was certain before very long to abandon the policy of systematic defiance, and adopt a more reasonable and less hostile attitude to the Russian Empire. He followed with a keen eye all the political and electoral manifestations of opinion in England, and, when the late Government was complacently counting upon a new lease of power, in return for 'Peace with Honour,' Skobeleff, with prophetic voice, declared that its days were numbered, and that it would be succeeded by a Government with which it would be possible for Russia to act in common. His prediction was literally fulfilled at Dulcigno.

Of Russia's policy in Egypt Skobeleff, of course, did not speak; the question only became urgent after his death. The views of the Russian Foreign Office on that question are clear and unmistakable. I will only reproduce the circular of M. de Giers :—

St. Petersburg, June $\frac{18}{30}$, 1882.

1. First and foremost, the maintenance of the European concert. Whatever solution is adopted should proceed from it.

2. As far as possible to re-establish and consolidate the *status quo*.[1]

3. It is desirable that a moral action should suffice to secure that end. In that case the results ought to be registered by the Conference, so as to give a new European confirmation to the public law of Europe.

4. If moral action does not suffice, the Powers in concert ought alone to pronounce upon the measures to be taken, and they ought only to be executed in virtue of its authority and under its control.

5. If the Porte persists in refusing to take part in the Conference, the Powers ought to come to an understanding to compel us to accept their decisions.

6. If a material intervention is indispensable, the most legal and the least dangerous would be that of the Sultan acting in virtue of a European delegation, and with the necessary guarantees that he does not overpass the limits of his commission.

7. If the Sultan refuses, and England and France, either singly or collectively, believe themselves obliged to act, this ought also to be undertaken, after an understanding with the Powers by their delegations, and with a clearly defined programme. The precedent of the military intervention of France in Syria should be consulted. The Powers should appoint special commissioners to accompany the expedition.

8. As for the final aim of the intervention, it ought to be the re-establishment of the *status quo*. But this *status quo* has inconveniences which have been revealed by experience. It may, perhaps, be necessary to modify it upon some points relating principally to the position of the Egyptian Government, *vis à vis* foreign Powers, and to the obligations by which it is bound. In admitting the principle, the obligation to respect the engagements

---

[1] It will be seen by the date that this despatch was written before the bombardment of Alexandria.

which it has contracted, opportunity may occur for modifying them by mutual consent.

The inconveniences of the exclusive Anglo-French Control have been revealed by events. To perpetuate them by force would be a sorry task.

It may, perhaps, be possible and just to give a character, not exclusive, but international, to this Control. It would thus acquire more moral authority, and more guarantees against the personal abuses of its agents.

The Commission of Liquidation and the mixed Tribunals have this international character, and they work well.

It may possibly be found just to restrain this Control within limits which would guarantee foreign interests, without constituting an interference in the administration of the country. All these questions ought to be the subject of detailed discussion in Conference.

To this I only need add one word. The English Government has repeatedly and solemnly declared: 'Her Majesty's Government will invite the aid of other Powers to make provisions for the future and good government of Egypt.'

That assurance was accepted in good faith, and in some way or other it will, of course, be fulfilled.

England is evidently anxious to settle the question entirely as she likes. Naturally enough she feels no inclination whatever to offer a preliminary scheme 'on approval.' Even members of Parliament are left in the dark as to the plans of the Cabinet, and it is not very difficult to recognise the necessity of such a mode of action. Still, Englishmen may, perhaps, understand better now why Russians cannot entirely forget the fate of the San Stefano Treaty.

CHAPTER VII.

SKOBELEFF AND CONSTITUTIONALISM.

Skobeleff's belief in autocracy—Detestation of Nihilism—Assassins in Ireland and in Russia—Prince Krapotkine's 'La Révolte'—A propaganda of anarchy—A Nihilist view of English society—London a nest of Nihilist assassins—A Russian view of autocracy—G. Samarine on Constitutionalism—Why unsuited to Russia—The Moscow address—Aksakoff on the assassination of the Emperor—The social Revolution the outcome of Constitutionalism—Autocracy responsible and irresponsible—Liberalism the negation of Christianity—Evils not constitutional but economic—M. Anatole Leroy-Beaulieu's prescription—Russian material progress—Self-government in England and in Russia—The one man power—Autocracy tempered by general elections—Rule of the minority in England—The abuses of elective government—Skobeleff and Russian democracy—Aksakoff's letter to the Prince of Bulgaria.

SKOBELEFF, as all Slavophils do, believed not only in autocracy, but he understood that the very source of Russia's greatness and power lay in that concentration of power which allows speedy and drastic reforms, and which, besides, has been for so many centuries the shape of government which accords with the views and traditions of his country. Autocracy does not impede local self-development; just the opposite; but its aim is to add unity and harmonious strength to all the branches of administration. In Russia at present without that unity and without that strength there would be anarchy. Any unprejudiced and intelligent Russian cannot fail seeing it. Russian

Nihilists understand that quite well, and that is precisely why they pretend sometimes that they are only craving for constitutionalism. In reality, their only wish is anarchy, pure and simple, without the slightest restriction. Thus, the elements which are the chief objects of their hatred and attacks are precisely those that the Slavophils are most anxious to support and to preserve—viz. orthodoxy and autocracy. These are the greatest securities of the Empire, therefore those who want to destroy the Empire naturally attack those principles.

Skobeleff detested Nihilism. It was contrary to his very nature; it made war against the national tradition which he revered. It would destroy everything in Russia except the soil—faith, fatherland, the very idea of that which we all consider our duty to uphold. Nihilists exist themselves, but want to bring destruction to everything else. 'I will live, but you shall die!' is their motto.

The world, of course, is rich in people who do not see the results of their doctrines, who do not realise themselves what category they belong to, *de facto*, if not always theoretically. Tell some of the real but unconscious Nihilists that, in order to be consistent, they have to become Hartmanns or Krapotkines, they will look perfectly shocked. They talk of '*nuances* of Nihilism.' But that was only possible as long as Nihilism only represented a certain tendency, and never assumed any definite shape. When Tourgenieff introduced that word on the Russian soil, it was little more than a tendency to destroy established views and authorities. Now, even in England, there are authorities, like public opinion and Mrs. Grundy,[1] which can and often ought to be attacked. But Russians, as is their nature, seldom stop half-way, and thus a tendency which seemed not criminal at first, has become a monstrous, illegal power which no cultivated society can, with impunity, tolerate. The extremes on one side strengthened the opposite side. Many people who were indifferent to the maintenance of the autocratic power in Russia have become passionately devoted to it now, going in that direction perhaps even too far. They see in every official a supporter of their political faith, and are afraid to injure their cause by denouncing his shortcomings. This, of course, is not the wisest way of serving the interests of the autocracy, and our Emperor is the very last man to admire that kind of devotion.

It is almost hopeless to make Englishmen under-

---

[1] A Russian friend, reading this page in proof, pencilled on the margin, 'For foreign readers. Explain in a footnote "Who is Mrs. Grundy?"' What an order! Mrs. Grundy is a mythological deity much worshipped in England, who is supposed to incarnate the prejudices of very censorious and intensely respectable old women of the middle class. She is more feared than loved. Mr. Locker, in his *London Lyrics*, sings :

'The world's an ugly world. Offend
Good people, how they wrangle
The manners that they never mend,
The characters they mangle.
They eat and drink, and scheme and plod,
And go to church on Sunday ;
And many are afraid of God,
And more of Mrs. Grundy.'

stand the indignation excited in Russia at the warm welcome they extend to the anarchists. Some English literary men make quite a hero of Prince Krapotkine, and are quite amazed that we should be hurt. What would they say, I wonder, if we lionised at St. Petersburg the murderers of Lord Frederick Cavendish?

'Oh!' exclaims one of my very credulous friends, 'but Krapotkine is only seeking liberty of speech, liberty from arbitrary arrest, and constitutional government; and if you refuse all these things, what can you expect but dynamite?' When remarks of that sort are made to me, I cannot help wondering if Englishmen actually suppose that we never see Irish papers? But, though we read them, we try to see what is in accordance with truth, or in flagrant opposition to it. Now the Irish papers complain precisely of 'arbitrary arrests.' They deplore that Irish meetings are dispersed by the police, and that the Irish newspapers are seized in the post-office; they allege these facts as an excuse for their crimes. But in neither case can assassins find a proper excuse. Even on democratic principles, what right has a minority, a miserable handful of a minority, to assassinate the representatives of a majority because the latter will not remodel its laws at its dictation?

Surely nobody, even in England, will deny that the Nihilists are in a minority. If we had a parliament elected by universal suffrage, do you think that in all Russia one single Nihilist, even one, would be elected by the people?

I was talking the other day to a very eminent Liberal statesman, who had just returned from a short tour in Russia. 'There are two things,' said he, 'which struck me. The Nihilists are like our Irish revolutionists in many things; but they differ from them in this: the Irish assassin is a coward. The Nihilist has absolutely no fear, no thought for himself. The other thing that struck me is, that when a Nihilist commits a murder, the people would delight to tear him to pieces. In Ireland the populace only thinks of screening the assassin.' I repeat the remark as it was made to me. Does it not seem to show that in Russia the Government, in punishing the Nihilists, is acting much more in accordance with popular feeling than England is when she is attempting to repress crime in Ireland?

There is no constitutional form of government which to Russians does not seem a bit of humbug. Several English friends of mine—not only Mr. Carlyle—agree with us on that point. But because they dislike that form of government, they do not play the part of Guy Fawkes. Besides, I cannot imagine how they could replace their government? Any other, I daresay, would work in England still worse. How can one help regarding criminals otherwise than as criminals—if one is not Mr. Cowen, who gave the cordial hand of greeting to men whose hands reek with the blood of the sovereign who emancipated our serfs and liberated Bulgaria?

We do not press anybody to adopt an autocracy,

and if we did, we should shrink from supporting a propaganda of dynamite. Why, then, should English Liberals persist in pressing upon us a system unsuited to us, and glorify propagandists whose idea of abolishing autocracy is to blow up an autocrat? But how little English people know of the Nihilists if they candidly imagine that their object is to procure a constitutional government in Russia! The Nihilists, knowing English pet crotchets, may tell them that kind of thing, and some people like to be deceived; but we know better. One of the Nihilist organs, published at Geneva, laughs at the foolish falsehoods accepted by the 'Fortnightly Review' of the constitutional aims of Prince Krapotkine. He is an anarchist, not a constitutionalist. His paper, 'La Révolte,' is the organ of the party of European anarchy. Even a Republic is not enough for him, for it still represents an authority, and insists upon order and discipline. He is avowedly an anarchist. Anybody, studying the history of our times, must understand the meaning of that word. It is a terrible word, and, when supported by deeds, the cause of unspeakable horrors and miseries, worse even than those of any unhappy war.

In all Europe where is there a Republic so near an ideal of the advanced Left as in France? There they have universal suffrage, triennial Chambers, peasant proprietorship, equality, liberty, and fraternity, inscribed on every public building. The workmen are free to combine; everyone, even (I beg pardon for uttering such a name) Louise Michel, is free to make speeches at all kinds of meetings. The press is quite at liberty to invent all kinds of fiction. But the anarchists are as dissatisfied there as anywhere in the world, even in Russia. Prince Krapotkine himself is as ready to recommend dynamite in the Republic as in the Empire. If anybody doubt that, let him or her read the 'Révolte.'

When dynamite was used at Monceau-les-Mines, the 'Révolte' exulted in the introduction of that explosive into French politics. 'France,' it exclaimed, 'is in full revolution. The movements at Monceau and Lyons are the preludes of a great popular rising, whose watchwords will be, "Vive la révolution sociale! vive l'anarchie! Mort aux bourgeois!" In all be against property and ownership. When the people this time take up arms, the revolution will be made for the expropriation of all social wealth, to put a final end to slavery. The *mot d'ordre* of the approaching revolution will not be one of those empty formulas which some wish to impose upon us. It will be the cry of " Vive l'anarchie!" a cry which sums up all the aspirations of the nineteenth century; to that all the true revolutionists will rally, and this time the revolution will not fail. It is the insurrection at Monceau which has produced this immense result.' A brilliant prospect, is it not? The very thing to imitate!

I should like to ask my English readers, is there any government in England—even if Mr. Cowen himself was Prime Minister—which would not suppress such a propaganda of anarchy when it began to strike terror by murder? No matter how faulty the government may be—and every government, without exception, has a very great many faults—it is justified in regarding such doctrines as intolerable, and in treating their professors as enemies of human kind. Society is not organised on principles of anarchy, and it is not the duty of authorities who are charged with its defence to capitulate to anarchists and assassins.

In England there is a curious idea that you may ignore such facts with safety. Truth remains truth even when people dislike accepting it, and there are fires which go across channels and seas. The old English saying, 'Experience is never worth aught till it has been dearly bought' seems to be forgotten in this country. England will have to pay some day for her mistake in making heroes of the cosmopolitan anarchists of the Continent. I am no authority on these matters, but it strikes me that in no city of the world are the extremes of abject poverty and enormous wealth so often seen as in London. It also seems to me that the landed proprietors are absolutely isolated against a sudden rush of the lawless proletariat. I wonder if Englishmen will be pleased to know that one of the tracts which the Nihilists circulate among our peasants is devoted almost entirely to describing the miserable lot of the poor in England. 'If the Russian people,' says the author of 'From Fire into Flame,' 'does not take care, it will soon be as badly off as the people of England, a land which, during the last sixty years, has become one great prison, only that men work harder there than in any gaol. In London, the richest city in the world, during the last ten years, 3,292 labourers have died of starvation.' The hero of another Nihilist romance, after seeing children plaiting straw in English villages, and sleeping in foul cellars after fifteen or eighteen hours' labour, goes to a revolutionary meeting, where he learns from English lips that 'there draws nigh the terrible deadly contest between the working people and their oppressors. Already over all the land are spread our friends and comrades. Already do they everywhere secretly sharpen knives and prepare matches. Like a torrent will blood flow, like a burning mountain will glow fires,' and so forth. Clearly, if London is allowed for the moment to be a nest of Nihilist assassins, it is from no admiration of your social system that they honour you with their presence, nor will you have long to wait before you experience some of the 'advantages' of your hospitality.

Skobeleff was the very opposite of a Nihilist. He was an idealist, full of faith and enthusiasm. He explained Nihilism by a defect in our system of education. 'Panslavism was founded,' he told a friend in Paris, 'upon faith in God and love for the brethren, both of which were embodied in the Orthodox Church.' With him, as with all of us, Church and country are indissolubly united. He who is false to one is seldom, can seldom be true to another, and a weakening of faith in the first is often preliminary to loss of faith in the other.

Skobeleff never expounded his political ideas at great length. He left that to others. To understand the system which he enthusiastically supported, read the speeches of M. Aksakoff, M. George Samarine, and others. Take, for instance, this very clear statement of the Russian view of autocracy, which was written by G. Samarine, in 1862, and presented to his Majesty privately (as is often done in Russia by people who occupy no political position whatsoever) at a time when there were rumours that a Constitution was to be promulgated.

A report is current, that an address has been drawn up for signature in Moscow, demanding a Constitution. I, for my part, refuse to believe it, and say to everyone that this is nonsense, a falsehood. But such impossible and unlooked for things take place in these days, that perhaps after all some insane parody or other is being played even on the theme in question. If true it be, then I propose to put down in writing and give currency to something of the following description. We deem ourselves in conscience bound to make a full and public statement of our views on the subject of contemporory rumours about a restriction of autocratic power in Russia.

We do not acknowledge the truths of the theory *de jure divino* elaborated by Western scholasticism and repeated at second hand by our own clergy. To affirm that the supreme imperial power pertains to any dynasty by right in virtue of the force of Divine law, that it belongs to it by *birth*, that a whole nation has been given over by God as an entailed property to one person or family—this, in our opinion, is blasphemy. The law of God blesses imperial power *in general*, and imposes on every person the duty of submitting to it, because the imperial order (*this or that*), as being the actual condition of social life, serves to accomplish ends foreordained for the good of mankind. In that sense, 'there is no power but of God.' But what is this *power*, and what are we to understand by acknowledging the *power*? The Church leaves this an open question. It does not affect her. The Saviour and the Apostles founded the Church and gave to mankind a doctrine bearing on the relation of man to God; but they did not constitute forms of government and did not write a Constitution. To elaborate for itself a form of government, a limited or an unlimited monarchy, one aristocratic or republican—that is the affair of the people itself. Every nation constitutes for itself a *power* according to its needs and convictions, and that power ordained by it, receives the significance of a power *binding* on each individual pertaining to that nation.

To declare our opinion in this matter and to set at rest misunderstanding, which might easily arise out of what follows, we address ourselves to the question agitated at the present time, and we openly affirm that we regard every attempt to limit the supreme power which is now being made in Russia as a foolish proceeding, because it is impossible, and if it were possible, it would rightly be called a calamity and a crime against the people.

We have called this impossible, because on Russian territory there is no power invested in which one could limit that of another— the autocracy. To whatever pitch of mental derangement adult minds may have reached at this time, it is impossible to reckon government schools, universities, or literary clubs, of this or that colour, as power. We will allow that all these can do much harm;

give rise in this country to a host of wild conceptions, pervert the common judgment, draw some generations aside from the historic path and render them unfit for life; but all this is but a manifestation of simply *negative* strength, not creative nor life-giving. Poison is also strength, but one which destroys and does not give life. We have an historic, positive strength—the nation and another power—the autocratic Tzar. The latter is also a positive historic power, but only in consequence of the people's strength having evolved it out of itself, and because the former strength recognises in the Tzar its personification, its outward expression. As long as autocracy embraces these two conditions it is lawful and invincible. God grant we may not live to experience his strength on some square opposed to some handful or other of discontented persons. But it is time to give a timely account to oneself of the consequences of the quarrel, in which passionate people are calling upon it to engage. Let us suppose that some hundred pupils of a government institute collect together, and let us suppose that this number is swelled by some dozens of persons who have not yet succeeded in reconciling themselves to the abolition of serfdom; suppose that a few noisy journalists join this body, along with a few neighbouring drunkards, and a handful of burgesses and valets thoroughly infected with the spirit of revolution; in a word, suppose that everyone who would wish to see the fall of autocracy has surrounded the Winter Palace. If the Tzar, summoned by their cries, should rise and merely glance over the heads of that sprinkling of people, and if the crowd behind it should understand that it has *offended* the Tzar, what then? Will he say, 'Well deserved!' or will he move a body of troops against it for self-defence? Those who find this question a doubtful one had better turn for information to the peaceful arbiters who for six months have been about among the people, and who are of all most likely to listen to a straightforward statement of its grievances and hopes. They will say, with one voice, that the aspirations of the people go straight to the heart of the Tzar, swift as an electric current, borne through all intermediate classes and institutions and social layers, and that *no person or thing* can arrest it on its course; that all such intermediate media, in the eyes of the people, serve only as an obstacle which stands in the way of its union with the Tzar, and that there has long been concluded between them a compact for mutual aid, not, indeed, enunciated in so many words, but well understood and intelligible to all. If—which God forbid—they should chance in the general re-action to meet with something in the way of opposition, would not that 'something' produce exactly the same result as that which would overtake a frail canoe caught between two billows advancing one against the other? But let us take another view of the matter; perhaps when a cry is raised in the square, and the sound is heard of broken panes of glass, they would take fright in the Winter Palace and come to terms; possibly in a moment of terror some concession might be extorted; or if the people are not duly fired by ideas of progress and civilisation, and by those who consider themselves in the van of enlightenment, is there perhaps not something else which would fire their enthusiasm, even supposing, for instance, they were promised the abolition of the law of recruiting, the abolition of taxes, &c.?[1] In other words, one can act without the people and one can deceive the people. Both these devices have been had recourse to. Anna Ivanovna signed the Constitution that had been thrust into her hands, and on the day following tore it to pieces; but the people of that day who advocated constitutions were more considerable in numbers than such advocates are now,

[1] We must not lose sight of the fact that this was written in 1862, before the abolition of the law of recruiting, and the introduction of many reforms.

though of a milder temperament. There is another example to the point: on December 14, on the strength of a *lying* order, two regiments of the Guards were led out on the Palace Square. What came of this incident? . . . The fraud was powerless to move the people. So, then, the limitation of the autocracy is impossible.

Besides, we remarked that, even if this were possible, we should deem it a calamity. We explain the reason. All contemporary ills which afflict our land may be said to come to this — our imperial order is not proportionate to our strength and growth; the government stands in need of more than the land produces, and little by little consumes the land. As a foil to that evil, a constitutional form of government would not only not effect a cure, but, on the contrary, would make matters worse. We know, by experience, that where constitutional forms take their rise, not as the spontaneous fruit of free development in the life of a people, but are borrowed from without, ready made, like the cut of a coat, they have this direct and inevitable result—the strengthening of centralisation, not merely administrative but intellectual, in the development of enlightenment among the people. One point, one town becomes the autocratic ruler of all the country; thence to that central point of political action tend the majority of the people, the bulk of capital and of means, attracted by the hope of a fine career by reason of an attractive stir; but meanwhile life in the provinces grows torpid, the spirit of independence is weakening, and little by little everything grows dependent on directions given from above. For the first instance centralisation was established as a consequence of that strong tendency of popular forces to one central point; subsequently it was strengthened unwillingly, as a consequence of a continuous exhaustion of the whole organism, as the sole means of filling the void and arresting the morbid torpor in its extremities. St. Petersburg, the centre of autocracy, is a heavy burden for Russia to bear; as a centre of constitutional government it would strangle her outright.

Further, the first condition of proper historic development is sincerity and uprightness. By this I understand a correspondence of that which finds its expression in words, deeds, institutions, customs, with that which constitutes the essence of a people's life. Every constitutional form of government is founded on the right of the majority, acknowledged as a fact of legal predominance—an undoubted power—over weakness, over partial attractions and interests. But, if the minority arrogate to itself the vocation and rights of the majority, it is evident that the whole representation of constitutionalism is turned into a seditious lie. Whatever character a limited monarchy might assume amongst us—for no particular form has been sketched out for it—the masses, as a material or instrument or lifeless substance, would be left *without* it. I think it is evident enough that the people could neither mediately nor immediately be active participators in any sort of constitution whatever. Firstly, the people do not wish for a Constitution, because they trust in the good intentions of their autocratic Tzar, and have absolutely no faith whatever in classes and cliques, for the benefit of which the absolute power might be subjected to limitation; secondly, the people are illiterate, the people are isolated and formed into other societies; by the reforms of Peter the people have been jerked out of the rut of historic development; they are unfitted to be so, they cannot take part in representative institutions. We cannot therefore have a popular Constitution, but one acting apart from the people—that is to say, a government by minorities, acting without the authority of the majority, is a lie and a fraud. We have enough and to spare of false progress, false enlightenment, and false culture; may God grant we may not live to see in our midst a false freedom and a false Constitution! The latter falsehood would work more bitter mischief than the former ones.

It is now scarcely needful to explain why we have called every attempt made at this present time to change the form of government amongst us a crime perpetrated against the people. Whoever puts forward such claims, under the impression that he is speaking for the people and in its name, we can only regard as an object of pity. He who thinks it of no consequence what the people think and feel, he who wilfully despises them, and by his own authority lays violent hands on what the people has created, and on what the people loves—that man is a usurper.

We are firmly persuaded that all the talk of the present day about introducing another form of government is nothing more nor less than vain twaddle, which can lay claim neither to justice nor to sincerity. It is not of this that Russia stands in need. After the liberation of the peasants, which could only have been peacefully and successfully carried out by an absolute monarch, what we want is, toleration in matters of religion, a cessation of discourses against dissent by police agents, publicity and independent courts of justice, freedom of the press, as the only means to drive out all infectious juices which poison our literature, and thereby to call out a free reaction of sincere convictions and honourable sound judgment; we need a simplification of local administration, a reform of taxation, free access to means of enlightenment, a limitation of unproductive expenditure, a reduction in Court attendants, &c. &c. And all this can be done not only without limiting the absolute power, but more speedily and more easily by an autocratic will, fearless and without suspicion, mindful of his absolute power, and therefore a careful guardian of the free expression of the people's mind and the people's needs.[1]

[1] *The Russ*, No. 29, May 30.

That paper was written twenty years ago, but the convictions which it expresses are unchanged to-day. When the present Emperor came to the throne, the citizens of Moscow presented him with an address, in which they asserted :

We firmly believe that the historical power which created the unity of Russia, with all her external strength, and has put the foundation to the emancipation of the serfs, endowed with landed property, will save Russia out of her temporary difficulties. We firmly believe that only in *the affectionate union between the Emperor and his people, and not in the sham conventional-constitutional forms* taken from abroad, *lies our salvation.* Using the words of our Church, we may say that we firmly believe that God will give you power, strength, and wisdom necessary for achieving your difficult task. We firmly believe that the real sons of Russia will defend with all their heart and soul the traditions of their fathers, and that the renovation, as it happened two and a half centuries ago, will be spread from Moscow over all the rest of Russia.

It is true that the assassination of the Emperor will seem incompatible with the devotion expressed by Moscow to the autocracy ; but we see in that parricide only the result of the apostasy from the national and traditional path of Russian development. I cannot do better than reproduce here the remarkable speech addressed by M. Aksakoff to the St. Petersburg Benevolent Slavonic Society, March, 1881, on this very subject. M. Aksakoff said :—

Gentlemen,—I came from Moscow to take part in your assembly, and to join my Moscow voice to yours. I should greatly like to convey to you what is said and thought at

Moscow, but it is beyond expression by spoken word. How, indeed, are we to define the impressions which fill our souls at this moment? It is sorrow, it is grief, it is shame and horror—a kind of solemn foreboding horror. Divine judgment is now risen up against us. It is God Himself, living in history, who is sending us His terrible revelations. We are now standing before Him, and called upon to answer. What is the answer we are giving? Is there any answer we could give? Let everyone appeal to his conscience. Is he not partly to be blamed for the infamy which has deserved the punishment of God and stained our country in the eyes of the whole world? Let us not deceive ourselves. We are on the edge of ruin. One step more in the fatal direction we followed with such criminal light-headedness, and we attain to blood and chaos! This is no exaggeration, no mere words. Do not flatter yourselves with dreams. If our country is mute, it is because she is wondering and amazed. Do you realise the meaning of the silent wondering of many millions of people? Their breast is swelling like an ocean, full of heavy thoughts. No external calamity could be compared to the moral burden caused by the villainy of March 1.

The Emperor is murdered; the same Emperor who was the greatest benefactor to his country, who emancipated, bestowing upon them human and civil rights, tens of millions of Russian peasants. He is murdered; not from personal vengeance, not for booty, but precisely because he is the Emperor, the crowned head, the representative, the first man of his country, that vital, single man, who personified the very essence, the whole image, the whole strength and power, of Russia. From time immemorial that power constituted the strength of the country. The attempt directed against the person of the Tzar is always directed against the whole people; but in this case the whole historical principle of the national life has been attacked, the autocratic power bestowed upon the Emperor by the country itself. Who are those who dared to bring that awful shame upon the people, and, as if by mockery, in the name of the people? Who are they? Is it merely a handful of criminals, blood-thirsty blockheads, enslaved by the demon of destruction? Where did they come from? Let us address that question sternly to ourselves. Is it not the product of our moral treason, of which is guilty almost all the so-called liberal press. Can it be anything else but the logical, extreme expression of that Westernism which, since the time of Peter the Great, demoralised both our government and our society, and has already marred all the spiritual manifestations of our national life? Not content to profit by all the riches of European thought and knowledge, we borrowed her spirit, developed by a foreign history and foreign religion. We began idolising Europe, worshipping her gods and her idols! Who is to be blamed? Some forty years ago has not Khomiakoff warned us, threatening us with Divine punishment for 'deserting all that is sacred to our hearts'? But really, what are these 'Anarchists,' 'Social Democrats,' and Revolutionists, as they call themselves? Have they the smallest particle of Russian spirit in all their aspirations and aims? Is there the slightest shade in their teachings of a protest against the real shortcomings of which Russia is suffering? Just the opposite; what they despise most is precisely the Russian people. In their servile imitation of foreign teaching and foreign idols, they only borrow what can easily be explained, if not excused, in Western Europe by historical and social conditions. There results of that kind are the natural protest caused by unequal partition of land, the unjust reign of the *bourgeoisie* over the fourth class—deprived of all civil organisation and political rights—a protest, therefore, against the present constitutional forms.

But that injustice is exactly what we do not possess. Thank God, and thanks to that very martyr-Emperor so brutally murdered, our 'fourth class,' or our peasantry, forming almost eighty per cent. of the whole realm, now possess land, organisation, and the most complete self-government. To this very day, that fourth class is the keeper of our historical instinct, of our religion, and of the whole element of our political organism. They, and not the so-called 'Intelligencia,' are the real supporters of our country. The memory of our 'Zemskie assemblies,' summoned by the will of the autocratic power, is not lost in our history, and no efforts of our *bureaucracy*, and the pseudo-liberal worshippers of the Western political organisation, will be strong enough to stop in the future the renovation of that precious homogeneous union between the sovereign and the land (*zemstvo*).

And is it not monstrous that now, when violent protests are heard everywhere in the West against constitutionalism and parliamentarism, that in Russia the so-called 'Intelligencia' should be craving for the constitutional rags that Europe will have the charity to throw to her valets!

Who accepts the causes has also to accept their logical consequences. Who accepts the Western Constitution has also to bear the last expression of Western political life, viz. social revolution with all its manifestations.

But can such be the result of the historical thousand years' harvest of the Russian people? Its patience conquered all, every kind of misfortune, and remained, in spite of all, faithful to its civil and moral principles. Worse than all the external calamities was the moral treason of its leading class, powerful through knowledge and development. The reforms of Peter the Great weakened our memory and disabled us from understanding our own history—so very different from that of the West. Conquest is not at the bottom of our historical life, as is the case in all the Western countries. Our history begins with quite a voluntary and rational appeal to power. The same appeal was repeated much later, in 1612, and gave the foundation to the present reigning dynasty, empowered with autocracy, and nothing and nobody could induce the country to alter that shape of government. Such was the will, such was the inspiration of the national spirit.

Our history does not possess, therefore, that fundamental fact, which characterises the political life of the Western Powers of Europe, the antagonism between the people and a power imposed by conquest. That antagonism, however, is the very foundation of Western constitutionalism. It is a mere agreement; a compromise between two camps hostile to each other, mistrusting each other; a kind of treaty, surrounded with all sorts of conditions. To evade those conditions *without contradicting the letter of the agreement*, constitutes the great talent of the rulers as well as of those who are ruled. Struggle for power—that is the real sense of the political life of European countries. The foundation of their administration is a kind of mechanical apparatus; the centre of power and mind, of an *unlimited power*, belongs to the majority of voices based upon the numbers of the representatives. Thus some ten voices—often bribed and bought—autocratically decide the destinies of the people, forming the actual majority, in comparison of which the parliamentary majority is a few grains of sand compared to the sandy wilderness of Sahara. But that autocrat, composed of several numerical units, bears no moral responsibility before its conscience and the country, responsibility which falls heavily on the one personal representative of the supreme power. More than that, the so-called lowest class, forming the great bulk of the country, is not even represented in the Chambers. It is simply excluded, it is despised by the Western 'Intelligencia.'

During the First Republic the French Representative Assembly declared—quite legally as far as the form was concerned, and in the name of the people—that the worship addressed to God was null, and replaced by adoration of the 'Goddess of Reason;' and all that in the face of tens of millions of true believers, but of men deprived of any legal voice, and thus unable to protest at all. The same thing happened in France the other day. It is ordered now to put in all the primary schools, instead of the word God, the word *Nature*. Is this not a study illustrative of popular Western representation? What is the use of political rights which allow, in the name of liberty and law, such a revolting infraction of freedom and truth?

Such are the kinds of freedom promised to Russia by worshippers of European liberal institutions. But the instincts and the notions of freedom in the Russian people are higher and broader than in any part of the world, because they are free from the conventional and formal element, and are based on *moral truth*. They are easily traced in our self-government, the broadest of Europe, and in the largest application of the *elective element*. There was no antagonism between our Emperor and the people, as our superior power has been voluntarily recognised by the whole country.

The Russian people has not entrusted full power to a heartless, soulless, mechanical apparatus, but to the 'holiest of beings'—to a man with a human soul, with a Russian heart, and a Christian conscience. The people know, and know well, the drawbacks of every human institution, but feel at the same time the power to overcome and improve them. And our former Tzars have not deceived their hopes and confidence ; they held majestically and rigorously their imperial title, and asked for advice the whole Russian land in the shape of our *Zemskié Sobory*, and the land never failed to bring in response the love and the truthful thoughts of the whole nation. There was no mentioning any political rights, or supporting any kind of political doctrine. It was the regular, the natural manifestation of national life itself. Neither the people nor the autocratic Tzar ever thought themselves otherwise than in a constant moral and intellectual alliance of unity. The superior power, far from finding itself attacked, was supported by millions of loving hearts and intellects. And therefore, after the destructive calamities which took place before the year 1612, after that epoch, it gradually became, to the amazement of the whole world, one of the most powerful countries. The Emperor Peter the Great's reforms have changed all that. I admit that change had its cause, its *raison d'être*; but now it exists no more; any obstinacy shown in that direction by the Government or the 'Intelligencia' would be fatal, and has already been the cause of our present state. But, if our administration has forsaken for a time its national traditions, the nation itself remains faithful.

There is, however, another side of the question, of which I beg permission to say a few words. All that Nihilism, Socialism, that last word of Western European life, has a moral underlining. The idea of a State could nowhere be developed with such fullness and consistency as in the heathen world, where it constituted the highest idea of truth. Christianity showing to the man the highest vocation outside and above the State, designated the principle of Divine truth as the moral source of every strength and power. But, as soon as the Christian world forgets the notion of God, the modern foundation of the State is shaken, as Christianity is the only great principle subduing, moderating in due limits, the development of mere State principle. Society, which repudiates Christianity, but at the same time is unable to give up the exigencies inspired by Christian truths, individual freedom, and other Christian ideals—such a society is doomed to search only in the State for the realisation of all these ideals, though they are perfectly unattainable in that region. In rejecting the spiritual weapon, that highest moral motive for good, based upon faith in supernatural truth, there remains only material force, however legal it may be.

But a Christian cannot simply cease to be a Christian; he will continually struggle with his former God, in his own soul and in the outside world. And the more he struggles the more discontented he becomes. Therefore the final fate of every Christian society which excluded Christ from itself is rebellion and revolution. But rebellion creates nothing, and from rebellion to rebellion you come to anarchy, to a complete self-negation. The beginning of all this is to be traced already in Western Europe. In denying the existence of God and his soul, the man deifies the body, and is subdued by animal instincts. Such is the political and spiritual path recommended to Russia. After she has been covered with the so-called Liberal constitutional organisation by our social revolutionists, and that part of our 'Intelligencia' who stupidly imagine that you may stop half-way, they try to displace from her historical and Christian ground that Russia, which to this moment we call 'Holy Russia,' and simple people generally designate themselves as 'Christians' and 'Orthodox world.'

No, that shall never happen! Our people is hostile to Liberalism preached along with the negation of Christian faith and Christian morality, and which expresses the greatest contempt for the political and spiritual belief of the Russian land.

The time is come for us to bethink ourselves. The time is come to fix our mobile heart, our mobile thoughts, on the rock of Divine and national truth. I am happy to have been able to express aloud, in the name of the Slavonic society, the civil and moral aims and ideals of the Russian people. But that is not sufficient. It is necessary—it is absolutely necessary—for us to implore our Emperor to allow us, the whole country, the whole nation, to surround his throne and to express fearlessly, openly to the whole world, our horror and indignation to all who dare to make any attempt against what is most sacred to our national feeling, the historical principle of the autocracy, which constitutes the very foundation of our political life. Yes; let us implore that the old union between the Emperor and the country shall be revived, based upon reciprocal, sincere confidence, love, and union of souls.

Possibly M. Aksakoff's terminology and modest thought may be too Russian to be appreciated in the West, or, perhaps, even to be understood. Let me, therefore, supplement his remarks by giving in an Appendix some extracts from a very good reply to Professor Dragamanoff, which Baron Nicholas Fredericks, of St. Petersburg, published within a few weeks of M. Aksakoff's speech. Baron Fredericks gives a more occidental—a more St. Petersburg view of the autocracy—but it is sufficiently Russian to deserve attention. Baron Fredericks is a man of experience, and for a St. Petersburger his views are decidedly worth hearing.[1]

We may be wrong, everybody is wrong some-

[1] Vide Appendix B.

times, about the constitutional question. But whether we are right or wrong, there can be no doubt that the conventionalities of the West seem to us mere cant—an element which to us is most repulsive. You might as well say that people take smallpox because of the colour of their eyes, as to attribute all the troubles from which we suffer to the lack of a Constitution.

It is really too absurd to read the grave lectures which are addressed to poor Russia by her sapient critics of the West. A mob, plundered to the bone by Jewish usurers, turns suddenly upon its oppressors and wrecks their houses and hunts them through the street. If this is on our side of the Carpathians, it is held up to the world as the natural consequence of despotism. 'What can you expect in a country so barbarous as to submit to an autocrat?' All protestations that the causes of the anti-Jewish movement are, not constitutional, but economic; that bad counsels, in some cases given by Nihilistic instigations, have resulted in illegal protests, are obstinately ignored. But, if the selfsame attacks on the Jews take place on the English side of the Carpathians, in constitutional Hungary, then, all at once, it is discovered that the anti-Jewish riots have no connection whatever with Magyar constitutionalism. They are due to any cause but the form of government of the State in which they occur. It is just the same with Nihilism. We have our Nihilists, our dynamitards, and so have other countries, even those blest with the freest institutions of the world. But when a

Nihilist explodes a bomb in Russia, he is the natural product of despotism. When he uses dynamite in France, he is merely a miscreant and a criminal. 'Virtue and vice,' says M. Taine, 'are products like vitriol and sugar ;' but what are we to think of this anomalous classification wherein the products change their character with their geographical locations? In the Baltic provinces, the peasants, imitating the exploits of the Irish, have also shot one of their landlords. This was fortunately a unique case. In Ireland this is the result of landlordism, and can be easily explained—some of my friends positively assert—by the history of Ireland. But in the Baltic provinces, when the same phenomenon occurs, it is attributed in some mysterious way to the Panslavists.

Now all this strikes us as so ridiculous, so transparently absurd, that we can hardly take seriously any remonstrances addressed to us by those who show such bad faith, or at least such *parti pris*. If English critics wish to be attended to, let them at least apply the canons of their criticisms impartially to Russians and to their neighbours. What is virtue in a Magyar cannot be vice in a Russian. Neither can the mere fact that he lives east or west of a certain parallel of latitude convert an assassin into a hero, or *vice versâ*.

A very distinguished friend of mine, M. Anatole Leroy Beaulieu, who has shown an exceptional energy and good faith in studying Russian history and Russian life, recently published, in the second volume of his very interesting work, 'L'Empire des Tzars,' a diagnosis of our social *malaise*, and a prescription for our cure. Of course the prescription was a Constitution. Has any Frenchman or Englishman, except Mr. Carlyle and Mr. Froude, ever seen a disease which a Constitution would not cure; of course always excepting in their own Eastern dominions? The countries for whose good government they are responsible, and the conditions of which they must know the best, are just those where our Western mentors most resolutely refuse to apply their constitutional instrument. Germans, with their usual scientific thoroughness, are more cautious in their liberal doctrines.

Two years ago, on my way to Moscow, I stopped for a few days at St. Petersburg. I went to see there an old friend of mine, a German by birth, Protestant by creed, but, having always been in close contact with thorough Russians, very devoted to Russia. 'Well,' said I, 'what have you been doing since we parted?' 'Sighing, sighing, and longing....' 'Oh, yes,' interrupted I, 'of course longing for constitutional freedom, for Western progress, as almost everybody in Petersburg?'

'Not in the least,' was the reply; 'nothing of the sort. What do we long for?—it is power, unity of power, harmony of power, confidence in power, fidelity to power.... St. Petersburg is carried away by shallow phrases, loud words. It is so opposed to the

Russian character to prefer words to deeds, sham to reality. But this is our present tendency. Life becomes intolerable, simply because one meets too many traitors to Russia, traitors to Russian views, traitors to Russian traditions, to real Russian interests. If I went abroad as often as you do, I would only implore our advisers to think of themselves, and to let us alone. But people naturally prefer thinking of others, especially if they fancy they can find causes for blame and noble indignation. *Cela n'oblige à rien, et néanmoins cela pose!'*

I had warmly praised M. Leroy Beaulieu's first volume, in an article written before the second appeared, and the words I had used about the first were ingeniously used by one of my critics to cover a laudatory *résumé* of M. Leroy Beaulieu's constitutional prescriptions. It was a clever trick, often used they tell me, by 'truthful' servants of good faith. In reality, I endorsed the first volume, and disagreed with several parts of the second, though M. Leroy Beaulieu is very moderate, and admits honestly so many difficulties in the use of his prescriptions, that one is not altogether sure about the way he would take himself, if suddenly he were changed into Jupiter, and obliged to organise Russia at a moment's notice.

Russia, thank God! is not on the verge of ruin or of revolution, as M. Leroy Beaulieu supposes. Those who have witnessed the great national exhibitions which we held this year at Moscow know that Russia, instead of decaying, is making gigantic strides in material progress. Against all the assertions of the Nihilists put this suggestive fact, recognised and stated by the 'Economist,' that in the first eight months of this year, the percentage of increase of traffic on the Russian railways has been seven times greater than that on English railways in the same period; eleven times as great as the French lines, and thrice as much as the most prosperous lines of Europe. An increase of twenty-three per cent. in railway receipts, I willingly admit, is no proof of other than material prosperity. Russians, at least, do not gauge everything by a metallic standard; but it is at least a proof that the universal bankruptcy and ruin which is supposed to be impending, is not visible from the railway.

What is the principle of a constitutional government? Is it a government of the people by the people? To that we have no objection. All our government is based upon that idea. All that we ask for is, that the people who govern shall be people who understand the affairs with which they have to do. Our peasants understand the affairs of their commune; they have therefore authority to govern the commune. They manage its affairs, because they are their own affairs. But they do not understand Kuldja treaties or Egyptian protectorates; they are even unable to understand the difference between Lord Beaconsfield and Mr. Gladstone. What better instance can I give of their incapacity for understanding? These questions are, therefore, left in the hands of those who are familiar with such things. In England, I willingly admit, the case is quite different. The English peasant has no voice in the government of his commune. He is consulted only about affairs of 'haute politique.' That does not seem to us the most sensible plan; but we are not so impertinent as to urge England to adopt Russian customs. Let everybody mind his own business and avoid foreign novelties. Few things pleased me more than a Court reception in England. Could anything be more picturesque and unlike what you see anywhere else? One felt as if old times came back at a moment's notice, and that England, in the face of the whole world and all its representatives, liked to be as she was before, firmly clinging to her own habits and tastes, proudly disdaining the whimsical fancies of fashion, the very nature of which is to be speedily replaced and speedily thrown to oblivion. Had the Russian Slavophils their own way, we also would look more old-fashioned and more like ourselves. But, I must apologise for those frivolous remarks, and listen to the solemn voices of our judges. 'We object to the one man power,' says one. 'We cannot tolerate the autocracy of an individual,' says the other. . . .' I feel amazed and puzzled. But really —surely it was not a dream which I saw from 1876 to 1880 ? Surely, England under Lord Beaconsfield's government did not seem so very much opposed herself to one man power ? My English

Liberal friends often urged me 'to admit that all that happened in those bad times was not England's doing, but that of her absolute ruler.' His will—not England's—was law. Even the majority of the nation could only protest when he led them from one extravagance to another. He put armies and fleets in motion without asking the consent of Parliament, and he got as much money from the country as he liked for the display of his forces. He adopted one policy after the other, without any control or restraint. In Afghanistan England's traditional policy was reversed. He reversed first England's traditional policy, and then his own, in the Balkan Peninsula; and all the time these antics were going on the majority of the English people could only sing hymns of despair, and wait till the English autocrat, deluded by his own power, made an imprudent step and committed political suicide by allowing a general election. Fortunately, the man who can be considered as Lord Beaconsfield's extreme came to power. But all the people I see, or at least all the people whose opinions have any weight, tell me that no man in Europe, not even excepting our own Emperor, is more absolute than Mr. Gladstone. At his bidding the House of Lords pass one measure after another which they most abhor; at his command the House of Commons reluctantly consents to impose—after twenty days' talking—the closure upon interminable debates, which formed a kind of concert which no impresario in the world would tolerate more than one night.

Mr. Gladstone's opponents are powerless. Queen, princes, lords, commons, all the estates of the realm are as nothing compared with him. It is no doubt a noble spectacle, the devotion of the English people to their greatest statesman; but what about 'the one man power'?

I shall be told, I daresay, the English can tolerate an autocrat when they can dismiss him at their pleasure. English autocracy is tempered by general election, as marriage is said to be moralised by divorce. The difference between the two autocracies is that which exists between countries where divorce is allowed and where it is forbidden. But it is just as unfair to conclude that all wives in the latter country are longing to be rid of their husbands as it is to suppose that, because we cannot dismiss our emperors, we are the victims of cruel and degrading despotism. We do not want the divorce.

The Nihilistic demonstrations form a passing malady. In cholera times, Russia loses also many victims; but the cases of that other new-fashioned malady are not numerous. They are not even such an appreciable minority of the nation as Fenians and assassins are of your country. Because English Ministers cannot walk in the street without a police escort, it does not prove that the nation wishes to overthrow the Government. Is it fair, is it just, is it wise, to give to criminals in Russia a political importance which Englishmen would be the first to deny them in England? They say tradespeople find that in the long run nothing pays so well as honesty and good name. Surely the same advantages should also guide politicians and servants of the press.

Who is it that has the right of dismissing the English autocrat? Clearly the majority of the whole nation. But in 1874, if I remember right, there was a very grave doubt whether the majority polled for the Liberals was not even greater than that polled for the Conservatives. So, at least, I was assured as a foreigner. I have not the means of verifying these facts by my own experience.

Is it not notorious that the majority of the American nation was against President Hayes? Yet, by some curious constitutionalism, the elect of the minority became President of the United States. But the renewal of our autocrat's term of office, if it were made terminable at intervals, would be secured by overwhelming majorities. They are so overwhelming, that it would be folly to take the vote. Not even Nihilists—who do not practise great veracity in their descriptions of Russia—would deny that plebiscites would result in majorities of millions for the autocracy. Why, then, can we not accept the fact for granted? Why do English doctrinaires deny us the benefit of their own doctrines?

There is another point I would like to refer to?

When people talk of democracies and the rule of majorities, how often is the real vote of the majority secured ? Not in Italy, where the electoral college, even when extended, is a mere fraction of the population. Not in France, where the abstention of electors from the poll is alarming good Republicans.

Is it in England ? Well, this year I have been in England during the School Board elections. Everyone, even the illiterate, has a vote, and the uneducated majority has the election of the educational parliament of the capital. No one can deny, however, the importance of the questions submitted to the electors. But what was the result? The new Board was elected after an expensive contest in every district in London, but not one of its members received the votes of one-half of the electors on the register. In some cases only one-fifth came to the poll, and members were elected by one-tenth of their constituents. Yet the candidates who received that fractional amount of support were authorised to act in the name and on behalf of the nine-tenths who either did not vote at all or voted against them. 'Quite right,' I am told, for the many who remained at home were content to delegate their rights to the few who voted. It is true that the latter did not recognise any responsibility for those who stayed away; but it was there all the same, and the handful were authorised to exercise what the French call 'the popular sovereignty.'

In Russia we accept that principle, only we carry

it a little further. Instead of entrusting the exercise of the national sovereignty to any chance fractional group of irresponsible electors, we vest it in a family trained generation after generation in the responsible exercise of that sovereign trust. The majority—be quite at ease about that—are very well content to leave it there. 'With us,' said M. Katkoff recently, in one of his leaders in the 'Moscow Gazette,' 'the people forms only one indissoluble governmental party,' and just as Liberals gave supreme power to Mr. Gladstone, and the Conservatives to Lord Beaconsfield, so Russians, regardless of party, give a free hand to their Emperor. A power, indeed, adorned by all the prestige of the Lord's anointed in the eyes of a deeply religious people.

We are not without experience of elective institutions in Russia, and our experience is not altogether satisfactory. The 'Golos' plays the part at St. Petersburg of a 'constitutional organ,' and it is daily misleading a great many readers. What did it admit, however reluctantly, the other day? 'One of the essential vices of our provincial self-government is the indifference of the elected to the discharge of the duties of their mandate. It sometimes happens that no sitting of the General Assembly can be held because there are not sufficient members of the Zemstvo present to transact business, although one-third forms a quorum. This was the case at Kishineff last October, although very important business ought to have been transacted.' Could this ever have happened if representative meetings of that kind suited our tastes and beliefs? It only shows that Russians have little faith in majorities and decisions based upon numbers and oratorical arguments. The representation of the people often falls into the hands of professional politicians, whose chief object is to obtain a salaried post in the offices of the delegation. This contingent of members of the Zemstvo, bound together by the strongest ties of self-interest, forms a ring against which the independent members are powerless. Something of the same kind of thing appears to exist on an even greater scale in the United States; but the ring, the machine, and the 'spoils system' are all to be found in an incipient state in the heart of our democracy. If this is so where the assembly deals only with the provinces, how would it be if it controlled the destinies and disposed of the patronage of the Empire? Of course, the constitutionalists might object that 'the insignificance of the questions discussed makes us indifferent and lazy in attending the Assemblies.' But that is a bad argument. There are no *insignificant questions* when anything concerned with your country is discussed.

But I am digressing unpardonably. Skobeleff admired England, and the English institutions for England, but not for Russia. He would have the Slavonic races develop their destinies as Slavs, and not as Germans or English. Russia has a nobility, but without any political privileges. Skobeleff, like all Russians, was a democrat, and believed, like the overwhelming majority of Russians, that our democracy required the supreme will of an autocratic concentrated power. He believed in the Emperor and the Mir. These summed up for him, as for most of us, his political and social creed.

Those who share a dream in some future of a fraternal tie which might lead all the Slavs to a like kind of federal organisation under the headship of Russia, will have to wait a very long time, and realise many other dreams, before that latter crowning of the edifice is likely to take place.

We prefer the autocracy for ourselves. We are firmly convinced that it suits us better than the Western systems, but in the wide field of the Slavonic family all systems of government flourish. No uniformity is insisted on. A unity of brotherly affection, that is all we seek for. At the same time we are free to advise our younger brethren as to the best form of government, and that M. Aksakoff has frequently done. This letter of his to the Prince of Bulgaria is an admirable treatise on the Slavonic theory of governments:—

Truly it is a difficult task to which Providence has called you, and great indeed is the responsibility which you have so courageously assumed. May God come to the aid of your Highness and give to you the great, the enormous fund of patience and of perseverance indispensable for directing the government of a State whose formation has hardly been outlined! What, in my opinion, is essential for the present moment is to imprint on the government an emphatically national type.

The aspirations of the Slavonic races are entirely democratic in the true sense of the word, not in the sense of the revolutionary theories so much in vogue in Europe. The historic mission of the English Tories, of the Conservative parties in the West, *die beharrende Kraft* as the Germans say, reposes among the Slav nations in the popular ranks. It is here and not in the *bourgeoisie*, in the population of the towns, in the *soi-disant* cultivated classes, that the Government ought to seek its centre of gravity. It is the good sense, it is the instinct of the people which ought to regulate the administrative balance and serve as compass in the devious roads that the State has to travel. In Europe it is quite otherwise. The tendency which becomes more and more manifest in the Constitutional States of the West is to give a monopoly of power to the class of doctrinaires and theorists, *die Literaten* in Germany. These are they who, in the name of the misleading principle of the 'sovereignty of the people,' seek to impose on the people the most tyrannical of yokes, to compel it to submit to the despotism of their doctrines, and to direct the helm of the State according to their passing whims and political passions. The example of contemporary France is very edifying. It is in the name of the people that a miserable minority of the country, taking advantage of the title of the representatives of the nation, and relying upon a parliamentary majority of some dozens of votes, contrive to outrage legally the religious beliefs of the real popular majority.

The Russian ideal, which is more or less common to all the Slav races, is that of local self-government without political powers, supported and crowned by a central and superior authority, a personal authority, free and untrammelled in the governmental sphere.

The rural autonomy in Russia is so great that the Russian communes resemble little republics, which govern themselves according to their own uses and customs.

The people do not want sovereignty, nor do they seek to govern the State; but that which they do desire is a Government which inspires them with confidence by its energy, its strength, its disinterestedness, and its national character. The reason why the Russian people know their Tzar is, because the Tzar is not in Russia what the king was formerly in France, *le premier gentilhomme du pays*; he belongs to no party and to no social position, he is above and beyond all, he is the first man of the country, and stands for the people as their own personification. The supreme authority in Russia is neither an apparatus, nor a collective body, nor a personal and abstract combination, as in constitutional countries. That which the Russian people want is an authority possessing a human heart, a living being whose mind and soul are substituted for the formalism of the bureaucracy and the dead letter of the laws. Before Peter the Great, who introduced into Russia Western notions about the relations between authority and the people, the jealousy of power was entirely unknown to Russian sovereigns; they had the good custom of convoking the delegates of the country of all classes of the people to consult with them when they wished to settle questions more or less weighty, or when they wished to secure the sincere support of the whole nation. Although autocrats, they did not believe themselves to be infallible, and they recognised without reserve the necessity for the Government to know the thought of the country. These assemblies naturally were only consultative, and only influenced the course of events by their moral force, without prejudice to the dignity and the authority of the Tzar. It is that which will rehabilitate Russia in a time not far distant.

I believe, monseigneur, that this exposition of the theory of the State among the Slav races, and especially in Russia, may perhaps be of some use to you in your political combinations. Such democracy, based on the autonomy of the communes, the people, the true people as centre of gravity, the national character recognised in every theory, the art to make yourself popular, the country often consulted, religion respected, and the clergy honoured—these, with God's help, will enable you to make Bulgaria strong and happy.

CHAPTER VIII.

DEATH.

Skobeleff's presentiment—Commander of the Fourth Army Corps—Over-exertion—Love for his parents—His views of married life—Respect for women—His sudden death—A national sorrow—Honours paid to the dead—His funeral.

SKOBELEFF, who had so often exposed his life in war, who led his troops into seventy actions, was fated after all to die in time of peace, and in peaceful Moscow. To me personally there was something terrible in that fact. Not long ago, talking to him of possible conflagrations and wars, I exclaimed, 'I only hope and trust Russia will have no ground for shedding new torrents of blood. We have sustained too many losses already. Men like yourself have to serve their country at home, and not be the victims of a bullet.' 'As to me,' said he, as if gazing at the future, and talking to himself in an absent and dreamy way, 'I am convinced that I shall not meet my death on a battle-field.' And here came an expression over Skobeleff's face which I do not think it is possible ever to forget. There was something prophetic and fatalistic at the same time. He looked as if, forgetting all the surrounding scene, he was brought into contact with destiny itself, and all the mysterious elements which surround our life. It seemed as if death was already in the room, and trying to seize its prey. I endeavoured to give another turn to our conversation, and said, trying to smile. 'Well, we are all mortals. The old philosopher was right. As long as we live, death is not there; and when it comes we do not feel it.' 'Of course,' he hastened to say, as if awaking suddenly from a heavy dream; and he began talking of the Roman Catholic propaganda in Bosnia and Herzegovina.

The real cause of his death has never been absolutely well defined. Late in the evening of the $\frac{21\ \text{June}}{6\ \text{July}}$, 1882, he was dining with some friends, talkative and gay, and all the time sketching plans and maps, as he was fond of doing. At 3 A.M. the next day he existed no more. Some ascribed it to the rupture of an aneurism, others believed it to have resulted from a contusion received in one of the fiercest of his many battles. While before Plevna, at the very time when the legend of his invulnerability was the most firmly believed by his soldiers, he was struck by the fragment of a bursting shell. Its force was broken by the fur which he wore under his uniform, but the blow was so violent that he lay senseless for a couple of hours. His wound was concealed from his troops, who believed him to be asleep; and their belief was confirmed when the next day they saw him going about the same as always in their midst. But the shell, although it had not pierced his body, is supposed to have left there the germ of a fatal weakness. Such a hero deserved to die under the folds of the flag which he had so gloriously served; but the course of history both in Europe and in Asia might have been different had he forgotten to put on that fur, on the day when the shell burst beneath him at Plevna. He was spared to his country for two glorious campaigns, and then—ah! then—the end came, when Skobeleff was only thirty-nine.

After his return from Paris, he resumed his military duties, and was appointed Commander of the Fourth Army Corps, whose head-quarters were at Wilna. In peace as in war, Skobeleff spared neither himself nor his men, and every garrison in his wide district felt the stimulus of his energy. As a specimen of his duties at home, I may be, I hope, allowed to give the following account of how he spent a few days in the last month of his life, as it illustrates the recklessness with which he exhausted his superb vitality.

At nine o'clock in the morning of the $\frac{4}{17}$ of June, Skobeleff set out on horseback from Wilna to review the 4th regiment of the Cossacks of the Don, who were stationed at Lida, a distance of ninety-six versts (64 miles). He rode through the long summer day, and reached Lida at ten o'clock at night. The moment he entered Lida, without pausing a moment for rest, he ordered the 'boot and saddle' to be sounded. The Cossacks formed into line and ready to take the field. He took the command, and put them through a nocturnal manœuvre, which they executed splendidly. Early next morning, he was again in the field, exercising the troops, the manœuvres on this occasion including the crossing a river by swimming. In the very middle of the review a despatch arrived, announcing the arrival of the Grand Duke Michael, the Grand-master of the Artillery, at Wilna. Skobeleff left the field, and set off at once for Wilna, joined the Grand Duke, and proceeded with him to Orany. The next morning the 4th regiment of the Cossacks of the Don, who had ridden during the night a forced march of seventy-five versts, presented themselves in excellent order before him, and were commanded to take part in the review. No one thought anything of this; Skobeleff least of all. It is the simple duty of a soldier to endure all things, and Skobeleff was soldier born. Whatever our shortcomings may be, Russians may at least be proud of an endurance that never fails, a courage that nothing can daunt, and a patient persistence in the midst of all adversity, which brings the hour of victory at a time when other nations would find only hopeless irrevocable defeat. We are many, we are strong, we have learned to suffer and to wait. Skobeleff thought nothing of hardships. These nights without sleep after days in the saddle were to him as natural as breathing. He did not speak of them. He simply did what he wanted, and laughed at those who warned him of the consequences. Had he been more careful, he might still have been spared to us; but if he had been more careful, he would not have been Skobeleff.

He had left Wilna after the close of the manœuvres at Warsaw on a 28 days' *congé*, in order to commemorate in the old house of Riazan the anniversary of the tragic death of his mother.[1] Skobeleff was deeply attached to his parents, who also doted on him. He could never speak of his mother's terrible death without deep emotion, which he tried in vain to control. It occurred in the region south of the Balkans, which had been the scene of her son's most heroic exploits. After the war, and the death of her husband, Madame Skobeleff had devoted her life to

[1] Mr. Rose writes, in the *Fortnightly Review*:—'Skobeleff's intercourse with his parents was peculiarly touching. It is rare that there is such perfect confidence and mutual regard as existed in the case of the older and the younger Skobeleff. The affection of Skobeleff for his mother and hers for him was extremely beautiful. I recollect at Philippopolis, in 1879, she spoke to me of her "noble, handsome boy." He was always a boy to her. And the fine mobile features of the stately, high-bred, and courteous dame worked with emotion as she deftly touched on the "deeds o' derring do" by which he had attained his well-merited fame. She had taken a deep interest in the Russo-Turkish campaign, both because husband and son were prominent figures in the great drama, and because, with Aksakoff, she believed that its results would be "the regeneration, not only of the Slavs of the Balkans, but of the whole Slavonic world." At the close of the war, her husband no more, she came to Bulgaria, and found at once consolation in her bereavement, and an outlet for her abounding energy, in the organisation of hospitals for Bulgarian children, and in the foundation of schools; for, like her son, she had an enthusiastic belief in education. When I met her she was in the midst of the preparations for establishing in the neighbourhood of the battle-field a school, hospital, and church, to be endowed out of her private estate, in memory of her son's great victory of Shenova.'

works of charity, and was spending large sums of money in providing for the destitute and the orphans in that part of Bulgaria which is temporarily still called Eastern Roumelia. Before starting for the East, she came to see me, and urged me to go with her and work together. My family duties compelling me to spend the greater part of the year at Moscow, I had to decline her kind offers. But she seemed so full of her scheme, so delighted to work for the Slavs, whom her son loved so dearly, that only imperative reasons could prevent anybody from uniting one's fate to hers. However, there it was. I remained comfortably at home, and she went to work, not with her pen or her word, but in bringing practical, immediate help to the Slavonic world. Almost on the point of reaching her destination, one of the men assassinated both her and her maid. The fatal news reached Skobeleff when he was far away, among the Tekke-Turcomans. It left a scar which time could never efface. As the year brought round the anniversary of her death, Skobeleff intended going to his country place, where he spent his childhood, and where his parents had generally spent their summers. Skobeleff, though a very good son, was not a supporter of family ties, and was not happy in his married life. He never blamed his wife, who deserved no kind of blame, but they lived apart. 'A man,' he used to say, 'cannot serve two deities. Marriage absorbs a man too much.' But with all these heterodox views, Skobeleff had a very great regard for women, especially Russian women. I came across, the other day, an extract from a letter in an American newspaper, from one who knew him, which is worth while quoting:—

'Skobeleff told me,' says the writer, 'that he was in sympathy neither with English Constitutionalism nor American Democracy, but he admired the quiet daring of the Americans, and loved in them their reverence for women. He thought the old American lady a more agreeable being to contemplate than the young. Old English Quakeresses he pronounced "most worshipful." The staring, stuck-up British peeress who "clipped her words and was half choked by her "R's"'' was his pet aversion. The Englishwoman whom he most admired was an English Quaker lady, who had a daughter married in some Danubian town where he was quartered, and used to lecture him on the sin of soldiering. Her sweet eloquence and venerable manner affected him and alarmed his conscience, which he lulled by resolving to consecrate himself to the emancipation of his Slav brethren.' But how could he support his Slav brethren without committing the 'sin of soldiering,' when that was the only means left for helping them? Does not Mr. John Bright, whose devotion to peace is sufficiently known, show in his 'XXXI. Manchester Address' that Russia was drawn into war by England's determination to refuse all her proposals for the peaceful solution of the

Eastern difficulties? Speaking at Birmingham of Lord Beaconsfield's Cabinet, Mr. Bright deprecated its being too much for peace.[1] 'They are willing to sacrifice the interests, the happiness, and the freedom of millions of the Christian population of the Turkish provinces. and I am afraid they would make another great sacrifice, the fair fame and the honour of this country!' Then again he says, 'People of this country joined the Crusaders and went to Palestine for the purpose of liberating the holy places from the possession of the infidel and the Mahomedan, and now what do we do?' Skobeleff could admire old Quakeresses, but he could never consent to sacrifice 'the fair name and the honour of Russia,' nor give up sympathising with those of his co-religionists 'who were suffering from the oppression of centuries.'

When at Moscow, Skobeleff stayed a few days to visit the National Exhibition of Russian Industry, a collection of manufactures which has astonished even the Russians themselves by the evidence it afforded of the extent of our resources and the rapid development of our industries. He had not been very well, but he seemed to have recovered, and he was in high spirits when he met some friends in the evening of the $\frac{7}{19}$ July. At one o'clock in the morning he lay dead—hardly thirty-nine years old.

It was the $\frac{25 \text{ June}}{7 \text{ July}}$, 1882—day ever to be remembered as one of the most disastrous in our history.

[1] Bright's Speeches, p. 300, XIX. Birmingham Address.

When the news of his death became known, Russia wept. It was a terrible blow to the Russian heart. Seldom was grief so universal, so bitter, so uncontrolled. Other great men have died and their country has mourned, but few have been snatched away so suddenly in the very prime and glory of their youth. Skobeleff had come to be regarded as the personification of Russia. Almost invincible in war, terrible to his enemies, devoted to his friends, the bravest of soldiers, the kindest of chiefs, he was one for whom hundreds would have been glad to die ; for it was easier to die for him than to live for others. All Russia, from the Emperor to the peasant, grieved that national loss. All we can say is but as nothing to what we felt. ' I am deeply shocked and afflicted,' wrote the Emperor to Skobeleff's sister, the Princess Bielosselsky, 'at the sudden death of your brother. His loss to the Russian army is one it is hard to replace, and it must be deeply lamented by all true soldiers. It is sad, very sad, to lose men so useful and so devoted to their mission.'

'A frightful news comes to us from Moscow,' said the 'Journal de St. Pétersbourg;' 'Skobeleff is dead.'

Frightful indeed was the news to Russians, nor in the intensity of our grief did we even notice the shameful exultation beyond our frontiers, over the untimely death of a dreaded foe. Nor was it only Russians who felt his death like a sword-stab ; from

Sofia, from Belgrade, from all parts of the Slavonic world, came sounds of lamentation over the death of the great Slav hero. 'He was the champion of the liberty of the Bulgarian people; our nation will preserve religiously the memory of the dead from generation to generation.' It seemed impossible, if it had not been true. Skobeleff appeared to be the very personification of youth and vigour. He had gone through a hundred fights, shielded from the hailstorm of bullets which swept down thousands of the soldiers. There seemed to be a charm about him which not only repelled death but made it powerless. How could he have died when Russia was at peace, and he was far from the scene of danger and of glory? It seemed so wrong that we felt it could not be, and yet it was; the serene and energetic expression still covered the face, but life was gone.

The body was laid out in a room in the Hotel Dusseaux, which had been converted into a *chapelle ardente*, crowded with people, and the beautiful singing during the prayers was often interrupted by passionate sobbing. Immense crowds would not leave the place till late at night; others remained all night. The next day, after embalming, the body was moved in the evening to the Church of Three Apostles. As the sad *cortège* passed slowly through the streets, all Moscow stood mourning around the dead. In the church the scene was, if possible, still more touching. Representatives from all parts of the country crowded the temple to do honour to the nero-patriot of Russia. Skobeleff's grandfather had laid the foundation-stone of the church in which unparalleled honours were being paid to the last of the race. It had rained fast all night, but hundreds had stood through the rain in order to take part in the ceremony of the morning. All the authorities of Moscow were present. Laurel crowns, enormous bouquets were heaped on the coffin, near which were his sword and twenty-nine decorations, records of his valour. Peasants brought simple flowers from their fields, to him 'who loved the poor and the little ones,' touching tokens of affection for the leader whom their sons had so often followed to victory. The highest and the lowest stood united in a common grief before his bier. There was a sound of sobbing almost as of women. How many hopes were buried in his grave! An old soldier, decorated with the Cross of Koulm, who had served against Napoleon, knelt down, and having kissed the forehead of the dead, placed his cross upon Skobeleff''s breast and went away. Another veteran, weak and decrepid, stood gazing long on his placid features. At last he said, 'God is angry with Russia. In His vengeance He has punished Russia as he punished Egypt in old times.' 'Skobeleff dead!' said another, who saw the crowd and asked what was the matter. 'It is impossible, he would not consent to die,' and he went away, happy in his mistaken faith. The church was full all night, the people would not go home; when any left, their place was immediately taken by others anxious to have one last look of the hero.

So great was the press that the daïs was damaged, and admission was suspended for half-an-hour while it was repaired.

On June $\frac{19}{12}$, at ten o'clock in the morning, the funeral mass began. All Moscow assembled round the church. The church itself was filled with dignataries, from the brother and uncle of the Emperor (both arriving for that purpose from St. Petersburg) downward. The Archbishop Ambroise officiated, assisted by all the clergy, and a magnificent choir of chanters. The service lasted three hours, during which all were standing in deepest grief; no one stirred or spoke; some murmured a prayer, others bitterly sobbed. At the close the Archbishop pronounced an *oraison funèbre*; his voice trembled with emotion, tears filled his eyes. How could he help it? How could we help it, as we stood for the last time around the bier of the hope, the glory, and the pride of Russia?

And then all was over; the coffin, a simple shell of polished chestnut, with a cross, was carried through the streets to the station, to be conveyed to the family resting-place near Riazan. The crowd in the church flung themselves on the flowers which had covered the bier, and he was counted happy indeed who bore away a faded rose or lily as a memorial of the dead.

The streets were full, every window was crowded,

men were standing on all the roofs. It was with difficulty the cortège made its way through the throng, which sorrowed as but with a single heart over the bravest of the brave.

The coffin, preceded by singers of the Tchoudovo monastery, was supported by the Grand Duke Nicholas, the Grand Duke Alexis, the Prince Eugene Romanoff'sky, Duke of Leuchtenberg (the husband of Skobeleff's sister), and several generals. After the relatives and friends of the dead came the military bands, playing a funeral march, and then the Cossacks closed the procession. All Russia could not be more fully represented in one feeling of homage to the dead.

When the cortège reached the station the coffin was placed on the mortuary car, and the cannon thundered forth a last farewell to our fallen chief. Several miles before reaching the family property (Spasskojé) the peasants of that place met the coffin, and carried it on their shoulders to the grave.

Skobeleff was honoured in his death as no young Russian has ever been before; but it was not thus that he would have been buried, if he could have had his wish. During the siege of Geok Tepé, when General Petrushévitch was killed, some one said the General ought to be buried apart, with all due honours. Skobeleff observed, 'If I am killed, I want to be put in the common grave with the privates, and without any privileges at all. It is a great honour to be buried with the soldiers on the battle-field.'

That 'great honour' was denied him, but such other honour as Russia could pay she rendered to her bravest son. He sleeps at Spasskojé, but his memory remains, and will remain as a lasting source of inspiration and of hope to the whole Slavonic world!

APPENDICES.

APPENDIX A.

SKOBELEFF'S ORDERS OF THE DAY.

I.

The Trenches before Plevna, October $\frac{5}{17}$, 1877. No. 335.

A TELEGRAPHIC despatch from the Commander-in-chief, his Imperial Highness the Grand Duke, announces the fact that a brilliant victory was won yesterday in Asia Minor. Mukhtar Pasha has been completely defeated, driven back from Kars, and put to flight. I congratulate my courageous fellow-soldiers of the 16th infantry division on this telegram.

The matter which induced the most peace-loving of monarchs to take up arms was a just one, which had the approval of God. It will have a glorious ending. I would remind the army that our own metal is likely soon to be put to the proof. I would have you all know this and fortify your minds by prayer, that you may be ready religiously to fulfil to the end whatever may be required of us by duty, by our oath, and by the honour of the Russian name.

The officers and soldiers who have lately arrived from Russia are especially called upon to reflect on the new duties which fortune has mapped out for them. Their late residence in our beloved country will serve as a great consolation to them while on active service. They have seen what sacrifices Russia bears for us who fight here, and what she expects at our hands.

II.

October $\frac{14}{26}$, 1877. *No.* 360.

ON this day the division entrusted to me, the 16th artillery brigade, the third battery of the 2nd artillery brigade, and a hundred men of the 38th regiment of Don Cossacks, roused up by a false alarm, were ready for action in less than twenty-five minutes.

Here is another striking proof afforded by my fine army that neither losses, nor privations, nor bloody engagements, nor the difficulties of a late autumn campaign, are able to shake their endurance.

To-day I looked with pride upon you, my lads, so dear to the whole of Russia, and thought with confidence of that day probably near at hand, when we shall again stand face to face with the enemy, again cheerfully show a bold front for the holy cause. The rapidity, the enthusiasm with which all officers and soldiers alike prepared for action, burning with desire to co-operate valiantly with our fellow-guardsmen, affords me a proof that the division, reinforced as it is at present, will prove equal, whatever it may be called upon to endure, to uphold the immortal renown of its glorious standards. Trust me, my lads, as I trust you, and then we shall soon again strive, for the glory of the Russian name, to win the thanks of our Father and sovereign.

I offer my sincere thanks to all in command of companies, especially to all officers and privates, who were at the front.

III.

Adrianople, January 10, 1878.

I CONGRATULATE the brave army entrusted to me on the capture of the Turkish capital second in importance. It is to your endurance, to your patience, and to your courage that this success must be ascribed.

The Commander-in-chief, the Grand Duke, has desired me to thank you all. You have gladdened his Majesty the Emperor, you have gladdened our most gracious leader, you have gladdened the whole of Russia.

In giving you the credit which is due to you, I must, however, tell you frankly that I have lately remarked some falling off in discipline. During the march yesterday from Haskio too many fell out from the ranks. I even noticed that some privates dishonoured their uniforms by straggling for the purpose of plunder.

I address myself to all in command of companies, to all officers, to all honourable soldiers of the valorous army entrusted to me, and I remind them that on us, fortunate that we are, the van of the army on active service, are fixed the eyes of the whole of Russia, of the whole world.

May the Lord deliver us from temptation. . . .

May we maintain in all its purity the glory of the Russian name and the glory of the regiments—the glory upheld in this war with the price of blood.

I warn all soldiers of the division entrusted to me, that for all wilful absence from the ranks, not to speak of pillage, drunkenness, and crimes set down in the articles of war, culprits will be handed over to the court-martial.

Every act of pillage I shall regard as a proof of dereliction of duty on the part of commanders of companies. This general order will be read before all companies, squadrons, and batteries.

IV.

St. George's Convent, February 22, 1878.

AFTER the glorious victory at Shenova, where you annihilated sixty hostile battalions and captured 104 guns, you did not march, but, so to say, flew up to the walls of Constantinople.

Your valour surmounted all difficulties, and when you threatened the enemy at the very gates of the capital, vanquished Turkey hastened to sue for peace. On February 19, at six o'clock in the evening, a glorious peace was signed between Turkey and Russia, one purchased with the costly price of your efforts and of your blood.

We are now on friendly soil. Our relations to a conquered people ought to be not only just in a legal sense, but also magnanimous, for the courageous Russian soldier was never known to strike a fallen foe.

I am firmly persuaded that all ranks of the army entrusted to me are fully alive to the new relations which, from the date of the conclusion of peace, should exist between ourselves and the inhabitants of the country occupied by Russian troops.

By order of his Imperial Highness, the Commander-in-chief, I make it known that every act of plundering or violence offered to such, however trivial or under whatever form, will be dealt with with all the rigour of the articles of war. Further, his Imperial Highness, the Commander-in-chief, will regard such an action as a proof of want of influence over his men on the part of their commander, and consequently, by his order, not only the soldier immediately inculpated, but the officer in command of the company in which such a breach of discipline shall have occurred, will be called to account.

I am convinced that the courageous army entrusted to me will not sully its immortal glory by improper conduct in time of peace, and, mindful of the fact that one diseased sheep will infect the whole flock, you will yourselves keep a watchful eye on those among you likely, by yielding to temptation, to lessen the high opinion in which we are held by his Highness, the Commander-in-chief—the opinion which we so highly prize.

V.
August 15, 1878.

GLORIOUS Cossacks of the Ural sotnia,—Hitherto your name struck terror in the steppes of Turkestan; at Makroni in the Caucasian campaign, at Baliksh and on the Ouldjibaj you cut your way through mounted Asiatic hordes and took guns and standards by scores; many's the time that you excited my admiration there. I have learnt to love and esteem you, my fine lads. In the present war you have seen a new country and have encountered a new enemy.

It has not often fallen to my lot to be your leader in this present war, but I witnessed your fearlessness, both as warriors and as rowers, when the passage took place at Sistova; I heard of your victories in the first campaign beyond the Balkans.

In conjunction with the Imetli detachment, the Ural sotnia, under my command, participated in the arduous and dangerous duty of reconnoitring the pass across the Balkans and mapping out the way by which was accomplished the glorious passage across the Balkans, crowned by the capture of the Turkish army; after this the sotnia participated in the rapid advance to the walls of Constantinople. Here, condemned to inactivity, the sotnia spent six months in laborious outpost duty, and distinguished itself by its zeal, alacrity, and exemplary discipline.

I offer my thanks to all Cossacks who upheld by their blood that renown already won by them in Turkestan.

Many Ural heroes lie in European Turkey, but the survivors and those now on their way back to the Ural will tell in their native home how the Ural cavalry of Turkestan renown were no less highly esteemed in the European war.

VI.

Adrianople, November 14, 1878.

By command of his Excellency, the Commander-in-chief, some companies of the army corps under my command are to be billeted in Adrianople and other places, by reason of the fact that for many causes difficulties would be experienced in the erection of huts.

I am well assured that the army, quartered for a time among Armenians, Greeks, and Turks, will leave behind it a good report, that they will treat with due respect their peculiarities in point of faith, nationality, and mode of life, and by an amiable and a winning behaviour towards such supply a further proof that the peaceable inhabitants of the conquered territory will never find an enemy in the Russian soldier, who has come hither with the sole purpose of delivering the weak from the will of the strong.

It must be borne in mind that good behaviour towards his hosts will serve as a motive to excite these also to acts of kindness, which will supply the soldier with many little additional comforts.

I hope that the officers in billeting their men will take all possible pains to quarter their soldiers in the best possible manner.

In view of this fact that the dwelling and condition in general of the soldier has a direct bearing on his health and strength, and consequently on his fitness for military service and on his life itself, I would have all in command bear in mind and apply all means calculated to promote the health of the soldier and improve the condition of his mind. I would have them see also to the maintenance of rigorous order in the quarters, where the soldier naturally escapes the eye of his commander. In furtherance of this end, I deem it advisable that the officers of companies should live within the circuit of their company.

The following points shall be attended to:—

(1) The quarters shall be selected with care; there must be no want in them of fresh air; they must be warm, clean, dry, and light; all chinks must be stopped up and broken panes replaced. There must be a stove in each quarter, and a supply of fresh water must always be within easy reach.

(2) Over every quarter there will be an inspector, who will be answerable for order in the dwelling; privates will retire to rest at twilight, the officer on duty in battalions and companies will often visit the dwellings, in each of which will be kept a list of the privates who inhabit it. Each company will have its own court or square for the purposes of drill.

(3) Officers in command will be careful that their men attend to personal cleanliness and to that of their dwellings. They must always wear clean linen, and all must bathe at stated intervals.

(4) Inactivity is productive of mental decay, of drunkenness and disease. The soldier must always be occupied; hence, besides frequent drilling, instruction in the articles of war and in the use of weapons, the officers will encourage the soldiers to read and set on foot divers sorts of games.

VII.

Douz-Oloum, November 13, 1880.

THE officer in command of the transport service has communicated to me a telegram from the commandant of the N—— station, under date of November 1, to the following effect: 'Rain fell in the night, the roads are heavy; by reason of this fact the supplies will not be moved on to-day.' A strange thing this to hear and to read, that an ordinary fall of rain should prevent the moving up of a military train. For the stoppage of the transport on such frivolous grounds I suspend Captain —— from his duties, and order him to be confined to his house under arrest for three days. Major ——, who permitted so irregular a proceeding in time of war, will be reprimanded. I make known to the army, that even in case of heavy rains the supplies must be moved up without interruption. Neither the difficulties of a winter campaign, nor illness in an aggravated form, nor bloody encounters with the enemy, may hinder the fulfilment of the sovereign will of his Majesty the Tzar. The army entrusted to me, strong in the determination to heroically fulfil the intentions of our beloved monarch, are ready to endure all things, to submit to all things . . . for God and the Tzar are with us.

There is yet time; let all who are moved by an honest conviction that strength of mind and strength of body is unequal to the task leave our valorous ranks. Our warlike undertaking shall be accomplished come what may; separated from those who are wanting in energy we shall be still more united, still stronger than before, and shall anew cover with glory the Russian standards entrusted by his Majesty the Emperor to our iron Russian endurance, to our Russian valour.

APPENDIX B.

BARON FREDERICKS addressed a long letter to the 'New York Herald' shortly after the Emperor's assassination, of which the following are the most interesting passages :—

My friends are all of the best educated classes; I am their most devoted adherent and strict follower in the study of all that concerns our rights, our domestic and public life, and therefore dare affirm and protest both in their and in my own name, that we are very glad to have an opportunity to assert, first of all, that we the educated classes, exactly as every individual of the other classes, are not so easily put into the condition of sufferers by any arbitrary proceedings, when we have not transgressed our rights or have not done anything prohibited by law. Most of us, of the educated classes, have visited many countries, observed many governments, and are convinced that the same conditions for individual suffering and exemption from suffering exist in every civilised country. Every one of us who has taken the trouble to read attentively the existing laws of his native country is perfectly aware that the provisions of the so justly admired Habeas Corpus Act have been reproduced in the first, tenth, and fourteenth and fifteenth tomes of the Russian code of laws (edition of 1837-1876). The most appreciated of those provisions—that which prohibits any arbitrary imprisonment, written in a more precise form than in the aforesaid venerable Act of 1679, which prohibited sending anyone to a prison beyond the sea—is included in Article 10 of our statutes of criminal proceedings of 1864, in the edition of 1876, as follows :—' Every judge and every attorney who in his circuit of jurisdiction has ascertained that anyone has been arrested without due sentence or order of an authorised tribunal or competent person must liberate him instantly.' This provision was confirmed by the truly liberal-minded Emperor Alexander II. of Russia.

All our well-educated men know that since the remote epoch of 1613, when, at the election of the Tzar Michael of the ancient noble house of Romanoff, the delegates of Moscow, in the name of the whole Russian nation solemnly promised him loyalty, which signifies, according to the definition of our forefathers, an engagement to furnish him with all necessaries, provided that he and his descendants undertake the arduous task to govern the country, combined with the still more difficult obligation themselves to select their coadjutors and counsellors. This obligation of loyalty meant that the nation and its posterity would consecrate to the Tzar their allegiance—not the blind obedience of a slave, but that of a conscientious and devoted co-operator; so that every individual of our educated classes is also perfectly aware that any needed alteration in such fundamental stipulations, on account, for instance, of their being superannuated, can only be effected by means of a reciprocal agreement. That this stipulation, in its time, was a perfect one is beyond doubt, because there are many and many proofs of it; and one of the most unquestionable is the wisdom of our monarchs, by which they were enabled during a period of more than two centuries and a half to prevent internal wars. The mutinies of the Strelitzs (1684), of Pugatshoff (1774), and the so-called Decembrists (1825), although rebellions which required armed force to quell them, cannot be classed as effective wars. The population has been led on gradually towards civilisation, and to enjoy the blessings of peace as long as the political circumstances allowed it. An emancipation from serfdom has been effected without the effusion of a single drop of blood (1861). When we compare the emancipation in the Russian Empire with the more recent one (1864) in the United States of North America, renowned on account of the political liberties enjoyed by its inhabitants, where the consequence was the awful war of secession, then the Russian Empire has no reason to complain. Every youth is admitted into the highest schools —the universities—at the insignificant expense of about 35 dollars a year, and this trifling payment is in general made by government or different private associations for the relief of the poor. Every one of these great measures has been met with approbation and opposition; but that the wisdom of our monarchs has been beneficial to the nation in the highest degree and deserving of the best thanks is beyond doubt, when we look upon the attachment and the faithful devotion, not of the courtiers, but of the whole Russian nation to its Emperor.

Now, a few words about the question whether our institutions, based on the principle of self-government, are perfect or not, and why. Having been for twenty-two years consecutively a member of the city Common Council (Douma, established 1847), and also, for the space of twelve years, a constant member of the Common Council of the Government (county) of St. Petersburg (opened 1868), the undersigned feels a right to express an opinion founded on some personal experience. The city and governmental Common Councils are not perfect, and for the following reasons:—First, we, their members, are not perfect beings, but ordinary mortals, who do their best, and only what can safely be done without augmenting the existing burdens; second, a great many of the inhabitants out of doors wish for and expect important improvements, which cannot be effected without additional expense and discovering new sources of income, and who criticise, if not curse, the councils, ascribing to them abuses which never existed and cannot exist; third, a divergence of opinions prevails which is sometimes rather difficult to conciliate. This is what concerns the interests of all the different classes who send their representatives into both the councils. . . .

Is it not evident to anyone who has read attentively the history of the world, that all the different denominations and forms of government are, were, and will for ever and ever only be, experiments of more or less stability? To anyone who has visited different countries it has become evident that the nominal form of a government does not constitute the sole reason for the public weal; that there are certain necessary principles, admitted or excluded, which influence more intensely the public weal, the happiness and the prosperity of a whole nation, than the mere denomination and form of a government. The most essential foundations for a good government are undoubtedly—first, the educational principle of instilling into the minds of the individuals of both sexes, during their tender age, that their first and most sacred duty towards their native country is to be obedient to the existing laws and to their superiors; to fulfil their duties, be they of a conspicuous or a modest order, as perfectly and as conscientiously as possible. If everyone will do the same, their country will always be in a prosperous state; if, on the contrary, they will neglect their duties toward their country, they will most assuredly ruin it, whether it be a republic or a monarchy. Another essential principle is that of centralisation or decentralisation: we see the system of centralisation established in France, a republic, and in many European monarchies, and that of decentralisation in the United States of North America, a glorious republic, and in Germany, a glorious empire. The above-mentioned exchange of opinions and wishes have been briefly enumerated here, with the intention of proving that the easy and educated classes have not neglected to discuss the problems of government with the greatest care. . . . We are all convinced that a great majority of our representatives in the councils, although they have not had an opportunity of being brought up in the high schools of the Empire, still are well disposed, highly honest men of business, with the best intentions, and would look upon a motion to petition to obtain a sanction of the right of calling public political meetings as a mockery. They know by the experience acquired in the crowded assemblies in some of our local credit institutions that at such meetings no member can ever express his own opinion, for one is always obliged to listen to the interminable and, in general, ambiguous speeches of the leaders of such a meeting. . . .

The numberless gangs of outlaws of so many different denominations who have usurped the title of political parties, but have never been acknowledged as such by anybody or anywhere, would at other times have been looked upon only as extremely shocking and ridiculous; but now their importance has been augmented by the circumstance that they pride themselves on that account. Russia is not, according to their boastful expression, 'the sole field of their action.' It is now universally known and recognised that the cynic Diogenes of the nineteenth century has his nest and his supporters at Paris. Another blamable oppressor, a German fugitive, a preacher of death and destruction, has till lately had his readers and supporters at London. A great many Russian runaways are established and supported at Zürich and Geneva. Their demeanour is at present rather odious, and may grow still more obnoxious if *laissez faire* is to be the rule regarding them. The intentions of these criminals are not only plainly defined in their denominations, but openly professed in print, in the face of the whole world. For instance, the fine denomination of 'Terrorists' proclaims the intention of frightening the easy and educated classes, not only in Russia, but all over the globe. They would make every individual belonging to these classes their slave and their victim. . . .

In conclusion, it may be mentioned that some of the members of our City Common Council, a short time after the horrid catastrophe of March 1, considered it their duty, in order to give a greater security to the movements in his capital of their Emperor, the son of the late beloved Emperor-Liberator, and acknowledging that local measures would be insufficient, were of opinion that it would be the best to submit the question of putting an end to such hideous crimes to the consideration of a European congress, whose care it would be to employ the numerous armed forces, which are still in existence in consequence of the superannuated principle of an armed neutrality, not against, but in aid of every one of the European States which would be exposed to the attacks and machinations of the occult band. First of all, such mutual aid would consist in the drawing of a perfect, and at the same time general measure, which would be adopted everywhere as a law. Considering that the above-mentioned criminal agitations are the result of quite modern inventions, they seem to require the establishment of new criminal proceedings and punishments which would be adequate to the enormity of the crimes which are now being committed. In the meantime, as it has now been discovered that the activity and measures of the whole force of the police are insufficient to eradicate the existing secret associations of political impostors, which are herding together from distant localities, both at home and abroad, the best means to solve the difficult problem would be to apply the efficacious measure which was decreed by the British Parliament, when the London police was no longer able to prevent the activity of the 'garroters.'

APPENDIX C.

*LETTER FROM WIDDIN ON THE BURIAL OF THE
REMAINS OF NICHOLAS KIRÉEFF.*

No. XXVI. 'Russ,' June 26, 1882.

FROM A CORRESPONDENT OF THE 'RUSS.'

[NOTE BY THE EDITOR.—We have already informed our readers of a report of the discovery near the village of Rakovitza of the remains of Nicholas Kiréeff, the first volunteer who died a glorious death in the war between Serbia and the Turks in 1876, under the leadership of Tchernayeff. The brother of the deceased, Alexander Kiréeff, desirous of making himself personally acquainted with the truth of the said report, visited the field of battle, the environs of the village, and the monastery of Rakovitza. This visit took place in the month of May. He was accompanied, among others, by the dragoman of the Russian Consul at Widdin, who forwarded us a description of this excursion, which we print just as it stands, in all its fulness and artless simplicity. It will give a better insight into the relations of the Russian people with Bulgaria than any inferences or conclusions based on this subject, and of the reality of that bond which has been established between Bulgaria and Russia; of the great and sacred significance of that heroic epoch (the part played by Russian volunteers in Serbia), which a certain section of our press has treated with such contempt—one which is loud in its professions of *liberalism*, and is by way of guiding the Russian people, leaving out of account its national characteristics, and therefore out of sympathy with its national aspirations.]

Widdin (Bulgaria), May 20 (O.S.), 1882

Three days ago A. Kiréeff, the brother of the late N. Kiréeff, arrived at Widdin, on a visit from Russia. We had already heard of the intention of this gentleman to visit our obscure parts. As is well known, in the southwest corner of the district of Widdin, not far from the boundary of Serbia, near the village of Rakovitza, an ex-officer of the Russian Imperial Guards, N. Kiréeff, died a heroic death, on July 6, 1876, in a battle between Serbian troops and the Turks. He fell, so to say, on the very boundary which lies between the two kindred peoples, the Bulgarians and the Serbians—failing to free his younger brethren.

On the day after the arrival of A. Kiréeff, it was decided to visit the village of Rakovitza and the monastery of this name. I will give you as simple an account as I can of what I saw and heard during this interesting excursion.

On May 17, A. Kiréeff visited his Holiness, the late Exarch of Bulgaria, the Metropolitan Anthimos. The Bulgarian chief pastor received his guest as a kinsman. Of questions about Russia there was no end. Calling to mind how the late Tzar, the Deliverer, had graciously received a Bulgarian deputation at Tzarskoe Selo, at the head of which was his Holiness Anphim, the aged Bulgarian chief pastor burst into tears. . . .

Being informed of A. Kiréeff's intention to visit Rakovitza, the Metropolitan exclaimed :

'That is well! I too will go thither! We will go together!'

'Has your Holiness some matter of business at Rakovitza?'

'Business! I wish to accompany you; I would wish to visit again the field of battle at Rakovitza,'[1] said Anthimos, in an animated tone; and it was found impossible to dissuade the aged Metropolitan from this purpose. He at once called for his coachman, and ordered him to prepare for the journey. It was decided to start on the following day, at five o'clock in the morning.

The distance from Widdin to the village of Rakovitza amounts to about fifty versts. When we drove off early in the morning to join the Metropolitan, he had already left. So we followed alone—A. Kiréeff, a Bulgarian Doctor J., and myself.

It was beautiful weather. The country through which

[1] His Holiness Anthimos had but just returned from this spot.

we passed is highly favoured by nature. The slopes of
the hills are covered with vines, and fruit-trees here and
there make a pleasing variety. Cherry-trees had already
doffed their bright green foliage. On this side and on
that, now peeping out into view, now lost again, were
seen in the depths of gardens the red-tiled roofs of the
white houses of the villagers. And yonder, there already
soared-up before us, seeming to float in mid air, the frown-
ing tops of the Balkans and their branches in Serbia.
The mountains were girded by a blue, thin mist, and
seemed to frown from their snow-capped summits on all
going on below at their feet in the verdant flowering valleys. . . . We see in the far distance Mount Rtau, which
faces Bani, in Serbia. This must be at least 150 versts
off, and from here it has all the appearance of a head of
sugar. . . . I looked behind me. The Danube glittered
from betwixt a vast luxuriant valley, burning in a silver
streak, like a white satin ribbon on dark green velvet.

'Look over there,' said our coachman; 'that is Mount
Vrshka-Chouka. From that point you find yourself in
Serbia. Not far to the left of that mountain is the village
we are bound for, Rakovitza,' resumed our driver, a Turk,
speaking Bulgarian.

'What do I see there? . . . Soldiers?' asked A.
Kiréeff, pointing to a group of people, moving about opposite a village on one side of us. The groups in motion
carried arms, but wore the dress of peasants.

'That's our " National Guard "; they are drilling,' explained Dr. J. 'To-day is one of their feast-days; on the
morning of such days, the militia are required to march
out and drill,' he added.

Soon we reached the neighbourhood of another village
in the vicinity of which more groups of villagers were
marching about.

'There are some more militiamen,' said our driver.

Our guest from Petersburg looked on with pleasure at

the nimble movements of the village militia; and viewed these 'guards' in their village costume going through their exercise, with perhaps the same curiosity and interest as that he would feel in evolutions gone through by our own splendid guards on the field of Mars.

'What capital guards you have! They are simple countrymen, yet how willing they appear to be to learn their drill. . . . See how earnestly they prepare to fire.'

The word of command, 'fire!' reaches our ears.

Again they march forward.

'Left—right! left—right!' exclaims the drill-instructor, in a surly voice. He is a soldier who has served his time. 'Right-about-face . . . march!'

The words of command are given in Russ. So far as the words of command are concerned, it is difficult to realise that the speaker is a Bulgarian, and not a Russian soldier.

'Shorter steps! shorter steps!' is uttered in a surly shout.

(The instructor of the militiamen is almost always an inhabitant of their own village. It often happens that he sees brothers, uncles, or other relatives in the ranks before him.)

Let me take this opportunity, while we are still on the road to Rakovitza, of giving you a short account of the peasant militia of Bulgaria.

How is this matter progressing in Bulgaria? Officers in the army will tell you that the peasant militia of Bulgaria will soon equal (and perhaps, they will add, even in time surpass) the peasant army of our neighbour, Serbia. In my opinion, should Bulgaria be hereafter in a position to defend her freedom by force of arms, it will succeed in doing so as well as its neighbours. The Russians, whose arms secured that freedom, strive to instruct and protect them. . . .

In the district of Widdin, the militia amounts to one

hundred chets, or compagnies, numbering about 12,000, all told. They use the Krinka system of firearms. Each chet has its instructor. He draws pay from the government—fifteen francs a month. The militia turns out to drill not only on Sundays, but also on holidays. As to so-called economy and administration, at the head of each chet is found a chetnik, appointed by the regiment, whose duty it is to see that the militiamen are punctual at drill. He settles, along with the podchetnik and desyatnik (the council, of which the chetnik is president), the fines inflicted on absentees. The chetnik acts in concert with 'the district committee of the peasant-militia,' which administers the economic and administrative affairs of the whole army of the district. The military part of the affair is in the hands of the military commander of the district. The latter, in all districts of the Principality, are Russian officers. In Bulgaria, at the present time, the militia amounts to more than 100,000 men. (The Turkish inhabitants are exempted from this service.)

In front of Rakovitza we were met by the chet of that village. Militiamen lined the road. They were without arms. The instructor, when he saw our carriage, gave the word 'Attention!' . . .

Here we are at Rakovitza.

We drove into the village. The Metropolitan had already arrived. We found him sitting on a bench, covered with a carpet, in an arbour formed of vine branches, in front of the little house to which our carriages had driven up. He had been expecting us some little time, as it seemed; had had time to rest a little and drink coffee. Round the arbour stood groups of villagers with uncovered heads. When they saw their guest, A. Kiréeff, who had come to see them from so great a distance, they made before him a deep bow. My God, with what a look of wondering, naïve curiosity . . . one may say with what reverence, they looked upon him, on the brother of that young man who, six years ago, was killed in action on their soil!

In the village of Rakovitza there are 300 houses. The Turks looked upon that village, situated opposite the Serbian boundary, as an important strategic position. They always kept a garrison here, about a hundred men strong, which occupied a large blockhouse which faces the village on this side of the little river of Rakovitza. The blockhouse is in a state of perfect preservation. It has two stories, and is constructed of strong materials. In the upper story the Turks stored arms and cannon, while below were barracks. The villagers are now minded to transform the blockhouse into a church, there being no place of worship in Rakovitza.

In a line with the village of Rakovitza the Turks established Tartar and Tcherkassian settlers, whose numbers equalled those of the Bulgarians themselves. There is now no trace of the village of these intruders. On the approach of the Russians the Tartars and Tcherkassians took to flight.

In five minutes' time horses had been saddled, and all the party, not excepting His Holiness, Anthimos, set forth on horseback to the field of battle. This is situated immediately behind Rakovitza. In order to reach it we had to cross the little river Rakovitza, which flows through a deep ravine, and then to ascend a somewhat precipitous ascent to a wide plain. On that plain, not far from the Turkish blockhouse, the battle took place, the site of which, along with the Russian volunteer killed, unhappily remained in the hands of the Turks. . . .

That plain is situated on a somewhat lower level than that on which stands the village of Rakovitza, from the houses of which the inhabitants could easily watch the battle and observe all that took place. Eye-witnesses relate how, with beating hearts, they observed the Serbian line of battle spread itself out; how the leader of the

Serbian detachments, clothed in white, advanced at its head, sword in hand; how, by and by, he dashed into the Turkish trenches, and how, at length, as they watched, the whole Serbian division suddenly retreated, unable even to secure in their hasty retreat the body of their courageous leader.

About twenty feet from the Turkish trenches, which are still preserved, we saw an enclosure of oak. The inhabitants of Rakovitza affirm that this is the very spot where was left the body of the brave Kiréeff.

General Kiréeff entered the enclosure, in the centre of which lay a large white stone cross. The villagers had not yet set it up. The brother of the deceased, when he stepped on the soil watered with his kinsman's blood, crossed himself, and, deep in thought, stood over the cross for a few minutes. . . . He could not conceal his agitation. . . . Villagers stood with uncovered heads crossing themselves. His Holiness, Anthimos, with head bowed down and burying his face in his hands, clasped over his pastoral staff, wept in silence.

'I thank you, my friends,' said Kiréeff, breaking silence, 'I thank you for your remembrance of my brother Nicholas. Should any fresh enemy rise up against you, perhaps another Kiréeff may be forthcoming. . . .

'God bless you.' . . . 'Let us give thanks,' were heard amid the crowd of villagers, who had perfectly well understood the Russian words uttered by Kiréeff.

I viewed the environs of the field of Rakovitza, which is now entirely sown over with maize. It is only round the monument that a small clear space is to be found, covered with green grass. The field of Rakovitza is for the most part level; it is enclosed on three sides by the river Rakovitza, behind which the ground begins to rise abruptly. On the fourth side, the western, descend, and as it were settle down on the plain, the feet of mountains, which extend beyond the boundary into Serbia. The view of these mountains is quite enchanting. They are thickly wooded with oak and lime trees; to look at them one would take them for gigantic green waves, quietly swelling and bursting over the plain of Rakovitza. To the south, in the far distance, the Balkans present a background of blue and white, bright with their snowy tops. To the north Mount Vrshka-Chouka rises up in solitary grandeur, and looks down on us. On its summit is seen an opening in a wood, which forms the limit between the Serbian kingdom and the principality of Bulgaria.

A. Kiréeff, standing at the enclosure, sketched in his note-book the environs of the field of Rakovitza for his mother.

Before our departure we visited the school. There we found no teacher; the pupils had already dispersed, but some of these latter, when they saw us on our way to the school, came in of their own accord. A. Kiréeff set two children to read a passage from the Gospels. One of these read pretty well, the other perfectly. A little girl also read some lines. She was very shy, but read distinctly. The children were praised, and promised a map from Moscow and some copies of the Gospels. The school meets in a low, but clean little house, where fifty boys and eight little girls are under instruction.

After midday we left the village of Rakovitza and went to the monastery of that name, dedicated to the Holy Trinity. It is distant five versts from the village of Rakovitza, and was reached in one hour. It lies at the feet of the mountains, facing the boundary of Serbia.

At the monastery we were met by Archimandrite Meletius, the head of that cloister. He is the only monk in this monastery, there being no other brethren.

This cloister is very poor. I had never seen so poor a one either in Russia, where I had visited a great many, or in Serbia, where, during my journeys in that country, I had visited nearly all its cloisters.

The church, by reason of its smallness, should rather be called an oratory; it is only large enough to accommodate about twenty worshippers. In the monastic enclosure there are two ancient wings, in one of which dwells the Archimandrite, in the other servants.

We entered the church, and there we saw a coffin on our right. It was placed on a shelf against the wall. In that coffin, covered with calico of a lilac hue, were preserved the remains dug out by the inhabitants of Rakovitza. These were found on the field of battle, and were held to be those of Kiréeff and the Serbian soldiers who had fallen in company with their chief.

General Kiréeff begged His Holiness to permit the remains to be interred opposite the church. A grave was prepared forthwith. The brother of the deceased gave directions in person as to its length and breadth, turned up the turf with a spade, and began to dig. Four villagers lent a hand in the work, and with their aid the grave was ready in a very short time.

The coffin was borne out from the church. His Holiness having vested, tapers were lit and the funeral service began. The choir was composed of the Archimandrite and two priests. . . . The mournful funeral chant, resounding through the monastic enclosure, was deeply affecting. I shall never forget that laying to rest of the mortal remains of heroes who fell in the cause of Slavonic freedom. . . . When His Holiness Anthimos read the prayer in which were commemorated the names of 'the servants of God, Nicholas and his companions,' the villagers, according to the custom here, exclaimed, ' Lord, have mercy!' They sang the hymn 'Eternal remembrance.' All the assembled worshippers knelt down. . . .

The coffin was let down into the grave.

In the porch of the church, high up against the wall, a portrait of the deceased was suspended in a golden frame, with the inscription, in the handwriting of his own brother, 'Nicholas Kiréeff.'

From the monastery we repaired to Widdin, but by another road, through the little town of Koula. . . .

Our postilion, a Turk, had put to the horses, and we had already completed our preparations with a view of commencing our return journey from the cloister to Widdin, when Kiréeff was asked for an interview by the Metropolitan Anthimos, and addressed as follows: 'Pray tarry a little, I have something to say to you. Here, not far from the monastery of Rakovitza, five versts off and close to the high road, lies a village; it is a new one, having been but lately peopled,—*it has not yet been named.* The villagers have begged me to visit their village, and to " baptize " it in the name of the deceased Kiréeff. Let us go out of our way a little in order to do this, which will not involve much loss of time. . . . The villagers will be highly gratified!'

The invitation was accepted, and we set out for the 'nameless' village.

Here is a short account of this hamlet. Two years ago, a few inhabitants of the village of Rakovitza addressed a petition to the Government, asking leave to settle on that site, which was left unpeopled from the time the Tartars and Tcherkassians fled before the advancing Russian army. This request was acceded to, and over one hundred families, of whom the greater number were straitened in their birthplace by lack of sufficient land, little by little transferred their dwelling-place to the new dependency. These settlers formed a new village. It was situated immediately under Mount Vrshka-Chouka on its southern side. From the summit of this mountain (where we find the boundary of Serbia) we see at its base, almost under our feet, this *new* hamlet, from whence we can enjoy the picturesque view it presents, and even observe all that is passing within it. . . . If one turn to the south, one can descry at the foot of Vrshka-Chouka, the little Serbian town of Zaitschar, and a bend of the river Timok. Zaitschar is the point from whence, in 1876, the Timok army advanced to action, and from whence N. Kiréeff with his division entered Turkish territory. From its summit the field of Rakovitza can be plainly discerned, and the *enclosed space* can be plainly detected with the naked eye—the open space where Kiréeff fell. . . . (There is much to be seen from this eminence, about half the kingdom of Serbia, and almost as much of the Principality of Bulgaria).

The idea of calling the village *Kiréeff* was not one of recent date. I can recall that about a year ago, when M. Popoff was governor of the district of Widdin, he informed me that these villagers had acquainted him of their desire to call their hamlet Kiréeff, when he, M. Popoff, was among them for the purpose of marking off their new lands and dependencies. . . . This matter was subsequently shelved (I could never ascertain the reason why), and the result was that the village remained nameless up to this very time. It was designated in different ways: some called it New Rakovitza, others New Village, &c.

Here we are, then, making a journey for an imposing object—to a 'baptism,' as the Metropolitan Anphim expressed it. Our way would now make a circuit through little forests of oak and nut, now it would issue forth into open ground, and wind through vineyards and between fields of maize; through meads, now and then being hemmed in by a little river. The road was narrow. Often now one horse, now another—we were drawn by three horses yoked abreast—would entangle itself in bushes of brambles or wild roses, causing them to cover us with their leaves and exhale their perfume.

We drive into the village. A great crowd had assembled

to meet us. Infirm old men, women with children at the breast; every inhabitant would seem to have come out into the streets.

The village is still in an unfinished state; everything was in a chaotic condition; there were scarcely any yards to be seen. The houses are wide, covered, or being covered over with tiles. Around the dwellings wander cattle and birds—buffaloes, oxen, sheep, pigs, geese, ducks, chickens. . . . All spoke of confusion and disorder. It was evening, the sun was setting. The household cattle, driven in for the night, pressed around the houses, rending the air with a concert of divers sounds discordant to our ears.

We stepped down from the carriage and went up to a table which had been placed in a street in the centre of the village. Here the Metropolitan offered prayers, sprinkled the villagers with holy water, and then declaimed: 'Length of days to the village henceforth called by the name of Kiréeff.'

When the prayers were over his Holiness Anphim turned to the villagers and made an address:—

'I am glad for your sakes, my children, for now you are free. Where are the Tcherkassians and Turks from whom you suffered such violence and outrage?' (His Holiness Anthimos lifted up his eyes as he spoke and looked out on the broad expanse before him, formerly peopled by Tcherkassian marauders.) 'Of Tcherkassian and Tartar villages there is left no trace! Turks, Pashas, and Zaptiehs will trouble you no more. . . . I rejoice for your sakes. But do not forget to whom you owe this gift of freedom. It is Russia that has made you free.' (Here the villagers raised a shout, 'Long live Russia! long live our deliverer!') 'And what has Russia sacrificed to give you this freedom? So great is the debt you owe this country, that Bulgaria could never pay so much as one thousandth part of that debt which is owed to her for the freedom you enjoy. . . .' (Again a shout is raised by the crowd, ' Long live Russia ! ') ' It is not of money that I speak. . . . Think of the many mothers and fathers in that great country who are mourning the loss of sons; think of the many widows who are weeping for the loss of husbands; of houseless orphans who mourn for lost fathers, sisters—for lost brothers ! And here on this day there is one amongst us' (here his Holiness Anphim turned to where Kiréeff was standing) ' who is mourning a brother, who fell in this *your own country* for the freedom of its people. . . . The news of the death of Kiréeff was nearly the death of his aged mother. How shall we console the unconsolable, who have lost their dear ones for our sake, to win for us our freedom ? . . .

' By calling your village by the name of the fallen hero Kiréeff, you have given a proof to his mother and relatives, and to the whole of Russia, our deliverer, that we do not forget—that *we cannot forget* those whose blood flowed for our freedom. . . . Never forget Russia' (here his Holiness raised his hand to emphasise these words) ' remember Russia, to whom you owe your deliverance. . . . Without Russia we were like fish without water.' (" Long live glorious Russia, our deliverer ! ' the crowd broke in.)

Words would fail to express the sensation produced on the crowd by this address. I will not attempt to describe the naïve ' ovations ' accorded by the villagers to their guest Kiréeff. . . . It would take up too much of your space. One thing, however, I must put on record; something original in the highest degree. The villagers ran after our carriage, escorting it far beyond the village; several times they stopped our horses, and running up asked us each time to drink a glass of wine. Meanwhile, greetings were heard to the brother of Kiréeff, and to their village ' baptized' in his name. . . .

In the brief history of the village called Kiréeff, that day will constitute a great epoch; tradition will no doubt perpetuate its remembrance from generation to generation so long as the village of Kiréeff shall stand.

The sun was already setting when we left the hamlet of Kiréeff on our way to Widdin. It was growing dark when we reached the little town of Kula. Its inhabitants were probably aware at an early hour that a guest would visit them in the evening, and, as it seemed, had early made preparations for his arrival.

At the very entrance of the town the street was lined on either side with townsmen who greeted us heartily as we entered. The streets were decorated with flags, and a mortar fired salutes on the town square. The whole population of Kula gathered together near the church. The pupils of schools for both sexes stood before their respective schools, and greeted their guest by singing the Russian National Air, the townsmen joining in with cries of 'Long live Kiréeff!' A senior pupil presented A. K. with a crown of roses and pinks, in the name of all the pupils. The Bulgarian National Hymn was struck up, and we repaired to a garden, where supper had been prepared for the guest. Here the chief townsmen stood behind the table, and waited on Kiréeff; everyone strove to pay their guest every possible attention. . . . Greetings were exchanged and prolonged, interspersed with the singing of national airs. . . . Suddenly a cry was heard: 'Everlasting remembrance! everlasting remembrance to Nicholas Kiréeff!' . . . A toast was drunk in his honour. . . . 'To the church! to the church!' exclaimed others. The church was rapidly filled, and a choir of pupils of either sex sang the hymns, 'Rest with the Saints,' and 'Eternal Remembrance.' When A. Kiréeff passed through the town to enter his carriage, all the townsmen and pupils escorted their guest, singing as they went. The road was covered with nosegays of roses and other flowers. Our carriage was so full of nosegays, that we literally had difficulty in sitting. . . .

We spent one hour and a half in Koula. At two o'clock in the night we were already in Widdin.

February 1885.

A CATALOGUE OF
WORKS IN GENERAL LITERATURE & SCIENCE
PUBLISHED BY
MESSRS. LONGMANS, GREEN, & CO.
39 PATERNOSTER ROW, LONDON, E.C.

Classified Index.

AGRICULTURE, HORSES, DOGS, and CATTLE.

Dog (The), by Stonehenge	21
Fitzwygram's Horses and Stables	10
Greyhound (The), by Stonehenge	21
Horses and Roads, by Free-Lance	12
Loudon's Encyclopædia of Agriculture	14
Lloyd's The Science of Agriculture	14
Miles' (W. H.) Works on Horses and Stables	17
Nevile's Farms and Farming	18
——— Horses and Riding	18
Scott's Farm-Valuer	20
Steel's Diseases of the Ox	21
Ville's Artificial Manures	23
Youatt on the Dog	24
——— Horse	24

ANATOMY and PHYSIOLOGY.

Ashby's Notes on Physiology	5
Buckton's Health in the House	7
Cooke's Tablets of Anatomy and Physiology	8
Gray's Anatomy, Descriptive and Surgical	11
Macalister's Vertebrate Animals	15
Owen's Comparative Anatomy and Physiology	18
Quain's Elements of Anatomy	20
Smith's Operative Surgery on the Dead Body	21

ASTRONOMY.

Ball's Elements of Astronomy	22
Herschel's Outlines of Astronomy	12
'Knowledge' Library (The)	13
Proctor's (R. A.) Works	19
Nelson's The Moon	13
Webb's Celestial Objects for Common Telescopes	23

BIOGRAPHY, REMINISCENCES, LETTERS, &c.

Bacon's Life and Works	5
Bagehot's Biographical Studies	5
Bray's Phases of Opinion	7
Carlyle's (T.) Life, by James A. Froude	7
——— Reminiscences	7
——— (*Mrs.*) Letters and Memorials	7
Cates Dictionary of General Biography	7
Cox's Lives of Greek Statesmen	8
D'Eon de Beaumont's Life, by Telfer	8
Fox (C. J.), Early History of, by G. O. Trevelyan	10
Grimston's (Hon. R.) Life, by Gale	11
Hamilton's (Sir W. R.) Life, by R. P. Graves	11
Havelock's Memoirs, by J. C. Marshman	11
Macaulay's Life and Letters, by G. O. Trevelyan	15
Malmesbury's Memoirs	16
Maunder's Biographical Treasury	16
Mendelssohn's Letters	17
Mill (*James*), a Biography, by A. Bain	6
Mill (*John Stuart*), a Criticism, by A. Bain	6
Mill's (J. S.) Autobiography	18
Mozley's Reminiscences of Oriel College, &c.	18
——— Towns, Villages, &c.	18
Müller's (*Max*) Biographical Essays	13
Newman's Apologia pro Vitâ Suâ	18
Pasolini's Memoir	18
Pasteur's Life and Labours	18
Shakespeare's Life, by J. O. Halliwell-Phillipps	21
Southey's Correspondence with Caroline Bowles	21
Stephen's Ecclesiastical Biography	21
Wellington's Life, by G. R. Gleig	23

BOTANY and GARDENING.

Allen's Flowers and their Pedigrees	4
De Caisne & Le Maout's Botany	8
Lindley's Treasury of Botany	14

BOTANY and GARDENING—*continued.*

Loudon's Encyclopædia of Gardening	14
——— Encyclopædia of Plants	14
Rivers' Orchard-House	20
——— Rose Amateur's Guide	20
Thomé's Botany	22

CHEMISTRY.

Armstrong's Organic Chemistry	22
Kolbe's Inorganic Chemistry	13
Miller's Elements of Chemistry	17
——— Inorganic Chemistry	17
Payen's Industrial Chemistry	18
Thorpe & Muir's Qualitative Analysis	22
——— 's Quantitative Analysis	22
Tilden's Chemical Philosophy	22
Watts' Dictionary of Chemistry	23

CLASSICAL LANGUAGES, LITERATURE, and ANTIQUITIES.

Aristophanes' The Acharnians, translated	5
Aristotle's Works	5
Becker's Charicles	6
——— Gallus	6
Cicero's Correspondence, by Tyrrell	7
Homer's Iliad, translated by Cayley	12
——— Green	12
Hort's The New Pantheon	12
Mahaffy's Classical Greek Literature	16
Perry's Greek and Roman Sculpture	19
Plato's Parmenides, by Maguire	19
Rich's Dictionary of Antiquities	20
Simcox's History of Latin Literature	21
Sophocles' Works	21
Virgil's Æneid, translated by Conington	
——— Poems	8
——— Works, with Notes by Kennedy	23
Witt's Myths of Hellas	24
——— The Trojan War	24
——— The Wanderings of Ulysses	24

COOKERY, DOMESTIC ECONOMY, &c.

Acton's Modern Cookery	4
Buckton's Food and Home Cookery	7
Reeve's Cookery and Housekeeping	20

ENCYCLOPÆDIAS, DICTIONARIES, and BOOKS of REFERENCE.

Ayre's Bible Treasury	5
Blackley's German Dictionary	6
Brande's Dict. of Science, Literature, and Art	6
Cabinet Lawyer (The)	7
Cates' Dictionary of Biography	7
Contanseau's French Dictionaries	8
Cresy's Encyclopædia of Civil Engineering	8
Gwilt's Encyclopædia of Architecture	11
Johnston's General Dictionary of Geography	13
Latham's English Dictionaries	13
Lindley & Moore's Treasury of Botany	14
Longman's German Dictionary	14
Loudon's Encyclopædia of Agriculture	14
——— Gardening	14
——— Plants	14
M'Culloch's Dictionary of Commerce	15
Maunder's Treasuries	16
Quain's Dictionary of Medicine	20
Rich's Dictionary of Antiquities	20
Roget's English Thesaurus	20
Ure's Dictionary of Arts, Manufactures, &c.	23
White's Latin Dictionaries	23
Willich's Popular Tables	23
Yonge's English-Greek Dictionary	24

ENGINEERING, MECHANICS, MANUFACTURES, &c.

Anderson's Strength of Materials	22
Barry & Bramwell's Railways, &c	6
——'s Railway Appliances	22
Black's Treatise on Brewing	6
Bourne's Works on the Steam Engine	6
Cresy's Encyclopædia of Civil Engineering	8
Culley's Handbook of Practical Telegraphy	8
Edwards' Our Seamarks	9
Fairbairn's Mills and Millwork	10
—— Useful Information for Engineers	10
Gossiot's Elements of Mechanism	11
—— Principles of Mechanics	11
Gore's Electro-Metallurgy	22
Gwilt's Encyclopædia of Architecture	11
Mitchell's Practical Assaying	17
Northcott's Lathes and Turning	18
Piesse's Art of Perfumery	19
Preece & Sivewright's Telegraphy	22
Sennett's Marine Steam Engine	21
Shelley's Workshop Appliances	22
Swinton's Electric Lighting	22
Unwin's Machine Design	22
Ure's Dictionary of Arts, Manufactures, & Mines	23

ENGLISH LANGUAGE and LITERATURE.

Arnold's English Poetry and Prose	5
—— Manual of English Literature	5
Latham's English Dictionaries	14
—— Handbook of English Language	14
Roget's English Thesaurus	20
Whately's English Synonyms	23

HISTORY, POLITICS, HISTORICAL MEMOIRS, and CRITICISM.

Abbey & Overton's Eng. Church in 18th Century	4
Amos' Fifty Years of the English Constitution	4
—— Primer of the English Constitution	4
Arnold's Lectures on Modern History	5
Beaconsfield's Selected Speeches	6
Boultbee's History of the Church of England	6
Bramston & Leroy's Historic Winchester	6
Buckle's History of Civilisation	7
Chesney's Waterloo Lectures	7
Cox's General History of Greece	8
—— Lives of Greek Statesmen	8
Creighton's History of the Papacy	8
De Witt's (John) Life, by Pontalis	8
De Tocqueville's Democracy in America	8
Doyle's The English in America	9
Epochs of Ancient History	9
—— Modern History	9
Freeman's Historical Geography of Europe	10
Froude's History of England	10
—— Short Studies	10
—— The English in Ireland	10
Gardiner's History of England, 1603-42	10
—— Outline of English History	11
Grant's University of Edinburgh	11
Greville's Journal	11
Hickson's Ireland in the 17th Century	12
Lecky's History of England	14
—— European Morals	14
—— Rationalism in Europe	14
—— Leaders of Public Opinion in Ireland	14
Lewes' History of Philosophy	14
Longman's (W.) Lectures on History of England	14
—— Life and Times of Edward III	14
—— (F. W.) Frederick the Great	14
Macaulay's Complete Works	15
—— Critical and Historical Essays	15
—— History of England	15
—— Speeches	15
Maunder's Historical Treasury	16
Maxwell's Don John of Austria	16
May's Constitutional Hist. of Eng. 1760-1870	16
—— Democracy in Europe	16
Merivale's Fall of the Roman Republic	17
—— General History of Rome	17
—— Romans under the Empire	17
—— The Roman Triumvirates	17
Rawlinson's Seventh Great Oriental Monarchy	20
Seebohm's The Oxford Reformers	20
—— The Protestant Revolution	20

HISTORY, POLITICS, HISTORICAL MEMOIRS and CRITICISM—cont.

Short's History of the Church of England	21
Smith's Carthage and the Carthaginians	21
Taylor's History of India	22
Walpole's History of England, 1815-41	23
Wylie's England under Henry IV	24

ILLUSTRATED BOOKS and BOOKS on ART.

Dresser's Japan: its Architecture, &c	9
Eastlake's Five Great Painters	9
—— Hints on Household Taste	9
—— Notes on Foreign Picture Galleries	9
Jameson's (Mrs.) Works	13
Lang's (L.) Princess Nobody, illus. by R. Doyle	14
Macaulay's (Lord) Lays, illustrated by Scharf	15
—— illustrated by Weguelin	15
Moore's Irish Melodies, illustrated by Maclise	18
—— Lalla Rookh, illustrated by Tenniel	18
New Testament (The, illustrated	18
Perry's Greek and Roman Sculpture	19

MEDICINE and SURGERY.

Bull's Hints to Mothers	7
—— Maternal Management of Children	7
Coats' Manual of Pathology	7
Dickinson On Renal and Urinary Affections	9
Erichsen's Concussion of the Spine	10
—— Science and Art of Surgery	10
Garrod's Materia Medica	10
—— Treatise on Gout	10
Haward's Orthopaedic Surgery	12
Hewitt's Diseases of Women	12
—— Mechanic. System of Uterine Pathology	12
Holmes' System of Surgery	12
Husband's Questions in Anatomy	12
Jones' The Health of the Senses	13
Little's In-Knee Distortion	14
Liveing's Works on Skin Diseases	14
Longmore's Gunshot Injuries	14
Mackenzie's Use of the Laryngoscope	15
Macnamara's Diseases of Himalayan Districts	16
Morehead's Disease in India	18
Murchison's Continued Fevers of Great Britain	18
—— Diseases of the Liver	18
Paget's Clinical Lectures and Essays	18
—— Lectures on Surgical Pathology	18
Pereira's Materia Medica	18
Quain's Dictionary of Medicine	20
Richardson's The Asclepaid	20
Salter's Dental Pathology and Surgery	20
Smith's Handbook for Midwives	21
Thomson's Conspectus, by Birkett	22
Watson's Principles and Practice of Physic	23
West's Diseases of Infancy and Childhood	23

MENTAL and POLITICAL PHILOSOPHY, FINANCE, &c.

Abbott's Elements of Logic	4
Amos' Science of Jurisprudence	4
Aristotle's Works	5
Bacon's Essays, with Notes, by Abbott	5
—— by Hunter	5
—— by Whately	5
—— Letters, Life, and Occasional Works	5
—— Promus of Formularies	5
—— Works	5
Bagehot's Economic Studies	5
Bain's (Prof.) Philosophical Works	6
De Tocqueville's Democracy in America	8
Dowell's History of Taxes	9
Hume's Philosophical Works	13
Jefferies' The Story of My Heart	13
Justinian's Institutes, by T. Sandars	13
Kant's Critique of Practical Reason	13
Lang's Custom and Myth	13
Lewis' Authority in Matters of Opinion	14
Lubbock's Origin of Civilisation	14
Macleod's (H. D.) Works	16
Mill's (James) Phenomena of the Human Mind	16
Mill's (J. S.) Logic, Killick's Handbook to	17
—— Works	17
Miller's Social Economy	17
Monck's Introduction to Logic	18
Morell's Handbook of Logic	17
Seebohm's English Village Community	20

MENTAL and POLITICAL PHILOSOPHY, FINANCE, &c.—continued.

Sully's Outlines of Psychology	22
Swinburne's Picture Logic	22
Thompson's A System of Psychology	22
Thomson's Laws of Thought	22
Twiss on the Rights and Duties of Nations	22
Webb's The Veil of Isis	23
Whately's Elements of Logic	23
—— Elements of Rhetoric	23
Wylie's Labour, Leisure, and Luxury	24
Zeller's Works on Greek Philosophy	24

MISCELLANEOUS WORKS.

Arnold's (Dr.) Miscellaneous Works	5
A. K. H. B., Essays and Contributions of	4
Bagehot's Literary Studies	5
Beaconsfield Birthday Book (The)	6
Beaconsfield's Wit and Wisdom	6
Evans' Bronze Implements of Great Britain	10
Farrar's Language and Languages	10
French's Drink in England	10
Hassell's Adulteration of Food	12
Johnson's Patentee's Manual	13
Longman's Magazine	14
Macaulay's (Lord) Works, Selections from	15
Müller's (Max) Works	18
Peel's A Highland Gathering	19
Smith's (Sydney) Wit and Wisdom	21

NATURAL HISTORY (POPULAR).

Dixon's Rural Bird Life	9
Hartwig's (Dr. G.) Works	11
Maunder's Treasury of Natural History	16
Stanley's Familiar History of Birds	21
Wood's (Rev. J. G.) Works	24

POETICAL WORKS.

Bailey's Festus	5
Dante's Divine Comedy, translated by Minchin	8
Goethe's Faust, translated by Birds	11
—— translated by Webb	11
—— with Notes by Selss	11
Homer's Iliad, translated by Cayley	12
—— translated by Green	12
Ingelow's Poetical Works	13
Macaulay's (Lord) Lays of Ancient Rome	15
Macdonald's A Book of Strife	15
Pennell's ' From Grave to Gay '	19
Reader's Voices from Flower-Land	20
Shakespeare, Bowdler's Family Edition	21
—— Hamlet, by George Macdonald	15
Southey's Poetical Works	21
Stevenson's Child's Garden of Poems	21
Virgil's Æneid, translated by Conington	23
—— Poems, translated by Conington	23

SPORTS and PASTIMES.

Dead Shot (The), by Marksman	8
Francis' Book on Angling	10
Jefferies' Red Deer	13
Longman's Chess Openings	14
Pole's The Modern Game of Whist	19
Ronalds' Fly-Fisher's Entomology	20
Verney's Chess Eccentricities	23
Walker's The Correct Card	23
Wilcocks' The Sea-Fisherman	24

SCIENTIFIC WORKS (General).

Arnott's Elements of Physics	5
Bauerman's Descriptive Mineralogy	22
—— Systematic Mineralogy	22
Brande's Dictionary of Science &c.	6
Ganot's Natural Philosophy	10
—— Physics	10
Grove's Correlation of Physical Forces	11
Haughton's Lectures on Physical Geography	11
Helmholtz Scientific Lectures	12
—— —— On the Sensation of Tone	12
Hullah's History of Modern Music	12
—— Transition Period of Musical History	12
Keller's Lake Dwellings of Switzerland	13
Kerl's Treatise on Metallurgy	13
'Knowledge' Library (The)	20
Lloyd's Treatise on Magnetism	14
Macfarren's Lectures on Harmony	15
Maunder's Scientific Treasury	16
Proctor's (R. A.) Works	19
Rutley's The Study of Rocks	22

SCIENTIFIC WORKS (General)—cont.

Smith's Air and Rain	21
Text-books of Science	22
Tyndall's (Prof.) Works	22, 23

THEOLOGY and RELIGION.

Arnold's (Dr.) Sermons	5
Ayre's Treasury of Bible Knowledge	5
Boultbee's Commentary on the 39 Articles	6
Browne's Exposition of the 39 Articles	7
Calvert's Wife's Manual	7
Colenso's Pentateuch and Book of Joshua	7
Conder's Handbook to the Bible	7
Conybeare and Howson's St. Paul	8
Davidson's Introduction to the New Testament	8
Dewes' Life and Letters of St. Paul	9
Edersheim's Jesus the Messiah	9
—— Warburton Lectures	9
Ellicott's Commentary on St. Paul's Epistles	9
—— Lectures on the Life of Our Lord	9
Ewald's Antiquities of Israel	10
—— History of Israel	10
Hobart's Medical Language of St. Luke	12
Hopkins' Christ the Consoler	12
Jukes' (Rev. A.) Works	13
Kalisch's Bible Studies	13
—— Commentary on the Old Testament	13
Lyra Germanica	15
Macdonald's Unspoken Sermons (second series)	15
Manning's Temporal Mission of the Holy Ghost	16
Martineau's Endeavours after the Christian Life	16
—— Hours of Thought	16
Monsell's Spiritual Songs	18
Müller's (Max) Origin and Growth of Religion	18
—— Science of Religion	18
Paley's Christian Evidences, &c., by Potts	18
Psalms (The) of David, translated by Seymour	21
Rogers' Defence of the Eclipse of Faith	20
—— The Eclipse of Faith	20
Sewell's Night Lessons from Scripture	21
—— Passing Thoughts on Religion	21
—— Preparation for Holy Communion	21
Smith's Shipwreck of St. Paul	21
Supernatural Religion	22
Taylor's (Jeremy) Entire Works	22

TRAVELS, ADVENTURES, GUIDE BOOKS, &c.

Aldridge's Ranch Notes	4
Alpine Club (The) Map of Switzerland	4
Baker's Eight Years in Ceylon	5
—— Rifle and Hound in Ceylon	5
Ball's Alpine Guide	4
Brassey's (Lady) Works	7
Crawford's Across the Pampas and the Andes	8
Dent's Above the Snow Line	8
Freeman's United States	10
Hassall's San Remo	12
Howitt's Visits to Remarkable Places	12
Johnston's Dictionary of Geography	13
Maritime Alps (The)	16
Maunder's Treasury of Geography	16
Melville's In the Lena Delta	16
Miller's Wintering in the Riviera	17
Three in Norway	22

WORKS of FICTION.

Anstey's The Black Poodle, &c.	5
Antinous, by George Taylor	5
Atelier du Lys (The)	17
Atherstone Priory	17
Beaconsfield's (Lord) Novels and Tales	6
Burgomaster's Family (The)	17
Elsa and her Vulture	17
Harte's (Bret) In the Carquinez Woods	17
—— On the Frontier	17
In the Olden Time	17
Mademoiselle Mori	17
Modern Novelist's Library (The)	17
Oliphant's (Mrs.) In Trust	18
—— Madam	18
Payn's Thicker than Water	17
Sewell's (Miss) Stories and Tales	21
Six Sisters of the Valleys (The)	17
Sturgis' My Friends and I	17
Trollope's (Anthony) Barchester Towers	17
—— The Warden	17
Unawares	17
Whyte-Melville's (Major) Novels	17

A CATALOGUE

OF

WORKS IN GENERAL LITERATURE & SCIENCE

PUBLISHED BY

MESSRS. LONGMANS, GREEN & CO.

39 PATERNOSTER ROW, LONDON, E.C.

ABBEY and OVERTON.—*THE ENGLISH CHURCH IN THE EIGHTEENTH CENTURY.* By the Rev. C. J. ABBEY and the Rev. J. H. OVERTON. 2 vols. 8vo. 36s.

ABBOTT. — *THE ELEMENTS OF LOGIC.* By T. K. ABBOTT, B.D. 12mo. 2s. 6d. sewed, or 3s. cloth.

ACTON. — *MODERN COOKERY FOR PRIVATE FAMILIES,* reduced to a System of Easy Practice in a Series of carefully tested Receipts. By ELIZA ACTON. With upwards of 150 Woodcuts. Fcp. 8vo. 4s. 6d.

A. K. H. B.—*THE ESSAYS AND CONTRIBUTIONS OF A. K. H. B.*—Uniform Cabinet Editions in crown 8vo.

Autumn Holidays, 3s. 6d.
Changed Aspects of Unchanged Truths, 3s. 6d.
Commonplace Philosopher, 3s. 6d.
Counsel and Comfort, 3s. 6d.
Critical Essays, 3s. 6d.
Graver Thoughts of a Country Parson. Three Series, 3s. 6d. each.
Landscapes, Churches, and Moralities, 3s. 6d.
Leisure Hours in Town, 3s. 6d.
Lessons of Middle Age, 3s. 6d.
Our Little Life. Two Series, 3s. 6d. each.
Present Day Thoughts, 3s. 6d.
Recreations of a Country Parson. Three Series, 3s. 6d. each.
Seaside Musings, 3s. 6d.
Sunday Afternoons, 3s. 6d.

ALDRIDGE. — *RANCH NOTES IN KANSAS, COLORADO, THE INDIAN TERRITORY AND NORTHERN TEXAS.* By REGINALD ALDRIDGE. Crown 8vo. with 4 Illustrations engraved on Wood by G. Pearson, 5s.

ALLEN.—*FLOWERS AND THEIR PEDIGREES.* By GRANT ALLEN. With 50 Illustrations engraved on Wood. Crown 8vo. 7s. 6d.

ALPINE CLUB (The).—*GUIDES AND MAPS.*

THE ALPINE GUIDE. By JOHN BALL, M.R.I.A. Post 8vo. with Maps and other Illustrations:—

THE EASTERN ALPS, 10s. 6d.

CENTRAL ALPS, including all the Oberland District, 7s. 6d.

WESTERN ALPS, including Mont Blanc, Monte Rosa, Zermatt, &c. 6s. 6d.

THE ALPINE CLUB MAP OF SWITZERLAND, on the Scale of Four Miles to an Inch. Edited by R. C. NICHOLS, F.R.G.S. 4 Sheets in Portfolio, 42s. coloured, or 34s. uncoloured.

ENLARGED ALPINE CLUB MAP OF THE SWISS AND ITALIAN ALPS, on the Scale of Three English Statute Miles to One Inch, in 8 Sheets, price 1s. 6d. each.

ON ALPINE TRAVELLING AND THE GEOLOGY OF THE ALPS. Price 1s. Either of the Three Volumes or Parts of the 'Alpine Guide' may be had with this Introduction prefixed, 1s. extra.

AMOS.—*WORKS BY SHELDON AMOS, M.A.*

A PRIMER OF THE ENGLISH CONSTITUTION AND GOVERNMENT. Crown 8vo. 6s.

A SYSTEMATIC VIEW OF THE SCIENCE OF JURISPRUDENCE. 8vo. 18s.

FIFTY YEARS OF THE ENGLISH CONSTITUTION, 1830-1880. Crown 8vo. 10s. 6d.

ANSTEY.—*The Black Poodle*, and other Stories. By F. ANSTEY, Author of 'Vice Versâ.' With Frontispiece by G. Du Maurier and Initial Letters by the Author. Crown 8vo. 6s.

ANTINOUS.—An Historical Romance of the Roman Empire. By GEORGE TAYLOR (Professor HAUSRATH). Translated from the German by J. D. M. Crown 8vo. 6s.

ARISTOPHANES. — *The Acharnians of Aristophanes.* Translated into English Verse by ROBERT YELVERTON TYRRELL, M.A. Dublin. Crown 8vo. 2s. 6d.

ARISTOTLE.—*The Works of.*
The Politics, G. Bekker's Greek Text of Books I. III. IV. (VII.) with an English Translation by W. E. BOLLAND, M.A.; and short Introductory Essays by A. LANG, M.A. Crown 8vo. 7s. 6d.
The Ethics; Greek Text, illustrated with Essays and Notes. By Sir ALEXANDER GRANT, Bart. M.A. LL.D. 2 vols. 8vo. 32s.
The Nicomachean Ethics, Newly Translated into English. By ROBERT WILLIAMS, Barrister-at-Law. Crown 8vo. 7s. 6d.

ARNOLD. — *Works by Thomas Arnold, D.D.* Late Head-master of Rugby School.
Introductory Lectures on Modern History, delivered in 1841 and 1842. 8vo. 7s. 6d.
Sermons Preached mostly in the Chapel of Rugby School. 6 vols. crown 8vo. 30s. or separately, 5s. each.
Miscellaneous Works. 8vo. 7s. 6d.

ARNOLD. — *Works by Thomas Arnold, M.A.*
A Manual of English Literature, Historical and Critical. By THOMAS ARNOLD, M.A. Crown 8vo. 7s. 6d.
English Poetry and Prose: a Collection of Illustrative Passages from the Writings of English Authors, from the Anglo-Saxon Period to the Present Time. Crown 8vo. 6s.

ARNOTT.—*The Elements of Physics or Natural Philosophy.* By NEIL ARNOTT, M.D. Edited by A. BAIN, LL.D. and A. S. TAYLOR, M.D. F.R.S. Woodcuts. Crown 8vo. 12s. 6d.

ASHBY. — *Notes on Physiology for the Use of Students Preparing for Examination.* With 120 Woodcuts. By HENRY ASHBY, M.D. Lond., Physician to the General Hospital for Sick Children, Manchester. Fcp. 8vo. 5s.

AYRE. –*The Treasury of Bible Knowledge;* being a Dictionary of the Books, Persons, Places, Events, and other matters of which mention is made in Holy Scripture. By the Rev. J. AYRE, M.A. With 5 Maps, 15 Plates, and 300 Woodcuts. Fcp. 8vo. 6s.

BACON.—*The Works and Life of.*
Complete Works. Collected and Edited by R. L. ELLIS, M.A. J. SPEDDING, M.A. and D. D. HEATH. 7 vols. 8vo. £3. 13s. 6d.
Letters and Life, including all his Occasional Works. Collected and Edited, with a Commentary, by J. SPEDDING. 7 vols. 8vo. £4. 4s.
The Essays; with Annotations. By RICHARD WHATELY, D.D., sometime Archbishop of Dublin. 8vo. 10s. 6d.
The Essays; with Introduction, Notes, and Index. By E. A. ABBOTT, D.D. 2 vols. fcp. 8vo. price 6s. The Text and Index only, without Introduction and Notes, in 1 vol. fcp. 8vo. price 2s. 6d.
The Essays; with Critical and Illustrative Notes, and other Aids for Students. By the Rev. JOHN HUNTER, M.A. Crown 8vo. 3s. 6d.
The Promus of Formularies and Elegancies, illustrated by Passages from SHAKESPEARE. By Mrs. H. POTT. Preface by E. A. ABBOTT, D.D. 8vo. 16s.

BAGEHOT. — *Works by Walter Bagehot, M.A.*
Biographical Studies. 8vo. 12s.
Economic Studies. 8vo. 10s. 6d.
Literary Studies. 2 vols. 8vo. Portrait. 28s.

BAILEY. — *Festus, a Poem.* By PHILIP JAMES BAILEY. Crown 8vo. 12s. 6d.

BAKER.—*Works by Sir Samuel W. Baker, M.A.*
Eight Years in Ceylon. Crown 8vo. Woodcuts. 5s.
The Rifle and the Hound in Ceylon. Crown 8vo. Woodcuts. 5s.

BAIN. — *Works by Alexander Bain, LL.D.*
Mental and Moral Science: a Compendium of Psychology and Ethics. Crown 8vo. 10s. 6d.
The Senses and the Intellect. 8vo. 15s.
The Emotions and the Will. 8vo. 15s.
Practical Essays. Crown 8vo. 4s. 6d.
Logic, Deductive and Inductive. PART I. *Deduction,* 4s. PART II. *Induction,* 6s. 6d.
James Mill; a Biography. Crown 8vo. 5s.
John Stuart Mill; a Criticism, with Personal Recollections. Crown 8vo. 2s. 6d.

BARRY & BRAMWELL. — *Railways and Locomotives:* a Series of Lectures delivered at the School of Military Engineering, Chatham. *Railways,* by J. W. BARRY, M. Inst. C.E. *Locomotives,* by Sir F. J. BRAMWELL, F.R.S., M. Inst. C.E. With 228 Wood Engravings. 8vo. 21s.

BEACONSFIELD. — *Works by the Earl of Beaconsfield, K.G.*
Novels and Tales. The Cabinet Edition. 11 vols. Crown 8vo. 6s. each.

Endymion.
Lothair.   Henrietta Temple.
Coningsby.   Contarini Fleming, &c.
Sybil.   Alroy, Ixion, &c.
Tancred.   The Young Duke, &c.
Venetia.   Vivian Grey, &c.

Novels and Tales. The Hughenden Edition. With 2 Portraits and 11 Vignettes. 11 vols. Crown 8vo. 42s.
Novels and Tales. Modern Novelist's Library Edition, complete in 11 vols. Crown 8vo. 22s. boards, or 27s. 6d. cloth.
Selected Speeches. With Introduction and Notes, by T. E. KEBBEL, M.A. 2 vols. 8vo. Portrait, 32s.
The Wit and Wisdom of Benjamin Disraeli, Earl of Beaconsfield. Crown 8vo. 3s. 6d.
The Beaconsfield Birthday-book: Selected from the Writings and Speeches of the Right Hon. the Earl of Beaconsfield, K.G. With 2 Portraits and 11 Views of Hughenden Manor and its Surroundings. 18mo. 2s. 6d. cloth, gilt; 4s. 6d. bound.

BECKER. — *Works by Professor Becker, translated from the German by the Rev. F. Metcalfe.*
Gallus; or, Roman Scenes in the Time of Augustus. Post 8vo. 7s. 6d.
Charicles; or, Illustrations of the Private Life of the Ancient Greeks. Post 8vo. 7s. 6d.

BLACK. — *Practical Treatise on Brewing;* with Formulæ for Public Brewers and Instructions for Private Families. By W. Black. 8vo. 10s. 6d.

BLACKLEY & FRIEDLÄNDER. — *A Practical Dictionary of the German and English Languages:* containing New Words in General Use not found in other Dictionaries. By the Rev. W. L. BLACKLEY, M.A. and C. M. FRIEDLÄNDER, Ph.D. Post 8vo. 3s. 6d.

BOULTBEE. — *Works by the Rev. T. P. Boultbee, LL.D.*
A Commentary on the 39 Articles, forming an introduction to the Theology of the Church of England. Crown 8vo. 6s.
A History of the Church of England; Pre-Reformation Period. 8vo. 15s.

BOURNE. — *Works by John Bourne, C.E.*
A Treatise on the Steam Engine, in its application to Mines, Mills, Steam Navigation, Railways, and Agriculture. With 37 Plates and 546 Woodcuts. 4to. 42s.
Catechism of the Steam Engine, in its various Applications to Mines, Mills, Steam Navigation, Railways, and Agriculture. With 89 Woodcuts. Crown 8vo. 7s. 6d.
Handbook of the Steam Engine; a Key to the Author's Catechism of the Steam Engine. With 67 Woodcuts. Fcp. 8vo. 9s.
Recent Improvements in the Steam Engine. With 124 Woodcuts. Fcp. 8vo. 6s.
Examples of Steam and Gas Engines of the most recent Approved Types. With 54 Plates and 356 Woodcuts. 4to. 70s.

BRAMSTON & LEROY. — *Historic Winchester;* England's First Capital. By A. R. BRAMSTON and A. C. LEROY. Cr. 8vo. 6s.

BRANDE'S *Dictionary of Science, Literature, and Art.* Re-edited by the Rev. Sir G. W. Cox, Bart., M.A. 3 vols. medium 8vo. 63s.

BRASSEY. — *Works by Lady Brassey.*

A VOYAGE IN THE 'SUNBEAM,' OUR HOME ON THE OCEAN FOR ELEVEN MONTHS. By Lady Brassey. With Map and 65 Wood Engravings. Library Edition, 8vo. 21s. Cabinet Edition, crown 8vo. 7s. 6d. School Edition, fcp. 2s. Popular Edition, 4to. 6d.

SUNSHINE AND STORM IN THE EAST; or, Cruises to Cyprus and Constantinople. With 2 Maps and 114 Illustrations engraved on Wood. Library Edition, 8vo. 21s. Cabinet Edition, cr. 8vo. 7s. 6d.

IN THE TRADES, THE TROPICS, AND THE 'ROARING FORTIES'; or, Fourteen Thousand Miles in the *Sunbeam* in 1883. By Lady Brassey. With 292 Illustrations engraved on Wood from drawings by R. T. Pritchett, and Eight Maps and Charts. Édition de Luxe, imperial 8vo. £3. 13s. 6d. Library Edition, 8vo. 21s.

BRAY. — *Phases of Opinion and Experience during a Long Life:* an Autobiography. By Charles Bray, Author of 'The Philosophy of Necessity' &c. Crown 8vo. 3s. 6d.

BROWNE. — *An Exposition of the 39 Articles,* Historical and Doctrinal. By E. H. Browne, D.D., Bishop of Winchester. 8vo. 16s.

BUCKLE. — *History of Civilisation in England and France, Spain and Scotland.* By Henry Thomas Buckle. 3 vols. crown 8vo. 24s.

BUCKTON. — *Works by Mrs. C. M. Buckton.*

FOOD AND HOME COOKERY; a Course of Instruction in Practical Cookery and Cleaning. With 11 Woodcuts. Crown 8vo. 2s. 6d.

HEALTH IN THE HOUSE: Twenty-five Lectures on Elementary Physiology. With 41 Woodcuts and Diagrams. Crown 8vo. 2s.

BULL. — *Works by Thomas Bull, M.D.*

HINTS TO MOTHERS ON THE MANAGEMENT OF THEIR HEALTH during the Period of Pregnancy and in the Lying-in Room. Fcp. 8vo. 1s. 6d.

THE MATERNAL MANAGEMENT OF CHILDREN IN HEALTH AND DISEASE. Fcp. 8vo. 1s. 6d.

CABINET LAWYER, The; a Popular Digest of the Laws of England, Civil, Criminal, and Constitutional. Fcp. 8vo. 9s.

CALVERT. — *The Wife's Manual;* or Prayers, Thoughts, and Songs on Several Occasions of a Matron's Life. By the late W. Calvert, Minor Canon of St. Paul's. Printed and ornamented in the style of *Queen Elizabeth's Prayer Book.* Crown 8vo. 6s.

CARLYLE. — *Thomas and Jane Welsh Carlyle.*

THOMAS CARLYLE, a History of the first Forty Years of his Life, 1795-1835. By J. A. Froude, M.A. With 2 Portraits and 4 Illustrations, 2 vols. 8vo. 32s.

THOMAS CARLYLE, a History of his Life in London: from 1834 to his death in 1881. By James A. Froude, M.A. with Portrait engraved on steel. 2 vols. 8vo. 32s.

REMINISCENCES. By Thomas Carlyle. Edited by J. A. Froude, M.A. 2 vols. crown 8vo. 18s.

LETTERS AND MEMORIALS OF JANE WELSH CARLYLE. Prepared for publication by Thomas Carlyle, and edited by J. A. Froude, M.A. 3 vols. 8vo. 36s.

CATES. — *A Dictionary of General Biography.* Fourth Edition, with Supplement brought down to the end of 1884. By W. L. R. Cates. 8vo. 28s. cloth; 35s. half-bound russia.
The Supplement, 1881-4, 2s. 6d.

CHESNEY. — *Waterloo Lectures;* a Study of the Campaign of 1815. By Col. C. C. Chesney, R.E. 8vo. 10s. 6d.

CICERO. — *The Correspondence of Cicero:* a revised Text, with Notes and Prolegomena. — Vol. I., The Letters to the end of Cicero's Exile. By Robert Y. Tyrrell, M.A., Fellow of Trinity College, Dublin, 12s.

COATS. — *A Manual of Pathology.* By Joseph Coats, M.D. Pathologist to the Western Infirmary and the Sick Children's Hospital, Glasgow; formerly Pathologist to the Royal Infirmary, and President of the Pathological and Clinical Society of Glasgow. With 339 Illustrations engraved on Wood. 8vo. 31s. 6d.

COLENSO. — *The Pentateuch and Book of Joshua Critically Examined.* By J. W. Colenso, D.D., late Bishop of Natal. Crown 8vo. 6s.

CONDER. — *A Handbook to the Bible,* or Guide to the Study of the Holy Scriptures derived from Ancient Monuments and Modern Exploration. By F. R. Conder, and Lieut. C. R. Conder, R.E. Post 8vo. 7s. 6d.

CONINGTON.—*Works by John Conington, M.A.*
  The Æneid of Virgil. Translated into English Verse. Crown 8vo. 9s.
  The Poems of Virgil. Translated into English Prose. Crown 8vo. 9s.

CONTANSEAU.—*Works by Professor Léon Contanseau.*
  A Practical Dictionary of the French and English Languages. Post 8vo. 3s. 6d.
  A Pocket Dictionary of the French and English Languages; being a careful Abridgment of the Author's 'Practical French and English Dictionary.' Square 18mo. 1s. 6d.

CONYBEARE & HOWSON.—*The Life and Epistles of St. Paul.* By the Rev. W. J. CONYBEARE, M.A., and the Very Rev. J. S. HOWSON, D.D. Dean of Chester.
  Library Edition, with all the Original Illustrations, Maps, Landscapes on Steel, Woodcuts, &c. 2 vols. 4to. 42s.
  Intermediate Edition, with a Selection of Maps, Plates, and Wood-cuts. 2 vols. square crown 8vo. 21s.
  Student's Edition, revised and condensed, with 46 Illustrations and Maps. 1 vol. crown 8vo. 7s. 6d.

COOKE.—*Tablets of Anatomy and Physiology.* By THOMAS COOKE, F.R.C.S. Being a Synopsis of Demonstrations given in the Westminster Hospital Medical School, A.D. 1871-1875. Anatomy, complete, Second Edition, 4to. 15s. Physiology, complete, Second Edition, 4to. 10s.
  *** *These* TABLETS *may still be had in separate Fasciculi as originally published.*

COX.—*Works by the Rev. Sir G. W. Cox, Bart., M.A.*
  A General History of Greece: from the Earliest Period to the Death of Alexander the Great; with a Sketch of the Subsequent History to the Present Time. With 11 Maps and Plans. Crown 8vo. 7s. 6d.
  Lives of Greek Statesmen. Solon-Themistocles. Fcp. 8vo. 2s. 6d.

CRAWFORD.—*Across the Pampas and the Andes.* By ROBERT CRAWFORD, M.A. With Map and 7 Illustrations. Crown 8vo. 7s. 6d.

CREIGHTON.—*History of the Papacy during the Reformation.* By the Rev. M. CREIGHTON, M.A. Vols. I. and II. 8vo. 32s.

CRESY.—*Encyclopædia of Civil Engineering,* Historical, Theoretical, and Practical. By EDWARD CRESY. With above 3,000 Woodcuts, 8vo. 25s.

CULLEY.—*Handbook of Practical Telegraphy.* By R. S. CULLEY, M. Inst. C.E. Plates and Woodcuts. 8vo. 16s.

DANTE.—*The Divine Comedy of Dante Alighieri.* Translated verse for verse from the Original into Terza Rima. By JAMES INNES MINCHIN. Crown 8vo. 15s.

DAVIDSON.—*An Introduction to the Study of the New Testament,* Critical, Exegetical, and Theological. By the Rev. S. DAVIDSON, D.D. LL.D. Revised Edition. 2 vols. 8vo. 30s.

DEAD SHOT, The, OR *Sportsman's Complete Guide;* a Treatise on the Use of the Gun, with Lessons in the Art of Shooting Game of all kinds, and Wild-Fowl, also Pigeon-Shooting, and Dog-Breaking. By MARKSMAN. With 13 Illustrations. Crown 8vo. 10s. 6d.

DECAISNE & LE MAOUT.—*A General System of Botany.* Translated from the French of E. LE MAOUT, M.D., and J. DECAISNE, by Lady HOOKER; with Additions by Sir J. D. HOOKER, C.B. F.R.S. Imp. 8vo. with 5,500 Woodcuts, 31s. 6d.

DENT.—*Above the Snow Line:* Mountaineering Sketches between 1870 and 1880. By CLINTON DENT, Vice-President of the Alpine Club. With Two Engravings by Edward Whymper and an Illustration by Percy Macquoid. Crown 8vo. 7s. 6d.

D'EON DE BEAUMONT.—*The Strange Career of the Chevalier D'Eon de Beaumont,* Minister Plenipotentiary from France to Great Britain in 1763. By Captain J. BUCHAN TELFER, R.N. F.S.A. F.R.G.S. With 3 Portraits. 8vo. 12s.

DE TOCQUEVILLE.—*Democracy in America.* By ALEXIS DE TOCQUEVILLE. Translated by H. REEVE. 2 vols. crown 8vo. 16s.

DE WITT.—*The Life of John de Witt, Grand Pensionary of Holland;* or, Twenty Years of a Parliamentary Republic in the 17th Century. By M. ANTONIN LEFÈVRE PONTALIS. Translated from the French by S. E. and A. STEPHENSON. 2 vols. 8vo.

DEWES.—*THE LIFE AND LETTERS OF ST. PAUL.* By ALFRED DEWES, M.A. LL.D. D.D. Vicar of St. Augustine's, Pendlebury. With 4 Maps. 8vo. 7s. 6d.

DICKINSON. — *ON RENAL AND URINARY AFFECTIONS.* By W. HOWSHIP DICKINSON, M.D. Cantab. F.R.C.P. &c. With 12 Plates and 122 Woodcuts. 3 vols. 8vo. £3. 4s. 6d.

*** The Three Parts may be had separately: PART I.—*Diabetes*, 10s. 6d. sewed, 12s. cloth. PART II. *Albuminuria*, 20s. sewed, 21s. cloth. PART III.—*Miscellaneous Affections of the Kidneys and Urine*, 30s. sewed, 31s. 6d. cloth.

DIXON.—*RURAL BIRD LIFE;* Essays on Ornithology, with Instructions for Preserving Objects relating to that Science. By CHARLES DIXON. With 45 Woodcuts. Crown 8vo. 5s.

DOWELL.—*A HISTORY OF TAXATION AND TAXES IN ENGLAND, FROM THE EARLIEST TIMES TO THE PRESENT DAY.* By STEPHEN DOWELL, Assistant Solicitor of Inland Revenue. 4 vols. 8vo. 48s.

DOYLE.—*THE ENGLISH IN AMERICA;* Virginia, Maryland, and the Carolinas. By J. A. DOYLE, Fellow of All Souls' College, Oxford. 8vo. Map, 18s.

DRESSER.—*JAPAN; ITS ARCHITECTURE, ART, AND ART MANUFACTURES.* By CHRISTOPHER DRESSER, Ph.D. F.L.S. &c. With 202 Graphic Illustrations engraved on Wood for the most part by Native Artists in Japan, the rest by G. Pearson, after Photographs and Drawings made on the spot. Square crown 8vo. 31s. 6d.

EASTLAKE.—*FIVE GREAT PAINTERS;* Essays on Leonardo da Vinci, Michael Angelo, Titian, Raphael, Albert Dürer. By LADY EASTLAKE. 2 vols. Crown 8vo. 16s.

EASTLAKE.—*WORKS BY C. L. EASTLAKE, F.R.S. B.A.*

HINTS ON HOUSEHOLD TASTE IN FURNITURE, UPHOLSTERY, &c. With 100 Illustrations. Square crown 8vo. 14s.

NOTES ON FOREIGN PICTURE GALLERIES. Crown 8vo.

The Louvre Gallery, *Paris*, with 114 Illustrations, 7s. 6d.
The Brera Gallery, *Milan*, with 55 Illustrations, 5s.
The Old Pinakothek, *Munich*, with 107 Illustrations, 7s. 6d.

EDERSHEIM.—*WORKS BY THE REV. ALFRED EDERSHEIM, D.D.*

THE LIFE AND TIMES OF JESUS THE MESSIAH. 2 vols. 8vo. 42s.

PROPHECY AND HISTORY IN RELATION TO THE MESSIAH: the Warburton Lectures, delivered at Lincoln's Inn Chapel, 1880–1884. 8vo. 12s.
[*Nearly ready.*

EDWARDS.—*OUR SEAMARKS.* By E. PRICE EDWARDS. With numerous Illustrations of Lighthouses, &c. engraved on Wood by G. H. Ford. Crown 8vo. 8s. 6d.

ELLICOTT. — *WORKS BY C. J. ELLICOTT, D.D.*, Bishop of Gloucester and Bristol.

A CRITICAL AND GRAMMATICAL COMMENTARY ON ST. PAUL'S EPISTLES. 8vo. Galatians, 8s. 6d. Ephesians, 8s. 6d. Pastoral Epistles, 10s. 6d. Philippians, Colossians, and Philemon, 10s. 6d. Thessalonians, 7s. 6d. 1. Corinthians
[*Nearly ready.*

HISTORICAL LECTURES ON THE LIFE OF OUR LORD JESUS CHRIST. 8vo. 12s.

EPOCHS OF ANCIENT HISTORY.
Edited by the Rev. Sir G. W. COX, Bart. M.A. and C. SANKEY, M.A.

Beesly's Gracchi, Marius and Sulla, 2s. 6d.
Capes's Age of the Antonines, 2s. 6d.
——— Early Roman Empire, 2s. 6d.
Cox's Athenian Empire, 2s. 6d.
——— Greeks and Persians, 2s. 6d.
Curteis's Macedonian Empire, 2s. 6d.
Ihne's Rome to its Capture by the Gauls, 2s. 6d.
Merivale's Roman Triumvirates, 2s. 6d.
Sankey's Spartan and Theban Supremacies, 2s. 6d.
Smith's Rome and Carthage, 2s. 6d.

EPOCHS OF MODERN HISTORY.
Edited by C. COLBECK, M.A.

Church's Beginning of the Middle Ages, 2s. 6d.
Cox's Crusades, 2s. 6d.
Creighton's Age of Elizabeth, 2s. 6d.
Gairdner's Lancaster and York, 2s. 6d.
Gardiner's Puritan Revolution, 2s. 6d.
——— Thirty Years' War, 2s. 6d.
——— (Mrs.) French Revolution, 2s. 6d.
Hale's Fall of the Stuarts, 2s. 6d.
Johnson's Normans in Europe, 2s. 6d.
Longman's Frederick the Great, 2s. 6d.
Ludlow's War of American Independence, 2s. 6d.
M'Carthy's Epoch of Reform, 1830-1850, 2s. 6d.
Morris's Age of Anne, 2s. 6d.
Seebohm's Protestant Revolution, 2s. 6d.
Stubbs' Early Plantagenets, 2s. 6d.
Warburton's Edward III. 2s. 6d.

ERICHSEN.—*Works by John Eric Erichsen, F.R.S.*

THE SCIENCE AND ART OF SURGERY: Being a Treatise on Surgical Injuries, Diseases, and Operations. Illustrated by Engravings on Wood. 2 vols 8vo. 42s.; or bound in half-russia, 60s.

ON CONCUSSION OF THE SPINE, NERVOUS SHOCKS, and other Obscure Injuries of the Nervous System in their Clinical and Medico-Legal Aspects. Crown 8vo. 10s. 6d.

EVANS.—*The Bronze Implements, Arms, and Ornaments of Great Britain and Ireland.* By John Evans, D.C.L. LL.D. F.R.S. With 540 Illustrations. 8vo. 25s.

EWALD.—*Works by Professor Heinrich Ewald, of Göttingen.*

THE ANTIQUITIES OF ISRAEL. Translated from the German by H. S. Solly, M.A. 8vo. 12s. 6d.

THE HISTORY OF ISRAEL. Translated from the German. Vols. I.–V. 8vo. 63s. Vol. VI. *Christ and his Times*, 8vo. 16s. Vol. VII. *The Apostolic Age*, 8vo. 21s.

FAIRBAIRN.—*Works by Sir W. Fairbairn, Bart, C.E.*

A TREATISE ON MILLS AND MILLWORK, with 18 Plates and 333 Woodcuts. 1 vol. 8vo. 25s.

USEFUL INFORMATION FOR ENGINEERS. With many Plates and Woodcuts. 3 vols. crown 8vo. 31s. 6d.

FARRAR.—*Language and Languages.* A Revised Edition of *Chapters on Language and Families of Speech.* By F. W Farrar, D.D. Crown 8vo. 6s.

FITZWYGRAM.—*Horses and Stables.* By Major-General Sir F. Fitzwygram, Bart. With 39 pages of Illustrations. 8vo. 10s. 6d.

FOX.—*The Early History of Charles James Fox.* By the Right Hon. G. O. Trevelyan, M.P. Library Edition, 8vo. 18s. Cabinet Edition, cr. 8vo. 6s.

FRANCIS.—*A Book on Angling;* or, Treatise on the Art of Fishing in every branch; including full Illustrated Lists of Salmon Flies. By Francis Francis. Post 8vo. Portrait and Plates, 15s.

FREEMAN.—*Works by E. A. Freeman, D.C.L.*

THE HISTORICAL GEOGRAPHY OF EUROPE. With 65 Maps. 2 vols. 8vo. 31s. 6d.

SOME IMPRESSIONS OF THE UNITED STATES. Crown 8vo. 6s.

FRENCH.—*Nineteen Centuries of Drink in England,* a History. By Richard Valpy French, D.C.L. LL.D. F.S.A.; Author of 'The History of Toasting' &c. Crown 8vo. 10s. 6d.

FROUDE.—*Works by James A. Froude, M.A.*

THE HISTORY OF ENGLAND, from the Fall of Wolsey to the Defeat of the Spanish Armada.
Cabinet Edition, 12 vols. cr. 8vo. £3. 12s.
Popular Edition, 12 vols. cr. 8vo. £2. 2s.

SHORT STUDIES ON GREAT SUBJECTS. 4 vols. crown 8vo. 24s.

THE ENGLISH IN IRELAND IN THE EIGHTEENTH CENTURY. 3 vols. crown 8vo. 18s.

THOMAS CARLYLE, a History of the first Forty Years of his Life, 1795 to 1835. 2 vols. 8vo. 32s.

THOMAS CARLYLE, a History of His Life in London from 1834 to his death in 1881. By James A. Froude, M.A. with Portrait engraved on steel. 2 vols. 8vo. 32s.

GANOT.—*Works by Professor Ganot.* Translated by E. Atkinson, Ph.D. F.C.S.

ELEMENTARY TREATISE ON PHYSICS, for the use of Colleges and Schools. With 5 Coloured Plates and 898 Woodcuts. Large crown 8vo. 15s.

NATURAL PHILOSOPHY FOR GENERAL READERS AND YOUNG PERSONS. With 2 Plates and 471 Woodcuts. Crown 8vo. 7s. 6d.

GARDINER.—*Works by Samuel Rawson Gardiner, LL.D.*

HISTORY OF ENGLAND, from the Accession of James I. to the Outbreak of the Civil War, 1603-1642. Cabinet Edition, thoroughly revised. 10 vols. crown 8vo. price 6s. each.

OUTLINE OF ENGLISH HISTORY, B.C. 55-A.D. 1880. With 96 Woodcuts, fcp. 8vo. 2s. 6d.

*** For Professor Gardiner's other Works, see 'Epochs of Modern History,' p. 9.

GARROD. — *Works by Alfred Baring Garrod, M.D. F.R.S.*

A TREATISE ON GOUT AND RHEUMATIC GOUT (RHEUMATOID ARTHRITIS). With 6 Plates, comprising 21 Figures (14 Coloured), and 27 Illustrations engraved on Wood. 8vo. 21s.

THE ESSENTIALS OF MATERIA MEDICA AND THERAPEUTICS. Revised and edited, under the supervision of the Author, by E. B. BAXTER, M.D. F.R.C.P. Professor of Materia Medica and Therapeutics in King's College, London. Crown 8vo. 12s. 6d.

GOETHE. — *Faust.* Translated by T. E. WEBB, LL.D. Reg. Prof. of Laws and Public Orator in the Univ. of Dublin. 8vo. 12s. 6d.

FAUST. A New Translation, chiefly in Blank Verse; with a complete Introduction and Copious Notes. By JAMES ADEY BIRDS, B.A. F.G.S. Large crown 8vo. 12s. 6d.

FAUST. The German Text, with an English Introduction and Notes for Students. By ALBERT M. SELSS, M.A. Ph.D. Crown 8vo. 5s.

GOODEVE. — *Works by T. M. Goodeve, M.A.*

PRINCIPLES OF MECHANICS. With 253 Woodcuts. Crown 8vo. 6s.

THE ELEMENTS OF MECHANISM. With 342 Woodcuts. Crown 8vo. 6s.

GRANT. — *Works by Sir Alexander Grant, Bart. LL.D. D.C.L. &c.*

THE STORY OF THE UNIVERSITY OF EDINBURGH during its First Three Hundred Years. With numerous Illustrations. 2 vols. 8vo. 36s.

THE ETHICS OF ARISTOTLE. The Greek Text illustrated by Essays and Notes. 2 vols. 8vo. 32s.

GREVILLE. — *Journal of the Reigns of King George IV. and King William IV.* By the late C. C. F. GREVILLE. Edited by H. REEVE, C.B. 3 vols. 8vo. 36s.

GRIMSTON. — *The Hon. Robert Grimston:* a Sketch of his Life. By FREDERICK GALE. With Portrait. Crown 8vo. 10s. 6d.

GRAY. — *Anatomy, Descriptive and Surgical.* By HENRY GRAY, F.R.S. late Lecturer on Anatomy at St. George's Hospital. With 557 large Woodcut Illustrations; those in the First Edition after Original Drawings by Dr. Carter, from Dissections made by the Author and Dr. Carter; the additional Drawings in the Second and subsequent Editions by Dr. Westmacott, and other Demonstrators of Anatomy. Re-edited by T. PICKERING PICK, Surgeon to St. George's Hospital. Royal 8vo. 30s.

GWILT. — *An Encyclopædia of Architecture,* Historical, Theoretical, and Practical. By JOSEPH GWILT, F.S.A. Illustrated with more than 1,100 Engravings on Wood. Revised, with Alterations and Considerable Additions, by WYATT PAPWORTH. Additionally illustrated with nearly 400 Wood Engravings by O. JEWITT, and nearly 200 other Woodcuts. 8vo. 52s. 6d.

GROVE. — *The Correlation of Physical Forces.* By the Hon. Sir W. R. GROVE, F.R.S. &c. 8vo. 15s.

HALLIWELL-PHILLIPPS. — *Outlines of the Life of Shakespeare.* By J. O. HALLIWELL-PHILLIPPS, F.R.S. 8vo. 7s. 6d.

HAMILTON. — *Life of Sir William R. Hamilton,* Kt. LL.D. D.C.L. M.R.I.A. &c. Including Selections from his Poems, Correspondence, and Miscellaneous Writings. By the Rev. R. P. GRAVES, M.A. Vol. I. 8vo. 15s.

HARTWIG. — *Works by Dr. G. Hartwig.*

THE SEA AND ITS LIVING WONDERS. 8vo. with many Illustrations, 10s. 6d.

THE TROPICAL WORLD. With about 200 Illustrations. 8vo. 10s. 6d.

THE POLAR WORLD; a Description of Man and Nature in the Arctic and Antarctic Regions of the Globe. Maps, Plates, and Woodcuts. 8vo. 10s. 6d.

THE ARCTIC REGIONS (extracted from the 'Polar World'). 4to. 6d. sewed.

THE SUBTERRANEAN WORLD. With Maps and Woodcuts. 8vo. 10s. 6d.

THE AERIAL WORLD; a Popular Account of the Phenomena and Life of the Atmosphere. Map, Plates, Woodcuts. 8vo. 10s. 6d.

HARTE.—*On the Frontier.* Three Stories. By BRET HARTE. 16mo. 1s.

HASSALL.—*Works by Arthur Hill Hassall, M.D.*

Food; its Adulterations and the Methods for their Detection. Illustrated. Crown 8vo. 24s.

San Remo, climatically and medically considered. With 30 Illustrations. Crown 8vo. 5s.

HAUGHTON.—*Six Lectures on Physical Geography,* delivered in 1876, with some Additions. By the Rev. SAMUEL HAUGHTON, F.R.S. M.D. D.C.L. With 23 Diagrams. 8vo. 15s.

HAVELOCK.—*Memoirs of Sir Henry Havelock, K.C.B.* By JOHN CLARK MARSHMAN. Crown 8vo. 3s. 6d.

HAWARD.—*A Treatise on Orthopædic Surgery.* By J. WARRINGTON HAWARD, F.R.C.S. Surgeon to St. George's Hospital. With 30 Illustrations engraved on Wood. 8vo. 12s. 6d.

HELMHOLTZ.—*Works by Professor Helmholtz.*

Popular Lectures on Scientific Subjects. Translated and edited by EDMUND ATKINSON, Ph.D. F.C.S. With a Preface by Professor TYNDALL, F.R.S. and 68 Woodcuts. 2 vols. Crown 8vo. 15s. or separately, 7s. 6d. each.

On the Sensations of Tone as a Physiological Basis for the Theory of Music. Translated by A. J. ELLIS, F.R.S. Second English Edition. Royal 8vo. 21s.

HERSCHEL.—*Outlines of Astronomy.* By Sir J. F. W. HERSCHEL, Bart. M.A. With Plates and Diagrams. Square crown 8vo. 12s.

HEWITT.—*Works by Graily Hewitt, M.D.*

The Diagnosis and Treatment of Diseases of Women, including the Diagnosis of Pregnancy. New Edition, in great part re-written and much enlarged, with 211 Engravings on Wood, of which 79 are new in this Edition. 8vo. 24s.

The Mechanical System of Uterine Pathology. With 31 Life-size Illustrations prepared expressly for this Work. Crown 4to. 7s. 6d.

HICKSON.—*Ireland in the Seventeenth Century;* or, The Irish Massacres of 1641-2, their Causes and Results. Illustrated by Extracts from the unpublished State Papers, the unpublished MSS. in the Bodleian Library, Lambeth Library, &c. ; a Selection from the unpublished Depositions relating to the Massacres, and the Reports of the Trials in the High Court of Justice, 1652-4, from the unpublished MSS. By MARY HICKSON. With a Preface by J. A. Froude, M.A. 2 vols. 8vo. 28s.

HOBART.—*The Medical Language of St. Luke;* a Proof from Internal Evidence that St. Luke's Gospel and the Acts were written by the same person, and that the writer was a Medical Man. By the Rev. W. K. HOBART, LL.D. 8vo. 16s.

HOLMES.—*A System of Surgery,* Theoretical and Practical, in Treatises by various Authors. Edited by TIMOTHY HOLMES, M.A. Surgeon to St. George's Hospital; and J. W. HULKE, F.R.S. Surgeon to the Middlesex Hospital. In 3 Volumes, with Coloured Plates and Illustrations on Wood. 3 vols. royal 8vo. price Four Guineas.

HOMER.—*The Iliad of Homer,* Homometrically translated by C. B. CAYLEY. 8vo. 12s. 6d.

The Iliad of Homer. The Greek Text, with a Verse Translation, by W. C. GREEN, M.A. Vol. I. Books I.-XII. Crown 8vo. 6s.

HOPKINS.—*Christ the Consoler;* a Book of Comfort for the Sick. By ELLICE HOPKINS. Fcp. 8vo. 2s. 6d.

HORSES AND ROADS; or How to Keep a Horse Sound on His Legs. By FREE-LANCE. Crown 8vo. 6s.

HORT.—*The New Pantheon,* or an Introduction to the Mythology of the Ancients. By W. J. HORT. 18mo. 2s. 6d.

HOWITT.—*Visits to Remarkable Places,* Old Halls, Battle-Fields, Scenes illustrative of Striking Passages in English History and Poetry. By WILLIAM HOWITT. With 80 Illustrations engraved on Wood. Crown 8vo. 7s. 6d.

HULLAH.—*Works by John Hullah, LL.D.*

Course of Lectures on the History of Modern Music. 8vo. 8s. 6d.

Course of Lectures on the Transition Period of Musical History. 8vo. 10s. 6d.

LONGMANS & CO.'S LIST OF GENERAL AND SCIENTIFIC BOOKS.   13

HUME.—*The Philosophical Works of David Hume.* Edited by T. H. Green, M.A. and the Rev. T. H. Grose, M.A. 4 vols. 8vo. 56s. Or separately, Essays, 2 vols. 28s. Treatise on Human Nature. 2 vols. 28s.

HUSBAND. — *Examination Questions in Anatomy, Physiology, Botany, Materia Medica, Surgery, Medicine, Midwifery, and State-Medicine.* Arranged by H. A. Husband, M.B. M.C. M.R.C.S. L.S.A. &c. 32mo. 4s. 6d.

INGELOW. —*Poetical Works of Jean Ingelow.* New Edition, reprinted, with Additional Matter, from the 23rd and 6th Editions of the two volumes respectively. With 2 Vignettes. 2 vols. Fcp. 8vo. 12s.

IN THE OLDEN TIME.—A Novel. By the Author of 'Mademoiselle Mori.' Crown 8vo. 6s.

JAMESON.—*Works by Mrs. Jameson.*
Legends of the Saints and Martyrs. With 19 Etchings and 187 Woodcuts. 2 vols. 31s. 6d.
Legends of the Madonna, the Virgin Mary as represented in Sacred and Legendary Art. With 27 Etchings and 165 Woodcuts. 1 vol. 21s.
Legends of the Monastic Orders. With 11 Etchings and 88 Woodcuts. 1 vol. 21s.
History of the Saviour, His Types and Precursors. Completed by Lady Eastlake. With 13 Etchings and 281 Woodcuts. 2 vols. 42s.

JEFFERIES.—*Works by Richard Jefferies.*
The Story of My Heart: My Autobiography. Crown 8vo. 5s.
Red Deer. Crown 8vo. 4s. 6d.

JOHNSON.—*The Patentee's Manual;* a Treatise on the Law and Practice of Letters Patent, for the use of Patentees and Inventors. By J. Johnson and J. H. Johnson. 8vo. 10s. 6d.

JOHNSTON.—*A General Dictionary of Geography,* Descriptive, Physical, Statistical, and Historical; a complete Gazetteer of the World. By Keith Johnston. Medium 8vo. 42s.

JONES. — *The Health of the Senses: Sight, Hearing, Voice, Smell and Taste, Skin;* with Hints on Health, Diet, Education, Health Resorts of Europe, &c. By H. Macnaughton Jones, M.D. Crown 8vo. 3s. 6d.

JUKES.—*Works by the Rev. Andrew Jukes.*
The New Man and the Eternal Life. Crown 8vo. 6s.
The Types of Genesis. Crown 8vo. 7s. 6d.
The Second Death and the Restitution of all Things. Crown 8vo. 3s. 6d.
The Mystery of the Kingdom. Crown 8vo. 2s. 6d.

JUSTINIAN.—*The Institutes of Justinian;* Latin Text, chiefly that of Huschke, with English Introduction, Translation, Notes, and Summary. By Thomas C. Sandars, M.A. Barrister-at-Law. 8vo. 18s.

KALISCH. — *Works by M. M. Kalisch, M.A.*
Bible Studies. Part I. The Prophecies of Balaam. 8vo. 10s. 6d. Part II. The Book of Jonah. 8vo. 10s. 6d.
Commentary on the Old Testament; with a New Translation. Vol. I. Genesis, 8vo. 18s. or adapted for the General Reader, 12s. Vol. II. Exodus, 15s. or adapted for the General Reader, 12s. Vol. III. Leviticus, Part I. 15s. or adapted for the General Reader, 8s. Vol. IV. Leviticus, Part II. 15s. or adapted for the General Reader, 8s.

KANT. — *Critique of Practical Reason,* and other Works on the Theory of Ethics. By Emmanuel Kant. Translated by Thomas Kingsmill Abbott, B.D. With Memoir and Portrait. 8vo. 12s. 6d.

KELLER.—*The Lake Dwellings of Switzerland,* and other Parts of Europe. By Dr. F. Keller, President of the Antiquarian Association of Zürich. Translated and arranged by John E. Lee, F.S.A. F.G.S. 2 vols. royal 8vo. with 206 Illustrations, 42s.

KERL.—*A Practical Treatise on Metallurgy.* By Professor Kerl. Adapted from the last German Edition by W. Crookes, F.R.S. &c. and E. Röhrig, Ph.D. 3 vols. 8vo. with 625 Woodcuts, £4. 19s.

KILLICK.—*Handbook to Mill's System of Logic.* By the Rev. A. H. Killick, M.A. Crown 8vo. 3s. 6d.

KOLBE.—*A Short Text-Book of Inorganic Chemistry.* By Dr. Hermann Kolbe. Translated from the German by T. S. Humpidge, Ph.D. With a Coloured Table of Spectra and 66 Illustrations. Crown 8vo. 7s. 6d.

LANG. — *Works by Andrew Lang, late Fellow of Merton College.*
CUSTOM AND MYTH: Studies of Early Usage and Belief. With 15 Illustrations. Crown 8vo. 7s. 6d.
THE PRINCESS NOBODY: a Tale of Fairyland. After the Drawings by Richard Doyle, printed in colours by Edmund Evans. Post 4to. 5s. boards.

LATHAM. — *Works by Robert G. Latham, M.A. M.D.*
A DICTIONARY OF THE ENGLISH LANGUAGE. Founded on the Dictionary of Dr. JOHNSON. Four vols. 4to. £7.
A DICTIONARY OF THE ENGLISH LANGUAGE. Abridged from Dr. Latham's Edition of Johnson's Dictionary. One Volume. Medium 8vo. 14s.
HANDBOOK OF THE ENGLISH LANGUAGE. Crown 8vo. 6s.

LECKY. — *Works by W. E. H. Lecky.*
HISTORY OF ENGLAND IN THE 18TH CENTURY. 4 vols. 8vo. 1700-1784, £3. 12s.
THE HISTORY OF EUROPEAN MORALS FROM AUGUSTUS TO CHARLEMAGNE. 2 vols. crown 8vo. 16s.
HISTORY OF THE RISE AND INFLUENCE OF THE SPIRIT OF RATIONALISM IN EUROPE. 2 vols. crown 8vo. 16s.
LEADERS OF PUBLIC OPINION IN IRELAND. — Swift, Flood, Grattan, O'Connell. Crown 8vo. 7s. 6d.

LEWES. — *The History of Philosophy*, from Thales to Comte. By GEORGE HENRY LEWES. 2 vols. 8vo. 32s.

LEWIS. — ON THE INFLUENCE OF AUTHORITY IN MATTERS OF OPINION. By Sir G. C. LEWIS, Bart. 8vo. 14s.

LINDLEY and MOORE. — THE TREASURY OF BOTANY, or Popular Dictionary of the Vegetable Kingdom. Edited by J. LINDLEY, F.R.S. and T. MOORE, F.L.S. With 274 Woodcuts and 20 Steel Plates. Two Parts, fcp. 8vo. 12s.

LIVEING. — *Works by Robert Liveing, M.A. and M.D. Cantab.*
HANDBOOK ON DISEASES OF THE SKIN. With especial reference to Diagnosis and Treatment. Fcp. 8vo. 5s.
NOTES ON THE TREATMENT OF SKIN DISEASES. 18mo. 3s.
ELEPHANTIASIS GRÆCORUM, OR TRUE LEPROSY. Crown 8vo. 4s. 6d.

LITTLE. ON IN-KNEE DISTORTION (Genu Valgum): Its Varieties and Treatment with and without Surgical Operation. By W. J. LITTLE, M.D. Assisted by MUIRHEAD LITTLE, M.R.C.S. With 40 Illustrations. 8vo. 7s. 6d.

LLOYD. — A TREATISE ON MAGNETISM, General and Terrestrial. By H. LLOYD, D.D. D.C.L. 8vo. 10s. 6d.

LLOYD. — THE SCIENCE OF AGRICULTURE. By F. J. LLOYD. 8vo. 12s.

LONGMAN. — *Works by William Longman, F.S.A.*
LECTURES ON THE HISTORY OF ENGLAND from the Earliest Times to the Death of King Edward II. Maps and Illustrations. 8vo. 15s.
HISTORY OF THE LIFE AND TIMES OF EDWARD III. With 9 Maps, 8 Plates, and 16 Woodcuts. 2 vols. 8vo. 28s.

LONGMAN. — *Works by Frederick W. Longman, Balliol College, Oxon.*
CHESS OPENINGS. Fcp. 8vo. 2s. 6d.
FREDERICK THE GREAT AND THE SEVEN YEARS' WAR. With 2 Coloured Maps. 8vo. 2s. 6d.
A NEW POCKET DICTIONARY OF THE GERMAN AND ENGLISH LANGUAGES. Square 18mo. 2s. 6d.

LONGMAN'S MAGAZINE. Published Monthly. Price Sixpence. Vols. 1-4, 8vo. price 5s. each.

LONGMORE. — GUNSHOT INJURIES; Their History, Characteristic Features, Complications, and General Treatment. By Surgeon-General T. LONGMORE, C.B. F.R.C.S. With 58 Illustrations. 8vo. price 31s. 6d.

LOUDON. — *Works by J. C. Loudon, F.L.S.*
ENCYCLOPÆDIA OF GARDENING; the Theory and Practice of Horticulture, Floriculture, Arboriculture, and Landscape Gardening. With 1,000 Woodcuts. 8vo. 21s.
ENCYCLOPÆDIA OF AGRICULTURE; the Laying-out, Improvement, and Management of Landed Property; the Cultivation and Economy of the Productions of Agriculture. With 1,100 Woodcuts. 8vo. 21s.
ENCYCLOPÆDIA OF PLANTS; the Specific Character, Description, Culture, History, &c. of all Plants found in Great Britain. With 12,000 Woodcuts. 8vo. 42s.

LUBBOCK.—*The Origin of Civilization and the Primitive Condition of Man.* By Sir J. Lubbock, Bart. M.P. F.R.S. 8vo. Woodcuts, 18s.

LYRA GERMANICA; Hymns Translated from the German by Miss C. Winkworth. Fcp. 8vo. 5s.

MACALISTER.—*An Introduction to the Systematic Zoology and Morphology of Vertebrate Animals.* By A. Macalister, M.D. With 28 Diagrams. 8vo. 10s. 6d.

MACAULAY.—*Works and Life of Lord Macaulay.*
HISTORY OF ENGLAND from the Accession of James the Second:
Student's Edition, 2 vols. crown 8vo. 12s.
People's Edition, 4 vols. crown 8vo. 16s.
Cabinet Edition, 8 vols. post 8vo. 48s.
Library Edition, 5 vols. 8vo. £4.

CRITICAL AND HISTORICAL ESSAYS, with LAYS of ANCIENT ROME, in 1 volume:
Authorised Edition, crown 8vo. 2s. 6d. or 3s. 6d. gilt edges.
Popular Edition, crown 8vo. 2s. 6d.

CRITICAL AND HISTORICAL ESSAYS:
Student's Edition, 1 vol. crown 8vo. 6s.
People's Edition, 2 vols. crown 8vo. 8s.
Cabinet Edition, 4 vols. post 8vo. 24s.
Library Edition, 3 vols. 8vo. 36s.

ESSAYS which may be had separately price 6d. each sewed, 1s. each cloth:
Addison and Walpole.
Frederick the Great.
Croker's Boswell's Johnson.
Hallam's Constitutional History.
Warren Hastings.
The Earl of Chatham (Two Essays).
Ranke and Gladstone.
Milton and Machiavelli.
Lord Bacon.
Lord Clive.
Lord Byron, and The Comic Dramatists of the Restoration.
The Essay on Warren Hastings annotated by S. Hales, 1s. 6d.
The Essay on Lord Clive annotated by H. Courthope-Bowen, M.A. 2s. 6d.

SPEECHES:
People's Edition, crown 8vo. 3s. 6d.

MISCELLANEOUS WRITINGS
Library Edition, 2 vols. 8vo. Portrait, 21s.
People's Edition, 1 vol. crown 8vo. 4s. 6d.

[*Continued above.*]

MACAULAY—*Works and Life of Lord Macaulay*—continued.

LAYS OF ANCIENT ROME, &c.
Illustrated by G. Scharf, fcp. 4to. 10s. 6d.
―――― Popular Edition, fcp. 4to. 6d. sewed, 1s. cloth.
Illustrated by J. R. Weguelin, crown 8vo. 3s. 6d. cloth extra, gilt edges.
Cabinet Edition, post 8vo. 3s. 6d.
Annotated Edition, fcp. 8vo. 1s. sewed, 1s. 6d. cloth, or 2s. 6d. cloth extra, gilt edges.

SELECTIONS FROM THE WRITINGS OF LORD MACAULAY. Edited, with Occasional Notes, by the Right Hon. G. O. Trevelyan, M.P. Crown 8vo. 6s.

MISCELLANEOUS WRITINGS AND SPEECHES:
Student's Edition, in One Volume, crown 8vo. 6s.
Cabinet Edition, including Indian Penal Code, Lays of Ancient Rome, and Miscellaneous Poems, 4 vols. post 8vo. 24s.

THE COMPLETE WORKS of Lord Macaulay. Edited by his Sister, Lady Trevelyan.
Library Edition, with Portrait, 8 vols. demy 8vo. £5. 5s.
Cabinet Edition, 16 vols. post 8vo. £4. 16s.

THE LIFE AND LETTERS of Lord Macaulay. By the Right Hon. G. O. Trevelyan, M.P.
Popular Edition, 1 vol. crown 8vo. 6s.
Cabinet Edition, 2 vols. post 8vo. 12s.
Library Edition, 2 vols. 8vo. with Portrait, 36s.

MACDONALD,—*Works by George Macdonald, LL.D.*

Unspoken Sermons. Second Series. Crown 8vo. 7s. 6d.

A Book of Strife, in the Form of The Diary of an Old Soul: Poems. 12mo. 6s.

Hamlet. A Study with the Texts of the Folio of 1623. 8vo. 12s.

MACFARREN.—*Lectures on Harmony,* delivered at the Royal Institution. By Sir G. A. Macfarren. 8vo. 12s.

MACKENZIE.—*On the Use of the Laryngoscope in Diseases of the Throat;* with an Appendix on Rhinoscopy. By Morell Mackenzie, M.D. Lond. With 47 Woodcut Illustrations. 8vo. 6s.

MACLEOD.—*Works by Henry D. Macleod, M.A.*

Principles of Economical Philosophy. In 2 vols. Vol. I. 8vo. 15s. Vol. II. Part I. 12s.

The Elements of Economics. In 2 vols. Vol. I. crown 8vo. 7s. 6d. Vol. II. crown 8vo.

The Elements of Banking. Crown 8vo. 5s.

The Theory and Practice of Banking. Vol. I. 8vo. 12s. Vol. II.

Elements of Political Economy. 8vo. 16s.

Economics for Beginners. 8vo. 2s. 6d.

Lectures on Credit and Banking. 8vo. 5s.

MACNAMARA.—*Himalayan and Sub-Himalayan Districts of British India*, their Climate, Medical Topography, and Disease Distribution. By F. N. MACNAMARA, M.D. With Map and Fever Chart. 8vo. 21s.

McCULLOCH.—*The Dictionary of Commerce and Commercial Navigation* of the late J. R. McCULLOCH, of H.M. Stationery Office. Latest Edition, containing the most recent Statistical Information by A. J. WILSON. 1 vol. medium 8vo. with 11 Maps and 30 Charts, price 63s. cloth, or 70s. strongly half-bound in russia.

MAHAFFY.—*A History of Classical Greek Literature.* By the Rev. J. P. MAHAFFY, M.A. Crown 8vo. Vol. I. Poets, 7s. 6d. Vol. II. Prose Writers, 7s. 6d.

MALMESBURY.—*Memoirs of an Ex-Minister*: an Autobiography. By the Earl of MALMESBURY, G.C.B. Cheap Edition, 1 vol. crown 8vo. 7s. 6d.

MANNING.—*The Temporal Mission of the Holy Ghost*; or, Reason and Revelation. By H. E. MANNING, D.D. Cardinal-Archbishop. Crown 8vo. 8s. 6d.

THE MARITIME ALPS AND THEIR SEABOARD. By the Author of 'Véra,' 'Blue Roses,' &c. With 14 Full-page Illustrations and 15 Woodcuts in the Text. 8vo. 21s.

MARTINEAU.—*Works by James Martineau, D.D.*

Hours of Thought on Sacred Things. Two Volumes of Sermons. 2 vols. crown 8vo. 7s. 6d. each.

Endeavours after the Christian Life. Discourses. Crown 8vo. 7s. 6d.

MAUNDER'S TREASURIES.

Biographical Treasury. Reconstructed, revised, and brought down to the year 1882, by W. L. R. CATES. Fcp. 8vo. 6s.

Treasury of Natural History; or, Popular Dictionary of Zoology. Fcp. 8vo. with 900 Woodcuts, 6s.

Treasury of Geography, Physical, Historical, Descriptive, and Political. With 7 Maps and 16 Plates. Fcp. 8vo. 6s.

Historical Treasury: Outlines of Universal History, Separate Histories of all Nations. Revised by the Rev. Sir G. W. COX, Bart. M.A. Fcp. 8vo. 6s.

Treasury of Knowledge and Library of Reference. Comprising an English Dictionary and Grammar, Universal Gazetteer, Classical Dictionary, Chronology, Law Dictionary, &c. Fcp. 8vo. 6s.

Scientific and Literary Treasury: a Popular Encyclopædia of Science, Literature, and Art. Fcp. 8vo. 6s.

MAXWELL.—*Don John of Austria*; or, Passages from the History of the Sixteenth Century, 1547-1578. By the late Sir WILLIAM STIRLING MAXWELL, Bart. K.T. With numerous Illustrations engraved on Wood taken from Authentic Contemporary Sources. Library Edition. 2 vols. royal 8vo. 42s.

MAY.—*Works by the Right Hon. Sir Thomas Erskine May, K.C.B.*

The Constitutional History of England since the Accession of George III. 1760-1870. 3 vols. crown 8vo. 18s.

Democracy in Europe; a History. 2 vols. 8vo. 32s.

MELVILLE.—*In the Lena Delta;* a Narrative of the Search for LIEUT.-COMMANDER DE LONG and his Companions, followed by an account of the Greely Relief Expedition, and a Proposed Method of reaching the North Pole. By GEORGE W. MELVILLE, Chief Engineer, U.S.N. Edited by MELVILLE PHILIPS. With Maps and Illustrations. 8vo. 14s.

MENDELSSOHN.—THE LETTERS OF FELIX MENDELSSOHN. Translated by Lady WALLACE. 2 vols. crown 8vo. 10s.

MERIVALE.—WORKS BY THE VERY REV. CHARLES MERIVALE, D.D. Dean of Ely.
HISTORY OF THE ROMANS UNDER THE EMPIRE. 8 vols. post 8vo. 48s.
THE FALL OF THE ROMAN REPUBLIC: a Short History of the Last Century of the Commonwealth. 12mo. 7s. 6d.
GENERAL HISTORY OF ROME FROM B.C. 753 TO A.D. 476. Crown 8vo. 7s. 6d.
THE ROMAN TRIUMVIRATES. With Maps. Fcp. 8vo. 2s. 6d.

MILES. — WORKS BY WILLIAM MILES.
THE HORSE'S FOOT, AND HOW TO KEEP IT SOUND. Imp. 8vo. 12s. 6d.
STABLES AND STABLE FITTINGS. Imp. 8vo. with 13 Plates, 15s.
REMARKS ON HORSES' TEETH, addressed to Purchasers. Post 8vo. 1s. 6d.
PLAIN TREATISE ON HORSE-SHOEING. Post 8vo. Woodcuts, 2s. 6d.

MILL.—ANALYSIS OF THE PHENOMENA OF THE HUMAN MIND. By JAMES MILL. With Notes, Illustrative and Critical. 2 vols. 8vo. 28s.

MILL.—WORKS BY JOHN STUART MILL.
PRINCIPLES OF POLITICAL ECONOMY. Library Edition, 2 vols. 8vo. 30s.
People's Edition, 1 vol. crown 8vo. 5s.
A SYSTEM OF LOGIC, Ratiocinative and Inductive.
Library Edition, 2 vols. 8vo. 25s.
People's Edition, crown 8vo. 5s.
ON LIBERTY. Crown 8vo. 1s. 4d.
ON REPRESENTATIVE GOVERNMENT. Crown 8vo. 2s.
AUTOBIOGRAPHY, 8vo. 7s. 6d.
ESSAYS ON SOME UNSETTLED QUESTIONS OF POLITICAL ECONOMY. 8vo. 6s. 6d.
UTILITARIANISM. 8vo. 5s.
THE SUBJECTION OF WOMEN. Crown 8vo. 6s.
EXAMINATION OF SIR WILLIAM HAMILTON'S PHILOSOPHY. 8vo. 16s.
DISSERTATIONS AND DISCUSSIONS. 4 vols. 8vo. £2. 6s. 6d.
NATURE, THE UTILITY OF RELIGION, AND THEISM. Three Essays. 8vo. 10s. 6d.

MILLER.—WORKS BY W. ALLEN MILLER, M.D. LL.D.
THE ELEMENTS OF CHEMISTRY, Theoretical and Practical Re-edited, with Additions, by H. MACLEOD, F.C.S. 3 vols. 8vo.
Part I. CHEMICAL PHYSICS, 16s.
Part II. INORGANIC CHEMISTRY, 24s.
Part III. ORGANIC CHEMISTRY, 31s. 6d.
AN INTRODUCTION TO THE STUDY OF INORGANIC CHEMISTRY. With 71 Woodcuts. Fcp. 8vo. 3s. 6d.

MILLER. — READINGS IN SOCIAL ECONOMY. By Mrs. F. FENWICK MILLER, Member of the London School Board. Library Edition, crown 8vo. 5s.
Cheap Edition for Schools and Beginners, crown 8vo. 2s.

MILLER.—WINTERING IN THE RIVIERA; with Notes of Travel in Italy and France, and Practical Hints to Travellers. By W. MILLER. With 12 Illustrations. Post 8vo. 7s. 6d.

MITCHELL.—A MANUAL OF PRACTICAL ASSAYING. By JOHN MITCHELL, F.C.S. Revised, with the Recent Discoveries incorporated. By W. CROOKES, F.R.S. 8vo. Woodcuts, 31s. 6d.

MODERN NOVELIST'S LIBRARY (THE). Price 2s. each boards, or 2s. 6d. each cloth :—
By the Earl of BEACONSFIELD, K.G.
    Endymion.
Lothair.   Henrietta Temple.
Coningsby.   Contarini Fleming, &c.
Sybil.   Alroy, Ixion, &c.
Tancred.   The Young Duke, &c.
Venetia.   Vivian Grey, &c.
By Mrs. OLIPHANT.
    In Trust.
By JAMES PAYN.
    Thicker than Water.
By BRET HARTE.
    In the Carquinez Woods.
By ANTHONY TROLLOPE.
    Barchester Towers.
    The Warden.
By Major WHYTE-MELVILLE.
    Digby Grand   Good for Nothing.
    General Bounce.   Holmby House.
    Kate Coventry.   The Interpreter.
    The Gladiators.   Queen's Maries.
By Various Writers.
    The Atelier du Lys.
    Atherstone Priory.
    The Burgomaster's Family.
    Elsa and her Vulture.
    Mademoiselle Mori.
    The Six Sisters of the Valleys.
    Unawares.

MONCK. — *An Introduction to Logic.* By WILLIAM H. STANLEY MONCK, M.A. Prof. of Moral Philos. Univ. of Dublin. Crown 8vo. 5s.

MONSELL. — *Spiritual Songs for the Sundays and Holidays throughout the Year.* By J. S. B. MONSELL, LL.D. Fcp. 8vo. 5s. 18mo. 2s.

MOORE. — *The Works of Thomas Moore.*
Lalla Rookh, TENNIEL'S Edition, with 68 Woodcut Illustrations. Crown 8vo. 10s. 6d.
Irish Melodies, MACLISE'S Edition, with 161 Steel Plates. Super-royal 8vo. 21s.

MOREHEAD. — *Clinical Researches on Disease in India.* By CHARLES MOREHEAD, M.D. Surgeon to the Jamsetjee Jeejeebhoy Hospital. 8vo. 21s.

MORELL. — *Handbook of Logic,* adapted especially for the Use of Schools and Teachers. By J. D. MORELL, LL.D. Fcp. 8vo. 2s.

MOZLEY. — *Works by the Rev. Thomas Mozley, M.A.*
Reminiscences chiefly of Oriel College and the Oxford Movement. 2 vols. crown 8vo. 18s.
Reminiscences chiefly of Towns, Villages, and Schools. 2 vols. crown 8vo. 18s.

MÜLLER. — *Works by F. Max Müller, M.A.*
Biographical Essays. Crown 8vo. 7s. 6d.
Selected Essays on Language, Mythology and Religion. 2 vols. crown 8vo. 16s.
Lectures on the Science of Language. 2 vols. crown 8vo. 16s.
India, What Can it Teach Us? A Course of Lectures delivered before the University of Cambridge. 8vo. 12s. 6d.
Hibbert Lectures on the Origin and Growth of Religion, as illustrated by the Religions of India. Crown 8vo. 7s. 6d.
Introduction to the Science of Religion: Four Lectures delivered at the Royal Institution; with Notes and Illustrations on Vedic Literature, Polynesian Mythology, the Sacred Books of the East, &c. Crown 8vo. 7s. 6d.
A Sanskrit Grammar for Beginners, in Devanagari and Roman Letters throughout. Royal 8vo. 7s. 6d.

MURCHISON. — *Works by Charles Murchison, M.D. LL.D. F.R.C.S. &c.*
A Treatise on the Continued Fevers of Great Britain. New Edition, revised by W. CAYLEY, M.D. Physician to the Middlesex Hospital. 8vo. with numerous Illustrations, 25s.
Clinical Lectures on Diseases of the Liver, Jaundice, and Abdominal Dropsy. New Edition, revised by T. LAUDER BRUNTON, M.D. 8vo. with numerous Illustrations. 24s.

NEISON. — *The Moon,* and the Condition and Configurations of its Surface. By E. NEISON, F.R.A.S. With 26 Maps and 5 Plates. Medium 8vo. 31s. 6d.

NEVILE. — *Works by George Nevile, M.A.*
Horses and Riding. With 31 Illustrations. Crown 8vo. 6s.
Farms and Farming. With 13 Illustrations. Crown 8vo. 6s.

NEWMAN. — *Apologia pro Vita Sua;* being a History of his Religious Opinions by Cardinal NEWMAN. Crown 8vo. 6s.

NEW TESTAMENT (THE) of our Lord and Saviour Jesus Christ. Illustrated with Engravings on Wood after Paintings by the Early Masters chiefly of the Italian School. New and Cheaper Edition. 4to. 21s. cloth extra, or 42s. morocco.

NORTHCOTT. — *Lathes and Turning,* Simple, Mechanical, and Ornamental. By W. H. NORTHCOTT. With 338 Illustrations. 8vo. 18s.

OLIPHANT. — *Madam.* A Novel. By Mrs. OLIPHANT. 3 vols. crown 8vo. 21s.

OWEN. — *The Comparative Anatomy and Physiology of the Vertebrate Animals.* By Sir RICHARD OWEN, K.C.B. &c. With 1,472 Woodcuts. 3 vols. 8vo. £3. 13s. 6d.

PAGET. — *Works by Sir James Paget, Bart. F.R.S. D.C.L. &c.*
Clinical Lectures and Essays. Edited by F. HOWARD MARSH, Assistant-Surgeon to St. Bartholomew's Hospital. 8vo. 15s.
Lectures on Surgical Pathology. Delivered at the Royal College of Surgeons of England. Re-edited by the AUTHOR and W. TURNER, M.B. 8vo. with 131 Woodcuts, 21s.

PALEY.—VIEW OF THE EVIDENCES OF CHRISTIANITY AND HORAE PAULINAE. By Archdeacon PALEY. With Notes and an Analysis, and a Selection of Questions. By ROBERT POTTS, M.A. 8vo. 10s. 6d.

PASOLINI.—MEMOIR OF COUNT GIUSEPPE PASOLINI, LATE PRESIDENT OF THE SENATE OF ITALY. Compiled by his SON. Translated and Abridged by the DOWAGER-COUNTESS OF DALHOUSIE. With Portrait. 8vo. 16s.

PASTEUR.—LOUIS PASTEUR, his Life and Labours. By his SON-IN-LAW. Translated from the French by Lady CLAUD HAMILTON. Crown 8vo. 7s. 6d.

PAYEN.—INDUSTRIAL CHEMISTRY; a Manual for Manufacturers and for Colleges or Technical Schools; a Translation of PAYEN's 'Précis de Chimie Industrielle.' Edited by B. H. PAUL. With 698 Woodcuts. Medium 8vo. 42s.

PEEL.—A HIGHLAND GATHERING. By E. LENNOX PEEL. With 31 Illustrations engraved on Wood by E. Whymper from original Drawings by Charles Whymper. Crown 8vo.

PENNELL.—'FROM GRAVE TO GAY'; a Volume of Selections from the complete Poems of H. CHOLMONDELEY-PENNELL, Author of 'Puck on Pegasus' &c. Fcp. 8vo. 6s.

PEREIRA.—MATERIA MEDICA AND THERAPEUTICS. By Dr. PEREIRA. Abridged, and adapted for the use of Medical and Pharmaceutical Practitioners and Students. Edited by Professor R. BENTLEY, M.R.C.S. F.L.S. and by Professor T. REDWOOD, Ph.D. F.C.S. With 126 Woodcuts, 8vo. 25s.

PERRY.—A POPULAR INTRODUCTION TO THE HISTORY OF GREEK AND ROMAN SCULPTURE, designed to Promote the Knowledge and Appreciation of the Remains of Ancient Art. By WALTER C. PERRY. With 268 Illustrations. Square crown 8vo. 31s. 6d.

PIESSE.—THE ART OF PERFUMERY, and the Methods of Obtaining the Odours of Plants; with Instructions for the Manufacture of Perfumes, &c. By G. W. S. PIESSE, Ph.D. F.C.S. With 96 Woodcuts, square crown 8vo. 21s.

PLATO. — THE PARMENIDES OF PLATO; with Introduction, Analysis, and Notes. By THOMAS MAGUIRE, LL.D. D.Lit. Fellow and Tutor, Trinity College, Dublin. 8vo. 7s. 6d.

POLE.—THE THEORY OF THE MODERN SCIENTIFIC GAME OF WHIST. By W. POLE, F.R.S. Fcp. 8vo. 2s. 6d.

PROCTOR.—WORKS BY R. A PROCTOR.

THE SUN; Ruler, Light, Fire, and Life of the Planetary System. With Plates and Woodcuts. Crown 8vo. 14s.

THE ORBS AROUND US; a Series of Essays on the Moon and Planets, Meteors and Comets. With Chart and Diagrams, crown 8vo. 7s. 6d.

OTHER WORLDS THAN OURS; The Plurality of Worlds Studied under the Light of Recent Scientific Researches. With 14 Illustrations, crown 8vo. 10s. 6d.

THE MOON; her Motions, Aspects, Scenery, and Physical Condition. With Plates, Charts, Woodcuts, and Lunar Photographs, crown 8vo. 10s. 6d.

UNIVERSE OF STARS; Presenting Researches into and New Views respecting the Constitution of the Heavens. With 22 Charts and 22 Diagrams, 8vo. 10s. 6d.

NEW STAR ATLAS for the Library, the School, and the Observatory, in 12 Circular Maps (with 2 Index Plates). Crown 8vo. 5s.

LARGER STAR ATLAS for the Library, in 12 Circular Maps, with Introduction and 2 Index Pages. Folio, 15s. or Maps only, 12s. 6d.

LIGHT SCIENCE FOR LEISURE HOURS; Familiar Essays on Scientific Subjects, Natural Phenomena, &c. 3 vols. crown 8vo. 7s. 6d. each.

STUDIES OF VENUS-TRANSITS; an Investigation of the Circumstances of the Transits of Venus in 1874 and 1882. With 7 Diagrams and 10 Plates. 8vo. 5s.

TRANSITS OF VENUS. A Popular Account of Past and Coming Transits from the First Observed by Horrocks in 1639 to the Transit of 2012. With 20 Lithographic Plates (12 Coloured) and 38 Illustrations engraved on Wood, 8vo. 8s. 6d.

ESSAYS ON ASTRONOMY. A Series of Papers on Planets and Meteors, &c. With 10 Plates and 24 Woodcuts, 8vo. 12s.

A TREATISE ON THE CYCLOID AND ON ALL FORMS OF CYCLOIDAL CURVES, and on the use of Cycloidal Curves in dealing with the Motions of Planets, Comets, &c. &c. With 161 Diagrams. Crown 8vo. 10s. 6d.

PLEASANT WAYS IN SCIENCE, with numerous Illustrations. Crown 8vo. 6s.

MYTHS AND MARVELS OF ASTRONOMY, with numerous Illustrations. Crown 8vo. 6s. [Continued on next page.

PROCTOR —*Works by R. A. Proctor continued.*

THE 'KNOWLEDGE' LIBRARY. Edited by RICHARD A. PROCTOR.

How to Play Whist: with the Laws and Etiquette of Whist: Whist-Whittlings, and Forty fully-annotated Games. By 'FIVE OF CLUBS' (R. A. Proctor). Crown 8vo. 5s.

Science Byways. A Series of Familiar Dissertations on Life in Other Worlds. By RICHARD A. PROCTOR. Crown 8vo. 6s.

The Poetry of Astronomy. A Series of Familiar Essays on the Heavenly Bodies. By RICHARD A. PROCTOR. Crown 8vo. 6s.

Nature Studies. Reprinted from *Knowledge.* By GRANT ALLEN, ANDREW WILSON, THOMAS FOSTER, EDWARD CLODD, and RICHARD A. PROCTOR. Crown 8vo. 6s.

Leisure Readings. Reprinted from *Knowledge.* By EDWARD CLODD, ANDREW WILSON, THOMAS FOSTER, A. C. RUNYARD, and RICHARD A. PROCTOR. Crown 8vo. 6s.

The Stars in their Seasons. An Easy Guide to a Knowledge of the Star Groups, in Twelve Large Maps. By RICHARD A. PROCTOR. Imperial 8vo. 5s.

QUAIN'S ELEMENTS of ANATOMY. The Ninth Edition. Re-edited by ALLEN THOMSON, M.D. LL.D. F.R.S.S. L. & E. EDWARD ALBERT SCHÄFER, F.R.S. and GEORGE DANCER THANE. With upwards of 1,000 Illustrations engraved on Wood, of which many are Coloured. 2 vols. 8vo. 18s. each.

QUAIN.—*A Dictionary of Medicine.* Including General Pathology, General Therapeutics, Hygiene, and the Diseases peculiar to Women and Children. By Various Writers. Edited by R. QUAIN, M.D. F.R.S. &c. With 138 Woodcuts. Medium 8vo. 31s. 6d. cloth, or 40s. half-russia; to be had also in 2 vols. 34s. cloth.

RAWLINSON. — *The Seventh Great Oriental Monarchy;* or, a History of the Sassanians. By G. RAWLINSON, M.A. With Map and 95 Illustrations. 8vo. 28s.

READER.—*Voices from Flowerland,* in Original Couplets. By EMILY E. READER. A Birthday-Book and Language of Flowers. 16mo. 2s. 6d. limp cloth; 3s. 6d. roan, gilt edges, or in vegetable vellum, gilt top.

REEVE. *Cookery and Housekeeping;* a Manual of Domestic Economy for Large and Small Families. By Mrs. HENRY REEVE. With 8 Coloured Plates and 37 Woodcuts. Crown 8vo. 7s. 6d.

RICH. *A Dictionary of Roman and Greek Antiquities.* With 2,000 Woodcuts. By A. RICH, B.A. Crown 8vo. 7s. 6d.

RICHARDSON. — *The Asclepaid:* a Book of Original Research and Observation in the Science, Art, and Literature of Medicine, Preventive and Curative. By BENJAMIN WARD RICHARDSON, M.D. F.R.S. Published Quarterly, price 2s. 6d. Vol. I. 1884. 8vo. 12s. 6d.

RIVERS. — *Works by Thomas Rivers.*

The Orchard-House; or, the Cultivation of Fruit Trees under Glass. Crown 8vo. with 25 Woodcuts, 5s.

The Rose Amateur's Guide. Fcp. 8vo. 4s. 6d.

ROGERS. — *Works by Henry Rogers.*

The Eclipse of Faith; or, a Visit to a Religious Sceptic. Fcp. 8vo. 5s.

Defence of the Eclipse of Faith. Fcp. 8vo. 3s. 6d.

ROGET.—*Thesaurus of English Words and Phrases,* classified and arranged so as to facilitate the expression of Ideas, and assist in Literary Composition. By PETER M. ROGET, M.D. Crown 8vo. 10s. 6d.

RONALDS. — *The Fly-Fisher's Entomology.* By ALFRED RONALDS. With 20 Coloured Plates. 8vo. 14s.

SALTER.—*Dental Pathology and Surgery.* By S. J. A. SALTER, M.B. F.R.S. With 133 Illustrations. 8vo. 18s.

SCOTT.—*The Farm-Valuer.* By JOHN SCOTT. Crown 8vo. 5s.

SEEBOHM. — *Works by Frederick Seebohm.*

The Oxford Reformers — John Colet, Erasmus, and Thomas More; a History of their Fellow-Work. 8vo. 14s.

The English Village Community Examined in its Relations to the Manorial and Tribal Systems, and to the Common or Openfield System of Husbandry. 13 Maps and Plates. 8vo. 16s.

The Era of the Protestant Revolution. With Map. Fcp. 8vo. 2s. 6d.

SENNETT.—*THE MARINE STEAM ENGINE*; a Treatise for the use of Engineering Students and Officers of the Royal Navy. By RICHARD SENNETT, Chief Engineer, Royal Navy. With 244 Illustrations. 8vo. 21s.

SEWELL.—*WORKS BY ELIZABETH M. SEWELL.*
STORIES AND TALES. Cabinet Edition, in Eleven Volumes, crown 8vo. 3s. 6d. each, in cloth extra, with gilt edges:—
   Amy Herbert. Gertrude.
   The Earl's Daughter.
   The Experience of Life.
   A Glimpse of the World.
   Cleve Hall. Ivors.
   Katharine Ashton.
   Margaret Percival.
   Laneton Parsonage. Ursula.
PASSING THOUGHTS ON RELIGION. Fcp. 8vo. 3s. 6d.
PREPARATION FOR THE HOLY COMMUNION; the Devotions chiefly from the works of JEREMY TAYLOR. 32mo. 3s.
NIGHT LESSONS FROM SCRIPTURE. 32mo. 3s. 6d.

SEYMOUR.—*THE PSALMS OF DAVID*; a new Metrical English Translation of the Hebrew Psalter or Book of Praises. By WILLIAM DIGBY SEYMOUR, Q.C. LL.D. Crown 8vo. 2s. 6d.

SHORT.—*SKETCH OF THE HISTORY OF THE CHURCH OF ENGLAND TO THE REVOLUTION OF 1688.* By T. V. SHORT, D.D. Crown 8vo. 7s. 6d.

SHAKESPEARE.—*BOWDLER'S FAMILY SHAKESPEARE.* Genuine Edition, in 1 vol. medium 8vo. large type, with 36 Woodcuts, 14s. or in 6 vols. fcp. 8vo. 21s.
OUTLINES OF THE LIFE OF SHAKESPEARE. By J. O. HALLIWELL-PHILLIPPS, F.R.S. 8vo. 7s. 6d.

SIMCOX.—*A HISTORY OF LATIN LITERATURE.* By G. A. SIMCOX, M.A. Fellow of Queen's College, Oxford. 2 vols. 8vo. 32s.

SMITH, Rev. SYDNEY.—*THE WIT AND WISDOM OF THE REV. SYDNEY SMITH.* Crown 8vo. 3s. 6d.

SMITH, R. BOSWORTH.—*CARTHAGE AND THE CARTHAGINIANS.* By R. BOSWORTH SMITH, M.A. Maps, Plans, &c. Crown 8vo. 10s. 6d.

SMITH, R. A.—*AIR AND RAIN*; the Beginnings of a Chemical Climatology. By R. A. SMITH, F.R.S. 8vo. 24s.

SMITH, JAMES.—*THE VOYAGE AND SHIPWRECK OF ST. PAUL.* By JAMES SMITH, of Jordanhill. With Dissertations on the Life and Writings of St. Luke, and the Ships and Navigation of the Ancients. With numerous Illustrations. Crown 8vo. 7s. 6d.

SMITH, T.—*A MANUAL OF OPERATIVE SURGERY ON THE DEAD BODY.* By THOMAS SMITH, Surgeon to St. Bartholomew's Hospital. A New Edition, re-edited by W. J. WALSHAM. With 46 Illustrations. 8vo. 12s.

SMITH, H. F.—*THE HANDBOOK FOR MIDWIVES.* By HENRY FLY SMITH, M.B. Oxon. M.R.C.S. late Assistant-Surgeon at the Hospital for Sick Women, Soho Square. With 41 Woodcuts. Crown 8vo. 5s.

SOPHOCLES.—*SOPHOCLIS TRAGŒDIÆ* superstites; recensuit et brevi Annotatione instruxit GULIELMUS LINWOOD, M.A. Ædis Christi apud Oxonienses nuper Alumnus. Editio Quarta, auctior et emendatior. 8vo. 16s.

SOUTHEY.—*THE POETICAL WORKS OF ROBERT SOUTHEY*, with the Author's last Corrections and Additions. Medium 8vo. with Portrait, 14s.
THE CORRESPONDENCE OF ROBERT SOUTHEY WITH CAROLINE BOWLES. Edited by EDWARD DOWDEN, LL.D. 8vo. Portrait, 14s.

STANLEY.—*A FAMILIAR HISTORY OF BIRDS.* By E. STANLEY, D.D. Revised and enlarged, with 160 Woodcuts. Crown 8vo. 6s.

STEEL.—*A TREATISE ON THE DISEASES OF THE OX*; being a Manual of Bovine Pathology specially adapted for the use of Veterinary Practitioners and Students. By J. H. STEEL, M.R.C.V.S. F.Z.S. With 2 Plates and 116 Woodcuts. 8vo. 15s.

STEPHEN.—*ESSAYS IN ECCLESIASTICAL BIOGRAPHY.* By the Right Hon. Sir J. STEPHEN, LL.D. Crown 8vo. 7s. 6d.

STEVENSON.—*THE CHILD'S GARDEN OF POEMS.* By ROBERT LOUIS STEVENSON. 1 vol. small fcp. 8vo. printed on hand-made paper, 5s.

'STONEHENGE.'—*THE DOG IN HEALTH AND DISEASE.* By 'STONEHENGE.' With 78 Wood Engravings. Square crown 8vo. 7s. 6d.
THE GREYHOUND. By 'STONEHENGE.' With 25 Portraits of Greyhounds, &c. Square crown 8vo. 15s.

STURGIS. *My Friends and I.* By JULIAN STURGIS. With Frontispiece. Crown 8vo. 5s.

SULLY.—*Outlines of Psychology,* with Special Reference to the Theory of Education. By JAMES SULLY, M.A. 8vo. 12s. 6d.

SUPERNATURAL RELIGION; an Inquiry into the Reality of Divine Revelation. Complete Edition, thoroughly revised. 3 vols. 8vo. 36s.

SWINBURNE. *Picture Logic;* an Attempt to Popularise the Science of Reasoning. By A. J. SWINBURNE, B.A. Post 8vo. 5s.

SWINTON.—*The Principles and Practice of Electric Lighting.* By ALAN A. CAMPBELL SWINTON. With 54 Illustrations engraved on Wood. Crown 8vo. 5s.

TAYLOR.—*Student's Manual of the History of India,* from the Earliest Period to the Present Time. By Colonel MEADOWS TAYLOR, C.S.I. Crown 8vo. 7s. 6d.

TEXT-BOOKS OF SCIENCE: a Series of Elementary Works on Science, Mechanical and Physical, forming a Series of Text-books of Science, adapted for the use of Students in Public and Science Schools. Fcp. 8vo. fully illustrated with Woodcuts.

Abney's Photography, 3s. 6d.
Anderson's Strength of Materials, 3s. 6d.
Armstrong's Organic Chemistry, 3s. 6d.
Ball's Elements of Astronomy, 6s.
Barry's Railway Appliances, 3s. 6d.
Bauerman's Systematic Mineralogy, 6s.
——— Descriptive Mineralogy, 6s.
Bloxam and Huntington's Metals, 5s.
Glazebrook's Physical Optics, 6s.
Glazebrook and Shaw's Practical Physics, 6s.
Gore's Electro-Metallurgy, 6s.
Griffin's Algebra and Trigonometry, 3s. 6d.
Jenkin's Electricity and Magnetism, 3s. 6d.
Maxwell's Theory of Heat, 3s. 6d.
Merrifield's Technical Arithmetic, 3s. 6d.
Miller's Inorganic Chemistry, 3s. 6d.
Preece and Sivewright's Telegraphy, 5s.
Rutley's Petrology, or Study of Rocks, 4s. 6d.
Shelley's Workshop Appliances, 4s. 6d.
Thome's Structural and Physiological Botany, 6s.
Thorpe's Quantitative Analysis, 4s. 6d.
Thorpe and Muir's Qualitative Analysis, 3s. 6d.
Tilden's Chemical Philosophy, 3s. 6d. With Answers to Problems, 4s. 6d.
Unwin's Machine Design, 6s.
Watson's Plane and Solid Geometry, 3s. 6d.

TAYLOR. *The Complete Works of Bishop Jeremy Taylor.* With Life by Bishop Heber. Revised and corrected by the Rev. C. P. EDEN. 10 vols. £5. 5s.

THOMSON.—*An Outline of the Necessary Laws of Thought;* a Treatise on Pure and Applied Logic. By W. THOMSON, D.D. Archbishop of York. Crown 8vo. 6s.

THOMSON'S CONSPECTUS *Adapted to the British Pharmacopœia.* By EDMUND LLOYD BIRKETT, M.D. &c. Latest Edition. 18mo. 6s.

THOMPSON.—*A System of Psychology.* By DANIEL GREENLEAF THOMPSON. 2 vols. 8vo. 36s.

THREE IN NORWAY. By Two of THEM. With a Map and 59 Illustrations on Wood from Sketches by the Authors. Crown 8vo. 6s.

TREVELYAN. — *Works by the Right Hon. G. O. Trevelyan, M.P.*

The Life and Letters of Lord Macaulay. By the Right Hon. G. O. TREVELYAN, M.P.
  LIBRARY EDITION, 2 vols. 8vo. 36s.
  CABINET EDITION, 2 vols. crown 8vo. 12s.
  POPULAR EDITION, 1 vol. crown 8vo. 6s.

The Early History of Charles James Fox. Library Edition, 8vo. 18s. Cabinet Edition, crown 8vo. 6s.

TWISS.—*Works by Sir Travers Twiss.*

The Rights and Duties of Nations, considered as Independent Communities in Time of War. 8vo. 21s.

On the Rights and Duties of Nations in Time of Peace. 8vo. 15s.

TYNDALL.—*Works by John Tyndall, F.R.S. &c.*

Fragments of Science. 2 vols. crown 8vo. 16s.

Heat a Mode of Motion. Crown 8vo. 12s.

Sound. With 204 Woodcuts. Crown 8vo. 10s. 6d.

Essays on the Floating-Matter of the Air in relation to Putrefaction and Infection. With 24 Woodcuts. Crown 8vo. 7s. 6d.

[Continued on next page.

LONGMANS & CO.'S LIST OF GENERAL AND SCIENTIFIC BOOKS. 23

TYNDALL.—*Works by John Tyndall F.R.S. &c.*—continued.

Lectures on Light, delivered in America in 1872 and 1873. With Portrait, Plate, and Diagrams. Crown 8vo. 7s. 6d.

Lessons in Electricity at the Royal Institution, 1875-76. With 58 Woodcuts. Crown 8vo. 2s. 6d.

Notes of a Course of Seven Lectures on Electrical Phenomena and Theories, delivered at the Royal Institution. Crown 8vo. 1s. sewed, 1s. 6d. cloth.

Notes of a Course of Nine Lectures on Light, delivered at the Royal Institution. Crown 8vo. 1s. sewed, 1s. 6d. cloth.

Faraday as a Discoverer. Fcp. 8vo. 3s. 6d.

URE.—*A Dictionary of Arts, Manufactures, and Mines.* By Dr. URE. Seventh Edition, re-written and enlarged by R. HUNT, F.R.S. With 2,064 Woodcuts. 4 vols. medium 8vo. £7. 7s.

VERNEY.—*Chess Eccentricities.* Including Four-handed Chess, Chess for Three, Six, or Eight Players, Round Chess for Two, Three, or Four Players, and several different ways of Playing Chess for Two Players. By Major GEORGE HOPE VERNEY. Crown 8vo. 10s. 6d.

VILLE.—*On Artificial Manures*, their Chemical Selection and Scientific Application to Agriculture. By GEORGES VILLE. Translated and edited by W. CROOKES, F.R.S. With 31 Plates. 8vo. 21s.

VIRGIL.—*Publi Vergili Maronis Bucolica, Georgica, Æneis;* the Works of VIRGIL, Latin Text, with English Commentary and Index. By B. H. KENNEDY, D.D. Crown 8vo. 10s. 6d.

The Æneid of Virgil. Translated into English Verse. By J. CONINGTON, M.A. Crown 8vo. 9s.

The Poems of Virgil. Translated into English Prose. By JOHN CONINGTON, M.A. Crown 8vo. 9s.

WALKER.—*The Correct Card;* or, How to Play at Whist; a Whist Catechism. By Major A. CAMPBELL-WALKER, F.R.G.S. Fcp. 8vo. 2s. 6d.

WALPOLE.—*History of England from the Conclusion of the Great War in 1815 to the Year 1841.* By SPENCER WALPOLE. 3 vols. 8vo. £2. 14s.

WATSON.—*Lectures on the Principles and Practice of Physic*, delivered at King's College, London, by Sir THOMAS WATSON, Bart. M.D. With Two Plates. 2 vols. 8vo. 36s.

WATTS.—*A Dictionary of Chemistry and the Allied Branches of other Sciences.* Edited by HENRY WATTS, F.R.S. 9 vols. medium 8vo. £15. 2s. 6d.

WEBB.—*Celestial Objects for Common Telescopes.* By the Rev. T. W. WEBB, M.A. Map, Plate, Woodcuts. Crown 8vo. 9s.

WEBB.—*The Veil of Isis:* a Series of Essays on Idealism. By THOMAS W. WEBB, LL.D. 8vo. 10s. 6d.

WELLINGTON.—*Life of the Duke of Wellington.* By the Rev. G. R. GLEIG, M.A. Crown 8vo. Portrait, 6s.

WEST.—*Lectures on the Diseases of Infancy and Childhood.* By CHARLES WEST, M.D. &c. Founder of, and formerly Physician to, the Hospital for Sick Children. 8vo. 18s.

WHATELY.—*English Synonyms.* By E. JANE WHATELY. Edited by her Father, R. WHATELY, D.D. Fcp. 8vo. 3s.

WHATELY.—*Works by R. Whately, D.D.*

Elements of Logic. 8vo. 10s. 6d. Crown 8vo. 4s. 6d.

Elements of Rhetoric. 8vo. 10s. 6d. Crown 8vo. 4s. 6d.

Lessons on Reasoning. Fcp. 8vo. 1s. 6d.

Bacon's Essays, with Annotations. 8vo. 10s. 6d.

WHITE.—*A Concise Latin-English Dictionary*, for the Use of Advanced Scholars and University Students. By the Rev. J. T. WHITE, D.D. Royal 8vo. 12s.

WHITE & RIDDLE.—*A Latin-English Dictionary.* By J. T. WHITE, D.D. Oxon. and J. J. E. RIDDLE, M.A. Oxon. Founded on the larger Dictionary of Freund. Royal 8vo. 21s.

WILCOCKS. *THE SEA FISHERMAN.* Comprising the Chief Methods of Hook and Line Fishing in the British and other Seas, and Remarks on Nets, Boats, and Boating. By J. C. WILCOCKS. Profusely Illustrated. New and Cheaper Edition, much enlarged, crown 8vo. 6s.

WILLICH. *POPULAR TABLES* for giving Information for ascertaining the value of Lifehold, Leasehold, and Church Property, the Public Funds, &c. By CHARLES M. WILLICH. Edited by MONTAGU MARRIOTT. Crown 8vo. 10s.

WITT.—*WORKS BY PROF. WITT,* Head Master of the Alstadt Gymnasium, Königsberg. Translated from the German by FRANCIS YOUNGHUSBAND.

THE TROJAN WAR. With a Preface by the Rev. W. G. RUTHERFORD, M.A. Head-Master of Westminster School. Crown 8vo. 2s.

MYTHS OF HELLAS; or, Greek Tales. Crown 8vo. 3s. 6d.

THE WANDERINGS OF ULYSSES. Crown 8vo. 3s. 6d.

WOOD.—*WORKS BY REV. J. G. WOOD.*

HOMES WITHOUT HANDS; a Description of the Habitations of Animals, classed according to the Principle of Construction. With about 140 Vignettes on Wood. 8vo. 10s. 6d.

INSECTS AT HOME; a Popular Account of British Insects, their Structure, Habits, and Transformations. 8vo. Woodcuts, 10s. 6d.

INSECTS ABROAD; a Popular Account of Foreign Insects, their Structure, Habits, and Transformations. 8vo. Woodcuts, 10s. 6d.

BIBLE ANIMALS; a Description of every Living Creature mentioned in the Scriptures. With 112 Vignettes. 8vo. 10s. 6d.

STRANGE DWELLINGS; a Description of the Habitations of Animals, abridged from 'Homes without Hands.' With Frontispiece and 60 Woodcuts. Crown 8vo. 5s. Popular Edition, 4to. 6d.

OUT OF DOORS; a Selection of Original Articles on Practical Natural History. With 6 Illustrations. Crown 8vo. 5s.

[*Continued above.*

WOOD.—*WORKS BY REV. J. G. WOOD*—continued.

COMMON BRITISH INSECTS: BEETLES, MOTHS, AND BUTTERFLIES. Crown 8vo. with 130 Woodcuts, 3s. 6d.

PETLAND REVISITED. With numerous Illustrations, drawn specially by Miss Margery May, engraved on Wood by G. Pearson. Crown 8vo. 7s. 6d.

WYLIE.—*HISTORY OF ENGLAND UNDER HENRY THE FOURTH.* By JAMES HAMILTON WYLIE, M.A. one of Her Majesty's Inspectors of Schools. Vol. 1, crown 8vo. 10s. 6d.

WYLIE.—*LABOUR, LEISURE, AND LUXURY;* a Contribution to Present Practical Political Economy. By ALEXANDER WYLIE, of Glasgow. Crown 8vo. 6s.

YONGE.—*THE NEW ENGLISH-GREEK LEXICON,* containing all the Greek words used by Writers of good authority. By CHARLES DUKE YONGE, M.A. 4to. 21s.

YOUATT. — *WORKS BY WILLIAM YOUATT.*

THE HORSE. Revised and enlarged by W. WATSON, M.R.C.V.S. 8vo. Woodcuts, 7s. 6d.

THE DOG. Revised and enlarged. 8vo. Woodcuts. 6s.

ZELLER. — *WORKS BY DR. E. ZELLER.*

HISTORY OF ECLECTICISM IN GREEK PHILOSOPHY. Translated by SARAH F. ALLEYNE. Crown 8vo. 10s. 6d.

THE STOICS, EPICUREANS, AND SCEPTICS. Translated by the Rev. O. J. REICHEL, M.A. Crown 8vo. 15s.

SOCRATES AND THE SOCRATIC SCHOOLS. Translated by the Rev. O. J. REICHEL, M.A. Crown 8vo. 10s. 6d.

PLATO AND THE OLDER ACADEMY. Translated by S. FRANCES ALLEYNE and ALFRED GOODWIN, B.A. Crown 8vo. 18s.

THE PRE-SOCRATIC SCHOOLS; a History of Greek Philosophy from the Earliest Period to the time of Socrates. Translated by SARAH F. ALLEYNE. 2 vols. crown 8vo. 30s.

www.ingramcontent.com/pod-product-compliance
Lightning Source LLC
Chambersburg PA
CBHW022135300426
44115CB00006B/187